OECD Insurance Statistics 2021

OECD
BETTER POLICIES FOR BETTER LIVES

This work is published under the responsibility of the Secretary-General of the OECD. The opinions expressed and arguments employed herein do not necessarily reflect the official views of OECD member countries.

This document, as well as any data and map included herein, are without prejudice to the status of or sovereignty over any territory, to the delimitation of international frontiers and boundaries and to the name of any territory, city or area.

The statistical data for Israel are supplied by and under the responsibility of the relevant Israeli authorities. The use of such data by the OECD is without prejudice to the status of the Golan Heights, East Jerusalem and Israeli settlements in the West Bank under the terms of international law.

Please cite this publication as:
OECD (2022), *OECD Insurance Statistics 2021*, OECD Publishing, Paris,
https://doi.org/10.1787/841fa619-en.

ISBN 978-92-64-87313-1 (print)
ISBN 978-92-64-45919-9 (pdf)

OECD Insurance Statistics
ISSN 2307-8421 (print)
ISSN 2307-843X (online)

Corrigenda to publications may be found on line at: *www.oecd.org/about/publishing/corrigenda.htm*.

Table of contents

Conventional signs and abbreviations

Signs and abbreviations

c	Confidential data
..	Not available
.	Decimal point
		Break in series

ISO country codes and abbreviations for currency

	ISO code	Currency	Abbreviation
Australia	AUS	dollar	AUD
Austria	AUT	euro	EUR
Belgium	BEL	euro	EUR
Canada	CAN	dollar	CAD
Chile	CHL	peso	CLP
Colombia	COL	peso	COP
Costa Rica	CRI	colon	CRC
Czech Republic	CZE	koruna	CZK
Denmark	DNK	krone	DKK
Estonia	EST	euro	EUR
Finland	FIN	euro	EUR
France	FRA	euro	EUR
Germany	DEU	euro	EUR
Greece	GRC	euro	EUR
Hungary	HUN	forint	HUF
Iceland	ISL	króna	ISK
Ireland	IRL	euro	EUR
Israel	ISR	sheqel	ILS
Italy	ITA	euro	EUR
Japan	JPN	yen	JPY
Korea	KOR	won	KRW
Latvia	LVA	euro	EUR
Lithuania	LTU	euro	EUR
Luxembourg	LUX	euro	EUR
Mexico	MEX	peso	MXN
Netherlands	NLD	euro	EUR
New Zealand	NZL	dollar	NZD
Norway	NOR	krone	NOK
Poland	POL	zloty	PLN
Portugal	PRT	euro	EUR
Slovak Republic	SVK	euro	EUR
Slovenia	SVN	euro	EUR
Spain	ESP	euro	EUR
Sweden	SWE	krona	SEK
Switzerland	CHE	franc	CHF
Turkey	TUR	lira	TRY
United Kingdom	GBR	pound	GBP
United States	USA	dollar	USD

Common definitions and notes

Notes on data sources

All the data in the statistical tables of each jurisdiction have been reported by the relevant national insurance authorities. Regarding comparative tables of indicators, the data are mainly drawn from the tables by jurisdiction. Data on exchange rates are taken from the IMF International Financial Statistics database. Data on population are taken from the IMF publication *World Economic Outlook*. Data on GDP come from the OECD Annual National Accounts database for OECD jurisdictions and from the IMF publication *World Economic Outlook* for all the other jurisdictions.

> To achieve greater clarity, the number of variables selected and displayed in this publication has been limited. Data have been extracted from the Global Insurance Statistics database. The complete database can be accessed online at the following link:
>
> OECD Insurance Statistics, *http://dx.doi.org/10.1787/ins-data-en.*

A significant effort has been made to achieve comparability among jurisdictions. Definitions, classifications, calculation methods, and units have been standardised as far as possible.

General notes

a) Life and non-life categories follow the definitions used in national law. However, the premiums for accident and sickness insurance underwritten by life companies should be included in non-life figures.

b) Up until 2008, the insurance business is broken down between life and non-life business. As of 2009, the insurance business is broken down between the business of pure life, pure non-life and composite undertakings. The insurance business of composite undertakings is further broken down between life and non-life components. Some jurisdictions do not allow for insurance undertakings to be active in both life and non-life insurance business and therefore composite insurance undertakings do not exist in these jurisdictions. In other jurisdictions (e.g., Austria, Hungary, Mexico, Spain) however, composite insurance undertakings account for more than 25% of all insurance undertakings operating in these jurisdictions. Therefore, to have comparable data across years for life business data (respectively non-life), one has to sum up the life (respectively non-life) business of pure life (respectively non-life) undertakings and the life (respectively non-life) business of composite undertakings as of 2009.

c) Figures provided for the number of companies and for insurance premiums should include all insurance companies licensed or authorised in the reporting jurisdiction, *including* professional reinsurers, whether or not these are controlled, but *excluding* any statutory system of social security administered by the State.

d) *Domestic companies* means those companies incorporated under national law, together with those companies in the reporting jurisdiction which are unincorporated, but excluding the branches and agencies of foreign companies.

e) *Foreign-controlled companies* means those domestic companies controlled by foreign interests, such "control" being defined according to national law (see the definition of foreign controlled companies in notes by jurisdiction). The data of *foreign-controlled companies* are part of those of *Domestic companies*.

f) *Foreign companies* means companies incorporated outside the reporting jurisdiction.

In 2016, a new supervisory framework for insurance and reinsurance companies was implemented in the European Union (EU) and the European Economic Area (EEA). This framework includes harmonised reporting requirements across EU/EEA jurisdictions. These requirements led to changes in national data collection, which may hamper the data comparability with the ones collected before 2016 for some jurisdictions which only collect data with the Solvency II framework.

International Comparisons:

Detailed metadata at: *http://metalinks.oecd.org/ins/20190221/0f8b*.

Country tables

In this part, the main insurance statistics are presented through separate tables for each OECD member jurisdiction. Figures refer to the calendar year. The premiums and other amounts are described in millions of the national currency unit.

International comparisons

Table 1. Balance sheet and income, direct insurance (All insurance companies)

2020

Million US dollars

	Gross claims payments	Gross operating expenses	Commissions	Outstanding claims provision (changes)	Total assets	Gross technical provisions	Gross technical provisions unit-linked	Shareholders' equity	Net income
Argentina	6 168	2 716	1 578	469	19 435	4 830	..	5 306	822
Australia	92 113	9 510	2 627	..	178 630	123 488	10 044	32 916	-480
Austria	17 184	..	..	..	..	..	..	..	..
Belgium	29 068	3 344	3 423	955	374 205	312 751	55 310	20 387	2 406
Bermuda	77 025	3 063	4 992	..	546 931	417 497	..	84 574	9 285
Bolivia	299	218	53	..	1 198	547	..	337	31
Brazil	9 662	10 161	5 067	571	254 315	224 983	186 983	18 497	3 463
Bulgaria	704	524	312	130	3 837	2 425	241	402	100
Canada	..	..	..	..	..	..	..	..	..
Chile	7 760	1 700	670	158	74 910	64 277	6 384	7 583	981
Colombia	4 142	3 047	693	-630	27 012	19 786	..	4 557	406
Costa Rica	627	315	236	-7	4 182	1 571	0	1 907	168
Cuba	..	..	..	..	..	..	..	..	..
Czech Republic	3 976	2 092	435	115	22 144	15 828	4 681	3 724	629
Denmark	28 686	2 506	309	..	659 472	526 998	240 304	33 017	2 241
Dominican Republic	..	..	..	..	..	..	..	..	..
Ecuador	..	..	..	..	..	..	..	..	..
Egypt	1 181	216	457	392	7 997	..	..	2 075	..
El Salvador	354	225	96	130	971	221	..	408	24
Estonia	471	185	..	..	2 484	1 525	777	464	73
Finland	7 786	1 304	306	128	96 353	84 606	..	8 855	1 125
France	286 914	62 244	..	0	3 710 481	2 927 688	511 440	239 923	10 999
Germany	192 381	17 704	24 426	6 950	2 175 171	1 982 111	161 495	79 690	2 378
Greece	2 424	1 213	..	..	24 283	18 088	3 770	4 734	..
Guatemala	481	306	162	..	1 503	720	..	558	145
Honduras	554	171	..	..	1 093	241	..	..	49
Hong Kong, China	..	..	..	..	..	..	..	..	..
Hungary	2 165	959	588	71	10 678	8 666	4 698	1 159	267
Iceland	405	103	..	..	1 532	740	64	596	117
India	..	..	..	..	..	..	..	..	..
Indonesia	12 400	2 823	2 739	107	53 084	34 244	17 423	8 710	370
Ireland	31 880	1 409	3 345	..	518 069	452 442	326 195	37 673	..
Israel[1]	13 447	2 168	2 178	166	202 303	176 643	126 308	9 760	1 107
Italy	112 745	16 038	12 645	116	1 186 380	1 026 571	216 889	91 185	9 805
Japan	334 417	75 119	13 669	19 880	4 010 424	3 031 357	..	147 590	22 590
Korea	115 290	27 770	..	..	1 200 334	815 163	9 488	128 620	4 981
Latvia	573	148	67	2	1 813	1 296	507	393	61
Lithuania	422	208	11	12	2 052	1 342	405	518	62
Luxembourg	25 927	5 205	3 505	1 805	324 830	294 844	186 251	13 636	472
Malaysia	9 501	2 720	1 386	224	94 045	72 051	16 909	9 426	1 844
Mexico	14 271	1 818	3 760	5 126	92 175	71 552	..	13 106	2 337
Montenegro	42	..	..	..	..	..	..	..	..
Morocco	..	..	..	..	..	..	..	..	..
Netherlands	87 096	..	..	..	..	..	..	..	..
New Zealand	3 665	..	..	..	..	..	..	..	..
Nicaragua	78	84	20	29	388	148	..	169	22
Norway	13 659	2 494	558	286	246 451	208 939	..	24 086	2 083
Panama	616	..	..	..	..	..	..	..	..
Paraguay	..	..	..	..	..	..	..	..	..
Peru	2 088	1 160	680	274	16 598	12 218	..	2 560	309
Poland	10 295	5 353	2 790	228	54 184	30 993	11 031	17 998	1 559
Portugal	11 712	2 009	957	322	66 399	35 849	16 123	7 638	519
Puerto Rico	..	..	..	..	..	..	..	..	..
Russia	9 378	..	4 746	..	..	32 694	..	..	..
Singapore	20 332	2 007	2 476	..	262 301	213 433	34 565	23 623	2 065
Slovak Republic	1 419	869	..	..	8 239	5 494	971	..	..
Slovenia	1 770	548	143	-1	9 905	7 070	1 603	2 120	173
South Africa	35 784	4 854	2 212	..	229 782	183 123	..	29 530	1 046
Spain	51 598	11 323	6 819	1 476	431 644	286 273	24 900	57 822	6 209
Sri Lanka	..	..	..	..	..	..	..	..	..
Sweden	..	..	..	..	..	..	..	..	..
Switzerland	57 211	5 280	5 891	2 130	529 841	388 109	24 973	60 916	7 142
Chinese Taipei	57 786	4 976	5 454	..	1 128 365	919 034	..	93 425	7 564
Thailand	..	..	..	..	..	..	..	..	..
Tunisia	455	..	..	..	..	..	..	..	..
Turkey	4 712	2 174	1 742	1 018	40 971	14 873	..	4 802	1 432
United Kingdom	347 083	46 606	..	-17 731	3 570 916	2 953 456	1 835 667	228 376	..
United States	1 538 658	444 116	153 360	160 196	7 565 702	1 348 824	..	1 643 334	126 701
Uruguay	516	267	168	519	5 596	4 680	..	638	123

.. Not available

Note: Detailed metadata at: *http://metalinks.oecd.org/ins/20220309/dc26.*

1. Information on data for Israel: *http://oe.cd/israel-disclaimer.*

Source: *Balance sheet and income, OECD Insurance Statistics (database)*

Table 2. Balance sheet and income, direct insurance (Life insurance companies)

2020

Million US dollars

	Gross claims payments	Gross operating expenses	Commissions	Outstanding claims provision (changes)	Total assets	Gross technical provisions	Gross technical provisions unit-linked	Shareholders' equity	Net income
Argentina	220	106	14	0	2 908	2 314	..	439	129
Australia	61 964	3 687	1 198	..	79 569	54 657	10 044	14 194	-280
Austria	1 190	..	..	..	..	..	..	..	..
Belgium	343	28	17	1	4 767	3 739	197	340	34
Bermuda	73 273	438	4 071	..	513 897	402 926	..	68 922	7 959
Bolivia	158	105	27	..	735	453	..	181	6
Brazil	447	1 268	158	-29	114 323	110 508	103 216	2 778	175
Bulgaria	1	2	1	0	10	4	0	7	0
Canada	..	..	..	..	..	..	..	..	..
Chile	5 644	975	358	198	66 623	58 278	6 384	5 965	727
Colombia	2 128	1 502	267	-514	16 944	13 117	..	2 789	246
Costa Rica	..	..	..	..	..	..	..	..	..
Cuba	..	..	..	..	..	..	..	..	..
Czech Republic	259	116	4	2	2 315	2 059	1 075	158	36
Denmark	21 519	807	49	..	629 550	511 017	240 304	23 522	977
Dominican Republic	..	..	..	..	..	..	..	..	..
Ecuador	..	..	..	..	..	..	..	..	..
Egypt	608	93	200	..	4 507	..	..	741	..
El Salvador	86	95	40	80	355	106	..	109	4
Estonia	.. c	.. c	..	..	.. c	.. c	.. c	..	..
Finland	4 778	420	109	85	77 761	72 168	..	3 732	626
France	159 092	19 507	..	0	577 847	496 847	95 914	45 403	1 531
Germany	84 763	4 311	6 499	230	1 456 575	1 370 043	161 424	22 954	363
Greece	322	56	..	..	4 819	4 129	411	573	..
Guatemala	..	..	..	..	..	..	..	..	..
Honduras	69	60	..	..	426	135	..	..	20
Hong Kong, China	..	..	..	..	..	..	..	..	..
Hungary	578	108	56	15	3 163	2 835	1 314	222	21
Iceland	17	11	..	..	164	78	64	49	21
India	..	..	..	..	..	..	..	..	..
Indonesia	9 817	1 891	1 637	44	40 772	28 968	17 423	3 825	-25
Ireland	25 494	724	1 754	..	429 814	396 730	326 195	18 551	..
Israel[1]	..	..	..	..	..	..	..	..	..
Italy	24 435	1 093	676	337	336 289	318 042	118 562	12 061	872
Japan	285 159	43 540	..	18 271	3 725 804	3 031 357	..	113 003	18 166
Korea	80 780	13 027	..	..	898 239	597 228	9 488	88 808	2 924
Latvia	..	..	..	..	..	..	..	..	..
Lithuania	35	20	0	0	454	397	335	49	11
Luxembourg	18 608	1 449	692	43	271 607	259 015	186 251	4 598	222
Malaysia	7 288	1 600	1 074	..	81 563	66 530	16 909	4 198	1 216
Mexico	1 064	72	120	97	20 451	18 581	..	1 598	199
Montenegro	9	..	..	..	..	..	..	..	..
Morocco	..	..	..	..	..	..	..	..	..
Netherlands	22 260	..	..	..	..	..	..	..	..
New Zealand	264	..	..	..	..	..	..	..	..
Nicaragua	..	..	..	..	..	..	..	..	..
Norway	6 886	911	105	..	214 680	193 446	..	14 035	820
Panama	103	..	..	..	..	..	..	..	..
Paraguay	..	..	..	..	..	..	..	..	..
Peru	331	168	91	43	2 070	1 596	..	295	24
Poland	4 410	1 457	686	235	25 796	16 679	11 031	7 223	566
Portugal	5 363	333	151	23	34 625	17 405	15 287	1 837	122
Puerto Rico	..	..	..	..	..	..	..	..	..
Russia	2 836	..	1 171	..	..	17 928	..	..	..
Singapore	10 604	628	1 280	..	143 657	121 847	22 977	8 311	838
Slovak Republic	84	121	..	..	917	374	248	..	..
Slovenia	..	0	..	0	17	0	..	17	0
South Africa	30 354	3 356	1 230	..	215 215	177 537	..	23 555	507
Spain	2 951	479	289	83	32 380	22 581	3 543	2 846	193
Sri Lanka	..	..	..	..	..	..	..	..	..
Sweden	..	..	..	..	..	..	..	..	..
Switzerland	30 257	1 184	950	-1 734	344 800	301 921	24 958	14 803	1 123
Chinese Taipei	54 474	3 803	4 581	..	1 113 893	911 188	..	88 343	7 054
Thailand	..	..	..	..	..	..	..	..	..
Tunisia	39	..	..	..	..	..	..	..	..
Turkey	779	757	580	67	27 970	2 585	..	1 515	583
United Kingdom	262 799	11 418	..	-31 305	2 997 397	2 585 291	1 763 232	131 133	..
United States	423 072	75 340	54 772	50 645	4 907 631	21 232	..	503 855	30 407
Uruguay	0	0	0	0	0	0	..	0	0

.. Not available; c Confidential data

Note: Detailed metadata at: *http://metalinks.oecd.org/ins/20220309/dc26*.

1. Information on data for Israel: *http://oe.cd/israel-disclaimer*.

Source: *Balance sheet and income, OECD Insurance Statistics (database)*

Table 3. Balance sheet and income, direct insurance (Non-life insurance companies)

2020

Million US dollars

	Gross claims payments	Gross operating expenses	Commissions	Outstanding claims provision (changes)	Total assets	Gross technical provisions	Gross technical provisions unit-linked	Shareholders' equity	Net income
Argentina	2 720	726	324	127	5 337	254	..	1 312	183
Australia	30 148	5 823	1 430	..	99 061	68 831	..	18 722	-200
Austria	1 393	..	..	..	..	..	..	..	..
Belgium	1 990	483	510	821	24 691	15 724	..	4 922	122
Bermuda	3 752	2 626	921	..	33 035	14 571	..	15 653	1 326
Bolivia	142	113	27	..	463	93	..	156	26
Brazil	1 768	1 335	748	226	7 649	5 127	0	1 296	258
Bulgaria	590	456	277	125	2 571	1 545	0	305	88
Canada	..	..	..	..	..	..	..	..	..
Chile	2 116	726	312	-40	8 287	5 998	..	1 618	52
Colombia	2 015	1 545	426	-116	10 067	6 669	..	1 767	160
Costa Rica	20	16	14	-2	104	50	0	35	6
Cuba	..	..	..	..	..	..	..	..	..
Czech Republic	234	159	41	9	764	362	0	234	26
Denmark	7 166	1 699	260	..	29 922	15 981	..	9 496	1 264
Dominican Republic	..	..	..	..	..	..	..	..	..
Ecuador	..	..	..	..	..	..	..	..	..
Egypt	573	123	258	392	3 490	..	..	1 334	..
El Salvador	149	54	22	17	255	38	..	140	11
Estonia	330	150	..	..	1 033	458	0	464	73
Finland	3 009	884	198	43	18 592	12 438	..	5 123	499
France	127 822	42 737	..	0	398 780	187 781	0	78 853	3 655
Germany	107 618	13 393	17 927	6 720	718 596	612 067	71	56 736	2 015
Greece	251	289	..	..	2 306	1 101	0	932	..
Guatemala	6	14	5	..	153	35	..	84	15
Honduras	484	111	..	..	667	107	..	..	29
Hong Kong, China	..	..	..	..	..	..	..	..	..
Hungary	111	74	41	20	446	210	0	159	21
Iceland	387	92	..	..	1 368	662	0	547	96
India	..	..	..	..	..	..	..	..	..
Indonesia	2 583	933	1 102	63	12 312	5 275	..	4 886	395
Ireland	6 386	685	1 591	..	88 255	55 712	..	19 122	..
Israel[1]	823	188	113	107	6 232	4 361	0	935	103
Italy	6 161	3 274	2 490	-328	33 469	19 785	..	9 468	1 042
Japan	49 259	31 579	13 669	1 609	284 620	..	..	34 587	4 424
Korea	34 510	14 743	..	..	302 095	217 935	..	39 812	2 056
Latvia	399	127	58	2	858	501	..	241	57
Lithuania	326	169	11	1	1 154	621	0	360	45
Luxembourg	7 319	3 756	2 812	1 762	53 223	35 829	0	9 038	249
Malaysia	2 213	1 121	312	224	12 482	5 521	0	5 228	628
Mexico	1 326	478	493	1 167	8 814	4 574	..	2 380	491
Montenegro	33	..	..	..	..	..	..	..	..
Morocco	..	..	..	..	..	..	..	..	..
Netherlands	64 836	..	..	..	..	..	..	..	..
New Zealand	2 897	..	..	..	..	..	..	..	..
Nicaragua	..	..	..	..	..	..	..	..	..
Norway	6 774	1 583	452	286	31 771	15 494	..	10 051	1 264
Panama	..	..	..	..	..	..	..	..	..
Paraguay	..	..	..	..	..	..	..	..	..
Peru	219	226	113	15	1 246	527	..	353	61
Poland	5 885	3 896	2 104	-7	28 388	14 314	0	10 775	993
Portugal	1 610	616	329	104	4 688	2 615	0	1 314	148
Puerto Rico	..	..	..	..	..	..	..	..	..
Russia	6 542	..	3 575	..	..	14 766	..	..	..
Singapore	3 179	686	129	..	21 712	10 808	0	7 439	347
Slovak Republic	..	..	..	..	..	..	..	..	..
Slovenia	484	62	6	1	466	196	..	219	21
South Africa	5 430	1 498	982	..	14 567	5 587	..	5 976	539
Spain	11 022	3 648	1 898	348	35 958	17 903	0	11 516	1 576
Sri Lanka	..	..	..	..	..	..	..	..	..
Sweden	..	..	..	..	..	..	..	..	..
Switzerland	26 954	4 096	4 941	3 864	185 041	86 188	15	46 113	6 019
Chinese Taipei	3 311	1 172	873	..	14 472	7 846	..	5 081	510
Thailand	..	..	..	..	..	..	..	..	..
Tunisia	94	..	..	..	..	..	..	..	..
Turkey	3 933	1 417	1 162	950	13 002	12 288	..	3 287	849
United Kingdom	13 250	7 340	..	-198	55 597	33 376	..	17 584	..
United States	1 115 586	368 776	98 588	109 551	2 658 071	1 327 592	..	1 139 479	96 294
Uruguay	14	12	4	4	65	25	..	30	3

.. Not available

Note: Detailed metadata at: *http://metalinks.oecd.org/ins/20220309/dc26*.

1. Information on data for Israel: *http://oe.cd/israel-disclaimer*.

Source: *Balance sheet and income, OECD Insurance Statistics (database)*

Table 4. Portfolio allocation, direct insurance (All insurance companies)

2020

Million US dollars

	Cash and deposits	Land and buildings	Equity	Bills and bonds	Loans	Collective investment schemes	Private equity funds	Hedge funds	Structured products	Assets for unit-linked contracts	Total investments
Argentina	423	579	1 081	6 952	60	4 828	0	0	0	0	15 412
Australia	6 907	3 408	7 693	60 321	1 760	10 297	..	..	..	17 787	108 803
Austria	..	..	..	..	..	..	..	..	..	..	..
Belgium	9 261	11 868	20 506	249 230	50 372	21 558	1 171	..	2 402	55 255	421 775
Bermuda	..	..	..	..	..	..	..	..	..	..	..
Bolivia	45	102	9	156	46	0	46	0	0	0	638
Brazil	418	249	575	21 500	88	14 144	4 337	412	0	185 339	227 067
Bulgaria	..	..	..	..	..	..	..	..	..	..	..
Canada	..	..	..	..	..	..	..	..	..	..	..
Chile	1 899	10 029	622	32 589	8 286	6 003	0	0	0	6 410	66 476
Colombia	808	213	1 474	15 643	18	863	563	0	59	0	19 960
Costa Rica	182	0	139	2 741	371	43	0	0	0	0	3 477
Cuba	..	..	..	..	..	..	..	..	..	..	..
Czech Republic	..	..	..	..	..	..	..	..	..	..	..
Denmark	13 638	1 736	169 769	130 249	6 686	20 321	..	..	..	252 194	659 473
Dominican Republic	..	..	..	..	..	..	..	..	..	..	..
Ecuador	..	..	..	..	..	..	..	..	..	..	..
Egypt	..	..	..	..	..	..	..	..	..	..	..
El Salvador	304	7	0	221	23	16	..	..	..	..	582
Estonia	..	..	..	..	..	..	..	..	..	..	..
Finland	5 642	1 628	3 864	17 254	1 747	6 760	..	..	..	53 120	92 352
France	..	..	..	..	..	..	..	..	..	..	..
Germany	19 587	39 389	191 767	1 020 336	139 942	836 187	11 082	..	20 737	160 088	2 443 184
Greece	1 257	854	214	14 454	228	1 542	0	0	7	3 731	22 789
Guatemala	269	49	17	552	9	..	..	..	..	..	1 009
Honduras	58	5	37	373	21	0	0	0	0	0	494
Hong Kong, China	..	..	..	..	..	..	..	..	..	..	..
Hungary	207	167	91	4 840	58	343	..	..	..	4 716	10 597
Iceland	38	21	451	577	17	163	..	..	..	64	1 331
India	..	..	..	..	..	..	..	..	..	..	..
Indonesia	4 283	858	11 499	10 659	13	12 293	..	..	..	1 649	41 357
Ireland	..	..	..	..	..	..	..	..	..	..	..
Israel[1]	4 632	2 825	2 095	34 295	6 521	2 358	2 781	133	127	127 630	185 396
Italy	10 919	5 914	75 040	636 876	5 642	..	..	..	..	217 107	1 110 769
Japan	..	..	..	..	..	..	..	..	..	..	..
Korea	15 929	16 360	53 918	428 658	207 219	..	..	..	..	108 136	1 145 840
Latvia	164	23	5	740	35	199	0	0	0	521	1 694
Lithuania	105	8	14	1 057	11	78	0	0	1	405	1 727
Luxembourg	4 570	290	2 880	45 988	210	8 340	..	..	..	187 465	315 714
Malaysia	5 719	1 227	8 516	40 250	2 921	..	..	..	..	18 078	87 734
Mexico	676	984	826	55 758	1 380	11 636	0	..	..	..	75 763
Montenegro	..	..	..	..	..	..	..	..	..	..	..
Morocco	..	..	..	..	..	..	..	..	..	..	..
Netherlands	..	..	..	..	..	..	..	..	..	..	..
New Zealand	..	..	..	..	..	..	..	..	..	..	..
Nicaragua	10	11	3	225	17	..	..	..	..	..	286
Norway	1 952	17 993	12 563	82 159	18 081	39 200	..	..	..	55 261	233 675
Panama	..	..	..	..	..	..	..	..	..	..	..
Paraguay	..	..	..	..	..	..	..	..	..	..	..
Peru	907	985	719	10 003	6	800	6	0	0	0	14 227
Poland	902	748	5 994	25 650	930	4 449	68	11	3	11 949	50 629
Portugal	1 159	575	3 799	35 250	286	2 839	122	25	432	16 145	60 610
Puerto Rico	..	..	..	..	..	..	..	..	..	..	..
Russia	9 649	815	2 928	24 909	262	140	..	..	..	..	38 529
Singapore	..	..	..	..	..	..	..	..	..	..	..
Slovak Republic	425	233	247	6 132	111	1 752	0	0	115	455	9 470
Slovenia	204	321	766	5 250	27	555	..	..	8	2 205	9 346
South Africa	15 517	633	30 400	42 011	5 986	111 106	0	1 154	4 164	0	232 136
Spain	22 688	14 348	20 396	282 749	2 483	17 342	993	979	6 893	31 315	391 593
Sri Lanka	..	..	..	..	..	..	..	..	..	..	..
Sweden	..	..	..	..	..	..	..	..	..	..	..
Switzerland	21 473	53 882	20 410	213 411	63 032	25 524	4 512	2 039	253	24 456	497 198
Chinese Taipei	32 456	56 833	90 829	650 385	44 897	54 320	12 825	..	757	83 106	1 098 875
Thailand	..	..	..	..	..	..	..	..	..	..	..
Tunisia	..	..	..	..	..	..	..	..	..	..	..
Turkey	6 875	146	556	5 056	77	171	..	..	..	1 151	12 325
United Kingdom	38 416	22 370	105 158	712 270	147 492	254 013	4 855	5 790	456	1 709 464	3 000 284
United States	323 937	43 018	764 440	4 679 640	743 740	..	..	39 465	3 810	..	7 059 805
Uruguay	539	13	7	4 213	0	0	0	0	0	0	5 121

.. Not available

Note: Detailed metadata at: *http://metalinks.oecd.org/ins/20220309/e230.*

1. Information on data for Israel: *http://oe.cd/israel-disclaimer.*

Source: *Outstanding investment by direct insurance companies, OECD Insurance Statistics (database)*

Table 5. Portfolio allocation, direct insurance (Life insurance companies)

2020

Million US dollars

	Cash and deposits	Land and buildings	Equity	Bills and bonds	Loans	Collective investment schemes	Private equity funds	Hedge funds	Structured products	Assets for unit-linked contracts	Total investments
Argentina	17	52	16	1 629	0	900	0	0	0	0	2 794
Australia	3 335	3 319	7 008	26 465	235	..	..	..	..	17 787	58 480
Austria	..	..	..	..	..	..	..	..	..	..	..
Belgium	881	373	524	5 204	2 526	1 469	10	..	34	360	11 678
Bermuda	..	..	..	..	..	..	..	..	..	..	..
Bolivia	29	74	4	112	46	0	39	0	0	0	455
Brazil	82	21	21	4 384	88	5 175	109	130	0	102 581	112 592
Bulgaria	..	..	..	..	..	..	..	..	..	..	..
Canada	..	..	..	..	..	..	..	..	..	..	..
Chile	1 357	9 962	599	30 854	8 268	5 854	0	0	0	6 410	63 858
Colombia	508	87	935	12 160	15	621	500	..	46	..	15 152
Costa Rica	..	..	..	..	..	..	..	..	..	..	..
Cuba	..	..	..	..	..	..	..	..	..	..	..
Czech Republic	..	..	..	..	..	..	..	..	..	..	..
Denmark	10 362	1 328	164 728	113 721	6 186	18 210	..	..	..	252 194	629 550
Dominican Republic	..	..	..	..	..	..	..	..	..	..	..
Ecuador	..	..	..	..	..	..	..	..	..	..	..
Egypt	..	..	..	..	..	..	..	..	..	..	..
El Salvador	132	6	0	102	2	5	..	..	..	..	249
Estonia	..	..	..	..	..	..	..	..	..	..	..
Finland	3 338	790	1 908	12 546	1 038	3 231	..	..	..	53 120	76 661
France	..	..	..	..	..	..	..	..	..	..	..
Germany	8 631	24 312	88 956	655 139	113 075	579 761	6 454	..	14 629	160 017	1 654 370
Greece	322	5	97	3 614	94	128	0	0	0	433	4 787
Guatemala	..	..	..	..	..	..	..	..	..	..	..
Honduras	22	1	12	151	10	0	0	0	0	0	196
Hong Kong, China	..	..	..	..	..	..	..	..	..	..	..
Hungary	43	14	11	1 715	4	111	..	..	..	1 329	3 238
Iceland	6	0	0	69	0	5	..	..	..	64	144
India	..	..	..	..	..	..	..	..	..	..	..
Indonesia	2 451	788	10 547	9 126	10	10 975	..	..	..	1 649	35 547
Ireland	..	..	..	..	..	..	..	..	..	..	..
Israel[1]	..	..	..	..	..	..	..	..	..	..	..
Italy	2 284	339	5 063	171 763	75	..	..	..	..	118 677	324 985
Japan	98 235	54 500	273 313	2 514 437	267 265	..	..	..	..	..	3 654 219
Korea	10 765	11 325	43 464	338 451	137 536	..	..	..	..	108 136	871 532
Latvia	..	..	..	..	..	..	..	..	..	..	..
Lithuania	28	0	0	81	0	2	0	0	0	335	448
Luxembourg	2 157	76	1 902	25 718	100	6 920	..	..	..	187 465	269 484
Malaysia	3 647	1 099	8 351	37 434	2 911	..	..	..	..	18 078	77 258
Mexico	11	21	16	18 720	258	15	0	..	..	..	20 146
Montenegro	..	..	..	..	..	..	..	..	..	..	..
Morocco	..	..	..	..	..	..	..	..	..	..	..
Netherlands	..	..	..	..	..	..	..	..	..	..	..
New Zealand	..	..	..	..	..	..	..	..	..	..	..
Nicaragua	..	..	..	..	..	..	..	..	..	..	..
Norway	860	17 247	10 400	70 650	17 633	35 036	..	..	..	55 261	212 932
Panama	..	..	..	..	..	..	..	..	..	..	..
Paraguay	..	..	..	..	..	..	..	..	..	..	..
Peru	175	148	87	1 299	3	58	0	0	0	0	1 789
Poland	489	171	584	9 819	404	1 844	0	0	3	11 949	25 264
Portugal	357	249	160	16 085	260	645	49	0	26	15 333	33 149
Puerto Rico	..	..	..	..	..	..	..	..	..	..	..
Russia	..	..	..	..	..	..	..	..	..	..	..
Singapore	..	..	..	..	..	..	..	..	..	..	..
Slovak Republic	59	1	47	903	2	577	0	0	0	238	1 827
Slovenia	16	0	0	0	0	0	..	..	0	0	16
South Africa	12 338	515	29 182	36 121	5 893	109 898	0	1 126	4 133	0	215 215
Spain	1 074	392	504	21 135	153	965	140	25	1 237	3 532	29 047
Sri Lanka	..	..	..	..	..	..	..	..	..	..	..
Sweden	..	..	..	..	..	..	..	..	..	..	..
Switzerland	6 232	45 268	13 611	166 429	48 502	12 825	2 820	1 063	150	24 442	336 324
Chinese Taipei	31 496	55 473	88 732	646 396	44 881	53 473	12 818	..	736	83 106	1 088 329
Thailand	..	..	..	..	..	..	..	..	..	..	..
Tunisia	..	..	..	..	..	..	..	..	..	..	..
Turkey	1 744	52	50	1 634	77	48	..	..	..	1 151	3 555
United Kingdom	22 007	17 795	81 478	464 188	130 995	211 811	4 423	4 329	327	1 704 540	2 639 831
United States	145 009	22 825	177 042	3 320 425	718 724	..	..	39 465	3 795	..	4 685 700
Uruguay	..	..	..	..	..	..	..	..	..	..	..

.. Not available

Note: Detailed metadata at: *http://metalinks.oecd.org/ins/20220309/e230.*

1. Information on data for Israel: *http://oe.cd/israel-disclaimer.*

Source: *Outstanding investment by direct insurance companies, OECD Insurance Statistics (database)*

Table 6. Portfolio allocation, direct insurance (Non-life insurance companies)

2020

Million US dollars

	Cash and deposits	Land and buildings	Equity	Bills and bonds	Loans	Collective investment schemes	Private equity funds	Hedge funds	Structured products	Assets for unit-linked contracts	Total investments
Argentina	88	136	117	1 921	1	1 510	0	0	0	0	4 417
Australia	3 572	89	685	33 856	1 525	10 297	..	..	..	..	50 323
Austria	..	..	..	..	..	..	..	..	..	..	..
Belgium	1 248	567	1 614	12 123	1 051	3 230	47	..	77	0	20 158
Bermuda	..	..	..	..	..	..	..	..	..	..	..
Bolivia	17	29	5	44	0	0	7	0	0	0	183
Brazil	60	55	3	1 855	0	462	1	24	0	0	2 461
Bulgaria	..	..	..	..	..	..	..	..	..	..	..
Canada	..	..	..	..	..	..	..	..	..	..	..
Chile	542	66	23	1 735	19	149	0	0	0	0	2 619
Colombia	300	126	539	3 484	3	242	63	..	13	..	4 808
Costa Rica	12	0	0	50	17	0	0	0	0	0	79
Cuba	..	..	..	..	..	..	..	..	..	..	..
Czech Republic	..	..	..	..	..	..	..	..	..	..	..
Denmark	3 276	408	5 041	16 528	500	2 110	..	..	..	..	29 922
Dominican Republic	..	..	..	..	..	..	..	..	..	..	..
Ecuador	..	..	..	..	..	..	..	..	..	..	..
Egypt	..	..	..	..	..	..	..	..	..	..	..
El Salvador	61	0	0	29	1	4	..	..	..	..	95
Estonia	196	0	1	715	4	0	0	0	0	0	918
Finland	2 304	838	1 956	4 708	709	3 529	..	..	..	..	15 691
France	..	..	..	..	..	..	..	..	..	..	..
Germany	10 956	15 077	102 811	365 197	26 867	256 426	4 628	..	6 108	71	788 814
Greece	303	202	38	1 156	6	299	0	0	2	0	2 057
Guatemala	43	3	0	58	6	..	..	..	..	..	127
Honduras	36	3	25	223	11	0	0	0	0	0	298
Hong Kong, China	..	..	..	..	..	..	..	..	..	..	..
Hungary	39	8	0	341	0	8	..	..	..	0	408
Iceland	33	21	451	507	17	158	..	..	..	0	1 187
India	..	..	..	..	..	..	..	..	..	..	..
Indonesia	1 832	69	953	1 533	3	1 317	..	..	..	..	5 810
Ireland	..	..	..	..	..	..	..	..	..	..	..
Israel[1]	515	93	131	2 010	272	1 075	141	20	7	..	4 317
Italy	1 179	523	2 456	16 755	49	..	..	..	..	..	24 037
Japan	18 823	7 696	62 354	61 234	13 905	..	..	..	..	..	255 911
Korea	5 164	5 035	10 455	90 207	69 683	..	..	..	..	0	274 309
Latvia	115	23	5	511	35	40	0	0	0	0	734
Lithuania	64	8	7	672	3	53	0	0	0	0	853
Luxembourg	2 413	214	977	20 270	111	1 421	..	..	..	0	46 230
Malaysia	2 072	129	165	2 817	10	..	..	..	..	..	10 475
Mexico	210	208	84	3 533	31	67	0	..	..	..	4 481
Montenegro	..	..	..	..	..	..	..	..	..	..	..
Morocco	..	..	..	..	..	..	..	..	..	..	..
Netherlands	..	..	..	..	..	..	..	..	..	..	..
New Zealand	..	..	..	..	..	..	..	..	..	..	..
Nicaragua	..	..	..	..	..	..	..	..	..	..	..
Norway	1 091	746	2 163	11 510	448	4 164	..	..	..	..	20 743
Panama	..	..	..	..	..	..	..	..	..	..	..
Paraguay	..	..	..	..	..	..	..	..	..	..	..
Peru	105	62	117	216	0	39	0	0	0	0	705
Poland	413	578	5 409	15 831	526	2 606	68	11	0	0	25 365
Portugal	332	105	34	2 606	22	217	15	1	23	0	3 354
Puerto Rico	..	..	..	..	..	..	..	..	..	..	..
Russia	..	..	..	..	..	..	..	..	..	..	..
Singapore	..	..	..	..	..	..	..	..	..	..	..
Slovak Republic	27	0	0	0	14	0	0	0	0	0	40
Slovenia	35	24	1	324	0	16	..	..	0	0	400
South Africa	3 093	111	1 209	4 674	93	1 207	0	28	31	0	14 567
Spain	3 699	2 467	2 762	10 740	512	5 589	190	152	147	0	26 346
Sri Lanka	..	..	..	..	..	..	..	..	..	..	..
Sweden	..	..	..	..	..	..	..	..	..	..	..
Switzerland	15 241	8 614	6 799	46 983	14 530	12 700	1 692	976	103	15	160 874
Chinese Taipei	960	1 360	2 097	3 988	16	847	7	..	21	0	10 545
Thailand	..	..	..	..	..	..	..	..	..	..	..
Tunisia	..	..	..	..	..	..	..	..	..	..	..
Turkey	5 132	93	505	3 422	0	124	..	..	..	0	8 770
United Kingdom	4 289	600	2 684	17 624	518	5 057	6	114	65	0	30 943
United States	178 928	20 193	587 398	1 359 215	25 016	..	..	0	15	..	2 374 105
Uruguay	9	0	0	27	0	0	0	0	0	0	39

.. Not available

Note: Detailed metadata at: *http://metalinks.oecd.org/ins/20220309/e230.*

1. Information on data for Israel: *http://oe.cd/israel-disclaimer.*

Source: *Outstanding investment by direct insurance companies, OECD Insurance Statistics (database)*

Table 7. Total gross premiums (Life and Non-life)

Million US dollars

	2013	2014	2015	2016	2017	2018	2019	2020
Argentina	16 643	18 622	19 376	19 749	18 519	20 137	12 574	12 387
Australia	87 591	97 011	78 796	74 145	72 339	69 991	61 277	57 397
Austria	25 084	25 102	21 091	20 647	20 485	21 880	21 090	..
Belgium	37 521	38 345	30 746	30 432	30 839	33 703	35 152	34 417
Bermuda	..	..	..	..	..	..	151 401	276 673
Bolivia	..	..	..	468	499	549	610	628
Brazil	..	69 867	55 519	58 914	66 431	61 462	62 990	48 672
Bulgaria	..	..	..	..	..	1 530	1 667	1 678
Canada	98 512	93 189	83 612	81 909	87 408	87 012	..	..
Chile	11 776	10 976	11 413	12 401	12 860	14 006	12 893	9 989
Colombia	10 207	9 690	8 003	8 050	8 978	9 409	9 392	8 417
Costa Rica	1 036	1 157	1 049	1 211	1 319	1 333	1 418	1 439
Cuba	..	..	..	..	..	..	..	..
Czech Republic	7 998	7 608	6 173	6 002	6 402	7 052	7 214	7 215
Denmark	..	37 098	31 997	33 498	37 549	40 976	38 589	40 999
Dominican Republic	..	..	..	..	..	1 222	..	..
Ecuador	..	..	2 316	2 135	..	..	1 797	..
Egypt	..	..	..	..	..	..	1 968	2 503
El Salvador	546	572	609	619	..	658	702	722
Estonia	774	839	764	815	924	1 092	1 102	1 070
Finland	13 061	14 125	11 917	10 012	10 084	5 156	6 744	4 611
France	275 750	294 033	250 873	314 251	314 319	338 708	332 471	302 729
Germany	333 713	338 764	293 086	294 660	311 208	335 669	344 268	365 897
Greece	5 407	5 056	3 964	3 908	4 213	4 485	4 538	4 690
Guatemala	683	749	804	856	953	964	1 006	1 048
Honduras	368	379	398	..	..	631	624	621
Hong Kong, China	37 856	43 121	47 901	59 301	64 310	69 089	..	..
Hungary	3 582	3 584	2 991	3 146	3 484	3 767	3 955	3 910
Iceland	419	444	420	487	611	652	612	545
India	..	..	70 878	..	100 841	..	107 818	..
Indonesia	15 782	14 325	14 629	17 290	19 483	18 967	19 763	18 098
Ireland	45 314	52 557	48 802	54 182	49 821	48 129	49 889	45 005
Israel[1]	13 941	14 366	14 117	15 142	17 427	18 560	19 324	19 513
Italy	161 161	193 455	165 854	151 423	150 732	163 781	158 241	155 752
Japan	349 905	347 080	313 822	434 737	390 096	402 773	399 088	385 035
Korea	169 166	187 090	183 675	185 593	189 491	192 869	..	198 780
Latvia	626	687	589	589	730	893	960	911
Lithuania	753	798	716	786	895	1 037	1 059	1 091
Luxembourg	24 705	28 945	21 278	20 289	24 314	24 539	28 130	24 174
Malaysia	16 974	17 588	15 346	15 100	15 156	16 716	17 667	18 068
Mexico	27 184	27 349	24 929	24 150	26 569	28 250	31 346	28 301
Montenegro	..	..	..	..	..	..	..	..
Morocco	..	..	..	..	..	..	..	..
Netherlands	51 142	48 603	37 399	77 358	80 465	86 997	..	..
New Zealand	5 139	5 359	4 657	4 753	5 144	..	7 258	..
Nicaragua	157	178	191	204	..	224	..	201
Norway	25 536	26 461	20 647	20 210	20 407	21 993	22 064	21 331
Panama	1 316	..	..	..	..	..	1 707	1 670
Paraguay	363	..	428	368	390	..	438	..
Peru	3 392	3 602	3 709	3 354	3 500	3 938	4 263	4 051
Poland	18 307	17 412	14 539	14 213	16 495	17 211	16 627	16 266
Portugal	17 003	18 667	13 945	12 079	12 941	14 868	13 338	11 050
Puerto Rico	9 610	9 108	11 145	13 470	..	..	..	..
Russia	..	26 658	17 299	18 218	22 517	24 301	23 675	22 206
Singapore	27 186	30 379	30 331	33 160	36 830	..	44 929	51 049
Slovak Republic	2 959	2 986	2 400	..	5 047	..	2 823	2 791
Slovenia	2 808	2 783	2 386	2 416	2 596	2 863	2 963	3 123
South Africa	54 268	51 527	47 054	42 473	..	..	..	43 650
Spain	77 177	76 604	65 514	73 655	74 242	78 578	74 106	71 530
Sri Lanka	..	746	931	..	1 128	1 147	..	..
Sweden	27 203	49 890	40 254	39 107	44 382	49 044	48 704	..
Switzerland	74 264	74 480	70 367	67 483	67 772	69 456	69 986	69 040
Chinese Taipei	..	..	..	..	..	207 626	204 499	114 520
Thailand	..	..	..	..	..	..	..	..
Tunisia	..	..	..	864	909	..	..	..
Turkey	13 212	12 314	11 775	13 718	13 074	11 333	12 126	12 215
United Kingdom	340 385	365 688	336 743	403 794	394 929	471 031	418 559	380 960
United States	2 289 921	2 431 323	2 621 083	2 703 793	2 836 293	2 632 284	2 773 916	2 934 829
Uruguay	1 208	1 303	1 277	..	1 576	..	1 554	1 463
OECD Total	4 876 013	4 961 919	4 852 388	5 215 044	5 346 884	5 311 380	5 031 220	5 225 019

.. Not available

Note: Detailed metadata at: *http://metalinks.oecd.org/ins/20220309/7297.*

1. Information on data for Israel: *http://oe.cd/israel-disclaimer.*

Source: *Insurance activity indicators, OECD Insurance Statistics (database)*

Table 8. Total gross premiums (Life)

Million US dollars

	2013	2014	2015	2016	2017	2018	2019	2020
Argentina	2 969	3 076	2 966	3 158	2 724	2 886	1 716	1 606
Australia	48 122	59 315	46 633	41 066	37 668	34 664	26 477	21 205
Austria	8 556	8 901	7 440	6 701	6 493	6 543	6 065	..
Belgium	21 651	21 664	17 045	16 560	16 547	18 437	18 181	16 819
Bermuda	..	..	..	..	..	..	80 400	198 854
Bolivia	..	..	..	157	202	238	274	296
Brazil	..	42 061	34 819	38 935	44 172	40 919	43 685	33 374
Bulgaria	..	..	..	..	..	216	212	209
Canada	32 379	26 712	24 001	23 795	25 754	26 213	..	..
Chile	7 830	7 224	7 795	8 726	8 930	9 633	8 641	5 956
Colombia	5 214	4 602	3 727	3 879	4 567	4 710	4 751	4 201
Costa Rica	139	142	133	186	194	215	227	215
Cuba	..	..	..	..	..	..	..	..
Czech Republic	3 657	3 429	2 537	2 435	2 451	2 583	2 314	2 229
Denmark	..	25 124	22 055	23 001	25 945	28 664	27 518	29 832
Dominican Republic	..	..	..	..	..	196	..	..
Ecuador	..	..	453	471	..	..	524	..
Egypt	..	..	..	..	..	..	860	1 157
El Salvador	146	147	156	153	..	165	180	196
Estonia	227	254	238	245	252	275	283	304
Finland	7 423	8 108	6 943	5 063	5 115	5 156	6 744	4 611
France	172 187	188 634	160 946	182 414	173 606	186 967	185 390	150 513
Germany	120 293	121 746	99 628	97 651	99 769	106 802	112 711	116 213
Greece	2 238	2 500	2 000	1 846	2 125	2 220	2 310	2 402
Guatemala	136	156	156	170	196	197	213	223
Honduras	114	134	145	..	..	210	201	195
Hong Kong, China	32 425	37 459	41 972	53 421	58 134	62 257	..	..
Hungary	1 951	1 965	1 529	1 559	1 679	1 742	1 751	1 722
Iceland	33	36	35	43	54	54	51	49
India	..	..	55 415	..	71 312	..	80 314	..
Indonesia	10 720	9 490	10 093	12 560	14 530	13 832	13 941	12 744
Ireland	36 525	43 221	38 853	37 127	39 617	36 272	35 902	34 465
Israel[1]	7 374	7 426	7 568	7 986	9 368	10 016	10 615	10 546
Italy	115 147	148 645	129 077	114 779	112 984	122 310	118 872	115 896
Japan	349 905	347 080	313 822	328 210	293 005	302 966	292 247	276 258
Korea	100 249	106 200	104 820	104 530	102 221	102 538	..	101 326
Latvia	118	142	128	137	164	171	255	275
Lithuania	241	286	262	273	261	293	303	332
Luxembourg	22 711	27 166	19 641	18 568	22 318	22 523	25 512	21 362
Malaysia	10 200	10 594	9 306	9 317	9 603	10 709	11 628	11 912
Mexico	12 523	12 812	11 530	11 266	11 421	12 672	14 118	12 856
Montenegro	..	..	..	..	..	..	..	..
Morocco	..	..	..	..	..	..	..	..
Netherlands	24 263	23 202	16 307	15 198	14 654	14 136	..	..
New Zealand	..	..	..	..	..	..	1 714	..
Nicaragua	27	32	33	38	..	46	..	38
Norway	13 838	14 629	11 383	11 202	11 313	12 291	12 351	11 277
Panama	523	..	..	..	..	..	428	429
Paraguay	44	..	57	1	54	..	58	..
Peru	1 587	1 768	1 794	1 519	1 644	1 909	2 082	1 908
Poland	9 892	9 087	7 302	6 051	6 499	6 009	5 541	5 322
Portugal	11 984	13 617	9 411	7 200	7 581	9 188	7 567	4 901
Puerto Rico	411	570	542	1 279	..	..	..	..
Russia	..	3 353	2 408	3 721	6 171	7 784	6 324	5 971
Singapore	18 449	20 808	21 033	23 739	27 593	..	30 926	38 835
Slovak Republic	1 642	1 621	1 229	..	3 712	..	1 372	1 334
Slovenia	629	637	552	545	582	621	617	596
South Africa	42 679	41 476	37 576	33 870	..	..	..	33 634
Spain	34 397	33 612	28 532	34 695	33 262	34 263	30 780	26 559
Sri Lanka	..	265	395	..	467	474	..	..
Sweden	14 190	34 734	29 507	29 302	33 761	37 087	36 812	..
Switzerland	35 791	36 140	34 407	31 672	30 486	30 835	30 562	26 668
Chinese Taipei	..	..	..	..	..	201 388	197 955	107 233
Thailand	..	..	..	..	..	..	..	..
Tunisia	..	..	..	175	179	..	..	..
Turkey	2 072	1 510	1 390	2 048	2 268	1 801	2 433	2 449
United Kingdom	246 475	268 267	246 702	277 703	272 461	339 319	304 010	268 534
United States	881 541	880 040	973 634	970 503	1 009 291	1 139 513	1 180 619	1 242 994
Uruguay	347	384	427	..	665	..	686	669
OECD Total	2 568 739	2 490 433	2 388 743	2 424 161	2 428 380	2 669 703	2 515 618	2 520 220

.. Not available

Note: Detailed metadata at: *http://metalinks.oecd.org/ins/20220309/7297*.

1. Information on data for Israel: *http://oe.cd/israel-disclaimer*.

Source: *Insurance activity indicators, OECD Insurance Statistics (database)*

Table 9. Total gross premiums (Non-life)

Million US dollars

	2013	2014	2015	2016	2017	2018	2019	2020
Argentina	13 673	15 546	16 410	16 591	15 795	17 251	10 859	10 781
Australia	39 469	37 695	32 163	33 079	34 671	35 328	34 800	36 192
Austria	16 527	16 201	13 651	13 946	13 992	15 337	15 025	..
Belgium	15 870	16 681	13 701	13 871	14 292	15 266	16 971	17 598
Bermuda	..	..	..	..	..	..	71 001	77 820
Bolivia	..	..	..	312	297	311	336	332
Brazil	..	27 806	20 699	19 979	22 258	20 543	19 305	15 297
Bulgaria	..	..	..	..	..	1 315	1 454	1 469
Canada	66 133	66 477	59 610	58 115	61 654	60 799	..	..
Chile	3 946	3 751	3 619	3 676	3 930	4 373	4 252	4 033
Colombia	4 993	5 088	4 276	4 171	4 411	4 699	4 640	4 216
Costa Rica	897	1 014	916	1 024	1 125	1 118	1 191	1 225
Cuba	..	..	..	..	..	..	..	..
Czech Republic	4 341	4 179	3 636	3 566	3 951	4 469	4 901	4 987
Denmark	10 445	11 974	9 943	10 497	11 604	12 312	11 071	11 166
Dominican Republic	..	..	..	..	..	1 026	..	..
Ecuador	..	..	1 864	1 665	..	..	1 274	..
Egypt	..	..	..	..	..	..	1 108	1 346
El Salvador	400	412	437	446	..	493	522	526
Estonia	547	584	526	570	672	817	818	766
Finland	5 638	6 017	4 974	4 949	4 968	..	..	..
France	103 563	105 399	89 928	131 837	140 713	151 741	147 082	152 216
Germany	213 420	217 018	193 459	197 010	211 439	228 866	231 557	249 684
Greece	3 169	2 556	1 964	2 063	2 088	2 265	2 227	2 287
Guatemala	547	593	648	685	757	767	792	825
Honduras	254	246	253	..	..	421	424	426
Hong Kong, China	5 431	5 661	5 929	5 880	6 177	6 832	..	..
Hungary	1 631	1 619	1 462	1 588	1 804	2 025	2 204	2 188
Iceland	385	408	384	444	556	598	561	496
India	..	..	15 463	..	29 529	..	27 504	..
Indonesia	5 062	4 835	4 537	4 730	4 954	5 136	5 823	5 354
Ireland	8 789	9 335	9 949	17 055	9 625	10 006	12 517	10 540
Israel[1]	6 567	6 940	6 548	7 156	8 059	8 544	8 709	8 967
Italy	46 013	44 811	36 777	36 645	37 748	41 470	39 369	39 855
Japan	..	..	..	106 527	97 090	99 808	106 841	108 777
Korea	68 917	80 890	78 855	81 063	87 270	90 330	..	97 453
Latvia	507	546	462	452	566	721	704	636
Lithuania	512	513	454	513	634	744	756	759
Luxembourg	1 993	1 779	1 637	1 720	1 996	2 016	2 618	2 812
Malaysia	6 773	6 994	6 041	5 782	5 553	6 007	6 039	6 156
Mexico	14 661	14 536	13 399	12 884	15 148	15 578	17 228	15 446
Montenegro	..	..	..	..	..	..	..	..
Morocco	..	..	..	..	..	..	..	..
Netherlands	26 878	25 401	21 093	62 160	64 818	71 621	..	..
New Zealand	5 139	5 359	4 657	4 753	5 144	..	5 544	..
Nicaragua	130	146	158	166	..	178	..	162
Norway	11 697	11 833	9 264	9 008	9 094	9 702	9 713	10 054
Panama	793	..	..	..	..	..	1 279	1 242
Paraguay	318	..	371	367	335	..	380	..
Peru	1 805	1 834	1 916	1 835	1 856	2 029	2 181	2 143
Poland	8 416	8 325	7 237	8 162	9 996	11 202	11 086	10 944
Portugal	5 018	5 050	4 534	4 879	5 360	5 680	5 771	6 149
Puerto Rico	9 199	8 538	10 603	12 191	..	..	..	..
Russia	..	16 937	14 891	14 497	16 346	16 518	17 352	16 236
Singapore	8 737	9 571	9 298	9 421	9 238	..	14 003	12 215
Slovak Republic	1 318	1 366	1 171	..	1 335	..	1 451	1 457
Slovenia	2 179	2 146	1 833	1 871	2 014	2 242	2 346	2 526
South Africa	11 589	10 051	9 478	8 602	..	..	..	10 016
Spain	42 780	42 992	36 982	38 959	40 979	44 315	43 325	44 971
Sri Lanka	..	481	535	..	661	673	..	..
Sweden	13 013	15 156	10 746	9 805	10 621	11 957	11 892	..
Switzerland	38 474	38 340	35 959	35 811	37 287	38 621	39 424	42 372
Chinese Taipei	..	..	..	..	..	6 238	6 544	7 288
Thailand	..	..	..	..	..	..	..	..
Tunisia	..	..	..	689	730	..	..	..
Turkey	11 140	10 804	10 386	11 670	10 806	9 532	9 693	9 765
United Kingdom	93 910	97 421	90 041	126 091	122 469	131 712	114 549	112 426
United States	1 408 380	1 551 283	1 647 449	1 733 290	1 827 002	1 492 771	1 593 297	1 691 835
Uruguay	862	918	850	..	911	..	868	794
OECD Total	2 307 274	2 471 485	2 463 645	2 790 883	2 916 932	2 638 586	2 514 131	2 704 799

.. Not available

Note: Detailed metadata at: *http://metalinks.oecd.org/ins/20220309/7297*.

1. Information on data for Israel: *http://oe.cd/israel-disclaimer*.

Source: *Insurance activity indicators, OECD Insurance Statistics (database)*

Table 10. Market share in OECD (Life and Non-life)

Per cent

	2013	2014	2015	2016	2017	2018	2019	2020
Australia	1.9	2.0	1.6	1.4	1.4	1.3	1.2	1.1
Austria	0.5	0.5	0.4	0.4	0.4	0.4	0.4	..
Belgium	0.8	0.8	0.6	0.6	0.6	0.6	0.7	0.7
Canada	2.1	1.9	1.7	1.6	1.6	1.6	..	..
Chile	0.3	0.2	0.2	0.2	0.2	0.3	0.3	0.2
Colombia	0.2	0.2	0.2	0.2	0.2	0.2	0.2	0.2
Costa Rica	0.0	0.0	0.0	0.0	0.0	0.0	0.0	0.0
Czech Republic	0.2	0.2	0.1	0.1	0.1	0.1	0.1	0.1
Denmark	..	0.7	0.7	0.6	0.7	0.8	0.8	0.8
Estonia	0.0	0.0	0.0	0.0	0.0	0.0	0.0	0.0
Finland	0.3	0.3	0.2	0.2	0.2	0.1	0.1	0.1
France	5.9	5.9	5.2	6.0	5.9	6.4	6.6	5.8
Germany	7.2	6.8	6.0	5.7	5.8	6.3	6.8	7.0
Greece	0.1	0.1	0.1	0.1	0.1	0.1	0.1	0.1
Hungary	0.1	0.1	0.1	0.1	0.1	0.1	0.1	0.1
Iceland	0.0	0.0	0.0	0.0	0.0	0.0	0.0	0.0
Ireland	1.0	1.1	1.0	1.0	0.9	0.9	1.0	0.9
Israel	0.3	0.3	0.3	0.3	0.3	0.3	0.4	0.4
Italy	3.5	3.9	3.4	2.9	2.8	3.1	3.1	3.0
Japan	7.5	7.0	6.5	8.3	7.3	7.6	7.9	7.4
Korea	3.6	3.8	3.8	3.6	3.5	3.6	..	3.8
Latvia	0.0	0.0	0.0	0.0	0.0	0.0	0.0	0.0
Lithuania	0.0	0.0	0.0	0.0	0.0	0.0	0.0	0.0
Luxembourg	0.5	0.6	0.4	0.4	0.5	0.5	0.6	0.5
Mexico	0.6	0.6	0.5	0.5	0.5	0.5	0.6	0.5
Netherlands	1.1	1.0	0.8	1.5	1.5	1.6	..	..
New Zealand	0.1	0.1	0.1	0.1	0.1	..	0.1	..
Norway	0.5	0.5	0.4	0.4	0.4	0.4	0.4	0.4
Poland	0.4	0.4	0.3	0.3	0.3	0.3	0.3	0.3
Portugal	0.4	0.4	0.3	0.2	0.2	0.3	0.3	0.2
Slovak Republic	0.1	0.1	0.0	..	0.1	..	0.1	0.1
Slovenia	0.1	0.1	0.0	0.0	0.0	0.1	0.1	0.1
Spain	1.7	1.5	1.4	1.4	1.4	1.5	1.5	1.4
Sweden	0.6	1.0	0.8	0.8	0.8	0.9	1.0	..
Switzerland	1.6	1.5	1.5	1.3	1.3	1.3	1.4	1.3
Turkey	0.3	0.2	0.2	0.3	0.2	0.2	0.2	0.2
United Kingdom	7.3	7.4	6.9	7.7	7.4	8.9	8.3	7.3
United States	49.2	49.0	54.0	51.8	53.0	49.6	55.1	56.2
OECD Total	100.0	100.0	100.0	100.0	100.0	100.0	100.0	100.0

.. Not available

Note: Detailed metadata at: *http://metalinks.oecd.org/ins/20220309/7297.*

Source: *Insurance activity indicators, OECD Insurance Statistics (database)*

Table 11. Market share in OECD (Life)

Per cent

	2013	2014	2015	2016	2017	2018	2019	2020
Australia	2.0	2.4	2.0	1.7	1.6	1.3	1.1	0.8
Austria	0.4	0.4	0.3	0.3	0.3	0.2	0.2	..
Belgium	0.9	0.9	0.7	0.7	0.7	0.7	0.7	0.7
Canada	1.4	1.1	1.0	1.0	1.1	1.0	..	..
Chile	0.3	0.3	0.3	0.4	0.4	0.4	0.3	0.2
Colombia	0.2	0.2	0.2	0.2	0.2	0.2	0.2	0.2
Costa Rica	0.0	0.0	0.0	0.0	0.0	0.0	0.0	0.0
Czech Republic	0.2	0.1	0.1	0.1	0.1	0.1	0.1	0.1
Denmark	..	1.0	0.9	0.9	1.1	1.1	1.1	1.2
Estonia	0.0	0.0	0.0	0.0	0.0	0.0	0.0	0.0
Finland	0.3	0.3	0.3	0.2	0.2	0.2	0.3	0.2
France	7.3	7.6	6.7	7.5	7.1	7.0	7.4	6.0
Germany	5.1	4.9	4.2	4.0	4.1	4.0	4.5	4.6
Greece	0.1	0.1	0.1	0.1	0.1	0.1	0.1	0.1
Hungary	0.1	0.1	0.1	0.1	0.1	0.1	0.1	0.1
Iceland	0.0	0.0	0.0	0.0	0.0	0.0	0.0	0.0
Ireland	1.6	1.7	1.6	1.5	1.6	1.4	1.4	1.4
Israel	0.3	0.3	0.3	0.3	0.4	0.4	0.4	0.4
Italy	4.9	6.0	5.4	4.7	4.7	4.6	4.7	4.6
Japan	14.9	13.9	13.1	13.5	12.1	11.3	11.6	11.0
Korea	4.3	4.3	4.4	4.3	4.2	3.8	..	4.0
Latvia	0.0	0.0	0.0	0.0	0.0	0.0	0.0	0.0
Lithuania	0.0	0.0	0.0	0.0	0.0	0.0	0.0	0.0
Luxembourg	1.0	1.1	0.8	0.8	0.9	0.8	1.0	0.8
Mexico	0.5	0.5	0.5	0.5	0.5	0.5	0.6	0.5
Netherlands	1.0	0.9	0.7	0.6	0.6	0.5	..	..
New Zealand	..	..	..	..	..	..	0.1	..
Norway	0.6	0.6	0.5	0.5	0.5	0.5	0.5	0.4
Poland	0.4	0.4	0.3	0.3	0.3	0.2	0.2	0.2
Portugal	0.5	0.5	0.4	0.3	0.3	0.3	0.3	0.2
Slovak Republic	0.1	0.1	0.1	..	0.2	..	0.1	0.1
Slovenia	0.0	0.0	0.0	0.0	0.0	0.0	0.0	0.0
Spain	1.5	1.4	1.2	1.4	1.4	1.3	1.2	1.1
Sweden	0.6	1.4	1.2	1.2	1.4	1.4	1.5	..
Switzerland	1.5	1.5	1.4	1.3	1.3	1.2	1.2	1.1
Turkey	0.1	0.1	0.1	0.1	0.1	0.1	0.1	0.1
United Kingdom	10.5	10.8	10.3	11.5	11.2	12.7	12.1	10.7
United States	37.5	35.3	40.8	40.0	41.6	42.7	46.9	49.3
OECD Total	100.0	100.0	100.0	100.0	100.0	100.0	100.0	100.0

.. Not available

Note: Detailed metadata at: *http://metalinks.oecd.org/ins/20220309/7297.*

Source: *Insurance activity indicators, OECD Insurance Statistics (database)*

Table 12. Market share in OECD (Non-life)

Per cent

	2013	2014	2015	2016	2017	2018	2019	2020
Australia	1.7	1.5	1.3	1.2	1.2	1.3	1.4	1.3
Austria	0.7	0.7	0.6	0.5	0.5	0.6	0.6	..
Belgium	0.7	0.7	0.6	0.5	0.5	0.6	0.7	0.7
Canada	2.9	2.7	2.4	2.1	2.1	2.3	..	..
Chile	0.2	0.2	0.1	0.1	0.1	0.2	0.2	0.1
Colombia	0.2	0.2	0.2	0.1	0.2	0.2	0.2	0.2
Costa Rica	0.0	0.0	0.0	0.0	0.0	0.0	0.0	0.0
Czech Republic	0.2	0.2	0.1	0.1	0.1	0.2	0.2	0.2
Denmark	0.5	0.5	0.4	0.4	0.4	0.5	0.4	0.4
Estonia	0.0	0.0	0.0	0.0	0.0	0.0	0.0	0.0
Finland	0.2	0.2	0.2	0.2	0.2	..	..	..
France	4.5	4.3	3.7	4.7	4.8	5.8	5.9	5.6
Germany	9.3	8.8	7.9	7.1	7.2	8.7	9.2	9.2
Greece	0.1	0.1	0.1	0.1	0.1	0.1	0.1	0.1
Hungary	0.1	0.1	0.1	0.1	0.1	0.1	0.1	0.1
Iceland	0.0	0.0	0.0	0.0	0.0	0.0	0.0	0.0
Ireland	0.4	0.4	0.4	0.6	0.3	0.4	0.5	0.4
Israel	0.3	0.3	0.3	0.3	0.3	0.3	0.3	0.3
Italy	2.0	1.8	1.5	1.3	1.3	1.6	1.6	1.5
Japan	..	..	..	3.8	3.3	3.8	4.3	4.0
Korea	3.0	3.3	3.2	2.9	3.0	3.4	..	3.6
Latvia	0.0	0.0	0.0	0.0	0.0	0.0	0.0	0.0
Lithuania	0.0	0.0	0.0	0.0	0.0	0.0	0.0	0.0
Luxembourg	0.1	0.1	0.1	0.1	0.1	0.1	0.1	0.1
Mexico	0.6	0.6	0.5	0.5	0.5	0.6	0.7	0.6
Netherlands	1.2	1.0	0.9	2.2	2.2	2.7	..	..
New Zealand	0.2	0.2	0.2	0.2	0.2	..	0.2	..
Norway	0.5	0.5	0.4	0.3	0.3	0.4	0.4	0.4
Poland	0.4	0.3	0.3	0.3	0.3	0.4	0.4	0.4
Portugal	0.2	0.2	0.2	0.2	0.2	0.2	0.2	0.2
Slovak Republic	0.1	0.1	0.0	..	0.0	..	0.1	0.1
Slovenia	0.1	0.1	0.1	0.1	0.1	0.1	0.1	0.1
Spain	1.9	1.7	1.5	1.4	1.4	1.7	1.7	1.7
Sweden	0.6	0.6	0.4	0.4	0.4	0.5	0.5	..
Switzerland	1.7	1.6	1.5	1.3	1.3	1.5	1.6	1.6
Turkey	0.5	0.4	0.4	0.4	0.4	0.4	0.4	0.4
United Kingdom	4.1	3.9	3.7	4.5	4.2	5.0	4.6	4.2
United States	61.0	62.8	66.9	62.1	62.6	56.6	63.4	62.5
OECD Total	100.0	100.0	100.0	100.0	100.0	100.0	100.0	100.0

.. Not available

Note: Detailed metadata at: *http://metalinks.oecd.org/ins/20220309/7297*.

Source: *Insurance activity indicators, OECD Insurance Statistics (database)*

Table 13. Density (Life and Non-life)

US dollar per inhabitant

	2013	2014	2015	2016	2017	2018	2019	2020
Argentina	393	405	418	422	393	428	264	258
Australia	3 350	3 688	2 926	2 660	2 540	2 383	2 012	1 835
Austria	2 603	2 657	2 227	2 143	2 176	2 284	2 219	2 285
Belgium	3 260	3 308	2 653	2 613	2 653	2 903	2 853	2 744
Bermuda	..	..	..	..	..	..	..	..
Bolivia	..	..	..	42	43	47	50	50
Brazil	337	346	273	287	321	295	300	230
Bulgaria	..	..	..	..	..	214	236	239
Canada	2 538	2 168	1 930	1 919	2 010	2 085	..	..
Chile	665	613	630	675	692	740	668	508
Colombia	214	199	163	162	179	185	183	162
Costa Rica	218	241	216	246	265	265	278	280
Cuba	..	..	..	..	..	..	..	..
Czech Republic	747	712	574	555	590	651	663	660
Denmark	6 079	6 543	5 610	5 699	6 315	6 842	6 486	6 911
Dominican Republic	..	..	..	..	..	119	..	..
Ecuador	..	..	139	127	98	100	103	..
Egypt	..	..	..	..	14	17	19	24
El Salvador	..	..	..	..	..	97	103	104
Estonia	587	638	581	619	702	826	830	805
Finland	2 371	2 556	2 150	1 797	1 803	935	1 221	835
France	3 893	4 110	3 554	4 108	4 246	4 560	4 461	4 062
Germany	3 112	3 131	2 597	2 602	2 838	3 049	3 090	3 233
Greece	480	457	361	359	388	414	419	435
Guatemala	43	46	48	50	55	54	56	57
Honduras	42	42	44	..	..	66	64	62
Hong Kong, China	5 003	5 658	6 259	7 652	8 266	8 803	..	..
Hungary	357	360	300	317	350	381	401	397
Iceland	1 270	1 329	1 245	1 436	1 783	1 840	1 684	1 495
India	..	..	54	62	71	..	78	..
Indonesia	60	55	56	66	73	71	72	65
Ireland	9 606	11 052	10 154	11 107	10 207	9 554	9 492	8 901
Israel[1]	1 731	1 749	1 685	1 772	2 001	2 090	2 135	2 117
Italy	2 600	3 125	2 678	2 445	2 437	2 645	2 595	2 549
Japan	2 545	2 580	2 370	3 201	2 893	3 010	2 989	2 890
Korea	3 181	3 503	3 418	3 437	3 483	3 506	3 532	3 631
Latvia	309	343	297	299	374	461	500	478
Lithuania	254	272	246	274	317	370	379	390
Luxembourg	45 569	51 995	37 506	35 103	41 043	40 668	43 263	36 152
Malaysia	520	530	454	441	439	481	508	508
Mexico	226	224	202	194	210	222	243	216
Montenegro	..	..	..	..	..	..	170	171
Morocco	..	..	..	..	115	124	..	..
Netherlands	3 002	2 846	2 176	4 532	4 626	4 971	4 857	5 035
New Zealand	1 148	1 178	971	989	1 012	..	1 455	1 240
Nicaragua	26	29	30	32	34	35	31	31
Norway	5 011	5 132	3 967	3 972	3 858	4 131	4 119	3 958
Panama	321	..	..	..	..	..	372	355
Paraguay	54	..	63	53	56	61	61	..
Peru	110	116	118	106	109	122	128	120
Poland	475	453	372	361	420	436	418	409
Portugal	1 570	1 735	1 293	1 110	1 189	1 369	1 225	997
Puerto Rico	2 661	2 552	3 182	3 927	..	..	..	..
Russia	..	176	115	120	149	161	156	145
Singapore	4 047	4 489	4 400	4 631	5 411	..	5 764	6 440
Slovak Republic	542	544	434	..	927	..	518	510
Slovenia	1 209	1 198	1 012	1 028	1 105	1 223	1 250	1 287
South Africa	986	923	830	733	..	..	..	702
Spain	1 529	1 521	1 295	1 456	1 467	1 550	1 447	1 354
Sri Lanka	..	35	44	..	51	52	..	..
Sweden	2 644	4 908	3 961	3 796	4 248	4 646	4 572	4 830
Switzerland	7 898	7 892	7 456	7 025	6 904	6 962	6 879	6 646
Chinese Taipei	..	..	..	..	..	5 181	4 991	4 798
Thailand	..	..	..	..	..	..	..	..
Tunisia	..	..	..	75	75	72	70	76
Turkey	168	151	145	162	152	126	131	130
United Kingdom	4 793	5 098	4 598	3 950	5 123	5 672	5 044	4 590
United States	5 687	5 971	6 307	6 503	6 721	7 093	7 500	7 929
Uruguay	351	377	368	..	451	425	442	414
OECD Total	3 016	3 172	3 037	3 186	3 293	3 489	3 556	3 600

.. Not available

Note: Detailed metadata at: *http://metalinks.oecd.org/ins/20220309/7297.*

1. Information on data for Israel: *http://oe.cd/israel-disclaimer.*

Source: *Insurance activity indicators, OECD Insurance Statistics (database)*

Table 14. Density (Life)

US dollar per inhabitant

	2013	2014	2015	2016	2017	2018	2019	2020
Argentina	70	70	67	70	60	63	37	34
Australia	1 898	2 321	1 781	1 521	1 335	1 180	848	638
Austria	1 007	1 039	860	765	735	735	683	683
Belgium	1 937	1 930	1 512	1 458	1 454	1 613	1 580	1 457
Bermuda	..	..	..	..	..	..	..	..
Bolivia	..	..	..	14	17	20	22	24
Brazil	204	209	171	190	214	196	208	158
Bulgaria	..	..	..	..	..	29	29	28
Canada	834	629	555	561	604	625	..	..
Chile	444	406	432	475	481	509	448	304
Colombia	111	96	77	80	93	94	94	83
Costa Rica	29	30	27	38	39	43	45	42
Cuba	..	..	..	..	..	..	..	..
Czech Republic	348	326	241	229	230	242	215	206
Denmark	4 236	4 443	3 878	4 006	4 495	4 939	4 719	5 098
Dominican Republic	..	..	..	..	..	19	..	..
Ecuador	..	..	28	28	27	30	30	..
Egypt	..	..	..	..	6	7	9	11
El Salvador	..	..	..	..	..	24	26	28
Estonia	172	193	181	186	191	208	213	229
Finland	1 366	1 485	1 268	923	929	935	1 221	835
France	2 486	2 684	2 344	2 391	2 449	2 636	2 580	2 116
Germany	1 445	1 456	1 180	1 148	1 197	1 282	1 350	1 383
Greece	203	228	184	171	197	207	215	224
Guatemala	9	10	9	10	11	11	12	12
Honduras	21	15	16	..	..	22	21	20
Hong Kong, China	4 446	5 082	5 644	7 041	7 642	8 149	..	..
Hungary	197	199	155	159	171	178	179	176
Iceland	103	111	107	128	161	155	142	134
India	..	..	42	47	53	..	59	..
Indonesia	43	38	39	49	56	52	52	47
Ireland	7 803	9 158	8 141	7 729	8 198	7 413	7 231	6 886
Israel[1]	915	904	903	935	1 076	1 128	1 173	1 144
Italy	1 866	2 413	2 096	1 864	1 837	1 994	1 963	1 919
Japan	2 545	2 580	2 370	2 496	2 252	2 348	2 277	2 163
Korea	1 966	2 070	2 032	2 015	1 962	1 952	1 946	1 957
Latvia	59	71	64	70	84	89	133	144
Lithuania	81	97	90	95	92	105	108	119
Luxembourg	41 868	48 768	34 604	32 123	37 673	37 331	39 401	32 104
Malaysia	333	340	294	290	295	325	354	358
Mexico	105	106	95	91	92	101	111	100
Montenegro	..	..	..	..	..	..	31	36
Morocco	..	..	..	..	51	55	..	..
Netherlands	1 446	1 378	964	895	857	823	804	803
New Zealand	..	..	..	..	..	..	343	271
Nicaragua	4	5	5	6	7	7	6	6
Norway	2 715	2 837	2 187	2 133	2 139	2 309	2 306	2 093
Panama	128	..	..	..	..	..	96	93
Paraguay	7	..	8	0	8	9	8	..
Peru	51	57	57	48	52	59	63	57
Poland	260	239	192	159	171	158	146	140
Portugal	1 146	1 309	908	697	736	893	736	476
Puerto Rico	114	161	156	373	..	..	..	..
Russia	..	23	16	25	42	53	43	41
Singapore	3 045	3 392	3 404	3 611	4 374	..	4 537	5 277
Slovak Republic	303	299	227	..	683	..	252	243
Slovenia	305	309	268	264	282	300	297	285
South Africa	794	760	678	602	..	..	..	564
Spain	729	712	606	736	705	722	643	521
Sri Lanka	..	13	19	..	22	22	..	..
Sweden	1 469	3 562	2 994	2 931	3 335	3 625	3 564	4 087
Switzerland	4 385	4 378	4 113	3 739	3 573	3 592	3 533	3 055
Chinese Taipei	..	..	..	..	..	4 948	4 749	4 529
Thailand	..	..	..	..	..	..	..	..
Tunisia	..	..	..	15	15	16	16	18
Turkey	26	19	17	25	27	21	28	28
United Kingdom	3 488	3 781	3 411	2 508	3 696	4 155	3 828	3 385
United States	2 473	2 476	2 577	2 588	2 642	2 783	2 948	3 134
Uruguay	101	111	123	..	190	169	195	189
OECD Total	1 673	1 755	1 636	1 590	1 643	1 741	1 765	1 734

.. Not available

Note: Detailed metadata at: *http://metalinks.oecd.org/ins/20220309/7297*.

1. Information on data for Israel: *http://oe.cd/israel-disclaimer*.

Source: *Insurance activity indicators, OECD Insurance Statistics (database)*

Table 15. Density (Non-life)

US dollar per inhabitant

	2013	2014	2015	2016	2017	2018	2019	2020
Argentina	323	335	351	352	333	365	227	224
Australia	1 453	1 367	1 145	1 139	1 206	1 203	1 164	1 197
Austria	1 596	1 617	1 367	1 377	1 441	1 550	1 536	1 602
Belgium	1 323	1 378	1 142	1 156	1 200	1 290	1 273	1 286
Bermuda	..	..	..	..	..	..	..	..
Bolivia	..	..	..	28	25	27	27	26
Brazil	133	138	102	97	108	99	92	72
Bulgaria	..	..	..	..	..	184	207	211
Canada	1 704	1 539	1 375	1 358	1 407	1 460	..	..
Chile	221	208	198	200	211	231	220	204
Colombia	103	103	85	83	86	91	88	80
Costa Rica	189	211	188	208	226	222	234	238
Cuba	..	..	..	..	..	..	..	..
Czech Republic	399	386	333	325	360	409	447	454
Denmark	1 843	2 101	1 732	1 692	1 820	1 903	1 767	1 813
Dominican Republic	..	..	..	..	..	100	..	..
Ecuador	..	..	112	98	71	71	73	..
Egypt	..	..	..	..	8	10	10	13
El Salvador	..	..	..	..	..	73	76	76
Estonia	415	444	400	433	510	618	617	577
Finland	1 005	1 071	882	875	873	..	..	..
France	1 407	1 427	1 209	1 717	1 797	1 924	1 880	1 946
Germany	1 667	1 674	1 417	1 454	1 641	1 767	1 740	1 850
Greece	277	229	177	188	190	207	204	210
Guatemala	34	36	39	40	43	43	44	44
Honduras	21	27	28	..	..	44	43	43
Hong Kong, China	557	577	615	611	624	654	..	..
Hungary	160	161	145	158	179	203	222	221
Iceland	1 166	1 217	1 138	1 308	1 621	1 685	1 542	1 361
India	..	..	11	15	18	..	20	..
Indonesia	17	18	17	17	18	18	20	17
Ireland	1 803	1 894	2 013	3 378	1 890	1 915	2 116	2 015
Israel[1]	815	845	782	838	925	962	962	973
Italy	735	712	582	581	600	651	632	631
Japan	..	..	..	705	641	662	712	727
Korea	1 215	1 433	1 386	1 421	1 521	1 554	1 586	1 674
Latvia	250	273	232	230	290	373	366	333
Lithuania	173	175	156	179	224	265	271	271
Luxembourg	3 700	3 227	2 902	2 980	3 370	3 337	3 862	4 048
Malaysia	187	190	160	150	144	156	155	150
Mexico	120	118	107	102	119	121	132	116
Montenegro	..	..	..	..	..	..	139	135
Morocco	..	..	..	..	64	69	..	..
Netherlands	1 556	1 467	1 212	3 637	3 768	4 148	4 053	4 233
New Zealand	1 148	1 178	971	989	1 012	..	1 111	969
Nicaragua	21	24	25	26	28	28	25	25
Norway	2 295	2 295	1 780	1 840	1 719	1 822	1 813	1 866
Panama	192	..	..	..	..	..	275	262
Paraguay	48	..	54	53	48	53	53	..
Peru	59	59	61	58	58	62	65	63
Poland	216	214	180	202	249	278	272	268
Portugal	424	426	385	413	454	476	490	521
Puerto Rico	2 546	2 391	3 026	3 554	..	..	..	..
Russia	..	110	98	95	107	108	113	105
Singapore	1 001	1 098	996	1 021	1 037	..	1 227	1 163
Slovak Republic	238	244	207	..	244	..	266	267
Slovenia	904	889	744	765	823	923	953	1 002
South Africa	192	163	152	131	..	..	..	138
Spain	800	809	690	721	763	828	804	833
Sri Lanka	..	22	25	..	30	30	..	..
Sweden	1 175	1 346	967	865	913	1 021	1 008	743
Switzerland	3 513	3 514	3 343	3 286	3 331	3 370	3 346	3 591
Chinese Taipei	..	..	..	..	..	233	243	269
Thailand	..	..	..	..	..	..	..	..
Tunisia	..	..	..	60	59	56	54	58
Turkey	141	131	128	137	125	105	103	102
United Kingdom	1 306	1 317	1 188	1 441	1 427	1 517	1 216	1 205
United States	3 215	3 496	3 731	3 914	4 079	4 310	4 552	4 796
Uruguay	250	266	245	..	261	256	247	225
OECD Total	1 343	1 417	1 401	1 596	1 650	1 747	1 790	1 866

.. Not available

Note: Detailed metadata at: *http://metalinks.oecd.org/ins/20220309/7297*.

1. Information on data for Israel: *http://oe.cd/israel-disclaimer*.

Source: *Insurance activity indicators, OECD Insurance Statistics (database)*

Table 16. Penetration (Life and Non-life)

Per cent

	2013	2014	2015	2016	2017	2018	2019	2020
Argentina	2.4	2.4	2.6	2.6	2.6	2.3	2.1	2.6
Australia	5.3	6.1	5.8	5.3	4.7	4.3	3.8	3.5
Austria	5.1	5.1	5.0	4.7	4.6	4.5	4.4	4.7
Belgium	7.0	6.9	6.4	6.2	6.0	6.1	6.1	6.1
Bermuda	..	..	..	..	..	..	..	..
Bolivia	..	..	..	1.4	1.3	1.3	1.4	1.5
Brazil	2.7	2.8	3.1	3.3	3.2	3.2	3.4	3.4
Bulgaria	..	..	..	..	..	2.3	2.4	2.4
Canada	4.8	4.2	4.4	4.5	4.4	4.5	..	..
Chile	4.2	4.2	4.6	4.9	4.6	4.7	4.6	3.9
Colombia	2.6	2.5	2.7	2.8	2.8	2.8	2.8	3.0
Costa Rica	2.0	2.2	1.9	2.1	2.2	2.1	2.2	2.3
Cuba	..	..	..	..	..	..	..	..
Czech Republic	3.7	3.6	3.2	3.0	2.9	2.8	2.8	2.9
Denmark	9.9	10.4	10.5	10.4	10.9	11.1	10.8	11.3
Dominican Republic	..	..	..	..	..	1.4	..	..
Ecuador	..	..	2.3	2.1	1.6	1.6	1.7	..
Egypt	..	..	..	..	0.7	0.7	0.6	0.7
El Salvador	..	..	..	..	..	2.4	2.5	2.7
Estonia	3.1	3.1	3.3	3.4	3.4	3.6	3.5	3.5
Finland	4.7	5.1	5.0	4.1	3.9	1.9	2.5	1.7
France	8.8	9.2	9.4	10.7	10.6	10.6	10.6	10.1
Germany	6.7	6.5	6.3	6.2	6.4	6.4	6.6	7.0
Greece	2.2	2.1	2.0	2.0	2.1	2.1	2.2	2.5
Guatemala	1.3	1.3	1.3	1.3	1.3	1.3	1.3	1.3
Honduras	2.0	1.9	1.9	..	..	2.6	2.5	2.6
Hong Kong, China	13.1	14.1	14.8	17.6	18.0	18.2	..	..
Hungary	2.6	2.5	2.4	2.4	2.4	2.3	2.4	2.5
Iceland	2.5	2.4	2.3	2.3	2.4	2.4	2.4	2.5
India	..	..	3.4	3.6	3.6	..	3.8	..
Indonesia	1.6	1.6	1.7	1.8	1.9	1.8	1.7	1.6
Ireland	18.7	19.9	16.4	17.7	14.7	12.1	11.8	10.4
Israel[1]	4.7	4.6	4.7	4.7	4.9	5.0	4.9	4.8
Italy	7.3	8.8	8.9	7.9	7.5	7.6	7.8	8.1
Japan	6.3	6.8	6.7	7.6	7.3	7.7	7.2	7.1
Korea	11.7	12.0	11.9	11.7	11.0	10.5	11.1	11.5
Latvia	2.1	2.2	2.2	2.1	2.4	2.6	2.8	2.7
Lithuania	1.6	1.6	1.7	1.8	1.9	1.9	1.9	2.0
Luxembourg	39.6	43.2	36.6	33.3	37.8	34.5	37.4	30.9
Malaysia	4.8	4.7	4.7	4.6	4.4	4.3	4.5	5.0
Mexico	2.1	2.0	2.1	2.2	2.3	2.3	2.4	2.6
Montenegro	..	..	..	..	..	..	1.9	2.2
Morocco	..	..	..	..	3.6	3.7	..	..
Netherlands	5.7	5.4	4.8	9.8	9.5	9.3	9.2	9.6
New Zealand	2.9	2.6	2.5	2.5	2.4	..	3.4	3.0
Nicaragua	1.4	1.5	1.5	1.5	1.6	1.7	1.6	1.7
Norway	4.9	5.3	5.4	5.7	5.1	5.0	5.4	5.9
Panama	2.7	..	..	..	..	..	2.3	2.9
Paraguay	0.9	..	1.0	1.0	1.0	1.1	1.1	..
Peru	1.7	1.8	1.9	1.7	1.6	1.7	1.8	2.0
Poland	3.5	3.2	3.0	2.9	3.0	2.8	2.7	2.6
Portugal	7.2	7.8	6.7	5.6	5.5	5.8	5.3	4.4
Puerto Rico	9.3	8.8	10.7	12.8	..	..	..	..
Russia	..	1.2	1.2	1.4	1.4	1.4	1.4	1.4
Singapore	7.1	7.8	7.9	8.1	8.8	..	8.8	10.9
Slovak Republic	3.0	2.9	2.7	..	5.3	..	2.7	2.7
Slovenia	5.1	4.9	4.8	4.7	4.7	4.7	4.8	5.0
South Africa	14.5	14.4	14.5	13.9	..	..	..	13.9
Spain	5.3	5.2	5.0	5.5	5.2	5.1	4.9	5.0
Sri Lanka	..	0.9	1.1	..	1.3	1.3	..	..
Sweden	4.3	8.2	7.7	7.4	7.9	8.6	8.8	9.3
Switzerland	8.9	8.7	8.7	8.4	8.3	8.0	8.0	7.6
Chinese Taipei	..	..	..	..	..	20.1	19.2	17.0
Thailand	..	..	..	..	..	..	..	..
Tunisia	..	..	..	2.0	2.2	2.1	2.1	2.3
Turkey	1.3	1.2	1.3	1.5	1.4	1.3	1.4	1.5
United Kingdom	11.0	10.7	10.2	9.6	12.7	13.2	11.9	11.4
United States	10.7	10.8	11.1	11.2	11.2	11.3	11.5	12.5
Uruguay	1.9	2.1	2.2	..	2.5	2.3	2.5	2.8
OECD Total	8.1	8.4	8.5	8.7	8.8	8.9	9.0	9.4

.. Not available

Note: Detailed metadata at: *http://metalinks.oecd.org/ins/20220309/7297*.

1. Information on data for Israel: *http://oe.cd/israel-disclaimer*.

Source: *Insurance activity indicators, OECD Insurance Statistics (database)*

Table 17. Penetration (Life)

Per cent

	2013	2014	2015	2016	2017	2018	2019	2020
Argentina	0.4	0.4	0.4	0.4	0.4	0.3	0.3	0.3
Australia	3.0	3.8	3.5	3.0	2.4	2.2	1.6	1.2
Austria	2.0	2.0	1.9	1.7	1.6	1.4	1.4	1.4
Belgium	4.1	4.0	3.7	3.5	3.3	3.4	3.4	3.3
Bermuda	..	..	..	..	..	..	..	..
Bolivia	..	..	..	0.5	0.5	0.6	0.6	0.7
Brazil	1.7	1.7	1.9	2.2	2.1	2.1	2.3	2.3
Bulgaria	..	..	..	..	..	0.3	0.3	0.3
Canada	1.6	1.2	1.3	1.3	1.3	1.3	..	..
Chile	2.8	2.8	3.2	3.4	3.2	3.2	3.1	2.3
Colombia	1.4	1.2	1.3	1.4	1.5	1.4	1.5	1.5
Costa Rica	0.3	0.3	0.2	0.3	0.3	0.3	0.4	0.3
Cuba	..	..	..	..	..	..	..	..
Czech Republic	1.7	1.6	1.3	1.2	1.1	1.0	0.9	0.9
Denmark	6.9	7.1	7.3	7.3	7.8	8.0	7.9	8.3
Dominican Republic	..	..	..	..	..	0.2	..	..
Ecuador	..	..	0.5	0.5	0.4	0.5	0.5	..
Egypt	..	..	..	..	0.3	0.3	0.3	0.3
El Salvador	..	..	..	..	..	0.6	0.6	0.7
Estonia	0.9	1.0	1.0	1.0	0.9	0.9	0.9	1.0
Finland	2.7	2.9	3.0	2.1	2.0	1.9	2.5	1.7
France	5.6	6.0	6.2	6.2	6.1	6.1	6.1	5.2
Germany	3.1	3.0	2.9	2.7	2.7	2.7	2.9	3.0
Greece	0.9	1.1	1.0	1.0	1.1	1.0	1.1	1.3
Guatemala	0.3	0.3	0.2	0.3	0.3	0.3	0.3	0.3
Honduras	1.0	0.7	0.7	..	..	0.9	0.8	0.8
Hong Kong, China	11.6	12.6	13.3	16.2	16.6	16.9	..	..
Hungary	1.4	1.4	1.2	1.2	1.2	1.1	1.1	1.1
Iceland	0.2	0.2	0.2	0.2	0.2	0.2	0.2	0.2
India	..	..	2.7	2.7	2.7	..	2.8	..
Indonesia	1.2	1.1	1.2	1.3	1.4	1.3	1.2	1.2
Ireland	15.2	16.5	13.2	12.3	11.8	9.4	9.0	8.1
Israel[1]	2.5	2.4	2.5	2.5	2.6	2.7	2.7	2.6
Italy	5.3	6.8	6.9	6.0	5.7	5.8	5.9	6.1
Japan	6.3	6.8	6.7	5.9	5.7	6.0	5.5	5.3
Korea	7.2	7.1	7.1	6.9	6.2	5.8	6.1	6.2
Latvia	0.4	0.5	0.5	0.5	0.5	0.5	0.8	0.8
Lithuania	0.5	0.6	0.6	0.6	0.5	0.5	0.6	0.6
Luxembourg	36.4	40.5	33.7	30.5	34.7	31.7	34.0	27.4
Malaysia	3.1	3.0	3.0	3.0	3.0	2.9	3.2	3.5
Mexico	1.0	1.0	1.0	1.0	1.0	1.0	1.1	1.2
Montenegro	..	..	..	..	..	..	0.3	0.5
Morocco	..	..	..	..	1.6	1.6	..	..
Netherlands	2.8	2.6	2.1	1.9	1.8	1.5	1.5	1.5
New Zealand	..	..	..	..	..	..	0.8	0.7
Nicaragua	0.2	0.3	0.3	0.3	0.3	0.4	0.3	0.3
Norway	2.6	2.9	3.0	3.0	2.8	2.8	3.0	3.1
Panama	1.1	..	..	..	..	..	0.6	0.8
Paraguay	0.1	..	0.1	0.0	0.1	0.1	0.1	..
Peru	0.8	0.9	0.9	0.8	0.8	0.8	0.9	0.9
Poland	1.9	1.7	1.5	1.3	1.2	1.0	0.9	0.9
Portugal	5.3	5.9	4.7	3.5	3.4	3.8	3.2	2.1
Puerto Rico	0.4	0.6	0.5	1.2	..	..	..	..
Russia	..	0.2	0.2	0.3	0.4	0.5	0.4	0.4
Singapore	5.3	5.9	6.1	6.4	7.1	..	6.9	9.0
Slovak Republic	1.7	1.6	1.4	..	3.9	..	1.3	1.3
Slovenia	1.3	1.3	1.3	1.2	1.2	1.1	1.1	1.1
South Africa	11.6	11.8	11.8	11.4	..	..	..	11.1
Spain	2.5	2.4	2.4	2.8	2.5	2.4	2.2	1.9
Sri Lanka	..	0.3	0.5	..	0.5	0.5	..	..
Sweden	2.4	6.0	5.8	5.7	6.2	6.7	6.9	7.8
Switzerland	4.9	4.9	4.8	4.5	4.3	4.1	4.1	3.5
Chinese Taipei	..	..	..	..	..	19.2	18.3	16.0
Thailand	..	..	..	..	..	..	..	..
Tunisia	..	..	..	0.4	0.4	0.5	0.5	0.5
Turkey	0.2	0.2	0.2	0.2	0.3	0.2	0.3	0.3
United Kingdom	8.0	8.0	7.6	6.1	9.2	9.7	9.0	8.4
United States	4.6	4.5	4.5	4.5	4.4	4.4	4.5	5.0
Uruguay	0.6	0.6	0.7	..	1.0	0.9	1.1	1.3
OECD Total	4.5	4.6	4.6	4.4	4.4	4.4	4.5	4.6

.. Not available

Note: Detailed metadata at: *http://metalinks.oecd.org/ins/20220309/7297.*

1. Information on data for Israel: *http://oe.cd/israel-disclaimer.*

Source: *Insurance activity indicators, OECD Insurance Statistics (database)*

Table 18. Penetration (Non-life)

Per cent

	2013	2014	2015	2016	2017	2018	2019	2020
Argentina	2.0	2.0	2.2	2.1	2.2	2.0	1.8	2.2
Australia	2.3	2.2	2.2	2.3	2.2	2.2	2.2	2.3
Austria	3.1	3.1	3.1	3.0	3.0	3.0	3.1	3.3
Belgium	2.8	2.9	2.8	2.7	2.7	2.7	2.7	2.9
Bermuda	..	..	..	..	..	..	..	..
Bolivia	..	..	..	0.9	0.8	0.8	0.8	0.8
Brazil	1.1	1.1	1.1	1.1	1.1	1.1	1.0	1.1
Bulgaria	..	..	..	..	..	1.9	2.1	2.1
Canada	3.2	3.0	3.2	3.2	3.1	3.1	..	..
Chile	1.4	1.4	1.5	1.4	1.4	1.5	1.5	1.6
Colombia	1.3	1.3	1.4	1.4	1.4	1.4	1.4	1.5
Costa Rica	1.8	1.9	1.6	1.7	1.9	1.8	1.9	2.0
Cuba	..	..	..	..	..	..	..	..
Czech Republic	2.0	1.9	1.9	1.8	1.7	1.7	1.9	2.0
Denmark	3.0	3.3	3.2	3.1	3.2	3.1	3.0	3.0
Dominican Republic	..	..	..	..	..	1.2	..	..
Ecuador	..	..	1.8	1.6	1.1	1.1	1.2	..
Egypt	..	..	..	..	0.4	0.4	0.3	0.3
El Salvador	..	..	..	..	..	1.8	1.8	2.0
Estonia	2.2	2.2	2.3	2.4	2.5	2.7	2.6	2.5
Finland	2.0	2.1	2.1	2.0	1.9	..	..	..
France	3.2	3.2	3.2	4.5	4.5	4.5	4.5	4.8
Germany	3.6	3.5	3.4	3.5	3.7	3.7	3.7	4.0
Greece	1.3	1.1	1.0	1.1	1.0	1.0	1.1	1.2
Guatemala	1.0	1.0	1.0	1.0	1.0	1.0	1.0	1.0
Honduras	1.0	1.2	1.2	..	..	1.8	1.7	1.8
Hong Kong, China	1.5	1.4	1.5	1.4	1.4	1.4	..	..
Hungary	1.2	1.1	1.1	1.2	1.2	1.2	1.3	1.4
Iceland	2.3	2.2	2.1	2.1	2.2	2.2	2.2	2.3
India	..	..	0.7	0.9	0.9	..	0.9	..
Indonesia	0.5	0.5	0.5	0.5	0.5	0.5	0.5	0.4
Ireland	3.5	3.4	3.3	5.4	2.7	2.4	2.6	2.4
Israel[1]	2.2	2.2	2.2	2.2	2.3	2.3	2.2	2.2
Italy	2.1	2.0	1.9	1.9	1.9	1.9	1.9	2.0
Japan	..	..	..	1.7	1.6	1.7	1.7	1.8
Korea	4.5	4.9	4.8	4.9	4.8	4.6	5.0	5.3
Latvia	1.7	1.7	1.7	1.6	1.9	2.1	2.1	1.9
Lithuania	1.1	1.1	1.1	1.2	1.3	1.4	1.4	1.4
Luxembourg	3.2	2.7	2.8	2.8	3.1	2.8	3.3	3.5
Malaysia	1.7	1.7	1.7	1.6	1.4	1.4	1.4	1.5
Mexico	1.1	1.1	1.1	1.2	1.3	1.2	1.3	1.4
Montenegro	..	..	..	..	..	..	1.6	1.8
Morocco	..	..	..	..	2.0	2.1	..	..
Netherlands	3.0	2.8	2.7	7.9	7.7	7.8	7.7	8.1
New Zealand	2.9	2.6	2.5	2.5	2.4	..	2.6	2.3
Nicaragua	1.2	1.2	1.2	1.3	1.3	1.4	1.3	1.3
Norway	2.2	2.4	2.4	2.6	2.3	2.2	2.4	2.8
Panama	1.6	..	..	..	..	..	1.7	2.1
Paraguay	0.8	..	0.9	1.0	0.9	0.9	0.9	..
Peru	0.9	0.9	1.0	0.9	0.9	0.9	0.9	1.0
Poland	1.6	1.5	1.4	1.6	1.8	1.8	1.7	1.7
Portugal	2.0	1.9	2.0	2.1	2.1	2.0	2.1	2.3
Puerto Rico	8.9	8.3	10.2	11.6	..	..	..	..
Russia	..	0.8	1.1	1.1	1.0	1.0	1.0	1.0
Singapore	1.8	1.9	1.8	1.8	1.7	..	1.9	2.0
Slovak Republic	1.3	1.3	1.3	..	1.4	..	1.4	1.4
Slovenia	3.8	3.7	3.6	3.5	3.5	3.5	3.7	3.9
South Africa	2.8	2.5	2.7	2.5	..	..	..	2.7
Spain	2.8	2.7	2.7	2.7	2.7	2.7	2.7	3.1
Sri Lanka	..	0.6	0.6	..	0.7	0.7	..	..
Sweden	1.9	2.3	1.9	1.7	1.7	1.9	2.0	1.4
Switzerland	4.0	3.9	3.9	3.9	4.0	3.9	3.9	4.1
Chinese Taipei	..	..	..	..	..	0.9	0.9	1.0
Thailand	..	..	..	..	..	..	..	..
Tunisia	..	..	..	1.6	1.7	1.6	1.6	1.8
Turkey	1.1	1.1	1.2	1.3	1.2	1.1	1.1	1.2
United Kingdom	3.0	2.8	2.6	3.5	3.5	3.5	2.9	3.0
United States	6.0	6.3	6.6	6.8	6.8	6.9	7.0	7.6
Uruguay	1.4	1.5	1.5	..	1.4	1.4	1.4	1.5
OECD Total	4.0	4.1	4.4	4.4	4.4	4.5	4.6	4.9

.. Not available

Note: Detailed metadata at: *http://metalinks.oecd.org/ins/20220309/7297*.

1. Information on data for Israel: *http://oe.cd/israel-disclaimer*.

Source: *Insurance activity indicators, OECD Insurance Statistics (database)*

Table 19. Life insurance share
Percentage of total insurance

Per cent

	2013	2014	2015	2016	2017	2018	2019	2020
Argentina	17.8	16.5	15.3	16.0	14.7	14.3	13.6	13.0
Australia	54.9	61.1	59.2	55.4	52.1	49.5	43.2	36.9
Austria	34.1	35.5	35.3	32.5	31.7	29.9	28.8	..
Belgium	57.7	56.5	55.4	54.4	53.7	54.7	51.7	48.9
Bermuda	..	..	..	..	..	..	53.1	71.9
Bolivia	..	..	..	33.5	40.4	43.3	44.9	47.2
Brazil	..	60.2	62.7	66.1	66.5	66.6	69.4	68.6
Bulgaria	..	..	..	..	..	14.1	12.7	12.5
Canada	32.9	28.7	28.7	29.1	29.5	30.1	..	..
Chile	66.5	65.8	68.3	70.4	69.4	68.8	67.0	59.6
Colombia	51.1	47.5	46.6	48.2	50.9	50.1	50.6	49.9
Costa Rica	13.4	12.3	12.7	15.4	14.7	16.1	16.0	14.9
Cuba	..	..	..	..	..	..	..	..
Czech Republic	45.7	45.1	41.1	40.6	38.3	36.6	32.1	30.9
Denmark	95.4	67.7	68.9	68.7	69.1	70.0	71.3	72.8
Dominican Republic	..	..	..	..	..	16.1	..	..
Ecuador	..	..	19.5	22.0	..	..	29.1	..
Egypt	..	..	..	..	..	..	43.7	46.2
El Salvador	26.7	25.7	25.6	24.7	..	25.1	25.6	27.1
Estonia	29.3	30.3	31.2	30.0	27.3	25.2	25.7	28.4
Finland	56.8	57.4	58.3	50.6	50.7	100.0	100.0	100.0
France	62.4	64.2	64.2	58.0	55.2	55.2	55.8	49.7
Germany	36.0	35.9	34.0	33.1	32.1	31.8	32.7	31.8
Greece	41.4	49.5	50.5	47.2	50.4	49.5	50.9	51.2
Guatemala	19.9	20.8	19.4	19.9	20.5	20.5	21.2	21.3
Honduras	30.9	35.3	36.4	..	..	33.3	32.2	31.4
Hong Kong, China	85.7	86.9	87.6	90.1	90.4	90.1	..	..
Hungary	54.5	54.8	51.1	49.5	48.2	46.2	44.3	44.0
Iceland	7.9	8.2	8.4	8.8	8.9	8.3	8.3	9.0
India	..	..	78.2	..	70.7	..	74.5	..
Indonesia	67.9	66.2	69.0	72.6	74.6	72.9	70.5	70.4
Ireland	80.6	82.2	79.6	68.5	79.5	75.4	72.0	76.6
Israel[1]	52.9	51.7	53.6	52.7	53.8	54.0	54.9	54.0
Italy	71.4	76.8	77.8	75.8	75.0	74.7	75.1	74.4
Japan	100.0	100.0	100.0	75.5	75.1	75.2	73.2	71.7
Korea	59.3	56.8	57.1	56.3	53.9	53.2	..	51.0
Latvia	18.9	20.6	21.6	23.2	22.5	19.2	26.6	30.2
Lithuania	32.0	35.8	36.6	34.7	29.2	28.3	28.6	30.4
Luxembourg	91.9	93.9	92.3	91.5	91.8	91.8	90.7	88.4
Malaysia	60.1	60.2	60.6	61.7	63.4	64.1	65.8	65.9
Mexico	46.1	46.8	46.3	46.7	43.0	44.9	45.0	45.4
Montenegro	..	..	..	..	..	..	..	..
Morocco	..	..	..	..	..	..	..	..
Netherlands	47.4	47.7	43.6	19.6	18.2	16.2	..	..
New Zealand	..	..	..	..	..	..	23.6	..
Nicaragua	17.2	17.8	17.4	18.6	..	20.4	..	19.2
Norway	54.2	55.3	55.1	55.4	55.4	55.9	56.0	52.9
Panama	39.7	..	..	..	..	..	25.1	25.7
Paraguay	12.2	..	13.3	0.2	13.9	..	13.3	..
Peru	46.8	49.1	48.4	45.3	47.0	48.5	48.8	47.1
Poland	54.0	52.2	50.2	42.6	39.4	34.9	33.3	32.7
Portugal	70.5	72.9	67.5	59.6	58.6	61.8	56.7	44.4
Puerto Rico	4.3	6.3	4.9	9.5	..	..	..	..
Russia	..	12.6	13.9	20.4	27.4	32.0	26.7	26.9
Singapore	67.9	68.5	69.3	71.6	74.9	..	68.8	76.1
Slovak Republic	55.5	54.3	51.2	..	73.6	..	48.6	47.8
Slovenia	22.4	22.9	23.1	22.5	22.4	21.7	20.8	19.1
South Africa	78.6	80.5	79.9	79.7	..	..	..	77.1
Spain	44.6	43.9	43.6	47.1	44.8	43.6	41.5	37.1
Sri Lanka	..	35.5	42.5	..	41.4	41.3	..	..
Sweden	52.2	69.6	73.3	74.9	76.1	75.6	75.6	..
Switzerland	48.2	48.5	48.9	46.9	45.0	44.4	43.7	38.6
Chinese Taipei	..	..	..	..	..	97.0	96.8	93.6
Thailand	..	..	..	..	..	..	..	..
Tunisia	..	..	..	20.3	19.7	..	..	..
Turkey	15.7	12.3	11.8	14.9	17.3	15.9	20.1	20.1
United Kingdom	72.4	73.4	73.3	68.8	69.0	72.0	72.6	70.5
United States	38.5	36.2	37.1	35.9	35.6	43.3	42.6	42.4
Uruguay	28.7	29.5	33.4	..	42.2	..	44.1	45.7
OECD Total	52.7	50.2	49.2	46.5	45.4	50.3	50.0	48.2

.. Not available

Note: Detailed metadata at: *http://metalinks.oecd.org/ins/20220309/7297.*

1. Information on data for Israel: *http://oe.cd/israel-disclaimer.*

Source: *Insurance activity indicators, OECD Insurance Statistics (database)*

Table 20. Direct total gross premiums per insurance company employee

US dollars

	2013	2014	2015	2016	2017	2018	2019	2020
Argentina	289 071	296 157	290 581	..	264 715	291 050	165 282	159 867
Australia	..	..	..	..	..	..	..	..
Austria	795 367	816 717	688 586	660 884	676 184	729 985	704 559	..
Belgium	..	..	..	..	..	..	..	..
Bermuda	..	..	..	..	..	..	..	..
Bolivia	..	..	..	112 942	99 464	101 913	106 567	152 952
Brazil	..	..	..	..	..	..	..	..
Bulgaria	..	..	..	..	..	..	..	..
Canada	..	..	..	..	..	..	..	..
Chile	493 638	454 677	495 261	510 666	519 672	558 276	512 932	466 063
Colombia	..	502 752	375 951	347 555	..	..	..	..
Costa Rica	..	..	..	..	..	..	..	..
Cuba	..	..	..	..	..	..	..	..
Czech Republic	..	..	..	..	..	..	..	..
Denmark	2 215 121	2 158 639	1 927 585	2 018 459	2 661 767	3 419 049	2 616 680	2 374 364
Dominican Republic	..	..	..	..	..	..	..	..
Ecuador	..	..	2 202 989	292 344	..	..	..	..
Egypt	..	..	..	..	..	..	40 536	..
El Salvador	..	..	..	..	..	195 773	..	206 498
Estonia	200 224	221 998	200 416	..	..	..	..	..
Finland	1 363 735	1 514 861	1 311 479	1 088 453	1 237 491	633 977	965 645	465 480
France	..	..	..	..	..	..	..	..
Germany	1 607 786	1 649 160	1 371 091	1 367 654	1 520 578	1 653 171	1 701 918	1 785 624
Greece	..	..	..	..	..	..	..	..
Guatemala	..	159 900	..	181 604	186 479	185 720	189 576	196 976
Honduras	267 721	183 148	217 165	..	..	1 497 747	1 768 927	270 945
Hong Kong, China	..	..	..	..	617 084	632 451	..	..
Hungary	157 425	161 509	147 122	169 626	168 073	197 023	177 672	208 722
Iceland	665 881	731 603	703 782	..	..	..	..	..
India	..	..	..	..	32 479	..	246 628	..
Indonesia	..	..	..	..	..	..	..	2 601 013
Ireland	5 005 661	..	..	..	..	..	..	..
Israel[1]	..	..	..	..	..	..	..	..
Italy	588 605	729 106	622 717	585 098	..	..	..	..
Japan	129 385	130 139	144 659	..	1 060 963	..	..	..
Korea	466 422	580 368	591 071	610 886	638 233	628 010	..	734 315
Latvia	198 764	237 445	301 825	..	..	..	..	..
Lithuania	128 847	136 520	120 842	130 040	147 705	172 038	179 804	206 601
Luxembourg	1 556 437	4 328 321	2 997 287	2 886 004	3 019 973	2 823 429	2 443 072	1 649 515
Malaysia	651 774	650 745	461 454	465 847	435 343	475 776	492 833	505 221
Mexico	436 528	403 458	330 532	410 335	423 179	..	..	..
Montenegro	..	..	..	..	..	..	..	..
Morocco	..	..	..	..	..	..	..	..
Netherlands	..	..	..	..	..	..	..	..
New Zealand	473 708	..	..	..	..	..	..	..
Nicaragua	1 704 849	119 312	2 050 664	..	..	..	..	107 031
Norway	..	..	..	..	..	..	..	..
Panama	392 524	..	..	..	..	..	243 877	234 721
Paraguay	382 149	..	124 344	..	..	..	..	..
Peru	285 142	301 442	290 594	..	..	295 065	306 299	310 374
Poland	169 341	183 458	167 678	..	..	..	375 376	1 648 107
Portugal	490 972	551 505	416 277	371 983	413 352	506 932	493 481	420 557
Puerto Rico	780 437	704 962	856 812	1 042 984	..	..	..	..
Russia	..	73 609	..	61 185	121 961	89 910	72 009	72 458
Singapore	..	..	..	..	..	..	..	..
Slovak Republic	..	403 610	..	..	..	..	..	..
Slovenia	..	..	..	..	..	..	..	..
South Africa	..	..	..	..	..	..	..	..
Spain	424 700	403 450	..	..	..	..	..	..
Sri Lanka	..	24 436	26 631	..	17 383	17 439	..	..
Sweden	1 210 867	2 042 276	1 771 433	..	1 686 900	1 927 908	2 031 531	..
Switzerland	..	..	..	..	..	..	..	..
Chinese Taipei	..	..	..	..	..	183 841	198 719	187 023
Thailand	..	..	..	..	..	..	..	..
Tunisia	..	..	..	173 680	..	..	..	..
Turkey	379 315	335 385	298 749	233 812	204 510	261 141	201 229	..
United Kingdom	..	..	..	..	..	..	..	..
United States	..	..	..	..	..	..	..	..
Uruguay	..	..	..	..	..	..	..	..
OECD Total	318 545	333 913	333 824	710 683	919 678	960 372	1 104 147	1 073 934

.. Not available

Note: Detailed metadata at: *http://metalinks.oecd.org/ins/20220309/7297*.

1. Information on data for Israel: *http://oe.cd/israel-disclaimer*.

Source: *Insurance activity indicators, OECD Insurance Statistics (database)*

Table 21. Retention ratio (Life and Non-life)

Per cent

	2013	2014	2015	2016	2017	2018	2019	2020
Argentina	90.6	86.5	87.5	88.4	88.7	89.3	87.3	86.3
Australia	84.5	86.0	83.8	80.4	77.1	77.9	74.1	69.4
Austria	81.3	83.6	84.2	81.1	82.7	87.2	86.4	..
Belgium	91.2	88.7	88.5	87.2	87.5	87.2	76.2	82.7
Bermuda	..	..	..	..	..	..	84.6	68.2
Bolivia	..	..	..	49.8	51.5	54.9	53.9	55.7
Brazil	..	95.2	95.4	95.8	95.7	95.6	95.5	94.3
Bulgaria	..	..	..	..	..	73.2	70.6	71.1
Canada	73.1	73.5	71.4	74.0	72.4	79.1	..	..
Chile	84.4	84.0	84.8	84.4	83.4	84.1	82.8	76.8
Colombia	82.9	82.5	81.5	80.1	81.6	81.1	80.4	78.2
Costa Rica	78.6	80.2	77.9	78.9	79.4	77.5	78.3	78.3
Cuba	..	..	..	..	..	..	..	..
Czech Republic	80.6	80.3	79.3	78.9	78.7	79.0	79.4	79.2
Denmark	99.4	97.2	97.1	96.9	96.7	97.2	97.8	98.4
Dominican Republic	..	..	..	..	..	69.1	..	..
Ecuador	..	..	72.4	72.3	..	..	67.0	..
Egypt	..	..	..	..	..	..	62.0	58.1
El Salvador	66.6	66.6	66.5	64.2	..	63.7	63.0	61.0
Estonia	..	..	..	..	..	..	..	..
Finland	97.4	97.6	97.7	97.3	97.4	99.5	99.5	99.2
France	89.3	91.0	88.6	84.8	88.0	87.7	87.0	84.9
Germany	89.7	89.0	87.7	87.9	87.5	86.1	86.4	85.7
Greece	79.8	87.6	87.2	88.8	89.2	88.7	89.6	89.8
Guatemala	66.3	64.2	64.9	67.8	67.2	65.2	65.6	64.7
Honduras	55.7	54.4	53.0	..	..	58.7	63.1	60.8
Hong Kong, China	87.0	87.7	88.3	90.4	90.4	90.7	..	..
Hungary	86.1	86.1	86.1	86.7	87.4	87.6	87.9	88.0
Iceland	93.9	94.4	94.8	95.4	96.0	95.9	96.3	95.9
India	..	..	95.2	..	91.8	..	91.0	..
Indonesia	85.5	83.8	84.8	86.0	87.3	86.8	85.6	85.0
Ireland	87.8	89.2	88.0	79.6	..	..	..	..
Israel[1]	87.3	88.5	88.4	84.9	86.5	85.8	85.3	84.1
Italy	96.2	97.1	97.2	96.4	96.3	96.2	96.5	96.3
Japan	94.9	94.3	94.6	89.5	89.8	88.8	85.1	85.5
Korea	94.7	94.7	94.7	94.7	94.3	94.0	..	93.5
Latvia	96.3	96.3	95.9	95.3	93.2	89.8	90.3	91.6
Lithuania	..	95.2	95.1	95.0	91.5	90.4	90.9	92.8
Luxembourg	74.9	71.8	84.1	82.2	85.8	76.8	73.0	80.9
Malaysia	87.8	87.8	87.9	88.3	88.6	89.2	89.9	89.4
Mexico	82.6	83.9	83.0	84.4	81.4	83.2	81.3	82.0
Montenegro	..	..	..	..	..	..	..	..
Morocco	..	..	..	..	..	..	..	..
Netherlands	92.3	89.4	91.7	98.3	97.6	98.0	..	..
New Zealand	107.9	111.2	112.7	107.0	106.8	..	70.3	..
Nicaragua	63.8	63.3	65.7	66.7	..	60.9	..	56.1
Norway	92.9	93.1	92.2	92.7	93.0	93.3	93.7	93.0
Panama	55.6	..	..	..	..	..	63.4	63.6
Paraguay	79.1	..	79.6	78.0	77.4	..	74.2	..
Peru	76.7	75.5	74.5	73.3	75.0	76.3	77.0	74.1
Poland	92.7	92.4	90.5	87.9	88.4	88.4	87.6	86.9
Portugal	91.1	92.0	90.5	88.9	88.6	89.4	86.3	81.7
Puerto Rico	99.6	98.6	92.9	93.9	..	..	..	..
Russia	..	86.9	88.6	88.9	91.7	92.4	91.9	90.7
Singapore	85.9	86.8	79.2	77.6	77.0	..	74.2	85.8
Slovak Republic	85.8	85.3	84.5	..	92.2	..	85.5	85.7
Slovenia	87.8	86.9	88.1	87.7	86.5	86.8	85.8	87.7
South Africa	87.6	88.2	89.7	88.9	..	..	..	88.2
Spain	90.0	91.3	91.3	91.0	90.6	91.0	89.6	83.8
Sri Lanka	..	87.0	86.6	..	85.6	87.9	..	..
Sweden	92.7	95.6	97.0	97.3	97.2	97.4	96.9	..
Switzerland	92.6	92.9	93.1	93.7	92.6	92.6	92.3	92.1
Chinese Taipei	..	..	..	..	..	98.9	98.8	98.2
Thailand	..	..	..	..	..	..	..	..
Tunisia	..	..	..	80.9	100.0	..	..	..
Turkey	75.6	75.0	74.8	76.1	72.0	70.9	71.5	70.9
United Kingdom	87.4	84.8	89.0	77.0	87.9	80.6	80.5	80.6
United States	71.3	74.9	72.8	72.5	71.4	83.7	84.4	83.1
Uruguay	91.2	90.8	91.5	..	92.9	..	91.9	91.1
OECD Total	81.5	82.5	80.7	79.4	79.6	85.6	85.0	84.3

.. Not available

Note: Detailed metadata at: *http://metalinks.oecd.org/ins/20220309/7297*.

1. Information on data for Israel: *http://oe.cd/israel-disclaimer*.

Source: *Insurance activity indicators, OECD Insurance Statistics (database)*

Table 22. Retention ratio (Life)

Per cent

	2013	2014	2015	2016	2017	2018	2019	2020
Argentina	96.6	97.1	97.2	96.7	96.8	96.8	95.7	94.1
Australia	92.3	92.5	91.3	89.3	82.5	84.2	76.5	67.1
Austria	96.7	97.4	97.6	97.4	97.8	97.8	97.8	..
Belgium	97.0	97.6	97.9	96.7	98.0	97.7	96.9	95.9
Bermuda	..	..	..	..	..	..	90.5	64.1
Bolivia	..	..	..	64.6	63.7	71.9	68.2	69.2
Brazil	..	99.6	99.5	99.6	99.5	99.6	99.6	99.6
Bulgaria	..	..	..	..	..	98.4	98.5	98.1
Canada	75.2	69.5	67.6	72.1	72.9	75.4	..	..
Chile	98.0	97.7	97.5	95.0	92.6	93.3	93.1	92.4
Colombia	94.4	94.2	94.7	93.9	92.8	92.0	91.2	90.9
Costa Rica	84.7	87.4	81.4	82.8	81.4	79.0	80.6	82.2
Cuba	..	..	..	..	..	..	..	..
Czech Republic	93.9	93.0	92.4	92.3	91.7	91.4	95.3	94.9
Denmark	100.0	99.8	99.8	99.8	99.8	99.9	99.9	99.9
Dominican Republic	..	..	..	..	..	76.5	..	..
Ecuador	..	..	81.6	99.2	..	..	99.0	..
Egypt	..	..	..	..	..	..	64.7	62.0
El Salvador	95.0	87.3	81.6	80.8	..	78.2	76.6	69.7
Estonia	..	..	..	..	..	..	..	..
Finland	99.4	99.5	99.5	99.3	99.4	99.5	99.5	99.2
France	92.5	94.1	90.7	86.5	93.2	93.9	93.1	92.6
Germany	96.8	97.0	97.0	96.6	97.0	96.2	97.3	97.2
Greece	94.8	95.6	95.9	96.2	95.0	95.1	95.7	96.4
Guatemala	75.3	76.6	76.9	80.9	79.9	78.1	79.2	78.7
Honduras	61.1	45.4	56.1	..	..	56.0	60.3	59.4
Hong Kong, China	90.0	90.5	91.0	92.8	92.7	93.4	..	..
Hungary	95.0	96.3	96.8	97.3	98.7	99.1	99.1	99.1
Iceland	83.9	82.3	83.7	85.2	85.9	85.0	85.6	86.1
India	..	..	99.6	..	99.5	..	99.4	..
Indonesia	97.2	96.7	96.8	97.3	97.4	97.1	96.8	96.6
Ireland	93.7	94.0	94.1	94.9	..	..	..	..
Israel[1]	95.3	95.2	95.5	95.1	95.2	95.4	95.8	95.4
Italy	98.8	99.0	99.1	99.1	99.1	99.1	99.5	99.6
Japan	94.9	94.3	94.6	93.1	93.6	92.7	88.2	88.7
Korea	98.8	98.8	98.7	98.6	98.4	98.4	..	98.2
Latvia	99.8	99.8	99.8	99.8	99.8	99.8	99.2	99.2
Lithuania	..	98.5	98.0	98.5	98.3	97.8	98.5	98.4
Luxembourg	76.4	72.1	85.3	83.6	87.4	77.4	73.5	81.9
Malaysia	97.3	96.9	96.7	96.6	95.9	96.0	95.8	95.0
Mexico	95.3	96.6	96.4	96.2	95.4	95.4	95.5	95.8
Montenegro	..	..	..	..	..	..	..	..
Morocco	..	..	..	..	..	..	..	..
Netherlands	95.4	89.6	94.0	97.2	96.4	97.7	..	..
New Zealand	..	..	..	..	..	..	60.6	..
Nicaragua	60.3	55.3	59.2	58.2	..	62.4	..	62.2
Norway	98.8	98.9	98.7	98.9	98.9	99.1	99.3	99.3
Panama	77.7	..	..	..	..	..	49.0	0.0
Paraguay	80.7	..	81.7	41.0	83.0	..	80.0	..
Peru	89.5	84.4	84.7	82.4	83.7	85.0	86.9	86.4
Poland	98.6	98.5	98.2	98.3	99.4	98.7	98.5	98.0
Portugal	97.0	97.7	97.2	96.5	96.5	96.9	96.5	95.0
Puerto Rico	103.3	100.0	56.0	78.0	..	..	..	..
Russia	..	98.4	98.6	98.8	99.2	99.3	99.7	99.7
Singapore	95.1	96.1	88.4	84.3	82.3	..	79.0	93.3
Slovak Republic	98.4	98.2	97.9	..	99.0	..	95.5	94.9
Slovenia	97.2	96.9	96.7	96.3	96.4	96.4	96.3	94.5
South Africa	92.5	93.2	95.2	94.6	..	..	..	95.7
Spain	93.9	96.4	96.8	97.3	96.2	97.1	97.0	83.4
Sri Lanka	..	96.3	96.3	..	96.0	99.5	..	..
Sweden	98.7	99.6	99.8	99.9	99.7	99.8	99.7	..
Switzerland	99.3	99.4	99.4	99.3	99.3	98.8	99.4	99.4
Chinese Taipei	..	..	..	..	..	99.7	99.6	99.9
Thailand	..	..	..	..	..	..	..	..
Tunisia	..	..	..	90.4	100.0	..	..	..
Turkey	95.7	94.8	95.1	95.8	96.2	95.5	96.0	96.2
United Kingdom	88.9	85.4	91.2	80.3	95.2	84.6	84.3	85.4
United States	77.4	88.3	80.4	80.0	77.8	75.2	78.6	75.2
Uruguay	97.5	97.6	97.6	..	97.4	..	97.5	97.4
OECD Total	88.7	91.6	88.6	86.7	87.6	84.9	85.1	83.3

.. Not available

Note: Detailed metadata at: *http://metalinks.oecd.org/ins/20220309/7297*.

1. Information on data for Israel: *http://oe.cd/israel-disclaimer*.

Source: *Insurance activity indicators, OECD Insurance Statistics (database)*

Table 23. Retention ratio (Non-life)

Per cent

	2013	2014	2015	2016	2017	2018	2019	2020
Argentina	89.3	84.4	85.7	86.8	87.3	88.0	86.0	85.1
Australia	75.0	75.7	73.0	69.3	71.3	71.8	72.3	70.8
Austria	73.2	76.0	77.0	73.3	75.8	82.7	81.7	..
Belgium	83.4	77.2	76.8	75.8	75.4	74.5	54.0	70.1
Bermuda	..	..	..	..	..	..	77.9	78.5
Bolivia	..	..	..	42.4	43.1	41.9	42.3	43.6
Brazil	..	88.5	88.5	88.4	88.3	87.7	86.4	82.7
Bulgaria	..	..	..	..	..	69.0	66.5	67.2
Canada	72.1	75.2	72.9	74.7	72.2	80.6	..	..
Chile	57.6	57.7	57.4	59.1	62.7	63.8	61.8	53.8
Colombia	70.8	72.0	69.9	67.3	70.1	70.2	69.3	65.6
Costa Rica	77.6	79.2	77.3	78.2	79.0	77.2	77.9	77.6
Cuba	..	..	..	..	..	..	..	..
Czech Republic	69.4	69.8	70.2	69.8	70.6	71.9	72.0	72.2
Denmark	88.1	91.7	91.1	90.6	89.9	91.1	92.5	94.3
Dominican Republic	..	..	..	..	..	67.7	..	..
Ecuador	..	..	70.1	64.7	..	..	53.8	..
Egypt	..	..	..	..	..	..	59.8	54.8
El Salvador	56.2	58.4	60.1	57.1	..	58.8	58.4	57.8
Estonia	..	..	..	..	..	..	..	..
Finland	94.7	95.0	95.2	95.3	95.4	..	..	..
France	84.1	85.3	84.8	82.4	81.7	80.1	79.2	77.3
Germany	85.7	84.6	82.9	83.7	83.0	81.3	81.1	80.4
Greece	69.1	79.8	78.3	82.2	83.3	82.5	83.2	83.0
Guatemala	64.0	61.0	62.0	64.5	63.9	61.8	62.0	60.9
Honduras	53.3	59.3	51.3	..	..	60.1	64.4	61.4
Hong Kong, China	69.3	69.0	69.8	68.9	68.7	65.8	..	..
Hungary	75.3	73.6	75.0	76.2	76.9	77.7	79.0	79.3
Iceland	94.7	95.5	95.8	96.3	97.0	96.9	97.2	96.9
India	..	..	79.5	..	73.1	..	66.4	..
Indonesia	60.8	58.4	58.3	55.7	57.6	58.9	58.8	57.5
Ireland	63.1	67.1	64.1	46.3	..	..	..	..
Israel[1]	78.2	81.2	80.2	73.6	76.4	74.6	72.6	70.7
Italy	89.9	90.5	90.6	87.9	87.8	87.6	87.3	86.8
Japan	..	..	..	78.4	78.2	76.9	76.6	77.4
Korea	88.6	89.5	89.4	89.8	89.5	88.9	..	88.7
Latvia	95.5	95.4	94.8	93.9	91.3	87.4	87.1	88.2
Lithuania	..	93.3	93.4	93.0	88.6	87.5	87.9	90.4
Luxembourg	58.5	65.9	68.9	66.7	67.7	69.2	68.3	72.8
Malaysia	73.6	74.0	74.4	74.9	76.0	77.0	78.4	78.6
Mexico	71.7	72.8	71.5	74.0	70.8	73.2	69.7	70.6
Montenegro	..	..	..	..	..	..	..	..
Morocco	..	..	..	..	..	..	..	..
Netherlands	89.5	89.2	89.9	98.5	98.1	98.3	..	..
New Zealand	77.5	80.0	80.5	73.8	74.4	..	73.4	..
Nicaragua	64.6	65.0	67.0	68.7	..	60.5	..	54.6
Norway	85.9	85.9	84.3	85.0	85.5	86.0	86.5	86.0
Panama	41.0	..	..	..	..	..	68.2	0.0
Paraguay	78.9	..	79.3	78.0	76.5	..	73.3	..
Peru	65.5	67.0	65.0	65.7	67.3	68.1	67.4	63.3
Poland	85.8	85.8	82.8	80.2	81.3	82.8	82.1	81.4
Portugal	76.9	76.8	76.6	77.7	77.4	77.1	72.8	71.1
Puerto Rico	99.5	98.5	94.8	95.5	..	..	..	..
Russia	..	82.0	87.0	86.4	88.9	89.2	89.1	87.4
Singapore	66.5	66.5	58.4	60.9	61.0	..	63.5	62.2
Slovak Republic	70.1	69.9	70.4	..	73.3	..	76.1	77.3
Slovenia	85.1	84.0	85.5	85.2	83.6	84.2	83.0	86.1
South Africa	69.8	67.7	68.0	66.8	..	..	..	62.8
Spain	86.8	87.3	87.0	85.3	86.0	86.2	84.3	83.9
Sri Lanka	..	81.9	79.4	..	78.3	79.8	..	..
Sweden	86.1	86.5	89.3	89.5	89.1	89.9	88.2	..
Switzerland	86.4	86.7	87.0	88.8	87.1	87.5	86.7	87.5
Chinese Taipei	..	..	..	..	..	72.7	73.0	72.6
Thailand	..	..	..	..	..	..	..	..
Tunisia	..	..	..	78.6	100.0	..	..	..
Turkey	71.9	72.2	72.1	72.7	66.9	66.2	65.3	64.6
United Kingdom	83.4	83.2	82.8	69.5	71.6	70.3	70.3	69.1
United States	67.4	67.3	68.2	68.3	67.9	90.1	88.8	88.9
Uruguay	88.7	87.9	88.4	..	89.7	..	87.4	85.7
OECD Total	73.5	73.4	73.0	73.0	72.9	86.3	85.0	85.2

.. Not available

Note: Detailed metadata at: *http://metalinks.oecd.org/ins/20220309/7297.*

1. Information on data for Israel: *http://oe.cd/israel-disclaimer.*

Source: *Insurance activity indicators, OECD Insurance Statistics (database)*

Table 24. Ratio of reinsurance accepted (Life and Non-life)

Per cent

	2013	2014	2015	2016	2017	2018	2019	2020
Argentina	0.3	7.2	7.0	6.7	6.6	5.5	5.5	5.4
Australia	10.9	10.1	10.9	12.5	13.0	14.3	16.1	17.7
Austria	12.0	9.6	8.9	9.3	6.4	7.2	6.8	..
Belgium	3.2	3.5	3.0	2.9	2.3	1.8	7.0	8.1
Bermuda	..	..	..	..	..	..	61.3	53.8
Bolivia	..	..	..	1.0	3.9	3.3	6.1	6.2
Brazil	..	0.0	0.0	0.0	0.0	0.0	0.0	0.0
Bulgaria	..	..	..	..	..	2.3	1.8	1.6
Canada	9.7	17.7	17.6	15.6	16.1	11.3	..	..
Chile	0.5	0.6	0.8	1.1	0.9	0.9	1.0	1.0
Colombia	1.3	1.9	2.0	1.8	1.9	2.0	2.0	1.9
Costa Rica	0.3	0.3	0.3	0.3	0.3	0.3	0.4	0.4
Cuba	..	..	..	..	..	..	..	..
Czech Republic	1.8	1.6	2.0	2.4	2.5	2.1	2.2	2.2
Denmark	84.9	0.8	0.8	2.9	3.3	3.5	2.4	1.8
Dominican Republic	..	..	..	..	..	..	..	..
Ecuador	..	..	2.0	1.7	..	..	0.6	..
Egypt	..	..	..	..	..	..	4.9	3.4
El Salvador	..	..	..	..	..	5.1	5.5	7.0
Estonia	..	..	..	..	..	0.0	0.0	..
Finland	1.5	1.4	1.3	1.5	1.6	0.0	0.1	0.0
France	10.1	10.5	8.9	15.7	12.7	12.7	12.8	12.6
Germany	22.4	22.4	24.6	24.5	24.6	24.7	25.4	26.5
Greece	2.3	1.2	1.1	1.0	0.9	0.9	0.9	0.7
Guatemala	2.7	2.7	3.1	2.9	2.9	3.4	2.8	3.1
Honduras	0.0	0.0	0.0	..	..	..	0.0	0.0
Hong Kong, China	4.7	4.8	4.5	4.8	4.7	4.6	..	..
Hungary	1.3	0.9	1.0	1.0	1.5	1.1	1.0	0.7
Iceland	2.3	2.5	2.4	1.7	1.4	1.7	1.7	0.1
India	..	..	0.7	..	5.8	..	0.5	..
Indonesia	4.9	2.5	2.1	2.0	1.8	1.8	2.2	3.6
Ireland	1.8	1.9	1.9	2.2	1.2	3.0	5.8	1.2
Israel[1]	..	..	..	0.0	..	..	..	..
Italy	2.4	1.8	1.8	2.1	2.1	2.3	1.0	1.4
Japan	7.4	5.5	4.1	6.5	6.0	5.5	5.5	5.6
Korea	5.2	5.0	5.1	5.2	5.6	6.2	..	5.4
Latvia	0.0	0.0	0.0	0.0	0.0	0.0	0.1	0.0
Lithuania	0.1	0.0	0.0	0.0	0.0	0.0	0.0	0.0
Luxembourg	0.9	1.2	0.8	0.3	0.2	0.2	5.6	6.4
Malaysia	7.4	7.5	7.7	7.7	7.2	6.7	6.5	7.4
Mexico	1.7	1.8	1.7	1.6	1.7	1.7	1.8	2.3
Montenegro	..	..	..	..	..	..	..	..
Morocco	..	..	..	..	..	..	..	..
Netherlands	1.5	1.5	1.7	0.5	1.8	1.8	..	..
New Zealand	0.6	0.6	3.8	1.8	5.3	..	0.1	..
Nicaragua	0.0	..	..	..	..	..	..	..
Norway	..	..	..	..	..	..	..	..
Panama	6.2	..	..	..	..	..	8.2	9.0
Paraguay	1.5	..	1.1	1.0	0.7	..	0.4	..
Peru	1.0	0.7	0.6	0.6	0.7	0.6	0.8	1.0
Poland	1.2	1.0	2.7	3.5	3.2	3.7	4.5	4.6
Portugal	3.5	3.3	3.9	5.1	5.3	5.3	5.5	7.1
Puerto Rico	0.5	0.9	0.8	0.6	..	..	..	..
Russia	..	3.5	2.8	3.0	2.7	2.9	3.4	3.9
Singapore	19.6	19.2	19.7	21.7	17.6	..	26.8	27.2
Slovak Republic	0.9	1.4	2.0	..	0.2	..	0.0	0.2
Slovenia	11.3	11.3	12.5	12.1	12.1	11.7	12.2	13.6
South Africa	2.3	2.3	2.2	2.9	..	..	..	4.1
Spain	7.7	7.8	8.2	8.2	8.1	7.8	8.1	10.8
Sri Lanka	..	2.2	1.5	..	2.4	2.2	..	..
Sweden	6.3	4.1	3.1	3.0	3.1	3.1	3.0	..
Switzerland	14.5	13.8	12.7	13.3	14.2	15.0	16.0	17.2
Chinese Taipei	..	..	..	..	..	41.1	42.4	1.1
Thailand	..	..	..	..	..	..	..	..
Tunisia	..	..	..	1.2	5.3	..	..	..
Turkey	2.7	5.0	3.1	5.9	6.0	8.5	10.0	8.5
United Kingdom	9.7	9.9	11.1	35.8	14.3	20.0	19.5	19.2
United States	21.5	21.8	22.8	22.3	23.0	11.9	11.2	10.8
Uruguay	0.0	0.0	0.0	..	0.0	..	0.0	0.0
OECD Total	15.4	15.4	16.6	18.4	17.2	11.8	11.8	11.6

.. Not available

Note: Detailed metadata at: *http://metalinks.oecd.org/ins/20220309/7297*.

1. Information on data for Israel: *http://oe.cd/israel-disclaimer*.

Source: *Insurance activity indicators, OECD Insurance Statistics (database)*

Table 25. Ratio of reinsurance accepted (Life)

Per cent

	2013	2014	2015	2016	2017	2018	2019	2020
Argentina	0.6	3.0	2.3	3.0	2.9	2.8	3.1	3.6
Australia	8.1	7.5	8.4	9.7	12.2	14.3	18.2	22.6
Austria	0.2	0.2	0.2	0.2	0.2	0.2	0.3	..
Belgium	0.4	0.4	0.3	0.4	0.3	0.3	0.5	0.2
Bermuda	..	..	..	..	..	..	38.3	41.2
Bolivia	..	..	..	0.0	3.3	4.8	6.1	5.5
Brazil	..	0.0	0.0	0.0	0.0	0.0	0.0	0.0
Bulgaria	..	..	..	..	..	5.0	5.8	6.1
Canada	9.7	16.6	17.5	15.0	14.4	11.8	..	..
Chile	0.0	0.1	0.4	1.0	0.8	0.8	0.9	0.8
Colombia	0.0	0.1	0.1	0.1	0.0	0.0	0.0	0.0
Costa Rica	0.0	0.0	0.0	0.0	0.0	0.0	0.0	0.0
Cuba	..	..	..	..	..	..	..	..
Czech Republic	0.0	0.0	0.0	0.6	0.6	0.7	0.9	1.0
Denmark	89.0	0.5	0.5	0.6	0.4	0.4	0.4	0.5
Dominican Republic	..	..	..	..	..	..	..	..
Ecuador	..	..	0.6	0.0	..	..	0.0	..
Egypt	..	..	..	..	..	..	0.3	0.3
El Salvador	..	..	..	..	..	5.0	5.1	7.5
Estonia	..	..	..	..	..	0.0	0.0	..
Finland	0.1	0.2	0.0	0.0	0.0	0.0	0.1	0.0
France	8.0	8.9	6.3	15.5	8.8	8.6	9.6	8.4
Germany	0.7	0.6	0.6	0.6	0.8	0.5	0.5	1.1
Greece	0.2	0.2	0.2	0.1	0.0	0.0	0.0	0.0
Guatemala	1.0	1.6	1.7	1.9	1.4	1.5	0.9	1.2
Honduras	0.0	0.0	0.0	..	..	..	0.0	0.0
Hong Kong, China	1.1	1.6	1.7	2.8	2.5	2.0	..	..
Hungary	0.0	0.0	0.0	0.0	0.0	0.0	0.0	0.0
Iceland	0.0	0.0	0.1	..	0.0	..	..	..
India	..	..	0.0	..	0.2	..	0.0	..
Indonesia	0.0	..	..	..	..	..	..	..
Ireland	1.1	1.1	1.2	0.7	0.2	0.1	0.3	0.2
Israel[1]	..	..	..	0.0	..	..	..	..
Italy	1.9	1.3	1.3	1.5	1.5	1.4	0.3	0.3
Japan	7.4	5.5	4.1	3.4	2.6	2.0	1.7	1.5
Korea	1.1	1.1	1.1	1.3	1.4	1.7	..	0.0
Latvia	0.0	0.0	0.0	0.0	0.0	0.0	0.0	0.0
Lithuania	0.0	0.0	0.0	0.0	0.0	0.0	0.0	0.0
Luxembourg	1.0	1.3	0.8	0.4	0.2	0.2	5.2	5.9
Malaysia	1.3	1.4	1.4	1.4	1.6	1.7	1.1	1.1
Mexico	0.6	0.7	0.4	0.5	0.6	0.4	0.6	0.7
Montenegro	..	..	..	..	..	..	..	..
Morocco	..	..	..	..	..	..	..	..
Netherlands	0.0	0.0	0.0	0.0	0.1	0.0	..	..
New Zealand	..	..	..	..	..	..	0.2	..
Nicaragua	0.0	..	..	..	..	..	..	..
Norway	..	..	..	..	..	..	..	..
Panama	5.5	..	..	..	..	..	5.2	7.0
Paraguay	0.8	..	0.7	0.0	0.2	..	0.0	..
Peru	1.2	0.6	0.5	0.3	0.1	0.0	0.2	0.2
Poland	0.1	0.1	0.1	0.1	0.1	0.0	0.0	0.0
Portugal	0.0	0.0	0.0	0.0	0.0	0.0	0.0	0.0
Puerto Rico	0.0	0.0	0.0	0.5	..	..	..	..
Russia	..	0.0	0.0	0.0	0.0	0.0	0.0	0.0
Singapore	10.9	10.8	10.4	14.7	11.0	..	16.3	21.6
Slovak Republic	0.0	0.0	0.0	..	0.0	..	0.0	0.5
Slovenia	..	..	..	..	..	..	..	..
South Africa	0.0	0.0	0.0	0.0	..	..	..	0.0
Spain	1.3	1.6	1.5	1.5	1.4	1.5	1.7	7.5
Sri Lanka	..	..	0.0	..	0.6	..	..	..
Sweden	0.2	0.0	0.0	0.0	0.0	0.0	0.0	..
Switzerland	1.5	1.4	1.5	1.7	1.3	1.2	1.2	1.4
Chinese Taipei	..	..	..	..	..	42.0	43.4	0.3
Thailand	..	..	..	..	..	..	..	..
Tunisia	..	..	..	1.5	1.5	..	..	..
Turkey	2.1	1.5	1.6	4.3	3.6	3.9	3.3	3.1
United Kingdom	9.3	9.0	10.0	40.7	10.4	18.7	15.9	15.4
United States	11.3	10.4	15.1	13.8	14.9	20.2	18.0	16.8
Uruguay	0.0	0.0	0.0	..	0.0	..	0.0	0.0
OECD Total	7.5	6.7	8.8	12.4	8.9	12.4	11.7	11.1

.. Not available

Note: Detailed metadata at: *http://metalinks.oecd.org/ins/20220309/7297*.

1. Information on data for Israel: *http://oe.cd/israel-disclaimer*.

Source: *Insurance activity indicators, OECD Insurance Statistics (database)*

Table 26. Ratio of reinsurance accepted (Non-life)

Per cent

	2013	2014	2015	2016	2017	2018	2019	2020
Argentina	0.3	8.0	7.8	7.5	7.2	6.0	5.9	5.6
Australia	14.2	14.3	14.7	16.0	13.9	14.3	14.5	14.9
Austria	18.2	14.7	13.6	13.7	9.2	10.2	9.4	..
Belgium	7.1	7.6	6.4	5.8	4.7	3.7	14.0	15.8
Bermuda	..	..	..	..	..	..	87.4	86.0
Bolivia	..	..	..	1.4	4.2	2.1	6.1	6.8
Brazil	..	0.1	0.0	0.0	0.0	0.0	0.0	0.0
Bulgaria	..	..	..	..	..	1.9	1.2	0.9
Canada	9.7	18.1	17.7	15.8	16.7	11.1	..	..
Chile	1.4	1.5	1.6	1.3	1.1	1.1	1.2	1.4
Colombia	2.5	3.5	3.7	3.5	3.8	3.9	4.0	3.7
Costa Rica	0.4	0.3	0.4	0.3	0.3	0.4	0.4	0.5
Cuba	..	..	..	..	..	..	..	..
Czech Republic	3.3	2.9	3.4	3.7	3.7	2.9	2.8	2.7
Denmark	1.1	1.3	1.4	8.0	9.8	10.7	7.3	5.4
Dominican Republic	..	..	..	..	..	..	..	..
Ecuador	..	..	2.4	2.2	..	..	0.9	..
Egypt	..	..	..	..	..	..	8.5	6.0
El Salvador	..	..	..	..	..	5.2	5.7	6.8
Estonia	..	..	..	..	..	0.0	0.0	..
Finland	3.3	3.0	3.0	3.0	3.3	..	..	..
France	13.4	13.3	13.5	16.1	17.4	17.8	16.9	16.7
Germany	34.6	34.7	37.0	36.4	35.9	36.0	37.6	38.4
Greece	3.7	2.2	1.9	1.8	1.8	1.7	1.7	1.5
Guatemala	3.2	3.0	3.4	3.2	3.3	3.9	3.3	3.6
Honduras	0.0	0.0	0.0	..	..	..	0.0	0.0
Hong Kong, China	26.0	26.1	24.2	23.3	25.1	28.3	..	..
Hungary	2.9	1.9	2.1	2.0	2.9	2.0	1.7	1.2
Iceland	2.5	2.7	2.6	1.9	1.5	1.9	1.8	0.1
India	..	..	3.0	..	19.4	..	2.0	..
Indonesia	15.2	7.3	6.8	7.5	7.2	6.6	7.3	12.1
Ireland	5.0	5.3	4.6	5.5	5.3	6.5	16.3	4.5
Israel[1]	..	..	..	0.0	..	..	..	..
Italy	3.4	3.4	3.8	3.9	3.7	5.1	3.1	4.7
Japan	..	..	..	16.0	16.3	16.1	15.9	15.9
Korea	11.1	10.1	10.3	10.2	10.5	11.2	..	11.0
Latvia	0.0	0.0	0.0	0.0	0.0	0.0	0.1	0.1
Lithuania	0.2	0.0	0.0	0.0	0.0	0.0	0.0	0.0
Luxembourg	0.3	0.2	0.2	0.2	0.2	0.4	9.4	9.9
Malaysia	16.5	16.7	17.3	17.8	16.8	15.8	16.8	19.6
Mexico	2.7	2.7	2.7	2.6	2.6	2.7	2.8	3.7
Montenegro	..	..	..	..	..	..	..	..
Morocco	..	..	..	..	..	..	..	..
Netherlands	2.9	2.8	2.9	0.6	0.7	0.5	..	..
New Zealand	0.6	0.6	3.8	1.8	5.3	..	0.0	..
Nicaragua	0.0	..	..	..	..	..	..	..
Norway	..	..	..	..	..	..	..	..
Panama	6.6	..	..	..	..	..	9.2	9.7
Paraguay	1.5	..	1.2	1.0	0.8	..	0.5	..
Peru	1.0	0.8	0.7	0.8	1.3	1.1	1.4	1.6
Poland	2.5	2.1	5.3	6.1	5.2	5.7	6.8	6.9
Portugal	11.7	12.3	12.1	12.6	12.9	13.8	12.7	12.8
Puerto Rico	0.5	1.0	0.9	0.6	..	..	..	..
Russia	..	5.0	3.3	3.7	3.7	4.2	4.6	5.3
Singapore	38.1	37.3	40.7	39.2	37.0	..	50.0	45.0
Slovak Republic	2.1	3.1	4.0	..	0.8	..	0.0	0.0
Slovenia	14.6	14.6	16.3	15.7	15.5	14.9	15.5	16.8
South Africa	10.8	11.6	11.1	14.2	..	..	..	17.9
Spain	12.9	12.6	13.5	14.1	13.4	12.7	12.6	12.8
Sri Lanka	..	3.5	2.6	..	3.7	3.7	..	..
Sweden	12.9	13.5	11.4	11.8	13.0	12.6	12.4	..
Switzerland	26.6	25.4	23.4	23.6	24.8	26.0	27.5	27.1
Chinese Taipei	..	..	..	..	..	11.9	12.4	12.7
Thailand	..	..	..	..	..	..	..	..
Tunisia	..	..	..	1.1	6.2	..	..	..
Turkey	2.8	5.4	3.3	6.1	6.5	9.3	11.7	9.9
United Kingdom	10.9	12.6	14.1	25.0	23.1	23.5	29.1	28.1
United States	27.8	28.2	27.4	27.0	27.4	5.6	6.2	6.4
Uruguay	0.0	0.0	0.0	..	0.0	..	0.0	0.0
OECD Total	23.4	24.1	24.2	23.6	24.0	11.0	11.8	12.0

.. Not available

Note: Detailed metadata at: *http://metalinks.oecd.org/ins/20220309/7297*.

1. Information on data for Israel: *http://oe.cd/israel-disclaimer*.

Source: *Insurance activity indicators, OECD Insurance Statistics (database)*

Table 27. Market share of foreign companies in the domestic market (Life)

Per cent

	2013	2014	2015	2016	2017	2018	2019	2020
Argentina	31.8	31.4	30.8	30.4	30.0	27.9	29.0	27.5
Australia	16.8	15.5	17.7	20.8	25.5	29.8	37.5	76.7
Austria	37.5	39.2	37.7	39.3	39.7	39.7	39.1	..
Belgium	..	..	..	..	..	..	..	..
Bermuda	..	..	..	..	..	..	..	..
Bolivia	..	..	..	29.9	20.8	27.8	28.0	27.4
Brazil	..	18.6	18.3	17.2	21.3	26.5	29.5	19.2
Bulgaria	..	..	..	..	..	97.2	97.2	96.7
Canada	5.6	26.0	21.0	18.7	18.1	15.2	..	..
Chile	46.7	45.0	41.8	41.6	44.5	43.0	45.0	42.4
Colombia	24.2	21.6	20.9	18.1	18.6	18.8	17.2	17.3
Costa Rica	12.4	17.0	23.0	25.0	33.9	37.2	37.3	36.5
Cuba	..	..	..	..	..	..	..	..
Czech Republic	96.8	96.7	96.3	96.8	96.4	95.9	97.1	96.5
Denmark	2.5	19.5	18.6	18.8	19.9	19.8	13.8	84.8
Dominican Republic	..	..	..	..	..	46.5	..	..
Ecuador	..	..	..	11.7	..	..	0.0	..
Egypt	..	..	..	..	..	..	..	..
El Salvador	17.4	9.6	9.4	9.6	..	10.3	9.9	8.1
Estonia	100.0	100.0	100.0	100.0	100.0	100.0	100.0	100.0
Finland	42.0	43.0	38.5	..	..	..	..	..
France	..	..	..	..	..	..	..	..
Germany	27.4	26.0	26.7	25.3	24.6	24.9	23.4	23.8
Greece	53.8	48.0	55.7	76.9	74.0	73.2	66.8	69.9
Guatemala	..	..	..	..	..	..	..	0.0
Honduras	13.8	59.6	62.2	..	..	62.7	59.6	57.6
Hong Kong, China	..	..	..	..	..	..	..	..
Hungary	95.6	96.2	95.8	96.9	96.6	96.3	96.4	96.2
Iceland	4.3	5.0	5.8	..	..	..	..	..
India	..	..	0.0	..	0.1	..	..	..
Indonesia	..	..	..	..	..	..	..	..
Ireland	4.9	4.5	4.7	..	5.3	2.5	1.3	..
Israel[1]	0.4	0.4	0.4	0.4	0.4	0.4	17.7	16.8
Italy	28.9	31.3	30.5	33.1	32.1	37.1	37.0	35.8
Japan	20.7	20.1	20.6	21.8	22.7	22.5	22.5	23.0
Korea	16.1	13.2	12.4	14.7	16.1	14.3	..	21.0
Latvia	91.8	91.0	89.8	90.8	91.3	91.6	91.8	90.0
Lithuania	97.0	97.4	97.4	97.5	97.1	97.3	97.2	97.2
Luxembourg	96.2	96.4	92.5	77.2	90.6	92.2	93.1	75.6
Malaysia	68.6	68.8	69.6	69.7	71.8	70.4	72.5	72.4
Mexico	6.3	74.0	72.3	70.6	68.0	68.8	68.5	65.6
Montenegro	..	..	..	..	..	..	..	..
Morocco	..	..	..	..	..	..	..	..
Netherlands	19.2	4.6	18.5	19.2	23.3	19.9	..	..
New Zealand	..	..	..	..	..	..	77.7	..
Nicaragua	29.1	26.6	26.4	18.0	..	25.8	..	27.3
Norway	12.3	13.3	15.1	0.7	0.7	0.5	0.4	0.3
Panama	59.9	..	..	..	..	..	39.9	42.8
Paraguay	6.2	..	0.0	0.0	5.5	..	5.6	..
Peru	23.5	30.7	56.8	28.1	27.6	23.4	35.0	36.3
Poland	48.8	50.0	50.7	54.3	45.2	44.0	44.6	46.7
Portugal	6.8	54.0	64.2	77.5	93.8	90.8	85.2	91.2
Puerto Rico	10.4	7.8	0.0	38.0	..	..	..	..
Russia	..	8.5	18.1	15.5	10.2	10.4	9.6	6.9
Singapore	67.2	71.3	70.6	70.0	53.3	..	53.3	54.0
Slovak Republic	90.4	90.0	89.0	..	5.6	..	87.8	91.0
Slovenia	17.6	17.2	17.0	17.1	15.7	15.4	25.3	27.0
South Africa	31.9	35.2	33.3	34.6	..	..	..	13.0
Spain	12.4	12.8	12.3	..	..	..	..	..
Sri Lanka	..	2.4	1.7	..	..	..	..	..
Sweden	19.5	7.9	8.8	11.2	12.2	13.2	12.3	..
Switzerland	31.2	27.9	26.9	25.6	25.3	26.1	10.6	8.3
Chinese Taipei	..	..	..	..	..	46.7	47.7	7.4
Thailand	..	..	..	..	..	..	..	..
Tunisia	..	..	..	..	..	..	..	..
Turkey	47.1	47.9	59.7	54.2	56.4	59.2	52.7	54.0
United Kingdom	23.3	16.0	16.9	..	..	..	..	..
United States	20.0	21.0	17.4	22.5	21.7	23.0	19.8	20.0
Uruguay	32.8	33.4	30.1	..	21.3	..	21.3	20.5

.. Not available

Note: Detailed metadata at: *http://metalinks.oecd.org/ins/20220309/7297.*

1. Information on data for Israel: *http://oe.cd/israel-disclaimer.*

Source: *Insurance activity indicators, OECD Insurance Statistics (database)*

Table 28. Market share of foreign undertakings in total domestic business (Life)

Branches or agencies

Per cent

	2013	2014	2015	2016	2017	2018	2019	2020
Argentina	1.8	3.9	3.2	3.4	3.5	3.7	5.0	5.3
Australia	..	..	..	..	..	..	..	..
Austria	0.0	0.0	0.0	0.0	0.0	0.0	0.0	..
Belgium	..	..	..	..	..	..	..	..
Bermuda	..	..	..	..	..	..	..	..
Bolivia	..	..	..	..	..	..	..	..
Brazil	..	..	0.0	0.0	0.0	0.0	0.0	0.0
Bulgaria	..	..	..	..	..	..	..	..
Canada	2.2	15.5	15.8	13.2	12.7	9.0	..	..
Chile	..	..	..	..	..	..	..	..
Colombia	..	0.0	..	..	..	..	..	..
Costa Rica	0.2	0.6	1.1	1.0	1.3	1.6	1.4	3.4
Cuba	..	..	..	..	..	..	..	..
Czech Republic	7.5	7.2	10.8	10.9	11.4	11.5	14.6	15.0
Denmark	..	..	..	..	..	..	..	..
Dominican Republic	..	..	..	..	..	..	..	..
Ecuador	..	..	..	..	..	..	0.0	..
Egypt	..	..	..	..	..	..	..	..
El Salvador	17.4	9.6	9.4	9.6	..	10.3	9.9	8.1
Estonia	2.5	2.7	2.8	2.2	3.1	5.2	8.3	10.9
Finland	..	..	..	..	..	..	..	..
France	..	..	..	..	..	..	..	..
Germany	4.0	3.9	4.0	3.9	4.0	3.8	3.7	4.4
Greece	0.0	0.0	0.0	0.0	0.0	0.0	0.0	0.0
Guatemala	..	..	..	..	..	..	..	0.0
Honduras	13.8	25.6	23.1	..	..	62.7	59.6	57.6
Hong Kong, China	..	..	..	..	..	..	..	..
Hungary	..	..	..	..	..	..	..	..
Iceland	..	..	..	..	..	..	..	..
India	..	..	0.0	..	0.1	..	..	..
Indonesia	..	..	..	..	..	..	..	..
Ireland	4.9	4.5	4.7	..	5.3	2.5	1.3	..
Israel[1]	..	..	..	..	..	..	..	..
Italy	0.0	0.0	0.0	0.0	0.0	..	..	..
Japan	4.9	4.2	4.1	4.3	4.5	0.1	0.1	0.2
Korea	2.2	2.4	0.2	2.0	2.1	2.3	..	..
Latvia	56.3	58.5	59.3	61.4	63.1	65.5	44.8	47.3
Lithuania	41.6	43.1	41.8	40.8	41.4	43.3	62.2	62.7
Luxembourg	0.5	0.1	0.1	0.1	0.1	0.1	5.1	5.8
Malaysia	0.5	0.5	0.5	0.5	0.6	0.7	..	..
Mexico	..	..	..	..	..	..	..	..
Montenegro	..	..	..	..	..	..	..	..
Morocco	..	..	..	..	..	..	..	..
Netherlands	2.0	0.0	0.0	..	..	..	..	..
New Zealand	..	..	..	..	..	..	20.8	..
Nicaragua	..	..	..	..	..	..	..	..
Norway	1.3	1.4	0.7	0.7	0.7	0.5	0.4	0.3
Panama	10.0	..	..	..	..	..	39.3	..
Paraguay	..	..	0.0	0.0	..	..	0.0	..
Peru	..	..	..	..	..	..	..	..
Poland	..	..	..	..	..	..	..	..
Portugal	0.0	0.0	0.0	0.0	0.0	0.0	0.0	0.0
Puerto Rico	..	..	..	..	..	..	..	..
Russia	..	..	..	..	0.0	0.0	0.0	0.0
Singapore	15.0	32.6	30.7	32.3	8.7	..	15.2	19.8
Slovak Republic	5.4	4.4	4.8	..	5.6	..	15.3	17.8
Slovenia	..	..	..	..	..	..	..	..
South Africa	0.0	..	..	..	..	..	..	0.0
Spain	0.0	0.0	0.0	..	..	..	..	..
Sri Lanka	..	..	0.0	..	..	..	..	..
Sweden	..	0.7	..	..	..	..	..	..
Switzerland	1.5	0.0	0.0	0.0	0.0	0.0	0.1	0.1
Chinese Taipei	..	..	..	..	..	43.9	45.3	3.0
Thailand	..	..	..	..	..	..	..	..
Tunisia	..	..	..	..	..	..	..	..
Turkey	..	..	..	0.0	0.0	0.0	..	0.0
United Kingdom	0.0	0.0	0.0	..	..	..	..	..
United States	..	..	..	0.0	0.0	0.0	0.0	0.0
Uruguay	0.0	0.0	0.0	..	0.0	..	0.0	0.0

.. Not available

Note: Detailed metadata at: *http://metalinks.oecd.org/ins/20220309/7297*.

1. Information on data for Israel: *http://oe.cd/israel-disclaimer*.

Source: *Insurance activity indicators, OECD Insurance Statistics (database)*

Table 29. Market share of foreign companies in the domestic market (Non-life)

Per cent

	2013	2014	2015	2016	2017	2018	2019	2020
Argentina	20.1	21.1	22.0	23.4	30.5	30.0	29.6	18.6
Australia	27.7	28.7	28.2	28.7	29.5	34.8	37.3	38.5
Austria	35.2	37.5	36.9	36.6	33.2	32.9	33.1	..
Belgium	..	..	..	..	..	..	..	..
Bermuda	..	..	..	..	..	..	..	..
Bolivia	..	..	..	27.9	29.1	25.5	25.1	25.8
Brazil	..	51.3	32.4	35.7	39.4	53.9	43.9	60.5
Bulgaria	..	..	..	..	..	47.2	44.7	42.5
Canada	27.9	44.8	41.6	40.9	41.3	37.5	..	..
Chile	63.7	63.5	62.7	79.0	75.6	73.8	73.5	72.0
Colombia	46.2	55.4	52.7	50.8	47.7	45.8	45.8	44.8
Costa Rica	10.0	14.2	17.5	20.5	22.8	25.4	25.4	27.1
Cuba	..	..	..	..	..	..	..	..
Czech Republic	88.2	89.4	90.0	89.1	88.6	87.8	86.9	86.6
Denmark	16.4	27.5	27.9	28.3	25.3	23.1	21.9	78.8
Dominican Republic	..	..	..	..	..	28.4	..	..
Ecuador	..	..	..	0.4	..	..	0.0	..
Egypt	..	..	..	..	..	..	..	..
El Salvador	0.0	0.0	0.0	0.0	..	4.5	4.2	3.8
Estonia	94.3	95.1	95.2	94.8	100.0	95.4	95.6	95.8
Finland	23.8	23.7	100.0	..	..	..	..	..
France	0.1	0.1	0.1	..	..	..	..	..
Germany	14.0	14.5	14.3	13.3	13.6	14.4	13.6	13.5
Greece	34.5	41.2	43.0	57.3	57.3	56.4	55.7	55.7
Guatemala	..	..	..	..	..	..	..	0.0
Honduras	10.5	40.3	42.8	..	..	49.3	47.3	48.3
Hong Kong, China	..	..	..	..	..	..	..	..
Hungary	94.9	94.7	92.8	91.7	91.4	91.4	91.4	92.5
Iceland	10.4	10.9	11.3	..	..	..	..	..
India	..	..	..	..	2.9	..	..	..
Indonesia	..	..	..	..	..	..	..	..
Ireland	14.3	24.3	22.2	..	17.1	16.6	22.8	..
Israel[1]	3.3	3.4	4.0	3.8	3.8	3.8	18.9	18.0
Italy	27.8	28.9	32.2	31.8	31.1	30.0	31.4	30.0
Japan	..	..	..	9.4	7.5	9.4	8.7	9.2
Korea	4.0	3.7	3.7	3.7	3.8	4.1	..	4.3
Latvia	49.4	48.7	57.1	79.0	77.2	79.5	83.5	86.7
Lithuania	98.8	99.0	99.0	99.3	99.5	99.5	99.6	99.6
Luxembourg	52.1	53.3	52.8	51.7	51.1	50.2	63.7	64.0
Malaysia	45.8	46.6	47.8	48.5	51.9	52.9	53.4	53.5
Mexico	9.7	48.7	52.2	48.5	50.3	48.1	49.5	46.8
Montenegro	..	..	..	..	..	..	..	..
Morocco	..	..	..	..	..	..	..	..
Netherlands	22.7	11.6	16.3	2.6	2.3	1.7	..	..
New Zealand	..	..	..	..	..	..	74.7	..
Nicaragua	25.7	24.7	25.7	26.0	..	29.4	..	30.8
Norway	43.4	41.1	40.2	40.3	37.8	37.3	37.3	36.2
Panama	47.0	..	..	..	..	..	43.4	45.4
Paraguay	26.4	..	0.0	22.8	24.7	..	27.5	..
Peru	19.9	20.6	45.9	24.8	25.7	25.0	40.1	40.1
Poland	61.3	61.3	61.8	59.1	58.4	59.1	60.2	60.2
Portugal	26.6	84.2	84.3	91.0	91.6	91.0	91.1	90.8
Puerto Rico	52.6	51.8	41.0	55.6	..	..	..	..
Russia	..	2.2	13.7	13.7	14.0	13.9	39.9	22.3
Singapore	86.2	89.0	89.2	90.2	80.0	..	79.0	78.6
Slovak Republic	93.8	93.6	93.2	..	8.3	..	96.8	98.5
Slovenia	5.1	5.2	5.3	5.7	5.9	5.8	18.3	17.8
South Africa	45.2	39.5	34.6	37.4	..	..	..	14.5
Spain	29.1	28.8	23.6	..	..	..	..	..
Sri Lanka	..	4.7	4.8	..	16.0	10.6	..	..
Sweden	57.6	55.4	44.8	46.7	48.0	52.6	52.3	..
Switzerland	20.6	19.6	20.3	20.1	18.7	17.4	16.9	16.0
Chinese Taipei	..	..	..	..	..	9.9	9.7	9.7
Thailand	..	..	..	..	..	..	..	..
Tunisia	..	..	..	..	..	..	..	..
Turkey	62.2	59.3	66.7	63.7	57.1	54.2	52.9	48.9
United Kingdom	58.0	57.8	57.5	0.3	0.5	0.5	0.7	0.8
United States	10.4	9.4	9.5	10.2	10.0	0.8	5.5	11.7
Uruguay	31.4	32.2	33.6	..	34.7	..	34.6	36.4

.. Not available

Note: Detailed metadata at: *http://metalinks.oecd.org/ins/20220309/7297*.

1. Information on data for Israel: *http://oe.cd/israel-disclaimer*.

Source: *Insurance activity indicators, OECD Insurance Statistics (database)*

Table 30. Market share of foreign undertakings in total domestic business (Non-life)

Branches or agencies

Per cent

	2013	2014	2015	2016	2017	2018	2019	2020
Argentina	0.1	3.2	2.5	2.4	2.6	2.1	2.2	2.2
Australia	9.7	10.1	9.1	9.9	9.6	11.9	13.2	15.1
Austria	0.1	0.1	0.0	0.0	0.1	0.1	0.1	..
Belgium	..	..	..	..	..	..	..	..
Bermuda	..	..	..	..	..	..	..	..
Bolivia	..	..	..	..	..	..	..	..
Brazil	..	..	0.0	0.0	0.0	0.0	0.0	0.0
Bulgaria	..	..	..	..	..	..	..	..
Canada	13.1	23.2	21.0	19.4	19.0	15.1	..	..
Chile	..	..	..	..	..	..	..	..
Colombia	..	0.0	..	..	..	..	..	..
Costa Rica	0.3	0.4	0.8	1.3	1.5	1.7	1.7	2.1
Cuba	..	..	..	..	..	..	..	..
Czech Republic	3.7	4.7	4.9	5.3	5.4	4.4	4.8	4.4
Denmark	..	..	..	..	..	..	..	..
Dominican Republic	..	..	..	..	..	..	..	..
Ecuador	..	..	..	..	..	..	0.0	..
Egypt	..	..	..	..	..	..	..	..
El Salvador	0.0	0.0	0.0	0.0	..	4.5	4.2	3.8
Estonia	13.6	14.8	13.5	15.0	15.1	15.3	15.9	21.8
Finland	..	..	..	..	..	..	..	..
France	0.1	0.1	0.1	..	..	..	..	..
Germany	2.7	3.2	3.5	3.1	3.8	4.0	3.6	3.8
Greece	0.0	0.0	0.0	0.0	0.0	0.0	0.0	0.0
Guatemala	..	..	..	..	..	..	..	0.0
Honduras	10.5	4.4	3.6	..	..	49.3	47.3	48.3
Hong Kong, China	..	..	..	..	..	..	..	..
Hungary	..	..	..	..	..	..	..	..
Iceland	..	..	..	..	..	..	..	..
India	..	..	..	..	2.9	..	..	..
Indonesia	..	..	..	..	..	..	..	..
Ireland	14.3	24.3	22.2	..	17.1	16.6	22.8	..
Israel[1]	..	..	..	..	..	..	..	..
Italy	1.1	1.1	1.4	1.6	1.5	1.6	1.7	1.7
Japan	..	..	..	2.3	2.5	2.8	2.3	3.3
Korea	3.1	2.3	2.3	2.3	2.4	2.8	..	3.0
Latvia	18.5	20.4	20.2	22.6	27.0	28.1	29.6	30.0
Lithuania	52.9	53.1	53.9	46.8	48.4	51.4	51.5	50.8
Luxembourg	6.5	3.6	3.6	3.5	3.3	3.6	11.7	10.9
Malaysia	6.7	7.3	8.4	9.6	8.9	8.8	10.0	12.6
Mexico	..	..	..	..	..	..	..	..
Montenegro	..	..	..	..	..	..	..	..
Morocco	..	..	..	..	..	..	..	..
Netherlands	0.3	0.3	0.0	..	..	..	..	..
New Zealand	..	..	..	..	..	..	13.0	..
Nicaragua	..	..	..	..	..	..	..	..
Norway	43.4	41.1	40.2	40.3	37.8	37.3	37.3	36.2
Panama	7.7	..	..	..	..	..	41.4	..
Paraguay	..	..	0.0	0.0	..	..	0.0	..
Peru	..	..	..	..	..	..	..	..
Poland	..	..	..	..	..	..	..	..
Portugal	0.0	0.0	0.0	0.0	0.0	0.0	0.0	0.0
Puerto Rico	..	..	..	..	..	..	..	..
Russia	..	..	..	0.1	0.0	0.0	0.0	0.0
Singapore	46.8	39.6	38.2	37.4	36.5	..	31.7	40.0
Slovak Republic	8.0	8.7	8.5	..	8.3	..	7.7	5.8
Slovenia	..	..	..	..	..	..	..	..
South Africa	0.0	..	..	..	..	..	..	0.0
Spain	0.0	0.0	0.0	..	..	..	..	..
Sri Lanka	..	..	0.0	..	..	..	..	..
Sweden	..	8.2	..	..	..	..	..	..
Switzerland	5.0	5.5	6.0	7.1	7.5	5.8	5.2	4.5
Chinese Taipei	..	..	..	..	..	3.3	3.4	3.3
Thailand	..	..	..	..	..	..	..	..
Tunisia	..	..	..	..	..	..	..	..
Turkey	0.3	0.3	0.4	0.4	0.5	0.7	1.0	1.2
United Kingdom	3.7	4.1	4.6	0.3	0.5	0.5	0.7	0.8
United States	0.0	0.0	0.1	0.1	0.1	0.1	0.0	0.0
Uruguay	0.0	0.0	0.0	..	0.0	..	0.0	0.0

.. Not available

Note: Detailed metadata at: *http://metalinks.oecd.org/ins/20220309/7297*.

1. Information on data for Israel: *http://oe.cd/israel-disclaimer*.

Source: *Insurance activity indicators, OECD Insurance Statistics (database)*

Country tables

AUSTRALIA

Table 1. Selected aggregates

Million AUD

	2013	2014	2015	2016	2017	2018	2019	2020
1.1 Insurance business written in the reporting country								
1.1.1 Insurance business, by ownership								
Gross premiums								
Domestic undertakings	86 754	103 414	100 992	95 348	90 032	88 064	81 517	75 436
Foreign controlled undertakings	15 722	17 983	19 150	19 836	21 498	24 659	26 308	35 921
Foreign companies (branches)	3 977	4 206	3 893	4 393	4 353	5 613	6 630	7 967
All undertakings	90 731	107 620	104 885	99 741	94 385	93 677	88 147	83 403
Premiums ceded								
Domestic undertakings	12 121	13 268	15 209	17 826	19 711	18 794	20 650	22 714
Foreign controlled undertakings	4 666	5 483	5 986	6 268	8 647	8 223	8 676	12 208
Foreign companies (branches)	1 947	1 842	1 739	1 759	1 873	1 875	2 155	2 770
All undertakings	14 068	15 110	16 948	19 585	21 584	20 669	22 805	25 484
Net written premiums								
Domestic undertakings	74 633	90 147	85 783	77 522	70 321	69 270	60 869	52 722
Foreign controlled undertakings	11 055	12 500	13 164	13 568	12 851	16 436	17 632	23 713
Foreign companies (branches)	2 030	2 365	2 154	2 634	2 480	3 738	4 475	5 197
All undertakings	76 663	92 511	87 937	80 156	72 801	73 008	65 344	57 919
1.1.2 Insurance business on foreign risks, gross premiums								
Life	574	686	701	711	706	880	1 176	1 156
Non-life	..	..	..	..	..	..	..	..
Composite total	..	..	..	..	..	..	..	..
Total	574	686	701	711	706	880	1 176	1 156
1.1.3 Life insurance payments, by class, gross premiums								
Annuities	..	..	..	..	..	..	..	..
Unit linked	..	..	..	..	..	..	..	..
Other life insurance	..	..	..	..	..	..	..	..
Total life insurance	45 794	60 881	56 868	49 890	43 141	39 741	31 149	23 860
***of which:** Pension contracts*	..	..	..	..	..	..	..	..
1.1.4 Non-life insurance payments, by class, gross premiums								
Motor vehicle insurance	12 924	13 467	13 749	14 512	15 447	15 789	16 471	16 885
Marine, aviation and other transport insurance	1 523	1 598	1 673	1 648	1 739	1 871	1 899	1 319
Freight insurance	..	..	..	..	..	..	..	..
Fire and other property damage insurance	12 038	11 836	12 031	12 297	12 713	13 428	14 391	15 736
Pecuniary loss insurance	1 258	1 454	1 493	1 443	1 352	1 230	1 169	1 076
General liability insurance	5 283	5 418	5 435	5 348	5 491	5 893	6 391	7 164
Accident and health	1 134	1 124	1 130	1 064	1 021	1 006	1 022	1 046
***of which:** Health*	..	..	..	..	..	..	..	..
Other non-life insurance	900	951	1 029	1 071	1 205	1 325	1 444	1 543
Treaty reinsurance	5 823	5 970	6 271	7 115	6 269	6 742	7 273	7 819
Total non-life insurance	40 884	41 818	42 811	44 498	45 237	47 283	50 060	52 588
1.2 Gross claims payments								
Life								
Domestic undertakings	47 647	64 828	56 547	59 350	47 307	46 989	43 814	94 607
Foreign controlled undertakings	5 212	5 876	6 681	7 133	9 207	8 564	9 141	80 540
Foreign companies (branches)	..	..	..	..	..	..	..	..
All undertakings	47 647	64 828	56 547	59 350	47 307	46 989	43 814	94 607
Non-life								
Domestic undertakings	24 141	26 293	29 311	28 026	29 946	30 252	33 037	40 491
Foreign controlled undertakings	4 542	5 446	6 183	5 534	6 453	8 199	8 425	11 044
Foreign companies (branches)	1 984	3 318	2 585	3 217	3 124	3 853	5 088	6 947
All undertakings	26 126	29 611	31 896	31 243	33 070	34 105	38 125	47 438
Composite, all undertakings	..	..	..	..	..	..	..	..
Total								
Domestic undertakings	71 788	91 121	85 858	87 376	77 253	77 241	76 851	135 098
Foreign controlled undertakings	9 754	11 322	12 864	12 667	15 660	16 763	17 566	91 584
Foreign companies (branches)	1 984	3 318	2 585	3 217	3 124	3 853	5 088	6 947
All undertakings	73 773	94 439	88 443	90 593	80 377	81 094	81 939	142 045
1.3 Commissions								
Life								
Domestic undertakings	3 015	3 118	3 087	3 129	2 514	2 402	2 052	1 740
Foreign controlled undertakings	447	451	460	464	494	483	470	1 347
Foreign companies (branches)	..	..	..	..	..	..	..	..
All undertakings	3 015	3 118	3 087	3 129	2 514	2 402	2 052	1 740
Non-life								
Domestic undertakings	506	566	816	1 038	1 070	1 310	1 338	1 418
Foreign controlled undertakings	239	270	276	308	341	418	452	534
Foreign companies (branches)	264	287	301	327	324	250	280	373
All undertakings	770	853	1 117	1 364	1 394	1 560	1 618	1 791
Composite, all undertakings	..	..	..	..	..	..	..	..
Total								
Domestic undertakings	3 521	3 684	3 903	4 167	3 584	3 712	3 390	3 158
Foreign controlled undertakings	686	721	736	772	835	901	923	1 881
Foreign companies (branches)	264	287	301	327	324	250	280	373
All undertakings	3 785	3 971	4 204	4 493	3 908	3 962	3 671	3 531

Table 1. Selected aggregates *(cont.)*

Million AUD

	2013	2014	2015	2016	2017	2018	2019	2020
1.4 Gross operating expenses								
Life								
Domestic undertakings	7 830	8 128	8 041	8 666	8 457	9 370	8 045	6 999
Foreign controlled undertakings	2 392	2 393	2 487	3 038	3 239	4 439	3 546	5 724
Foreign companies (branches)	..	..	..	..	..	..	..	..
All undertakings	7 830	8 128	8 041	8 666	8 457	9 370	8 045	6 999
Non-life								
Domestic undertakings	7 361	7 502	7 497	7 368	7 475	7 517	7 979	8 354
Foreign controlled undertakings	1 618	1 704	1 850	1 829	1 975	2 378	2 710	2 782
Foreign companies (branches)	597	629	660	618	563	790	1 003	1 109
All undertakings	7 959	8 131	8 157	7 987	8 038	8 307	8 982	9 463
Composite, all undertakings	..	..	..	..	..	..	..	..
Total								
Domestic undertakings	15 191	15 630	15 538	16 034	15 932	16 887	16 024	15 353
Foreign controlled undertakings	4 010	4 097	4 337	4 867	5 214	6 817	6 256	8 505
Foreign companies (branches)	597	629	660	618	563	790	1 003	1 109
All undertakings	15 789	16 259	16 198	16 653	16 495	17 677	17 027	16 462
1.5 Insurance business written abroad by branches, gross premiums								
Life								
Branches and agencies	..	..	..	..	..	..	..	..
Subsidaries	..	..	..	..	..	..	..	..
Total	..	..	..	..	..	..	..	..
Non-life								
Branches and agencies	..	..	..	..	..	..	..	..
Subsidaries	..	..	..	..	..	..	..	..
Total	..	..	..	..	..	..	..	..
Composite total	..	..	..	..	..	..	..	..
Total								
Branches and agencies	..	..	..	..	..	..	..	..
Subsidaries	..	..	..	..	..	..	..	..
Total	..	..	..	..	..	..	..	..

.. Not available

Note: Detailed metadata at: *http://metalinks.oecd.org/ins/20220309/d7ab.*

Source: *OECD Insurance Statistics (database)*

AUSTRALIA

Table 2. Number of companies and employees

	2013	2014	2015	2016	2017	2018	2019	2020
2.1 Number of companies								
Life								
Domestic undertakings	28	28	28	29	29	29	28	28
Foreign controlled undertakings	14	14	13	13	13	14	13	21
Foreign companies (branches)	..	..	..	..	..	..	..	..
All undertakings	28	28	28	29	29	29	28	28
Non-life								
Domestic undertakings	75	74	70	68	58	58	58	58
Foreign controlled undertakings	18	19	19	17	15	17	16	16
Foreign companies (branches)	29	29	29	31	28	28	27	27
All undertakings	104	103	99	99	86	86	85	85
Composite, all undertakings	..	..	0	..	..	..	..	..
Reinsurance								
Domestic undertakings	3	3	2	2	2	2	2	2
Foreign controlled undertakings	1	1	1	1	1	1	2	2
Foreign companies (branches)	9	9	9	8	8	8	9	9
All undertakings	12	12	11	10	10	10	11	11
Total								
Domestic undertakings	106	105	100	99	89	89	88	88
Foreign controlled undertakings	33	34	33	31	29	32	31	39
Foreign companies (branches)	38	38	38	39	36	36	36	36
All undertakings	144	143	138	138	125	125	124	124
2.2 Number of employees								
Insurance undertakings	..	..	..	..	..	..	..	..
Intermediaries	..	..	..	..	..	..	..	..
Total	..	..	..	..	..	..	..	..

.. Not available

Note: Detailed metadata at: *http://metalinks.oecd.org/ins/20220309/d7ab.*

Source: OECD *Insurance Statistics (database)*

AUSTRIA

Table 1. Selected aggregates

Million EUR

	2013	2014	2015	2016	2017	2018	2019	2020
1.1 Insurance business written in the reporting country								
1.1.1 Insurance business, by ownership								
Gross premiums								
Domestic undertakings	18 879	18 889	19 003	18 647	18 126	18 520	18 831	..
Foreign controlled undertakings	6 781	7 196	7 060	6 979	6 390	6 467	6 549	..
Foreign companies (branches)	8	6	6	6	7	8	8	..
All undertakings	18 887	18 895	19 009	18 653	18 134	18 527	18 839	..
Premiums ceded								
Domestic undertakings	3 539	3 102	2 996	3 521	3 130	2 376	2 570	..
Foreign controlled undertakings	1 127	1 171	1 113	1 636	1 280	475	549	..
Foreign companies (branches)	0	0	0	0	0	0	0	..
All undertakings	3 539	3 102	2 996	3 522	3 131	2 376	2 571	..
Net written premiums								
Domestic undertakings	15 340	15 787	16 007	15 126	14 996	16 144	16 261	..
Foreign controlled undertakings	5 654	6 024	5 948	5 343	5 110	5 991	6 000	..
Foreign companies (branches)	8	6	6	6	7	7	8	..
All undertakings	15 348	15 793	16 013	15 131	15 003	16 151	16 268	..
1.1.2 Insurance business on foreign risks, gross premiums								
Life	157	22	20	14	3	4	23	..
Non-life	717	726	702	753	777	931	858	..
Composite	595	489	391	371	363	358	387	..
of which:								
Life	202	158	111	95	89	82	80	..
Non-life	393	331	280	276	274	276	306	..
Total	1 469	1 237	1 114	1 138	1 143	1 293	1 268	..
1.1.3 Life insurance payments, by class, gross premiums								
Annuities	1 441	1 822	1 946	1 531	1 434	1 367	1 361	..
Unit linked	1 248	1 011	933	864	812	972	1 013	..
Other life insurance	3 738	3 852	3 812	3 646	3 488	3 188	3 029	..
Total life insurance	6 427	6 685	6 692	6 041	5 735	5 527	5 403	..
***of which:** Pension contracts*	997	1 116	1 031	940	964	923	831	..
1.1.4 Non-life insurance payments, by class, gross premiums								
Motor vehicle insurance	1 487	1 447	3 920	4 043	3 980	4 207	4 292	..
Marine, aviation and other transport insurance	174	138	11	9	10	9	6	..
Freight insurance	..	..	155	148	137	165	164	..
Fire and other property damage insurance	1 081	1 058	3 153	3 178	3 013	3 030	3 170	..
Pecuniary loss insurance	174	183	178	176	166	169	168	..
General liability insurance	860	886	889	905	868	903	932	..
Accident and health	3 150	3 143	3 257	3 391	3 473	3 627	3 780	..
***of which:** Health*	1 841	1 905	2 007	2 096	2 167	2 264	2 374	..
Other non-life insurance	5 517	5 340	742	749	739	877	910	..
Treaty reinsurance	..	..	..	..	..	..	..	..
Total non-life insurance	12 444	12 195	12 303	12 599	12 386	12 987	13 421	..
1.2 Gross claims payments								
Life								
Domestic undertakings	358	1 110	1 254	947	977	933	956	..
Foreign controlled undertakings	140	714	837	920	959	914	938	..
Foreign companies (branches)	0	0	0	0	0	0	0	..
All undertakings	358	1 110	1 254	947	977	933	956	..
Non-life								
Domestic undertakings	1 107	1 632	2 072	2 203	1 939	1 936	1 995	..
Foreign controlled undertakings	905	873	1 288	2 620	1 893	1 862	1 936	..
Foreign companies (branches)	4	3	2	3	3	3	4	..
All undertakings	1 111	1 636	2 075	2 206	1 942	1 939	2 000	..
Composite								
Domestic undertakings	11 676	11 289	12 780	12 440	12 173	11 700	12 554	..
Foreign controlled undertakings	3 846	3 026	3 760	10 479	9 813	9 865	11 072	..
Foreign companies (branches)	0	0	0	0	0	0	0	..
All undertakings	11 676	11 289	12 780	12 440	12 173	11 700	12 554	..
of which:								
Life	6 011	5 955	7 193	6 817	6 194	5 688	6 294	..
Domestic undertakings	6 011	5 955	7 193	6 817	6 194	5 688	6 294	..
Foreign controlled undertakings	2 274	1 630	2 235	3 500	3 281	3 307	3 710	..
Foreign companies (branches)	0	0	0	0	0	0	0	..
All undertakings	6 011	5 955	7 193	6 817	6 194	5 688	6 294	..
Non-life	5 665	5 335	5 588	5 623	5 980	6 012	6 261	..
Domestic undertakings	5 665	5 335	5 588	5 623	5 980	6 012	6 261	..
Foreign controlled undertakings	1 572	1 396	1 525	6 979	6 532	6 558	7 362	..
Foreign companies (branches)	0	0	0	0	0	0	0	..
All undertakings	5 665	5 335	5 588	5 623	5 980	6 012	6 261	..
Total								
Domestic undertakings	13 141	14 032	16 107	15 590	15 089	14 568	15 506	..
Foreign controlled undertakings	4 891	4 613	5 885	14 018	12 665	12 641	13 945	..
Foreign companies (branches)	4	3	2	3	3	3	4	..
All undertakings	13 145	14 036	16 109	15 593	15 092	14 572	15 510	..

Table 1. Selected aggregates *(cont.)*

Million EUR

	2013	2014	2015	2016	2017	2018	2019	2020
1.3 Commissions								
Life								
Domestic undertakings	99	98	98	80	73	73	73	..
Foreign controlled undertakings	5	70	70	79	72	72	72	..
Foreign companies (branches)	0	0	0	0	0	0	0	..
All undertakings	99	98	98	80	73	73	73	..
Non-life								
Domestic undertakings	354	398	386	399	408	411	416	..
Foreign controlled undertakings	319	329	341	348	352	350	350	..
Foreign companies (branches)	2	1	1	1	2	2	2	..
All undertakings	356	399	387	400	410	413	418	..
Composite								
Domestic undertakings	2 285	2 279	2 354	2 392	2 365	2 335	2 402	..
Foreign controlled undertakings	752	666	739	734	725	706	747	..
Foreign companies (branches)	0	0	0	0	0	0	0	..
All undertakings	2 285	2 279	2 354	2 392	2 365	2 335	2 402	..
of which:								
Life	644	624	623	579	538	454	463	..
Domestic undertakings	644	624	623	579	538	454	463	..
Foreign controlled undertakings	238	163	188	163	149	106	112	..
Foreign companies (branches)	0	0	0	0	0	0	0	..
All undertakings	644	624	623	579	538	454	463	..
Non-life	1 641	1 655	1 731	1 812	1 827	1 881	1 939	..
Domestic undertakings	1 641	1 655	1 731	1 812	1 827	1 881	1 939	..
Foreign controlled undertakings	514	503	551	571	576	600	635	..
Foreign companies (branches)	0	0	0	0	0	0	0	..
All undertakings	1 641	1 655	1 731	1 812	1 827	1 881	1 939	..
Total								
Domestic undertakings	2 738	2 775	2 839	2 871	2 846	2 819	2 891	..
Foreign controlled undertakings	1 076	1 065	1 150	1 161	1 149	1 128	1 170	..
Foreign companies (branches)	2	1	1	1	2	2	2	..
All undertakings	2 740	2 776	2 840	2 872	2 848	2 821	2 893	..
1.4 Gross operating expenses								
Life								
Domestic undertakings	120	43	40	37	42	37	34	..
Foreign controlled undertakings	14	30	30	36	41	37	33	..
Foreign companies (branches)	0	0	0	0	0	0	0	..
All undertakings	120	43	40	37	42	37	34	..
Non-life								
Domestic undertakings	697	153	143	192	191	210	218	..
Foreign controlled undertakings	414	116	92	111	105	103	99	..
Foreign companies (branches)	3	1	1	1	1	1	1	..
All undertakings	700	154	144	193	192	210	219	..
Composite								
Domestic undertakings	2 306	623	678	702	696	741	777	..
Foreign controlled undertakings	699	167	185	177	181	178	183	..
Foreign companies (branches)	0	0	0	0	0	0	0	..
All undertakings	2 306	623	678	702	696	741	777	..
of which:								
Life	848	194	202	223	224	236	238	..
Domestic undertakings	848	194	202	223	224	236	238	..
Foreign controlled undertakings	323	61	68	63	58	60	63	..
Foreign companies (branches)	0	0	0	0	0	0	0	..
All undertakings	848	194	202	223	224	236	238	..
Non-life	1 458	428	476	479	472	505	539	..
Domestic undertakings	1 458	428	476	479	472	505	539	..
Foreign controlled undertakings	376	106	117	114	123	118	120	..
Foreign companies (branches)	0	0	0	0	0	0	0	..
All undertakings	1 458	428	476	479	472	505	539	..
Total								
Domestic undertakings	3 124	819	861	930	929	988	1 028	..
Foreign controlled undertakings	1 128	313	308	324	328	318	315	..
Foreign companies (branches)	3	1	1	1	1	1	1	..
All undertakings	3 127	820	862	931	930	989	1 029	..

Table 1. Selected aggregates *(cont.)*

Million EUR

	2013	2014	2015	2016	2017	2018	2019	2020
1.5 Insurance business written abroad by branches, gross premiums								
Life								
Branches and agencies	157	22	19	13	11	10	29	..
Subsidaries	..	..	..	..	..	..	..	..
Total	157	22	19	13	11	10	29	..
Non-life								
Branches and agencies	159	198	204	217	215	220	245	..
Subsidaries	..	..	..	..	..	..	..	..
Total	159	198	204	217	215	220	245	..
Composite								
Branches and agencies	480	368	284	251	275	279	261	..
Subsidaries	..	..	..	..	..	..	..	..
Total	480	368	284	251	275	279	261	..
of which:								
Life	140	103	78	83	78	73	71	..
Branches and agencies	140	103	78	83	78	73	71	..
Subsidaries	..	..	..	..	..	..	..	..
Total	140	103	78	83	78	73	71	..
Non-life	340	266	206	168	198	206	190	..
Branches and agencies	340	266	206	168	198	206	190	..
Subsidaries	..	..	..	..	..	..	..	..
Total	340	266	206	168	198	206	190	..
Total								
Branches and agencies	796	587	507	481	501	510	535	..
Subsidaries	..	..	..	..	..	..	..	..
Total	796	587	507	481	501	510	535	..

.. Not available

Note: Detailed metadata at: *http://metalinks.oecd.org/ins/20220309/5fbc.*

Source: OECD *Insurance Statistics (database)*

AUSTRIA

Table 2. Number of companies and employees

	2013	2014	2015	2016	2017	2018	2019	2020
2.1 Number of companies								
Life								
Domestic undertakings	3	7	7	6	6	6	6	..
Foreign controlled undertakings	1	3	3	4	4	4	4	..
Foreign companies (branches)	0	0	0	0	0	0	0	..
All undertakings	3	7	7	6	6	6	6	..
Non-life								
Domestic undertakings	14	12	12	12	12	12	12	..
Foreign controlled undertakings	7	8	8	8	8	7	7	..
Foreign companies (branches)	1	1	1	1	1	1	1	..
All undertakings	15	13	13	13	13	13	13	..
Composite								
Domestic undertakings	26	21	20	17	17	16	16	..
Foreign controlled undertakings	9	6	5	4	4	4	4	..
Foreign companies (branches)	0	0	0	0	0	0	0	..
All undertakings	26	21	20	17	17	16	16	..
Reinsurance								
Domestic undertakings	3	3	2	3	2	1	1	..
Foreign controlled undertakings	1	2	1	1	0	0	0	..
Foreign companies (branches)	0	0	0	0	0	0	0	..
All undertakings	3	3	2	3	2	1	1	..
Total								
Domestic undertakings	46	43	41	38	37	35	35	..
Foreign controlled undertakings	18	19	17	17	16	15	15	..
Foreign companies (branches)	1	1	1	1	1	1	1	..
All undertakings	47	44	42	39	38	36	36	..
2.2 Number of employees								
Insurance undertakings	27 738	27 791	27 911	28 336	28 367	27 804	27 903	..
Intermediaries	..	..	..	..	..	..	..	..
Total	27 738	27 791	27 911	28 336	28 367	27 804	27 903	..

.. Not available

Note: Detailed metadata at: *http://metalinks.oecd.org/ins/20220309/5fbc.*

Source: *OECD Insurance Statistics (database)*

BELGIUM

Table 1. Selected aggregates

Million EUR

	2013	2014	2015	2016	2017	2018	2019	2020
1.1 Insurance business written in the reporting country								
1.1.1 Insurance business, by ownership								
Gross premiums								
Domestic undertakings	28 251	28 863	27 712	27 493	27 299	28 539	31 400	30 132
Foreign controlled undertakings	..	..	..	..	..	..	..	..
Foreign companies (branches)	..	..	..	..	..	..	..	..
All undertakings	28 251	28 863	27 712	27 493	27 299	28 539	31 400	30 132
Premiums ceded								
Domestic undertakings	2 474	3 251	3 183	3 520	3 412	3 656	7 478	5 223
Foreign controlled undertakings	..	..	..	..	..	..	..	..
Foreign companies (branches)	..	..	..	..	..	..	..	..
All undertakings	2 474	3 251	3 183	3 520	3 412	3 656	7 478	5 223
Net written premiums								
Domestic undertakings	25 777	25 612	24 529	23 973	23 887	24 882	23 923	24 910
Foreign controlled undertakings	..	..	..	..	..	..	..	..
Foreign companies (branches)	..	..	..	..	..	..	..	..
All undertakings	25 777	25 612	24 529	23 973	23 887	24 882	23 923	24 910
1.1.2 Insurance business on foreign risks, gross premiums								
Life	25	15	24	20	17	6	15	0
Non-life	268	563	436	515	553	611	453	458
Composite	218	223	321	331	331	378	580	543
of which:								
Life	53	39	38	23	17	14	15	18
Non-life	165	184	282	308	313	364	565	524
Total	511	801	781	866	901	995	1 048	1 001
1.1.3 Life insurance payments, by class, gross premiums								
Annuities	..	..	..	..	..	..	..	..
Unit linked	2 743	2 524	3 008	2 221	3 182	3 520	3 341	3 352
Other life insurance	13 501	13 723	12 302	12 674	11 424	12 051	12 826	11 351
Total life insurance	16 244	16 247	15 310	14 895	14 606	15 571	16 167	14 703
***of which:** Pension contracts*	..	..	..	..	..	..	..	..
1.1.4 Non-life insurance payments, by class, gross premiums								
Motor vehicle insurance	3 487	3 542	3 585	..	..	..	..	..
Marine, aviation and other transport insurance	71	69	81	..	..	..	..	..
Freight insurance	104	100	73	..	..	..	..	..
Fire and other property damage insurance	2 696	2 755	2 708	..	..	..	..	..
Pecuniary loss insurance	404	725	598	..	..	..	..	..
General liability insurance	770	785	762	..	..	..	..	..
Accident and health	3 592	3 695	3 653	..	..	..	..	..
***of which:** Health*	1 618	1 708	1 849	..	..	..	..	..
Other non-life insurance	825	885	888	..	..	..	..	..
Treaty reinsurance	..	..	..	..	..	..	..	..
Total non-life insurance	11 949	12 556	12 349	12 532	12 652	12 926	15 159	15 407
1.2 Gross claims payments								
Life								
Domestic undertakings	528	626	469	642	521	731	694	300
Foreign controlled undertakings	..	..	..	..	..	..	..	..
Foreign companies (branches)	..	..	..	..	..	..	..	..
All undertakings	528	626	469	642	521	731	694	300
Non-life								
Domestic undertakings	1 960	2 272	2 363	2 539	2 316	1 489	1 989	2 397
Foreign controlled undertakings	..	..	..	..	..	..	..	..
Foreign companies (branches)	..	..	..	..	..	..	..	..
All undertakings	1 960	2 272	2 363	2 539	2 316	1 489	1 989	2 397
Composite								
Domestic undertakings	23 890	24 323	25 926	25 229	24 184	22 308	22 683	23 407
Foreign controlled undertakings	..	..	..	..	..	..	..	..
Foreign companies (branches)	..	..	..	..	..	..	..	..
All undertakings	23 890	24 323	25 926	25 229	24 184	22 308	22 683	23 407
of which:								
Life	17 746	17 418	19 244	18 328	17 466	16 063	15 914	17 108
Domestic undertakings	17 746	17 418	19 244	18 328	17 466	16 063	15 914	17 108
Foreign controlled undertakings	..	..	..	..	..	..	..	..
Foreign companies (branches)	..	..	..	..	..	..	..	..
All undertakings	17 746	17 418	19 244	18 328	17 466	16 063	15 914	17 108
Non-life	6 144	6 905	6 682	6 901	6 717	6 244	6 770	6 299
Domestic undertakings	6 144	6 905	6 682	6 901	6 717	6 244	6 770	6 299
Foreign controlled undertakings	..	..	..	..	..	..	..	..
Foreign companies (branches)	..	..	..	..	..	..	..	..
All undertakings	6 144	6 905	6 682	6 901	6 717	6 244	6 770	6 299
Total								
Domestic undertakings	26 378	27 222	28 758	28 410	27 020	24 527	25 366	26 104
Foreign controlled undertakings	..	..	..	..	..	..	..	..
Foreign companies (branches)	..	..	..	..	..	..	..	..
All undertakings	26 378	27 222	28 758	28 410	27 020	24 527	25 366	26 104

Table 1. Selected aggregates *(cont.)*

Million EUR

	2013	2014	2015	2016	2017	2018	2019	2020
1.3 Commissions								
Life								
Domestic undertakings	55	45	47	55	56	64	67	15
Foreign controlled undertakings	..	..	..	..	..	..	..	..
Foreign companies (branches)	..	..	..	..	..	..	..	..
All undertakings	55	45	47	55	56	64	67	15
Non-life								
Domestic undertakings	391	450	550	616	607	303	287	265
Foreign controlled undertakings	..	..	..	..	..	..	..	..
Foreign companies (branches)	..	..	..	..	..	..	..	..
All undertakings	391	450	550	616	607	303	287	265
Composite								
Domestic undertakings	2 446	2 478	2 493	2 484	2 536	2 161	2 442	2 514
Foreign controlled undertakings	..	..	..	..	..	..	..	..
Foreign companies (branches)	..	..	..	..	..	..	..	..
All undertakings	2 446	2 478	2 493	2 484	2 536	2 161	2 442	2 514
of which:								
Life	875	852	833	765	756	730	735	757
Domestic undertakings	875	852	833	765	756	730	735	757
Foreign controlled undertakings	..	..	..	..	..	..	..	..
Foreign companies (branches)	..	..	..	..	..	..	..	..
All undertakings	875	852	833	765	756	730	735	757
Non-life	1 572	1 626	1 660	1 719	1 779	1 431	1 707	1 758
Domestic undertakings	1 572	1 626	1 660	1 719	1 779	1 431	1 707	1 758
Foreign controlled undertakings	..	..	..	..	..	..	..	..
Foreign companies (branches)	..	..	..	..	..	..	..	..
All undertakings	1 572	1 626	1 660	1 719	1 779	1 431	1 707	1 758
Total								
Domestic undertakings	2 892	2 973	3 090	3 155	3 198	2 529	2 797	2 793
Foreign controlled undertakings	..	..	..	..	..	..	..	..
Foreign companies (branches)	..	..	..	..	..	..	..	..
All undertakings	2 892	2 973	3 090	3 155	3 198	2 529	2 797	2 793
1.4 Gross operating expenses								
Life								
Domestic undertakings	58	41	45	47	51	61	60	25
Foreign controlled undertakings	..	..	..	..	..	..	..	..
Foreign companies (branches)	..	..	..	..	..	..	..	..
All undertakings	58	41	45	47	51	61	60	25
Non-life								
Domestic undertakings	386	643	618	641	678	382	363	426
Foreign controlled undertakings	..	..	..	..	..	..	..	..
Foreign companies (branches)	..	..	..	..	..	..	..	..
All undertakings	386	643	618	641	678	382	363	426
Composite								
Domestic undertakings	2 084	2 197	2 205	2 320	2 402	2 306	2 425	2 480
Foreign controlled undertakings	..	..	..	..	..	..	..	..
Foreign companies (branches)	..	..	..	..	..	..	..	..
All undertakings	2 084	2 197	2 205	2 320	2 402	2 306	2 425	2 480
of which:								
Life	830	833	824	859	869	883	895	922
Domestic undertakings	830	833	824	859	869	883	895	922
Foreign controlled undertakings	..	..	..	..	..	..	..	..
Foreign companies (branches)	..	..	..	..	..	..	..	..
All undertakings	830	833	824	859	869	883	895	922
Non-life	1 254	1 364	1 382	1 461	1 533	1 423	1 529	1 557
Domestic undertakings	1 254	1 364	1 382	1 461	1 533	1 423	1 529	1 557
Foreign controlled undertakings	..	..	..	..	..	..	..	..
Foreign companies (branches)	..	..	..	..	..	..	..	..
All undertakings	1 254	1 364	1 382	1 461	1 533	1 423	1 529	1 557
Total								
Domestic undertakings	2 528	2 881	2 868	3 008	3 130	2 749	2 847	2 931
Foreign controlled undertakings	..	..	..	..	..	..	..	..
Foreign companies (branches)	..	..	..	..	..	..	..	..
All undertakings	2 528	2 881	2 868	3 008	3 130	2 749	2 847	2 931

Table 1. Selected aggregates *(cont.)*

Million EUR

	2013	2014	2015	2016	2017	2018	2019	2020
1.5 Insurance business written abroad by branches, gross premiums								
Life								
Branches and agencies	2	2	0	0	0	0	0	0
Subsidaries	..	..	..	..	..	..	..	..
Total	2	2	..	0	0	0	0	0
Non-life								
Branches and agencies	727	1 572	1 931	1 854	1 843	1 912	991	3 544
Subsidaries	..	..	..	..	..	..	..	..
Total	727	1 572	1 931	1 854	1 843	1 912	991	3 544
Composite								
Branches and agencies	448	1 121	1 156	1 197	1 337	1 246	2 622	2 049
Subsidaries	..	..	..	..	..	..	..	..
Total	448	1 121	1 156	1 197	1 337	1 246	2 622	2 049
of which:								
Life	28	16	16	14	61	57	559	683
Branches and agencies	28	16	16	14	61	57	559	683
Subsidaries	..	..	..	..	..	..	..	..
Total	28	16	16	14	61	57	559	683
Non-life	421	1 105	1 141	1 183	1 276	1 189	2 063	1 366
Branches and agencies	421	1 105	1 141	1 183	1 276	1 189	2 063	1 366
Subsidaries	..	..	..	..	..	..	..	..
Total	421	1 105	1 141	1 183	1 276	1 189	2 063	1 366
Total								
Branches and agencies	1 178	2 696	3 087	3 051	3 181	3 158	3 614	5 592
Subsidaries	..	..	..	..	..	..	..	..
Total	1 178	2 696	3 087	3 051	3 181	3 158	3 614	5 592

.. Not available

Note: Detailed metadata at: *http://metalinks.oecd.org/ins/20220309/231b.*

Source: *OECD Insurance Statistics (database)*

BELGIUM

Table 2. Number of companies and employees

	2013	2014	2015	2016	2017	2018	2019	2020
2.1 Number of companies								
Life								
Domestic undertakings	16	15	15	12	10	9	9	8
Foreign controlled undertakings	..	..	..	..	..	..	..	..
Foreign companies (branches)	7	8	8	10	10	7	7	6
All undertakings	23	23	23	22	20	16	16	14
Non-life								
Domestic undertakings	44	42	41	38	34	36	35	35
Foreign controlled undertakings	..	..	..	..	..	..	..	..
Foreign companies (branches)	36	36	32	32	33	36	36	29
All undertakings	80	78	73	70	67	72	71	64
Composite								
Domestic undertakings	23	23	23	22	23	22	22	21
Foreign controlled undertakings	..	..	..	..	..	..	..	..
Foreign companies (branches)	2	2	2	2	2	2	2	2
All undertakings	25	25	25	24	25	24	24	23
Reinsurance								
Domestic undertakings	1	1	1	1	1	2	2	2
Foreign controlled undertakings	..	..	..	..	..	..	..	..
Foreign companies (branches)	1	1	1	1	1	1	0	0
All undertakings	2	2	2	2	2	3	2	2
Total								
Domestic undertakings	84	81	80	73	68	69	68	66
Foreign controlled undertakings	..	..	..	..	..	..	..	..
Foreign companies (branches)	46	47	43	45	46	46	45	37
All undertakings	130	128	123	118	114	115	113	103
2.2 Number of employees								
Insurance undertakings	..	..	..	..	..	..	..	..
Intermediaries	..	..	..	..	..	..	..	..
Total	..	..	..	..	..	..	..	..

.. Not available

Note: Detailed metadata at: *http://metalinks.oecd.org/ins/20220309/231b*.

Source: *OECD Insurance Statistics (database)*

CANADA

Table 1. Selected aggregates

Million CAD

	2013	2014	2015	2016	2017	2018	2019	2020
1.1 Insurance business written in the reporting country								
1.1.1 Insurance business, by ownership								
Gross premiums								
Domestic undertakings	91 830	81 347	86 082	89 439	93 962	97 815	..	..
Foreign controlled undertakings	11 237	18 957	17 321	18 250	19 658	19 804	..	..
Foreign companies (branches)	9 651	21 604	20 840	19 141	19 488	14 937	..	..
All undertakings	101 481	102 951	106 922	108 580	113 450	112 752	..	..
Premiums ceded								
Domestic undertakings	25 176	22 771	25 855	23 885	26 759	19 135	..	..
Foreign controlled undertakings	2 504	5 070	4 912	5 107	7 154	6 751	..	..
Foreign companies (branches)	2 094	4 469	4 735	4 370	4 568	4 467	..	..
All undertakings	27 270	27 240	30 590	28 255	31 327	23 602	..	..
Net written premiums								
Domestic undertakings	66 655	58 576	60 227	65 554	67 204	78 680	..	..
Foreign controlled undertakings	8 733	13 888	12 410	13 142	12 504	13 053	..	..
Foreign companies (branches)	7 557	17 135	16 104	14 771	14 920	10 470	..	..
All undertakings	74 212	75 710	76 331	80 325	82 123	89 150	..	..
1.1.2 Insurance business on foreign risks, gross premiums								
Life	..	..	..	..	..	..	..	..
Non-life	..	..	..	..	..	..	..	..
Composite	..	..	..	..	..	..	..	..
of which:								
Life	..	..	..	..	..	..	..	..
Non-life	..	..	..	..	..	..	..	..
Total	..	..	..	..	..	..	..	..
1.1.3 Life insurance payments, by class, gross premiums								
Annuities	6 263	5 562	5 539	5 966	6 558	7 390	..	..
Unit linked	..	..	..	..	..	..	..	..
Other life insurance	..	..	..	..	..	..	..	..
Total life insurance	..	..	..	..	..	..	..	..
***of which:** Pension contracts*	..	..	..	..	..	..	..	..
1.1.4 Non-life insurance payments, by class, gross premiums								
Motor vehicle insurance	22 857	21 007	21 426	21 938	23 234	24 519	..	..
Marine, aviation and other transport insurance	630	773	716	769	700	1 143	..	..
Freight insurance	..	..	..	..	..	..	..	..
Fire and other property damage insurance	16 687	18 994	19 992	20 599	21 593	28 429	..	..
Pecuniary loss insurance	1 748	2 271	2 613	2 659	2 708	2 559	..	..
General liability insurance	5 267	5 830	6 289	6 339	6 398	10 463	..	..
Accident and health	20 262	25 708	26 370	25 944	26 471	24 315	..	..
***of which:** Health*	..	..	..	..	..	..	..	..
Other non-life insurance	32	138	275	368	440	170	..	..
Treaty reinsurance	..	..	..	..	..	..	..	..
Total non-life insurance	67 482	74 721	77 682	78 616	81 545	91 598	..	..
1.2 Gross claims payments								
Life								
Domestic undertakings	0	0	0	3	..	3	..	..
Foreign controlled undertakings	0	0	0	0	..	0	..	..
Foreign companies (branches)	36	41	13	3	3	3	..	..
All undertakings	36	41	13	6	3	6	..	..
Non-life								
Domestic undertakings	28 506	25 194	25 500	30 110	29 433	30 596	..	..
Foreign controlled undertakings	5 566	8 332	8 552	11 171	11 043	11 435	..	..
Foreign companies (branches)	5 242	5 901	4 694	6 748	4 566	6 479	..	..
All undertakings	33 748	31 095	30 193	36 858	33 999	37 075	..	..
Composite								
Domestic undertakings	11 227	9 477	10 030	11 984	12 753	18 600	..	..
Foreign controlled undertakings	736	881	303	336	396	435	..	..
Foreign companies (branches)	159	7 182	7 161	5 671	5 797	1 025	..	..
All undertakings	11 386	16 659	17 190	17 654	18 549	19 626	..	..
of which:								
Life	4 969	5 480	5 747	5 919	6 342	6 699	..	..
Domestic undertakings	4 869	3 858	4 186	4 581	4 981	6 073	..	..
Foreign controlled undertakings	190	344	188	210	256	301	..	..
Foreign companies (branches)	99	1 622	1 561	1 339	1 361	626	..	..
All undertakings	4 969	5 480	5 747	5 919	6 342	6 699	..	..
Non-life	6 417	11 179	11 444	11 735	12 207	12 927	..	..
Domestic undertakings	6 357	5 620	5 844	7 403	7 772	12 528	..	..
Foreign controlled undertakings	546	537	115	127	139	134	..	..
Foreign companies (branches)	60	5 560	5 600	4 332	4 435	399	..	..
All undertakings	6 417	11 179	11 444	11 735	12 207	12 927	..	..
Total								
Domestic undertakings	39 733	34 671	35 529	42 097	42 186	49 199	..	..
Foreign controlled undertakings	6 301	9 213	8 854	11 508	11 439	11 870	..	..
Foreign companies (branches)	5 437	13 124	11 867	12 422	10 366	7 507	..	..
All undertakings	45 170	47 795	47 396	54 518	52 552	56 706	..	..

CANADA

Table 1. Selected aggregates *(cont.)*

Million CAD

	2013	2014	2015	2016	2017	2018	2019	2020
1.3 Commissions								
Life								
Domestic undertakings	0	..	0	0	0	..	..	..
Foreign controlled undertakings	0	..	..	..	..	..	..	..
Foreign companies (branches)	10	..	0	0	0	..	..	..
All undertakings	10	..	0	0	0	..	..	..
Non-life								
Domestic undertakings	4 781	..	5 441	5 666	5 434	6 103	..	..
Foreign controlled undertakings	1 092	..	1 882	1 938	2 087	2 182	..	..
Foreign companies (branches)	1 095	..	1 104	1 177	1 299	1 492	..	..
All undertakings	5 876	..	6 545	6 843	6 733	7 595	..	..
Composite								
Domestic undertakings	5 558	..	4 787	5 363	5 218	5 127	..	..
Foreign controlled undertakings	239	..	97	94	97	150	..	..
Foreign companies (branches)	145	..	193	156	197	174	..	..
All undertakings	5 703	..	4 980	5 519	5 416	5 301	..	..
of which:								
Life	4 291	..	3 572	4 059	3 893	3 812	..	..
Domestic undertakings	4 213	..	3 457	3 982	3 801	3 734	..	..
Foreign controlled undertakings	173	..	65	72	75	93	..	..
Foreign companies (branches)	78	..	115	77	93	78	..	..
All undertakings	4 291	..	3 572	4 059	3 893	3 812	..	..
Non-life	1 412	..	1 408	1 460	1 522	1 489	..	..
Domestic undertakings	1 345	..	1 330	1 381	1 418	1 393	..	..
Foreign controlled undertakings	66	..	32	22	22	57	..	..
Foreign companies (branches)	67	..	78	79	105	97	..	..
All undertakings	1 412	..	1 408	1 460	1 522	1 489	..	..
Total								
Domestic undertakings	10 339	..	10 228	11 029	10 653	11 230	..	..
Foreign controlled undertakings	1 331	..	1 979	2 032	2 184	2 332	..	..
Foreign companies (branches)	1 249	..	1 298	1 333	1 496	1 666	..	..
All undertakings	11 588	..	11 526	12 362	12 149	12 896	..	..
1.4 Gross operating expenses								
Life								
Domestic undertakings	23	24	22	30	29	25	..	..
Foreign controlled undertakings	..	0	0	0	0	0	..	..
Foreign companies (branches)	27	28	15	10	9	10	..	..
All undertakings	50	52	37	40	38	36	..	..
Non-life								
Domestic undertakings	6 023	4 032	4 493	4 725	4 694	4 658	..	..
Foreign controlled undertakings	1 409	1 385	1 488	1 756	1 635	1 548	..	..
Foreign companies (branches)	1 017	855	689	673	672	704	..	..
All undertakings	7 040	4 887	5 182	5 398	5 366	5 362	..	..
Composite								
Domestic undertakings	13 728	12 612	14 400	17 159	17 966	19 399	..	..
Foreign controlled undertakings	571	736	187	194	248	251	..	..
Foreign companies (branches)	117	206	272	518	713	259	..	..
All undertakings	13 845	12 818	14 672	17 677	18 679	19 658	..	..
of which:								
Life	..	..	..	..	..	..	..	..
Domestic undertakings	..	..	..	..	..	..	..	..
Foreign controlled undertakings	..	..	..	..	..	..	..	..
Foreign companies (branches)	..	..	..	..	..	..	..	..
All undertakings	..	..	..	..	..	..	..	..
Non-life	..	..	..	..	..	..	..	..
Domestic undertakings	..	..	..	..	..	..	..	..
Foreign controlled undertakings	..	..	..	..	..	..	..	..
Foreign companies (branches)	..	..	..	..	..	..	..	..
All undertakings	..	..	..	..	..	..	..	..
Total								
Domestic undertakings	19 774	16 668	18 915	21 914	22 689	24 082	..	..
Foreign controlled undertakings	1 981	2 121	1 675	1 950	1 883	1 799	..	..
Foreign companies (branches)	1 161	1 089	976	1 201	1 394	973	..	..
All undertakings	20 934	17 757	19 891	23 115	24 083	25 055	..	..

Table 1. Selected aggregates *(cont.)*

Million CAD

	2013	2014	2015	2016	2017	2018	2019	2020
1.5 Insurance business written abroad by branches, gross premiums								
Life								
Branches and agencies	..	..	..	..	..	..	..	..
Subsidaries	..	..	..	..	..	..	..	..
Total	..	0	0	0	0	0	..	..
Non-life								
Branches and agencies	..	..	..	..	..	..	..	..
Subsidaries	..	..	..	..	..	..	..	..
Total	1 018	1 320	1 500	1 502	1 522	2 658	..	..
Composite								
Branches and agencies	..	..	..	..	..	..	..	..
Subsidaries	..	..	..	..	..	..	..	..
Total	7 942	31 162	40 235	50 713	54 040	57 636	..	..
of which:								
Life	..	27 224	..	..	..	..	..	..
Branches and agencies	..	..	..	..	..	..	..	..
Subsidaries	..	..	..	..	..	..	..	..
Total	..	27 224	..	..	..	..	..	..
Non-life	..	3 939	..	..	..	..	..	..
Branches and agencies	..	..	..	..	..	..	..	..
Subsidaries	..	..	..	..	..	..	..	..
Total	..	3 939	..	..	..	..	..	..
Total								
Branches and agencies	..	..	..	..	..	..	..	..
Subsidaries	..	..	..	..	..	..	..	..
Total	8 959	32 482	41 736	52 215	55 562	60 294	..	..

.. Not available

Note: Detailed metadata at: *http://metalinks.oecd.org/ins/20220309/3eda.*

Source: *OECD Insurance Statistics (database)*

Table 2. Number of companies and employees

	2013	2014	2015	2016	2017	2018	2019	2020
2.1 Number of companies								
Life								
Domestic undertakings	1	1	1	3	3	3	..	..
Foreign controlled undertakings	0	0	0	0	0	0	..	..
Foreign companies (branches)	5	5	5	2	2	2	..	..
All undertakings	6	6	6	5	5	5	..	..
Non-life								
Domestic undertakings	60	66	66	63	61	57	..	..
Foreign controlled undertakings	22	28	28	27	27	25	..	..
Foreign companies (branches)	60	60	58	54	54	54	..	..
All undertakings	120	126	124	117	115	111	..	..
Composite								
Domestic undertakings	34	34	33	31	31	29	..	..
Foreign controlled undertakings	10	9	7	7	8	7	..	..
Foreign companies (branches)	26	23	22	20	20	20	..	..
All undertakings	60	57	55	51	51	49	..	..
Reinsurance								
Domestic undertakings	6	5	5	5	5	5	..	..
Foreign controlled undertakings	6	5	5	5	5	5	..	..
Foreign companies (branches)	28	25	26	28	28	28	..	..
All undertakings	34	30	31	33	33	33	..	..
Total								
Domestic undertakings	101	106	105	102	100	94	..	..
Foreign controlled undertakings	38	42	40	39	40	37	..	..
Foreign companies (branches)	119	113	111	104	104	104	..	..
All undertakings	220	219	216	206	204	198	..	..
2.2 Number of employees								
Insurance undertakings	..	..	..	..	..	..	..	..
Intermediaries	..	..	..	..	..	..	..	..
Total	..	..	..	..	..	..	..	..

.. Not available

Note: Detailed metadata at: *http://metalinks.oecd.org/ins/20220309/3eda*.

Source: *OECD Insurance Statistics (database)*

CHILE

Table 1. Selected aggregates

Million CLP

	2013	2014	2015	2016	2017	2018	2019	2020
1.1 Insurance business written in the reporting country								
1.1.1 Insurance business, by ownership								
Gross premiums								
Domestic undertakings	5 832 221	6 260 019	7 465 743	8 394 971	8 344 320	8 981 504	9 062 220	7 918 466
Foreign controlled undertakings	3 056 166	3 211 682	3 614 011	4 422 880	4 504 671	4 722 316	4 929 006	4 303 271
Foreign companies (branches)	..	..	..	..	..	..	..	..
All undertakings	5 832 221	6 260 019	7 465 743	8 394 971	8 344 320	8 981 504	9 062 220	7 918 466
Premiums ceded								
Domestic undertakings	906 942	998 507	1 135 872	1 310 392	1 382 346	1 428 339	1 561 858	1 835 991
Foreign controlled undertakings	647 814	676 439	749 522	953 240	901 373	921 260	1 052 698	1 243 020
Foreign companies (branches)	..	..	..	..	..	..	..	..
All undertakings	906 942	998 507	1 135 872	1 310 392	1 382 346	1 428 339	1 561 858	1 835 991
Net written premiums								
Domestic undertakings	4 925 279	5 261 513	6 329 871	7 084 578	6 961 974	7 553 165	7 500 362	6 082 475
Foreign controlled undertakings	2 408 352	2 535 243	2 864 489	3 469 640	3 603 299	3 801 056	3 876 308	3 060 251
Foreign companies (branches)	..	..	..	..	..	..	..	..
All undertakings	4 925 279	5 261 513	6 329 871	7 084 578	6 961 974	7 553 165	7 500 362	6 082 475
1.1.2 Insurance business on foreign risks, gross premiums								
Life	..	..	..	..	..	..	..	..
Non-life	..	..	..	..	..	..	..	..
Composite total	..	..	..	..	..	..	..	..
Total	..	..	..	..	..	..	..	..
1.1.3 Life insurance payments, by class, gross premiums								
Annuities	1 729 819	1 692 693	2 343 736	2 759 473	2 456 649	2 767 820	2 455 785	1 142 205
Unit linked	318 975	475 508	613 110	712 539	728 441	582 074	547 256	593 921
Other life insurance	1 827 419	1 948 628	2 123 123	2 373 130	2 560 094	2 775 274	3 016 938	2 945 626
Total life insurance	3 876 213	4 116 829	5 079 969	5 845 142	5 745 185	6 125 167	6 019 980	4 681 752
***of which:** Pension contracts*	..	..	..	..	..	..	..	..
1.1.4 Non-life insurance payments, by class, gross premiums								
Motor vehicle insurance	467 370	509 632	554 020	607 928	658 852	741 818	776 970	736 081
Marine, aviation and other transport insurance	117 884	129 698	148 074	132 318	134 870	152 066	172 407	201 879
Freight insurance	0	0	0	0	0	0	0	0
Fire and other property damage insurance	711 066	788 536	901 636	926 988	899 548	999 817	1 123 188	1 409 387
Pecuniary loss insurance	55 877	62 708	73 291	81 763	83 750	89 411	93 093	87 538
General liability insurance	52 154	56 828	41 342	34 468	30 188	41 483	46 072	52 866
Accident and health	25 789	30 296	46 180	53 105	66 796	74 322	78 869	80 419
***of which:** Health*	1 349	6 186	2 268	8 145	7 442	15 661	4 707	5 386
Other non-life insurance	524 059	561 863	602 569	651 596	675 973	705 464	697 812	628 887
Treaty reinsurance	0	0	0	0	0	0	0	0
Total non-life insurance	1 954 198	2 139 562	2 367 113	2 488 165	2 549 976	2 804 382	2 988 410	3 197 056
1.2 Gross claims payments								
Life								
Domestic undertakings	3 714 398	4 027 828	2 853 170	3 342 724	3 838 076	4 106 073	4 387 098	4 479 889
Foreign controlled undertakings	1 551 286	1 580 430	1 020 903	1 219 666	1 524 203	1 999 198	1 833 862	1 756 966
Foreign companies (branches)	..	..	..	..	..	..	..	..
All undertakings	3 714 398	4 027 828	2 853 170	3 342 724	3 838 076	4 106 073	4 387 098	4 479 889
Non-life								
Domestic undertakings	896 672	260 092	1 421 296	1 491 740	1 515 015	1 432 942	1 475 444	1 677 063
Foreign controlled undertakings	541 982	157 970	889 183	1 193 951	1 168 469	1 032 572	1 053 771	1 214 440
Foreign companies (branches)	..	..	..	..	..	..	..	..
All undertakings	896 672	260 092	1 421 296	1 491 740	1 515 015	1 432 942	1 475 444	1 677 063
Composite, all undertakings	..	..	..	..	..	..	..	..
Total								
Domestic undertakings	4 611 070	4 287 920	4 274 466	4 834 464	5 353 090	5 539 015	5 862 542	6 156 953
Foreign controlled undertakings	2 093 268	1 738 400	1 910 087	2 413 617	2 692 672	3 031 770	2 887 633	2 971 406
Foreign companies (branches)	..	..	..	..	..	..	..	..
All undertakings	4 611 070	4 287 920	4 274 466	4 834 464	5 353 090	5 539 015	5 862 542	6 156 953
1.3 Commissions								
Life								
Domestic undertakings	248 645	263 060	301 418	318 445	330 472	360 325	349 461	284 087
Foreign controlled undertakings	131 550	139 650	164 172	159 299	171 055	186 888	181 279	151 525
Foreign companies (branches)	..	..	..	..	..	..	..	..
All undertakings	248 645	263 060	301 418	318 445	330 472	360 325	349 461	284 087
Non-life								
Domestic undertakings	230 945	260 092	287 918	312 001	322 793	360 936	368 082	247 360
Foreign controlled undertakings	140 238	157 970	171 469	242 835	238 778	261 147	261 710	242 482
Foreign companies (branches)	..	..	..	..	..	..	..	..
All undertakings	230 945	260 092	287 918	312 001	322 793	360 936	368 082	247 360
Composite, all undertakings	..	..	..	..	..	..	..	..
Total								
Domestic undertakings	479 590	523 153	589 336	630 445	653 265	721 261	717 542	531 447
Foreign controlled undertakings	271 787	297 621	335 641	402 134	409 832	448 035	442 989	394 006
Foreign companies (branches)	..	..	..	..	..	..	..	..
All undertakings	479 590	523 153	589 336	630 445	653 265	721 261	717 542	531 447

Table 1. Selected aggregates *(cont.)*

Million CLP

	2013	2014	2015	2016	2017	2018	2019	2020
1.4 Gross operating expenses								
Life								
Domestic undertakings	549 344	583 313	612 178	664 997	732 176	776 679	883 091	772 695
Foreign controlled undertakings	268 515	284 692	308 320	316 103	364 993	390 610	413 417	351 006
Foreign companies (branches)	..	..	..	..	..	..	..	..
All undertakings	549 344	583 313	612 178	664 997	732 176	776 679	883 091	772 695
Non-life								
Domestic undertakings	359 066	382 886	412 676	457 861	501 804	533 252	569 035	575 211
Foreign controlled undertakings	251 791	266 721	288 658	367 114	406 682	414 288	431 095	421 765
Foreign companies (branches)	..	..	..	..	..	..	..	..
All undertakings	359 066	382 886	412 676	457 861	501 804	533 252	569 035	575 211
Composite, all undertakings	..	..	..	..	..	..	..	..
Total								
Domestic undertakings	908 410	966 199	1 024 854	1 122 857	1 233 980	1 309 931	1 452 126	1 347 906
Foreign controlled undertakings	520 306	551 413	596 978	683 216	771 674	804 898	844 512	772 772
Foreign companies (branches)	..	..	..	..	..	..	..	..
All undertakings	908 410	966 199	1 024 854	1 122 857	1 233 980	1 309 931	1 452 126	1 347 906
1.5 Insurance business written abroad by branches, gross premiums								
Life								
Branches and agencies	..	..	..	..	..	..	..	..
Subsidaries	..	..	..	..	..	..	..	..
Total	..	..	..	..	..	..	..	..
Non-life								
Branches and agencies	..	..	..	..	..	..	..	..
Subsidaries	..	..	..	..	..	..	..	..
Total	..	..	..	..	..	..	..	..
Composite total	..	..	..	..	..	..	..	..
Total								
Branches and agencies	..	..	..	..	..	..	..	..
Subsidaries	..	..	..	..	..	..	..	..
Total	..	..	..	..	..	..	..	..

.. Not available

Note: Detailed metadata at: *http://metalinks.oecd.org/ins/20220309/056a.*

Source: *OECD Insurance Statistics (database)*

Table 2. Number of companies and employees

	2013	2014	2015	2016	2017	2018	2019	2020
2.1 Number of companies								
Life								
Domestic undertakings	33	34	36	36	36	37	37	35
Foreign controlled undertakings	12	12	13	13	15	16	13	13
Foreign companies (branches)	..	..	..	0	..	..	..	..
All undertakings	33	34	36	36	36	37	37	35
Non-life								
Domestic undertakings	29	29	30	30	32	32	34	34
Foreign controlled undertakings	18	17	18	11	19	17	18	18
Foreign companies (branches)	..	..	..	0	..	..	..	..
All undertakings	29	29	30	30	32	32	34	34
Composite, all undertakings	**0**	**0**	**0**	**0**	..	..	..	..
Reinsurance								
Domestic undertakings	1	1	1	1	1	1	1	1
Foreign controlled undertakings	1	1	..	1	1	1	1	1
Foreign companies (branches)	..	..	..	0	..	..	..	..
All undertakings	1	1	1	1	1	1	1	1
Total								
Domestic undertakings	63	64	67	67	69	70	72	70
Foreign controlled undertakings	31	30	31	25	35	33	32	32
Foreign companies (branches)	..	..	..	0	..	..	..	..
All undertakings	63	64	67	67	69	70	72	70
2.2 Number of employees								
Insurance undertakings	16 686	17 039	15 368	16 414	16 859	16 908	16 891	15 049
Intermediaries	7 046	6 959	7 499	7 599	7 663	7 945	7 997	6 159
Total	23 732	23 998	22 867	24 013	24 522	24 853	24 888	21 208

.. Not available

Note: Detailed metadata at: *http://metalinks.oecd.org/ins/20220309/056a*.

Source: *OECD Insurance Statistics (database)*

COLOMBIA

Table 1. Selected aggregates

Million COP

	2013	2014	2015	2016	2017	2018	2019	2020
1.1 Insurance business written in the reporting country								
1.1.1 Insurance business, by ownership								
Gross premiums								
Domestic undertakings	19 075 213	19 396 882	21 943 459	24 585 330	26 496 734	27 809 761	30 812 229	31 099 908
Foreign controlled undertakings	6 665 400	7 635 672	8 309 246	8 622 786	8 718 250	8 981 678	9 654 677	9 654 677
Foreign companies (branches)	..	0	..	..	..	..	..	..
All undertakings	19 075 213	19 396 882	21 943 459	24 585 330	26 496 734	27 809 761	30 812 229	31 099 908
Premiums ceded								
Domestic undertakings	3 264 752	3 392 593	4 062 439	4 883 531	4 863 385	5 257 745	6 045 450	6 767 555
Foreign controlled undertakings	1 537 641	1 762 391	1 871 332	2 075 143	1 676 354	1 762 454	2 052 794	2 052 794
Foreign companies (branches)	..	0	..	..	..	..	..	..
All undertakings	3 264 752	3 392 593	4 062 439	4 883 531	4 863 385	5 257 745	6 045 450	6 767 555
Net written premiums								
Domestic undertakings	15 810 461	16 004 289	17 881 020	19 701 798	21 633 350	22 552 017	24 766 779	24 332 353
Foreign controlled undertakings	5 127 759	5 873 280	6 437 914	6 547 643	7 041 896	7 219 224	7 601 883	7 601 883
Foreign companies (branches)	..	0	..	..	..	..	..	..
All undertakings	15 810 461	16 004 289	17 881 020	19 701 798	21 633 350	22 552 017	24 766 779	24 332 353
1.1.2 Insurance business on foreign risks, gross premiums								
Life	..	..	..	..	..	..	..	..
Non-life	..	..	..	..	..	..	..	..
Composite	..	..	..	..	..	..	..	..
of which:								
Life	..	..	..	..	..	..	..	..
Non-life	..	..	..	..	..	..	..	..
Total	..	..	..	..	..	..	..	..
1.1.3 Life insurance payments, by class, gross premiums								
Annuities	2 437 934	814 432	1 096 967	1 759 549	2 019 643	2 204 084	2 452 253	2 120 094
Unit linked	..	..	..	..	..	..	..	..
Other life insurance	7 301 890	8 389 995	9 114 695	10 077 271	11 453 593	11 714 575	13 136 500	13 400 560
Total life insurance	9 739 824	9 204 427	10 211 663	11 836 820	13 473 236	13 918 659	15 588 754	15 520 655
***of which:** Pension contracts*	2 278 534	642 645	904 089	1 559 392	1 854 412	2 031 168	2 264 302	1 977 198
1.1.4 Non-life insurance payments, by class, gross premiums								
Motor vehicle insurance	2 198 323	2 389 604	2 628 864	2 982 278	3 365 337	3 491 141	3 668 192	3 441 435
Marine, aviation and other transport insurance	55 827	96 118	134 015	140 118	142 304	135 408	183 512	201 882
Freight insurance	266 931	264 282	285 223	301 591	290 964	293 469	315 021	316 943
Fire and other property damage insurance	1 394 129	1 984 995	2 388 974	2 596 551	2 592 128	2 787 985	2 992 325	3 320 280
Pecuniary loss insurance	1 210 196	1 876 165	2 171 112	2 173 155	2 035 235	2 188 222	2 421 701	2 555 692
General liability insurance	738 250	782 424	834 365	913 075	922 751	1 073 809	1 273 279	1 444 796
Accident and health	343 025	431 508	480 854	588 263	543 225	482 136	610 901	538 817
***of which:** Health*	52 173	55 613	59 071	60 349	60 216	62 250	63 711	64 807
Other non-life insurance	3 124 590	2 359 305	2 800 552	3 044 763	3 126 668	3 436 491	3 758 816	3 759 407
Treaty reinsurance	0	..	..	..	..	..	..	..
Total non-life insurance	9 331 270	10 184 400	11 723 960	12 739 794	13 018 612	13 888 659	15 223 747	15 579 253
1.2 Gross claims payments								
Life								
Domestic undertakings	4 208 328	4 732 708	5 219 437	5 850 532	6 614 108	7 506 898	7 797 284	7 860 957
Foreign controlled undertakings	1 074 648	1 102 287	1 246 232	1 223 887	1 289 528	1 379 180	1 393 943	1 249 680
Foreign companies (branches)	..	..	..	..	..	..	..	..
All undertakings	4 208 328	4 732 708	5 219 437	5 850 532	6 614 108	7 506 898	7 797 284	7 860 957
Non-life								
Domestic undertakings	4 219 440	4 266 391	5 013 568	6 555 550	6 355 609	6 662 371	8 175 580	7 443 559
Foreign controlled undertakings	1 811 255	2 261 082	2 565 529	3 043 646	2 668 837	2 829 971	3 777 045	3 156 618
Foreign companies (branches)	..	..	..	..	..	..	..	..
All undertakings	4 219 441	4 266 391	5 013 568	6 555 550	6 355 609	6 662 371	8 175 580	7 443 559
Composite								
Domestic undertakings	..	..	..	..	..	..	..	..
Foreign controlled undertakings	..	..	..	..	..	..	..	..
Foreign companies (branches)	..	..	..	..	..	..	..	..
All undertakings	..	..	..	..	..	..	..	..
of which:								
Life	..	..	..	..	..	..	..	..
Domestic undertakings	..	..	..	..	..	..	..	..
Foreign controlled undertakings	..	..	..	..	..	..	..	..
Foreign companies (branches)	..	..	..	..	..	..	..	..
All undertakings	..	..	..	..	..	..	..	..
Non-life	..	..	..	..	..	..	..	..
Domestic undertakings	..	..	..	..	..	..	..	..
Foreign controlled undertakings	..	..	..	..	..	..	..	..
Foreign companies (branches)	..	..	..	..	..	..	..	..
All undertakings	..	..	..	..	..	..	..	..
Total								
Domestic undertakings	8 427 768	8 999 099	10 233 005	12 406 082	12 969 717	14 169 269	15 972 864	15 304 517
Foreign controlled undertakings	2 885 903	3 363 369	3 811 761	4 267 533	3 958 365	4 209 152	5 170 989	4 406 298
Foreign companies (branches)	..	..	..	..	..	..	..	..
All undertakings	8 427 768	8 999 099	10 233 005	12 406 082	12 969 717	14 169 269	15 972 864	15 304 517

Table 1. Selected aggregates *(cont.)*

Million COP

	2013	2014	2015	2016	2017	2018	2019	2020
1.3 Commissions								
Life								
Domestic undertakings	..	..	..	..	..	..	..	..
Foreign controlled undertakings	..	..	..	..	..	..	..	..
Foreign companies (branches)	..	..	..	..	..	..	..	..
All undertakings	..	..	..	..	..	..	..	..
Non-life								
Domestic undertakings	..	..	..	..	..	..	..	..
Foreign controlled undertakings	..	..	..	..	..	..	..	..
Foreign companies (branches)	..	..	..	..	..	..	..	..
All undertakings	..	..	..	..	..	..	..	..
Composite								
Domestic undertakings	..	..	..	..	..	..	..	..
Foreign controlled undertakings	..	..	..	..	..	..	..	..
Foreign companies (branches)	..	..	..	..	..	..	..	..
All undertakings	..	..	..	..	..	..	..	..
of which:								
Life	..	..	..	..	..	..	..	..
Domestic undertakings	..	..	..	..	..	..	..	..
Foreign controlled undertakings	..	..	..	..	..	..	..	..
Foreign companies (branches)	..	..	..	..	..	..	..	..
All undertakings	..	..	..	..	..	..	..	..
Non-life	..	..	..	..	..	..	..	..
Domestic undertakings	..	..	..	..	..	..	..	..
Foreign controlled undertakings	..	..	..	..	..	..	..	..
Foreign companies (branches)	..	..	..	..	..	..	..	..
All undertakings	..	..	..	..	..	..	..	..
Total								
Domestic undertakings	..	..	..	..	..	..	..	..
Foreign controlled undertakings	..	..	..	..	..	..	..	..
Foreign companies (branches)	..	..	..	..	..	..	..	..
All undertakings	..	..	..	..	..	..	..	..
1.4 Gross operating expenses								
Life								
Domestic undertakings	1 324 845	3 306 113	3 596 035	3 847 673	4 227 762	4 582 318	5 170 933	5 550 438
Foreign controlled undertakings	384 239	708 464	1 077 766	1 100 785	1 280 372	1 383 239	1 421 144	1 366 545
Foreign companies (branches)	..	..	..	..	..	..	..	..
All undertakings	1 324 845	3 306 113	3 596 035	3 847 673	4 227 762	4 582 318	5 170 933	5 550 438
Non-life								
Domestic undertakings	1 957 574	3 907 054	4 067 473	4 555 295	4 738 383	4 996 774	5 709 898	5 708 230
Foreign controlled undertakings	1 052 070	2 331 832	2 418 659	2 624 752	2 729 921	2 665 162	3 071 224	2 886 040
Foreign companies (branches)	..	..	..	..	..	..	..	..
All undertakings	1 957 574	3 907 054	4 067 473	4 555 295	4 738 383	4 996 774	5 709 898	5 708 230
Composite								
Domestic undertakings	..	..	..	..	..	..	..	..
Foreign controlled undertakings	..	..	..	..	..	..	..	..
Foreign companies (branches)	..	..	..	..	..	..	..	..
All undertakings	..	..	..	..	..	..	..	..
of which:								
Life	..	..	..	..	..	..	..	..
Domestic undertakings	..	..	..	..	..	..	..	..
Foreign controlled undertakings	..	..	..	..	..	..	..	..
Foreign companies (branches)	..	..	..	..	..	..	..	..
All undertakings	..	..	..	..	..	..	..	..
Non-life	..	..	..	..	..	..	..	..
Domestic undertakings	..	..	..	..	..	..	..	..
Foreign controlled undertakings	..	..	..	..	..	..	..	..
Foreign companies (branches)	..	..	..	..	..	..	..	..
All undertakings	..	..	..	..	..	..	..	..
Total								
Domestic undertakings	3 282 419	7 213 167	7 663 508	8 402 968	8 966 145	9 579 092	10 880 831	11 258 668
Foreign controlled undertakings	1 436 309	3 040 295	3 496 425	3 725 536	4 010 293	4 048 401	4 492 368	4 252 585
Foreign companies (branches)	..	..	..	..	..	..	..	..
All undertakings	3 282 419	7 213 167	7 663 508	8 402 968	8 966 145	9 579 092	10 880 831	11 258 668

Table 1. Selected aggregates *(cont.)*

Million COP

	2013	2014	2015	2016	2017	2018	2019	2020
1.5 Insurance business written abroad by branches, gross premiums								
Life								
Branches and agencies	..	..	..	..	..	..	..	..
Subsidaries	..	..	..	..	..	..	..	..
Total	..	..	..	..	..	..	..	..
Non-life								
Branches and agencies	..	..	..	..	..	..	..	..
Subsidaries	..	..	..	..	..	..	..	..
Total	..	..	..	..	..	..	..	..
Composite								
Branches and agencies	..	..	..	..	..	..	..	..
Subsidaries	..	..	..	..	..	..	..	..
Total	..	..	..	..	..	..	..	..
of which:								
Life	..	..	..	..	..	..	..	..
Branches and agencies	..	..	..	..	..	..	..	..
Subsidaries	..	..	..	..	..	..	..	..
Total	..	..	..	..	..	..	..	..
Non-life	..	..	..	..	..	..	..	..
Branches and agencies	..	..	..	..	..	..	..	..
Subsidaries	..	..	..	..	..	..	..	..
Total	..	..	..	..	..	..	..	..
Total								
Branches and agencies	..	..	..	..	..	..	..	..
Subsidaries	..	..	..	..	..	..	..	..
Total	..	..	..	..	..	..	..	..

.. Not available
Note: Detailed metadata at: *http://metalinks.oecd.org/ins/20220309/9db3*.
Source: OECD *Insurance Statistics (database)*

Table 2. Number of companies and employees

	2013	2014	2015	2016	2017	2018	2019	2020
2.1 Number of companies								
Life								
Domestic undertakings	19	19	19	19	20	20	18	18
Foreign controlled undertakings	8	9	9	9	10	10	9	9
Foreign companies (branches)	..	0	0	0	0	0	0	0
All undertakings	19	19	19	19	20	20	18	18
Non-life								
Domestic undertakings	25	26	28	26	26	26	26	25
Foreign controlled undertakings	15	18	19	17	17	17	17	16
Foreign companies (branches)	..	0	0	0	0	0	0	0
All undertakings	25	26	28	26	26	26	26	25
Composite								
Domestic undertakings	..	..	..	..	..	..	..	0
Foreign controlled undertakings	..	..	..	..	..	..	..	0
Foreign companies (branches)	..	..	..	..	..	..	..	0
All undertakings	..	..	..	..	..	..	..	0
Reinsurance								
Domestic undertakings	..	0	0	0	..	..	0	0
Foreign controlled undertakings	..	0	0	0	..	..	0	0
Foreign companies (branches)	..	..	..	0	..	..	..	0
All undertakings	..	0	0	0	..	..	0	0
Total								
Domestic undertakings	44	45	47	45	46	46	44	43
Foreign controlled undertakings	23	27	28	26	27	27	26	25
Foreign companies (branches)	..	0	0	0	0	0	0	0
All undertakings	44	45	47	45	46	46	44	43
2.2 Number of employees								
Insurance undertakings	..	18 913	20 862	22 734	24 073	28 043	27 322	24 697
Intermediaries	..	..	..	..	..	..	..	..
Total	..	18 913	20 862	22 734	..	..	..	..

.. Not available

Note: Detailed metadata at: *http://metalinks.oecd.org/ins/20220309/9db3*.

Source: *OECD Insurance Statistics (database)*

COSTA RICA

Table 1. Selected aggregates

Million CRC

	2013	2014	2015	2016	2017	2018	2019	2020
1.1 Insurance business written in the reporting country								
1.1.1 Insurance business, by ownership								
Gross premiums								
Domestic undertakings	516 179	620 043	556 143	651 302	737 832	756 535	819 389	822 288
Foreign controlled undertakings	51 851	87 914	97 325	131 352	172 203	197 174	214 166	220 614
Foreign companies (branches)	1 553	2 549	4 820	8 124	10 859	12 731	13 588	19 582
All undertakings	517 731	622 592	560 964	659 425	748 691	769 266	832 977	841 870
Premiums ceded								
Domestic undertakings	110 550	123 137	123 797	138 584	153 940	172 213	180 275	181 144
Foreign controlled undertakings	30 133	51 318	51 490	67 548	86 837	102 855	109 389	107 388
Foreign companies (branches)	318	287	378	571	624	606	436	1 559
All undertakings	110 868	123 423	124 175	139 155	154 564	172 819	180 711	182 703
Net written premiums								
Domestic undertakings	405 629	496 907	432 347	512 718	583 892	584 322	639 113	641 143
Foreign controlled undertakings	21 718	36 596	45 835	63 804	85 366	94 320	104 777	113 226
Foreign companies (branches)	1 235	2 262	4 442	7 553	10 235	12 125	13 152	18 023
All undertakings	406 864	499 169	436 789	520 270	594 126	596 447	652 266	659 166
1.1.2 Insurance business on foreign risks, gross premiums								
Life	..	..	..	..	..	..	..	..
Non-life	..	..	..	..	..	..	..	..
Composite	..	..	..	..	..	..	..	..
of which:								
Life	..	..	..	..	..	..	..	..
Non-life	..	..	..	..	..	..	..	..
Total	..	..	..	..	..	..	..	..
1.1.3 Life insurance payments, by class, gross premiums								
Annuities	0	0	0	0	0	0	..	..
Unit linked	0	0	0	0	0	0	..	..
Other life insurance	69 602	76 618	71 125	101 364	110 272	124 136	133 588	125 495
Total life insurance	69 602	76 618	71 125	101 364	110 272	124 136	133 588	125 495
***of which:** Pension contracts*	..	..	0	0	0	0	..	..
1.1.4 Non-life insurance payments, by class, gross premiums								
Motor vehicle insurance	120 201	139 654	146 734	163 204	170 987	169 973	176 027	166 349
Marine, aviation and other transport insurance	1 456	1 723	1 801	1 874	2 111	2 437	3 065	2 307
Freight insurance	6 339	8 495	7 413	7 330	7 999	8 314	8 004	8 155
Fire and other property damage insurance	90 865	97 862	100 909	107 910	121 283	116 697	118 241	128 285
Pecuniary loss insurance	14 040	16 284	15 253	28 143	33 154	26 704	30 597	46 252
General liability insurance	8 532	10 040	10 506	10 270	14 075	15 981	17 967	19 109
Accident and health	206 691	271 915	207 219	239 328	288 806	305 020	345 483	345 917
***of which:** Health*	..	..	55 740	69 536	81 856	91 160	159 361	141 194
Other non-life insurance	0	0	0	0	0	0	0	0
Treaty reinsurance	0	0	0	0	..	..	..	..
Total non-life insurance	448 124	545 972	489 835	558 059	638 416	645 127	699 385	716 375
1.2 Gross claims payments								
Life								
Domestic undertakings	0	0	0	0	..	..	..	..
Foreign controlled undertakings	0	0	0	0	..	..	..	..
Foreign companies (branches)	0	0	0	0	..	..	..	..
All undertakings	0	0	0	0	..	..	..	..
Non-life								
Domestic undertakings	1 389	4 619	6 862	13 836	25 561	17 809	14 783	11 791
Foreign controlled undertakings	1 389	4 619	6 862	13 836	25 561	17 809	14 783	11 791
Foreign companies (branches)	0	0	0	0	0	0	..	..
All undertakings	1 389	4 619	6 862	13 836	25 561	17 809	14 783	11 791
Composite								
Domestic undertakings	254 137	310 662	334 327	342 248	329 870	366 280	381 042	346 144
Foreign controlled undertakings	15 198	21 033	33 023	30 239	39 000	52 410	57 067	57 646
Foreign companies (branches)	395	588	1 521	2 265	4 799	5 787	7 104	8 630
All undertakings	254 532	311 250	335 848	344 513	334 668	372 067	388 145	354 774
of which:								
Life	32 703	34 501	34 008	43 740	50 670	56 210	68 489	67 465
Domestic undertakings	32 703	34 501	34 008	43 740	50 664	56 070	68 315	67 232
Foreign controlled undertakings	1 077	1 651	2 244	4 374	8 530	12 043	15 707	13 375
Foreign companies (branches)	0	0	0	0	6	141	174	233
All undertakings	32 703	34 501	34 008	43 740	50 670	56 210	68 489	67 465
Non-life	221 830	276 749	301 840	300 773	283 999	315 857	319 657	287 309
Domestic undertakings	221 435	276 161	300 318	298 508	279 206	310 211	312 727	278 912
Foreign controlled undertakings	14 121	19 382	30 779	25 866	30 471	40 367	41 360	44 271
Foreign companies (branches)	395	588	1 521	2 265	4 793	5 646	6 930	8 397
All undertakings	221 830	276 749	301 840	300 773	283 999	315 857	319 657	287 309
Total								
Domestic undertakings	255 527	315 281	341 189	356 084	355 430	384 089	395 825	357 935
Foreign controlled undertakings	16 587	25 652	39 885	44 075	64 561	70 219	71 851	69 437
Foreign companies (branches)	395	588	1 521	2 265	4 799	5 787	7 104	8 630
All undertakings	255 922	315 869	342 710	358 349	360 229	389 876	402 928	366 565

Table 1. Selected aggregates *(cont.)*

Million CRC

	2013	2014	2015	2016	2017	2018	2019	2020
1.3 Commissions								
Life								
Domestic undertakings	0	0	..	..	..	..	..	..
Foreign controlled undertakings	0	0	..	..	..	..	..	..
Foreign companies (branches)	0	0	..	..	..	..	..	..
All undertakings	0	0	..	..	..	..	..	..
Non-life								
Domestic undertakings	392	785	..	..	..	..	..	..
Foreign controlled undertakings	392	785	..	..	..	..	..	..
Foreign companies (branches)	0	0	..	..	0	0	..	..
All undertakings	392	785	..	..	..	..	..	..
Composite								
Domestic undertakings	36 881	42 598	..	..	..	..	..	..
Foreign controlled undertakings	3 830	5 657	..	..	..	..	..	..
Foreign companies (branches)	402	437	..	..	..	..	..	..
All undertakings	37 284	43 035	..	..	..	..	..	..
of which:								
Life	..	..	..	..	..	..	..	..
Domestic undertakings	..	..	..	..	..	..	..	..
Foreign controlled undertakings	..	..	..	..	..	..	..	..
Foreign companies (branches)	..	..	..	..	..	..	..	..
All undertakings	..	..	..	..	..	..	..	..
Non-life	..	..	..	..	..	..	..	..
Domestic undertakings	..	..	..	..	..	..	..	..
Foreign controlled undertakings	..	..	..	..	..	..	..	..
Foreign companies (branches)	..	..	..	..	..	..	..	..
All undertakings	..	..	..	..	..	..	..	..
Total								
Domestic undertakings	37 273	43 383	..	..	..	..	..	..
Foreign controlled undertakings	4 222	6 443	..	..	..	..	..	..
Foreign companies (branches)	402	437	..	..	0	0	..	..
All undertakings	37 676	43 820	..	..	..	..	..	..
1.4 Gross operating expenses								
Life								
Domestic undertakings	0	0	0	0	..	..	..	..
Foreign controlled undertakings	0	0	0	0	..	..	..	..
Foreign companies (branches)	0	0	0	0	..	..	..	..
All undertakings	0	0	0	0	..	..	..	..
Non-life								
Domestic undertakings	1 650	3 618	3 133	5 210	6 934	7 901	8 241	9 307
Foreign controlled undertakings	1 650	3 618	3 133	5 210	6 934	7 901	8 241	9 307
Foreign companies (branches)	0	0	0	0	0	0	0	..
All undertakings	1 650	3 618	3 133	5 210	6 934	7 901	8 241	9 307
Composite								
Domestic undertakings	241 306	209 755	122 357	117 143	136 707	151 705	173 182	168 577
Foreign controlled undertakings	13 585	18 563	17 025	23 243	26 834	29 811	35 093	38 454
Foreign companies (branches)	1 181	1 566	2 196	3 395	3 987	4 818	5 298	6 565
All undertakings	242 487	211 320	124 553	120 538	140 694	156 522	178 480	175 142
of which:								
Life	..	..	19 351	23 644	28 303	31 698	36 077	36 125
Domestic undertakings	..	..	18 985	23 091	27 759	30 943	35 083	34 350
Foreign controlled undertakings	..	..	4 411	5 270	8 141	9 285	10 528	10 638
Foreign companies (branches)	..	..	367	553	544	755	993	1 775
All undertakings	..	..	19 351	23 644	28 303	31 698	36 077	36 125
Non-life	..	..	105 202	96 894	112 391	124 824	142 403	139 017
Domestic undertakings	..	..	103 372	94 052	108 948	120 762	138 099	134 227
Foreign controlled undertakings	..	..	12 614	17 973	18 693	20 526	24 565	27 816
Foreign companies (branches)	..	..	1 830	2 842	3 443	4 062	4 304	4 790
All undertakings	..	..	105 202	96 894	112 391	124 824	142 403	139 017
Total								
Domestic undertakings	242 956	213 373	125 490	122 353	143 640	159 606	181 423	177 885
Foreign controlled undertakings	15 235	22 180	20 158	28 453	33 768	37 712	43 334	47 761
Foreign companies (branches)	1 181	1 566	2 196	3 395	3 987	4 818	5 298	6 565
All undertakings	244 137	214 938	127 686	125 748	147 628	164 423	186 721	184 450

Table 1. Selected aggregates *(cont.)*

Million CRC

	2013	2014	2015	2016	2017	2018	2019	2020
1.5 Insurance business written abroad by branches, gross premiums								
Life								
Branches and agencies	..	..	..	..	..	..	..	..
Subsidaries	..	..	..	..	..	..	..	..
Total	..	..	..	..	..	..	..	..
Non-life								
Branches and agencies	..	..	..	..	..	..	..	..
Subsidaries	..	..	..	..	..	..	..	..
Total	..	..	..	..	..	..	..	..
Composite								
Branches and agencies	..	..	..	..	..	..	..	..
Subsidaries	..	..	..	..	..	..	..	..
Total	..	..	..	..	..	..	..	..
of which:								
Life	..	..	..	..	..	..	..	..
Branches and agencies	..	..	..	..	..	..	..	..
Subsidaries	..	..	..	..	..	..	..	..
Total	..	..	..	..	..	..	..	..
Non-life	..	..	..	..	..	..	..	..
Branches and agencies	..	..	..	..	..	..	..	..
Subsidaries	..	..	..	..	..	..	..	..
Total	..	..	..	..	..	..	..	..
Total								
Branches and agencies	..	..	..	..	..	..	..	..
Subsidaries	..	..	..	..	..	..	..	..
Total	..	..	..	..	..	..	..	..

.. Not available

Note: Detailed metadata at: *http://metalinks.oecd.org/ins/20220309/96dc.*

Source: *OECD Insurance Statistics (database)*

Table 2. Number of companies and employees

	2013	2014	2015	2016	2017	2018	2019	2020
2.1 Number of companies								
Life								
Domestic undertakings	0	0	0	0	..	..	..	..
Foreign controlled undertakings	0	0	0	0	..	..	..	..
Foreign companies (branches)	0	0	0	0	..	..	..	..
All undertakings	0	0	0	0	..	..	..	..
Non-life								
Domestic undertakings	2	3	3	3	3	3	3	3
Foreign controlled undertakings	2	3	3	3	3	3	3	3
Foreign companies (branches)	0	0	0	0	0	0	0	0
All undertakings	2	3	3	3	3	3	3	3
Composite								
Domestic undertakings	8	8	8	8	8	8	8	8
Foreign controlled undertakings	6	6	6	6	6	6	6	6
Foreign companies (branches)	2	2	2	2	2	2	2	2
All undertakings	10	10	10	10	10	10	10	10
Reinsurance								
Domestic undertakings	0	0	0	0	0	0	0	0
Foreign controlled undertakings	0	0	0	0	0	0	0	0
Foreign companies (branches)	0	0	0	0	0	0	0	0
All undertakings	0	0	0	0	0	0	0	0
Total								
Domestic undertakings	10	11	11	11	11	11	11	11
Foreign controlled undertakings	8	9	9	9	9	9	9	9
Foreign companies (branches)	2	2	2	2	2	2	2	2
All undertakings	12	13	13	13	13	13	13	13
2.2 Number of employees								
Insurance undertakings	..	..	..	..	..	2	1 965	3 330
Intermediaries	..	..	..	..	..	..	..	..
Total	..	..	..	..	..	..	..	..

.. Not available

Note: Detailed metadata at: *http://metalinks.oecd.org/ins/20220309/96dc.*

Source: *OECD Insurance Statistics (database)*

CZECH REPUBLIC

Table 1. Selected aggregates

Million CZK

	2013	2014	2015	2016	2017	2018	2019	2020
1.1 Insurance business written in the reporting country								
1.1.1 Insurance business, by ownership								
Gross premiums								
Domestic undertakings	147 955	148 755	140 688	135 581	138 186	142 473	152 231	154 641
Foreign controlled undertakings	135 671	137 200	129 432	124 165	125 585	128 377	136 031	137 284
Foreign companies (branches)	8 567	9 164	11 159	11 102	11 459	10 768	13 208	12 830
All undertakings	156 522	157 919	151 846	146 683	149 645	153 241	165 439	167 470
Premiums ceded								
Domestic undertakings	29 333	29 915	29 857	28 913	30 449	31 057	32 569	33 265
Foreign controlled undertakings	26 054	26 601	26 578	25 450	26 230	26 704	27 639	27 948
Foreign companies (branches)	1 016	1 250	1 561	1 993	1 484	1 048	1 450	1 562
All undertakings	30 349	31 165	31 418	30 905	31 933	32 105	34 018	34 827
Net written premiums								
Domestic undertakings	118 623	118 839	110 831	106 669	107 737	111 416	119 662	121 376
Foreign controlled undertakings	109 617	110 598	102 854	98 714	99 356	101 673	108 393	109 336
Foreign companies (branches)	7 550	7 914	9 598	9 109	9 976	9 720	11 758	11 268
All undertakings	126 173	126 754	120 429	115 778	117 713	121 136	131 421	132 644
1.1.2 Insurance business on foreign risks, gross premiums								
Life	0	0	0	0	0	0	0	0
Non-life	741	993	524	274	738	874	1 906	1 329
Composite	1 780	2 121	1 867	1 843	2 777	3 561	3 503	3 708
of which:								
Life	37	360	4	0	1 805	1 897	2 099	2 216
Non-life	1 742	1 761	1 863	1 843	972	1 664	1 404	1 492
Total	2 521	3 113	2 390	2 117	3 515	4 435	5 408	5 037
1.1.3 Life insurance payments, by class, gross premiums								
Annuities	1 775	1 505	1 413	..	..	..	..	..
Unit linked	34 764	37 632	35 125	26 131	25 608	25 199	19 296	17 682
Other life insurance	35 030	32 042	25 876	33 110	31 425	30 653	33 652	33 535
Total life insurance	71 569	71 179	62 414	59 240	57 033	55 852	52 948	51 217
***of which:** Pension contracts*	..	..	..	..	0	0	0	.. c
1.1.4 Non-life insurance payments, by class, gross premiums								
Motor vehicle insurance	35 804	37 855	39 633	38 212	40 533	44 078	48 204	51 677
Marine, aviation and other transport insurance	214	294	331	912	1 073	1 072	1 056	933
Freight insurance	393	461	466	0	..	..	..	..
Fire and other property damage insurance	21 442	21 687	22 655	23 042	24 244	24 997	26 621	27 852
Pecuniary loss insurance	5 920	4 933	3 770	3 959	4 030	3 309	3 805	3 166
General liability insurance	12 869	13 164	13 810	13 609	14 559	15 207	16 661	17 283
Accident and health	5 482	5 342	5 393	5 136	5 460	5 802	13 242	12 739
***of which:** Health*	0	0	0	0	2 474	2 575	3 260	2 460
Other non-life insurance	2 825	3 002	3 374	2 223	2 364	2 489	2 432	2 088
Treaty reinsurance	0	0	0	0	..	..	..	..
Total non-life insurance	84 950	86 738	89 431	87 092	92 263	96 954	112 021	115 738
1.2 Gross claims payments								
Life								
Domestic undertakings	765	1 307	702	.. c	.. c	.. c	.. c	.. c
Foreign controlled undertakings	765	1 307	702	.. c	.. c	.. c	.. c	0
Foreign companies (branches)	7 219	6 044	6 376	6 094	6 249	5 572	6 169	5 967
All undertakings	7 984	7 352	7 077	6 456	6 567	5 875	6 176	6 004
Non-life								
Domestic undertakings	5 208	6 045	2 285	2 103	2 172	2 681	3 159	3 595
Foreign controlled undertakings	2 171	1 734	1 288	1 072	1 070	1 349	1 507	1 577
Foreign companies (branches)	1 184	1 353	1 216	1 674	1 764	1 344	1 778	1 837
All undertakings	6 392	7 398	3 501	3 777	3 936	4 025	4 937	5 432
Composite								
Domestic undertakings	86 244	90 284	84 909	81 024	80 221	80 773	87 779	80 849
Foreign controlled undertakings	81 355	84 712	79 681	75 835	75 301	75 653	82 528	74 838
Foreign companies (branches)	0	0	0	0	0	0	..	0
All undertakings	86 244	90 284	84 909	81 024	80 221	80 773	87 779	80 849
of which:								
Life	43 395	50 972	44 105	37 676	36 087	37 421	37 517	31 915
Domestic undertakings	43 395	50 972	44 105	37 676	36 087	37 421	37 517	31 915
Foreign controlled undertakings	42 174	49 092	42 631	36 570	35 018	36 422	37 483	31 018
Foreign companies (branches)	0	0	0	0	0	0	..	0
All undertakings	43 395	50 972	44 105	37 676	36 087	37 421	37 517	31 915
Non-life	42 849	39 312	40 805	43 348	44 134	43 352	50 263	48 934
Domestic undertakings	42 849	39 312	40 805	43 348	44 134	43 352	50 263	48 934
Foreign controlled undertakings	39 180	35 620	37 050	39 265	40 283	39 231	45 044	43 820
Foreign companies (branches)	0	0	0	0	0	0	..	0
All undertakings	42 849	39 312	40 805	43 348	44 134	43 352	50 263	48 934
Total								
Domestic undertakings	92 217	97 636	87 896	83 490	82 712	83 757	90 945	84 480
Foreign controlled undertakings	84 291	87 754	81 671	77 269	76 690	77 305	84 035	76 415
Foreign companies (branches)	8 403	7 397	7 592	7 767	8 012	6 916	7 947	7 804
All undertakings	100 620	105 033	95 488	91 257	90 724	90 673	98 892	92 285

Table 1. Selected aggregates *(cont.)*

Million CZK

	2013	2014	2015	2016	2017	2018	2019	2020
1.3 Commissions								
Life								
Domestic undertakings	..	..	..	..	..	..	..	..
Foreign controlled undertakings	..	..	..	..	..	..	..	..
Foreign companies (branches)	..	..	..	..	..	..	..	..
All undertakings	..	..	..	..	..	..	..	..
Non-life								
Domestic undertakings	..	..	..	..	..	..	..	..
Foreign controlled undertakings	..	..	..	..	..	..	..	..
Foreign companies (branches)	..	..	..	..	..	..	..	..
All undertakings	..	..	..	..	..	..	..	..
Composite								
Domestic undertakings	..	..	..	..	..	..	..	..
Foreign controlled undertakings	..	..	..	..	..	..	..	..
Foreign companies (branches)	..	..	..	..	..	..	..	..
All undertakings	..	..	..	..	..	..	..	..
of which:								
Life	..	..	..	..	..	..	..	..
Domestic undertakings	..	..	..	..	..	..	..	..
Foreign controlled undertakings	..	..	..	..	..	..	..	..
Foreign companies (branches)	..	..	..	..	..	..	..	..
All undertakings	..	..	..	..	..	..	..	..
Non-life	..	..	..	..	..	..	..	..
Domestic undertakings	..	..	..	..	..	..	..	..
Foreign controlled undertakings	..	..	..	..	..	..	..	..
Foreign companies (branches)	..	..	..	..	..	..	..	..
All undertakings	..	..	..	..	..	..	..	..
Total								
Domestic undertakings	..	..	..	..	..	..	..	..
Foreign controlled undertakings	..	..	..	..	..	..	..	..
Foreign companies (branches)	..	..	..	..	..	..	..	..
All undertakings	..	..	..	..	..	..	..	..
1.4 Gross operating expenses								
Life								
Domestic undertakings	748	759	739	.. c	.. c	.. c	.. c	.. c
Foreign controlled undertakings	748	759	739	.. c	.. c	.. c	.. c	0
Foreign companies (branches)	1 587	1 459	2 036	2 015	1 894	1 905	2 451	2 581
All undertakings	2 335	2 219	2 775	2 520	2 251	2 232	2 485	2 694
Non-life								
Domestic undertakings	1 795	1 805	1 571	1 203	2 170	2 988	2 902	3 313
Foreign controlled undertakings	987	937	883	622	979	1 044	1 424	1 509
Foreign companies (branches)	715	841	1 203	1 224	1 412	1 401	1 767	370
All undertakings	2 510	2 646	2 773	2 427	3 582	4 389	4 669	3 683
Composite								
Domestic undertakings	21 863	22 207	20 341	21 319	36 095	41 260	40 228	42 178
Foreign controlled undertakings	20 499	21 233	19 120	19 893	32 685	36 930	36 082	37 560
Foreign companies (branches)	0	0	0	0	0	0	..	0
All undertakings	21 863	22 207	20 341	21 319	36 095	41 260	40 228	42 178
of which:								
Life	11 670	11 475	9 613	9 217	11 707	12 405	10 887	11 607
Domestic undertakings	11 670	11 475	9 613	9 217	11 707	12 405	10 887	11 607
Foreign controlled undertakings	11 231	11 050	9 059	8 637	10 795	11 445	10 249	10 933
Foreign companies (branches)	0	0	0	0	0	0	..	0
All undertakings	11 670	11 475	9 613	9 217	11 707	12 405	10 887	11 607
Non-life	10 193	10 733	10 728	12 102	24 388	28 855	29 341	30 571
Domestic undertakings	10 193	10 733	10 728	12 102	24 388	28 855	29 341	30 571
Foreign controlled undertakings	9 268	10 184	10 061	11 256	21 890	25 485	25 833	26 627
Foreign companies (branches)	0	0	0	0	0	0	..	0
All undertakings	10 193	10 733	10 728	12 102	24 388	28 855	29 341	30 571
Total								
Domestic undertakings	24 407	24 772	22 650	23 027	38 621	44 574	43 164	45 605
Foreign controlled undertakings	22 234	22 929	20 742	21 020	34 020	38 301	37 505	39 069
Foreign companies (branches)	2 302	2 301	3 239	3 239	3 307	3 307	4 218	2 950
All undertakings	26 708	27 072	25 889	26 266	41 928	47 881	47 382	48 555

Table 1. Selected aggregates *(cont.)*

Million CZK

	2013	2014	2015	2016	2017	2018	2019	2020
1.5 Insurance business written abroad by branches, gross premiums								
Life								
Branches and agencies	0	0	0	0	0	0	0	0
Subsidaries	..	..	..	..	..	..	..	..
Total	0	0	0	..	0	0	0	0
Non-life								
Branches and agencies	323	313	351	377	596	804	1 076	1 290
Subsidaries	..	..	..	..	..	..	..	..
Total	323	313	351	377	596	804	1 076	1 290
Composite								
Branches and agencies	3 714	4 528	5 164	1 697	1 805	1 897	2 099	2 216
Subsidaries	..	..	..	..	..	..	..	..
Total	3 714	4 528	5 164	1 697	1 805	1 897	2 099	2 216
of which:								
Life	1 737	1 434	1 460	1 697	1 805	1 897	2 099	2 216
Branches and agencies	1 737	1 434	1 460	1 697	1 805	1 897	2 099	2 216
Subsidaries	..	..	..	..	..	..	..	..
Total	1 737	1 434	1 460	1 697	1 805	1 897	2 099	2 216
Non-life	1 977	3 095	3 704	..	0	0	0	0
Branches and agencies	1 977	3 095	3 704	0	0	0	0	0
Subsidaries	..	..	..	..	..	..	..	..
Total	1 977	3 095	3 704	..	0	0	0	0
Total								
Branches and agencies	4 037	4 841	5 516	2 074	2 401	2 700	3 175	3 507
Subsidaries	..	..	..	..	..	..	..	..
Total	4 037	4 841	5 516	2 074	2 401	2 700	3 175	3 507

.. Not available; c Confidential data
Note: Detailed metadata at: *http://metalinks.oecd.org/ins/20220309/5614.*
Source: *OECD Insurance Statistics (database)*

Table 2. Number of companies and employees

	2013	2014	2015	2016	2017	2018	2019	2020
2.1 Number of companies								
Life								
Domestic undertakings	2	2	2	1	1	1	1	1
Foreign controlled undertakings	2	2	2	1	1	1	0	0
Foreign companies (branches)	3	4	5	5	5	6	6	4
All undertakings	5	6	7	6	6	7	7	5
Non-life								
Domestic undertakings	16	15	15	13	11	11	11	11
Foreign controlled undertakings	8	7	5	4	3	3	3	3
Foreign companies (branches)	15	16	18	19	17	14	13	13
All undertakings	31	31	33	32	28	25	24	24
Composite								
Domestic undertakings	15	15	14	14	14	14	13	13
Foreign controlled undertakings	12	12	11	11	11	11	10	10
Foreign companies (branches)	0	0	0	0	0	0	1	0
All undertakings	15	15	14	14	14	14	14	13
Reinsurance								
Domestic undertakings	1	1	1	1	1	1	1	1
Foreign controlled undertakings	1	1	1	1	1	1	1	1
Foreign companies (branches)	..	..	..	..	0	0	0	0
All undertakings	1	1	1	1	1	1	1	1
Total								
Domestic undertakings	34	33	32	29	27	27	26	26
Foreign controlled undertakings	23	22	19	17	16	16	14	14
Foreign companies (branches)	18	20	23	24	22	20	20	17
All undertakings	52	53	55	53	49	47	46	43
2.2 Number of employees								
Insurance undertakings	..	..	..	..	..	..	11 545	11 403
Intermediaries	..	..	..	..	..	..	..	..
Total	..	..	..	..	..	..	..	..

.. Not available

Note: Detailed metadata at: *http://metalinks.oecd.org/ins/20220309/5614.*

Source: *OECD Insurance Statistics (database)*

DENMARK

Table 1. Selected aggregates

Million DKK

	2013	2014	2015	2016	2017	2018	2019	2020
1.1 Insurance business written in the reporting country								
1.1.1 Insurance business, by ownership								
Gross premiums								
Domestic undertakings	1 268 025	208 213	215 276	225 500	247 934	258 749	257 368	268 220
Foreign controlled undertakings	39 736	46 022	46 192	49 042	53 373	53 706	41 503	222 991
Foreign companies (branches)	..	..	..	..	..	..	..	..
All undertakings	1 268 025	208 213	215 276	225 500	247 934	258 749	257 368	268 220
Premiums ceded								
Domestic undertakings	7 417	5 875	6 309	6 943	8 079	7 160	5 780	4 388
Foreign controlled undertakings	3 199	2 080	2 462	2 355	2 024	1 666	794	3 568
Foreign companies (branches)	..	..	..	..	..	..	..	..
All undertakings	7 417	5 875	6 309	6 943	8 079	7 160	5 780	4 388
Net written premiums								
Domestic undertakings	1 260 608	202 338	208 966	218 557	239 855	251 589	251 588	263 831
Foreign controlled undertakings	36 537	43 942	43 730	46 687	51 349	52 040	40 709	219 423
Foreign companies (branches)	..	..	..	..	..	..	..	..
All undertakings	1 260 608	202 338	208 966	218 557	239 855	251 589	251 588	263 831
1.1.2 Insurance business on foreign risks, gross premiums								
Life	1 125	631	631	..	..	..	..	..
Non-life	14 611	23 099	22 611	..	..	..	..	..
Composite total	..	..	..	..	..	..	..	..
Total	15 737	23 730	23 242	..	..	..	..	..
1.1.3 Life insurance payments, by class, gross premiums								
Annuities	..	..	..	..	..	..	..	..
Unit linked	..	..	..	..	..	..	..	..
Other life insurance	..	..	..	..	..	..	..	..
Total life insurance	133 294	140 314	147 662	153 907	170 623	180 289	182 733	194 220
***of which:** Pension contracts*	..	..	..	..	..	..	..	..
1.1.4 Non-life insurance payments, by class, gross premiums								
Motor vehicle insurance	16 304	19 310	19 146	21 247	23 487	25 929	21 607	19 813
Marine, aviation and other transport insurance	1 263	1 174	1 105	1 857	1 844	1 769	1 763	1 575
Freight insurance	..	..	0	..	..	..	..	0
Fire and other property damage insurance	20 737	22 855	22 642	25 107	26 732	26 184	26 145	26 724
Pecuniary loss insurance	372	402	417	1 113	2 045	1 921	2 086	2 334
General liability insurance	2 061	2 377	2 314	3 203	3 411	3 494	3 659	3 845
Accident and health	12 611	15 063	15 282	15 965	16 727	16 051	16 759	17 015
***of which:** Health*	1 051	1 265	1 337	4 498	4 657	4 129	4 641	4 703
Other non-life insurance	4 659	5 156	5 052	1 635	1 759	1 710	1 808	1 790
Treaty reinsurance	653	867	937	538	616	687	11	11
Total non-life insurance	58 661	67 204	66 895	70 665	76 621	77 745	73 838	73 052
1.2 Gross claims payments								
Life								
Domestic undertakings	111 119	124 323	98 376	115 270	112 996	128 844	128 044	140 781
Foreign controlled undertakings	24 154	24 385	20 765	23 573	22 740	25 299	19 923	23 259
Foreign companies (branches)	..	..	..	..	..	..	..	..
All undertakings	111 119	124 323	98 376	115 270	112 996	128 844	128 044	140 781
Non-life								
Domestic undertakings	43 547	46 601	47 833	44 773	45 620	46 939	47 270	47 399
Foreign controlled undertakings	6 731	13 007	13 316	11 816	11 605	11 136	10 436	10 585
Foreign companies (branches)	..	..	..	..	..	..	..	..
All undertakings	43 547	46 601	47 833	44 773	45 620	46 939	47 270	47 399
Composite, all undertakings	..	..	..	..	..	..	..	..
Total								
Domestic undertakings	154 666	170 924	146 209	160 043	158 616	175 783	175 314	188 180
Foreign controlled undertakings	30 885	37 392	34 081	35 389	34 345	36 435	30 359	33 844
Foreign companies (branches)	..	..	..	..	..	..	..	..
All undertakings	154 666	170 924	146 209	160 043	158 616	175 783	175 314	188 180
1.3 Commissions								
Life								
Domestic undertakings	182	195	199	175	207	246	209	269
Foreign controlled undertakings	43	60	36	34	26	30	0	..
Foreign companies (branches)	..	..	..	..	..	..	..	..
All undertakings	182	195	199	175	207	246	209	269
Non-life								
Domestic undertakings	1 380	1 613	1 879	1 361	1 320	1 262	1 350	1 329
Foreign controlled undertakings	361	579	891	494	463	446	465	417
Foreign companies (branches)	..	..	..	..	..	..	..	..
All undertakings	1 380	1 613	1 879	1 361	1 320	1 262	1 350	1 329
Composite, all undertakings	..	..	..	..	..	..	..	..
Total								
Domestic undertakings	1 562	1 808	2 079	1 536	1 527	1 508	1 559	1 598
Foreign controlled undertakings	405	639	927	528	489	476	465	417
Foreign companies (branches)	..	..	..	..	..	..	..	..
All undertakings	1 562	1 808	2 079	1 536	1 527	1 508	1 559	1 598

Table 1. Selected aggregates *(cont.)*

Million DKK

	2013	2014	2015	2016	2017	2018	2019	2020
1.4 Gross operating expenses								
Life								
Domestic undertakings	4 954	4 887	4 570	4 788	4 971	5 138	5 428	5 278
Foreign controlled undertakings	1 326	1 377	1 284	1 268	1 386	1 349	1 133	923
Foreign companies (branches)	..	..	..	..	..	..	..	..
All undertakings	4 954	4 887	4 570	4 788	4 971	5 138	5 428	6 201
Non-life								
Domestic undertakings	10 391	11 564	11 856	12 050	12 003	11 298	11 258	11 154
Foreign controlled undertakings	2 200	3 867	4 065	3 780	3 542	2 778	2 666	2 597
Foreign companies (branches)	..	..	..	..	..	..	..	..
All undertakings	10 391	11 564	11 856	12 050	12 003	11 322	11 258	13 751
Composite, all undertakings	..	..	..	..	..	..	..	..
Total								
Domestic undertakings	15 345	16 451	16 426	16 838	16 974	16 436	16 686	16 432
Foreign controlled undertakings	3 526	5 244	5 349	5 048	4 928	4 127	3 799	3 520
Foreign companies (branches)	..	..	..	..	..	..	..	..
All undertakings	15 345	16 451	16 426	16 838	16 974	16 460	16 686	19 952
1.5 Insurance business written abroad by branches, gross premiums								
Life								
Branches and agencies	..	..	..	..	..	..	..	..
Subsidaries	..	..	..	..	..	..	..	..
Total	..	..	..	..	..	..	..	..
Non-life								
Branches and agencies	10 031	9 286	8 607	19 043	19 072	18 499	18 804	18 699
Subsidaries	..	..	..	..	..	..	..	..
Total	10 031	9 286	8 607	19 043	19 072	18 499	18 804	18 699
Composite total	..	..	..	..	..	..	..	..
Total								
Branches and agencies	10 031	9 286	8 607	19 043	19 072	18 499	18 804	18 699
Subsidaries	..	..	..	..	..	..	..	..
Total	10 031	9 286	8 607	19 043	19 072	18 499	18 804	18 699

.. Not available

Note: Detailed metadata at: *http://metalinks.oecd.org/ins/20220309/88a4.*

Source: *OECD Insurance Statistics (database)*

Table 2. Number of companies and employees

	2013	2014	2015	2016	2017	2018	2019	2020
2.1 Number of companies								
Life								
Domestic undertakings	39	37	33	33	33	31	29	28
Foreign controlled undertakings	5	4	4	4	4	4	3	3
Foreign companies (branches)	1	1	1	1	2	2	3	6
All undertakings	40	38	34	34	35	33	32	34
Non-life								
Domestic undertakings	77	63	63	63	59	55	52	53
Foreign controlled undertakings	6	6	6	6	6	5	4	4
Foreign companies (branches)	48	49	49	53	56	67	58	35
All undertakings	125	112	112	116	115	122	110	88
Composite, all undertakings	**0**	**0**	**0**	**0**	..	..	..	..
Reinsurance								
Domestic undertakings	7	7	7	5	6	5	5	3
Foreign controlled undertakings	..	..	..	0	..	..	..	..
Foreign companies (branches)	..	..	..	..	..	..	..	3
All undertakings	7	7	7	5	6	5	5	6
Total								
Domestic undertakings	123	107	103	101	98	91	86	84
Foreign controlled undertakings	11	10	10	10	10	9	7	7
Foreign companies (branches)	49	50	50	54	58	69	61	44
All undertakings	172	157	153	155	156	160	147	128
2.2 Number of employees								
Insurance undertakings	15 377	17 057	16 472	16 112	13 640	11 568	14 391	16 950
Intermediaries	..	..	..	..	..	..	..	..
Total	15 377	17 057	16 472	16 112	13 640	11 568	14 391	16 950

.. Not available

Note: Detailed metadata at: *http://metalinks.oecd.org/ins/20220309/88a4*.

Source: *OECD Insurance Statistics (database)*

ESTONIA

Table 1. Selected aggregates

Million EUR

	2013	2014	2015	2016	2017	2018	2019	2020
1.1 Insurance business written in the reporting country								
1.1.1 Insurance business, by ownership								
Gross premiums								
Domestic undertakings	523	561	619	654	721	807	847	762
Foreign controlled undertakings	499	539	596	627	721	775	815	734
Foreign companies (branches)	60	70	70	82	97	118	137	175
All undertakings	583	631	689	736	818	925	984	937
Premiums ceded								
Domestic undertakings	27	28	29	31	31	45	48	44
Foreign controlled undertakings	18	2	20	22	22	34	38	35
Foreign companies (branches)	..	..	..	..	..	..	..	..
All undertakings	..	..	..	..	..	..	..	..
Net written premiums								
Domestic undertakings	496	534	590	624	690	762	799	718
Foreign controlled undertakings	481	217	576	605	670	741	777	699
Foreign companies (branches)	..	..	..	..	..	..	..	..
All undertakings	..	..	..	..	..	..	..	..
1.1.2 Insurance business on foreign risks, gross premiums								
Life	..	..	..	..	..	..	..	..
Non-life	..	..	..	..	..	..	..	..
Composite	..	..	..	..	..	..	..	..
of which:								
Life	..	..	..	..	..	..	..	..
Non-life	..	..	..	..	..	..	..	..
Total	..	..	..	..	..	..	..	..
1.1.3 Life insurance payments, by class, gross premiums								
Annuities	17	19	24	27	27	..	..	..
Unit linked	87	109	118	116	116	120	137	141
Other life insurance	66	63	72	80	80	113	116	125
Total life insurance	171	191	215	221	223	233	253	266
***of which:** Pension contracts*	33	37	36	40	39	39	..	..
1.1.4 Non-life insurance payments, by class, gross premiums								
Motor vehicle insurance	229	244	259	292	345	404	409	362
Marine, aviation and other transport insurance	2	2	2	6	6	6	8	13
Freight insurance	3	4	4	..	..	..	..	..
Fire and other property damage insurance	99	107	115	127	140	159	174	172
Pecuniary loss insurance	8	9	9	12	17	21	27	26
General liability insurance	15	16	19	21	22	26	27	27
Accident and health	40	42	42	54	43	70	81	67
***of which:** Health*	9	..	..	..	..	20	25	25
Other non-life insurance	9	16	23	4	7	6	5	4
Treaty reinsurance	8	..	..	..	..	..	0	0
Total non-life insurance	412	440	474	515	580	692	731	671
1.2 Gross claims payments								
Life								
Domestic undertakings	101	..	97	87	.. c	.. c	.. c	.. c
Foreign controlled undertakings	101	..	97	87	.. c	.. c	.. c	77
Foreign companies (branches)	..	..	..	0	2	12	6	5
All undertakings	101	..	97	87	93	80	78	..
Non-life								
Domestic undertakings	197	..	230	243	270	315	343	289
Foreign controlled undertakings	184	..	217	228	253	297	323	274
Foreign companies (branches)	33	..	40	43	49	55	67	80
All undertakings	230	246	271	287	319	370	410	369
Composite								
Domestic undertakings	..	..	..	38	36	48	53	46
Foreign controlled undertakings	..	..	..	38	36	48	53	46
Foreign companies (branches)	..	..	..	3	4	4	8	18
All undertakings	..	..	..	42	40	52	61	..
of which:								
Life	..	..	..	34	40	39	46	..
Domestic undertakings	..	..	..	31	36	35	38	31
Foreign controlled undertakings	..	..	..	31	36	35	38	31
Foreign companies (branches)	..	..	..	3	4	4	8	17
All undertakings	..	..	..	34	40	39	46	..
Non-life	..	..	..	8	0	13	15	..
Domestic undertakings	..	..	..	8	0	13	15	15
Foreign controlled undertakings	..	..	..	8	0	13	15	15
Foreign companies (branches)	..	..	..	0	0	0	0	1
All undertakings	..	..	..	8	0	13	15	..
Total								
Domestic undertakings	298	..	328	369	397	431	468	412
Foreign controlled undertakings	285	..	314	354	380	413	448	397
Foreign companies (branches)	33	..	40	47	55	71	81	103
All undertakings	331	246	368	416	452	502	549	369

ESTONIA

Table 1. Selected aggregates *(cont.)*

Million EUR

	2013	2014	2015	2016	2017	2018	2019	2020
1.3 Commissions								
Life								
Domestic undertakings	19	21	23	..	..	..	..	..
Foreign controlled undertakings	19	21	23	..	..	..	..	..
Foreign companies (branches)	..	..	..	..	..	..	..	..
All undertakings	19	..	23	..	..	..	..	..
Non-life								
Domestic undertakings	72	73	78	..	..	..	..	..
Foreign controlled undertakings	67	69	73	..	..	..	..	..
Foreign companies (branches)	..	..	..	..	..	..	..	..
All undertakings	72	..	78	..	..	..	..	..
Composite								
Domestic undertakings	..	..	..	..	..	..	..	..
Foreign controlled undertakings	..	..	..	..	..	..	..	..
Foreign companies (branches)	..	..	..	..	..	..	..	..
All undertakings	..	..	..	..	..	..	..	..
of which:								
Life	..	..	..	..	..	..	..	..
Domestic undertakings	..	..	..	..	..	..	..	..
Foreign controlled undertakings	..	..	..	..	..	..	..	..
Foreign companies (branches)	..	..	..	..	..	..	..	..
All undertakings	..	..	..	..	..	..	..	..
Non-life	..	..	..	..	..	..	..	..
Domestic undertakings	..	..	..	..	..	..	..	..
Foreign controlled undertakings	..	..	..	..	..	..	..	..
Foreign companies (branches)	..	..	..	..	..	..	..	..
All undertakings	..	..	..	..	..	..	..	..
Total								
Domestic undertakings	90	94	101	..	..	..	..	..
Foreign controlled undertakings	86	89	95	..	..	..	..	..
Foreign companies (branches)	..	..	..	..	..	..	..	..
All undertakings	90	..	101	..	..	..	..	..
1.4 Gross operating expenses								
Life								
Domestic undertakings	9	9	11	..	..	.. c	.. c	.. c
Foreign controlled undertakings	9	9	11	..	..	.. c	.. c	10
Foreign companies (branches)	..	..	..	..	..	..	..	..
All undertakings	9	..	11	..	..	..	..	10
Non-life								
Domestic undertakings	27	30	27	115	137	153	157	131
Foreign controlled undertakings	25	29	26	..	..	142	148	123
Foreign companies (branches)	..	..	..	..	..	..	..	..
All undertakings	27	..	27	..	..	..	..	131
Composite								
Domestic undertakings	..	..	..	..	..	25	25	21
Foreign controlled undertakings	..	..	..	..	..	25	25	21
Foreign companies (branches)	..	..	..	..	..	..	..	..
All undertakings	..	..	..	..	..	..	..	21
of which:								
Life	..	..	..	..	..	..	..	18
Domestic undertakings	..	..	..	..	..	21	21	18
Foreign controlled undertakings	..	..	..	..	..	21	21	18
Foreign companies (branches)	..	..	..	..	..	..	..	..
All undertakings	..	..	..	..	..	..	..	18
Non-life	..	..	..	..	..	..	..	3
Domestic undertakings	..	..	..	..	..	4	4	3
Foreign controlled undertakings	..	..	..	..	..	4	4	3
Foreign companies (branches)	..	..	..	..	..	..	..	..
All undertakings	..	..	..	..	..	..	..	3
Total								
Domestic undertakings	37	40	38	115	137	188	191	162
Foreign controlled undertakings	35	38	36	..	..	177	182	154
Foreign companies (branches)	..	..	..	..	..	..	..	..
All undertakings	37	..	38	..	..	..	..	162

Table 1. Selected aggregates *(cont.)*

Million EUR

	2013	2014	2015	2016	2017	2018	2019	2020
1.5 Insurance business written abroad by branches, gross premiums								
Life								
Branches and agencies	94	114	130	96	..	84	94	97
Subsidaries	..	..	..	..	..	..	..	..
Total	94	114	130	96	..	..	94	..
Non-life								
Branches and agencies	170	174	190	201	243	289	307	266
Subsidaries	..	..	..	..	..	..	..	..
Total	170	174	190	201	243	289	307	266
Composite								
Branches and agencies	..	..	..	52	..	73	88	107
Subsidaries	..	..	..	..	..	..	..	..
Total	..	..	..	52	..	..	88	..
of which:								
Life	..	..	..	42	..	..	67	..
Branches and agencies	..	..	..	42	..	56	67	86
Subsidaries	..	..	..	..	..	..	..	..
Total	..	..	..	42	..	..	67	..
Non-life	..	..	..	10	..	..	21	..
Branches and agencies	..	..	..	10	..	17	21	21
Subsidaries	..	..	..	..	..	..	..	..
Total	..	..	..	10	..	..	21	..
Total								
Branches and agencies	264	288	320	349	243	446	489	471
Subsidaries	..	..	..	..	..	..	..	..
Total	264	288	320	349	243	289	489	266

.. Not available; c Confidential data
Note: Detailed metadata at: *http://metalinks.oecd.org/ins/20220309/4eef*.
Source: OECD *Insurance Statistics (database)*

ESTONIA

Table 2. Number of companies and employees

	2013	2014	2015	2016	2017	2018	2019	2020
2.1 Number of companies								
Life								
Domestic undertakings	4	4	4	2	1	1	1	1
Foreign controlled undertakings	4	4	4	2	1	1	1	1
Foreign companies (branches)	1	1	1	0	1	1	1	1
All undertakings	5	5	5	2	2	2	2	2
Non-life								
Domestic undertakings	8	8	8	8	7	7	7	6
Foreign controlled undertakings	5	5	5	5	4	4	4	3
Foreign companies (branches)	4	4	3	4	4	6	6	6
All undertakings	12	12	11	12	11	13	13	12
Composite								
Domestic undertakings	0	0	0	2	2	2	1	1
Foreign controlled undertakings	0	0	0	2	2	2	1	1
Foreign companies (branches)	0	0	0	1	1	1	2	2
All undertakings	0	0	0	3	3	3	3	3
Reinsurance								
Domestic undertakings	0	0	0	0	0	0	0	..
Foreign controlled undertakings	0	0	0	0	..	0	0	..
Foreign companies (branches)	..	..	0	0	..	0	0	..
All undertakings	..	..	0	0	..	0	0	..
Total								
Domestic undertakings	12	12	12	12	10	10	9	8
Foreign controlled undertakings	9	9	9	9	7	7	6	5
Foreign companies (branches)	5	5	4	5	6	8	9	9
All undertakings	17	17	16	17	16	18	18	17
2.2 Number of employees								
Insurance undertakings	2 596	2 561	2 581	..	..	..	..	..
Intermediaries	1 271	1 217	1 232	..	..	..	..	..
Total	3 867	3 778	3 813	..	..	..	..	..

.. Not available

Note: Detailed metadata at: *http://metalinks.oecd.org/ins/20220309/4eef.*

Source: *OECD Insurance Statistics (database)*

FINLAND

Table 1. Selected aggregates

Million EUR

	2013	2014	2015	2016	2017	2018	2019	2020
1.1 Insurance business written in the reporting country								
1.1.1 Insurance business, by ownership								
Gross premiums								
Domestic undertakings	9 834	10 632	10 741	9 045	8 926	7 922	9 620	7 865
Foreign controlled undertakings	3 357	3 698	6 892	..	..	..	..	..
Foreign companies (branches)	..	..	..	..	..	..	..	..
All undertakings	9 834	10 632	10 741	9 045	8 926	4 366	6 024	4 037
Premiums ceded								
Domestic undertakings	257	259	246	241	230	-251	341	264
Foreign controlled undertakings	19	15	217	..	..	..	..	..
Foreign companies (branches)	..	..	..	..	..	..	..	..
All undertakings	257	259	246	241	230	-24	24	31
Net written premiums								
Domestic undertakings	9 577	10 373	10 495	8 804	8 696	7 671	9 271	7 601
Foreign controlled undertakings	3 338	3 683	6 675	..	..	..	..	..
Foreign companies (branches)	..	..	..	..	..	..	..	..
All undertakings	9 577	10 373	10 495	8 804	8 696	4 342	5 992	4 006
1.1.2 Insurance business on foreign risks, gross premiums								
Life	..	..	..	..	..	..	..	..
Non-life	..	..	..	..	..	..	..	..
Composite total	..	..	..	..	..	..	..	..
Total	..	..	..	..	..	..	..	..
1.1.3 Life insurance payments, by class, gross premiums								
Annuities	2 458	2 544	2 287	694	621	608	2 235	592
Unit linked	2 509	2 929	3 224	2 446	2 265	1 757	2 230	1 457
Other life insurance	614	619	745	1 433	1 641	2 000	1 554	1 988
Total life insurance	5 581	6 092	6 256	4 573	4 527	4 365	6 020	4 037
***of which:** Pension contracts*	819	756	597	675	2 265	593	638	581
1.1.4 Non-life insurance payments, by class, gross premiums								
Motor vehicle insurance	1 520	1 591	1 639	1 639	1 586	1 213	1 228	1 267
Marine, aviation and other transport insurance	70	70	68	73	69	69	84	95
Freight insurance	55	56	52	57	55	43	45	44
Fire and other property damage insurance	929	985	1 030	1 028	972	790	800	832
Pecuniary loss insurance	33	30	28	22	20	19	19	21
General liability insurance	239	392	385	234	218	193	79	175
Accident and health	1 048	1 060	1 058	1 119	1 183	957	1 029	1 034
***of which:** Health*	264	299	290	368	395	343	387	415
Other non-life insurance	144	152	88	163	151	124	129	138
Treaty reinsurance	149	135	135	136	144	148	150	173
Total non-life insurance	4 187	4 471	4 483	4 471	4 398	3 556	3 563	3 779
1.2 Gross claims payments								
Life								
Domestic undertakings	3 927	3 871	3 957	4 324	4 233	4 632	7 239	4 183
Foreign controlled undertakings	1 399	1 160	1 124	.. c	.. c	.. c	.. c	.. c
Foreign companies (branches)	..	..	..	..	..	..	..	..
All undertakings	3 927	3 871	3 957	4 324	4 233	4 632	7 239	4 183
Non-life								
Domestic undertakings	2 858	2 939	2 872	3 103	3 179	2 538	2 625	2 634
Foreign controlled undertakings	741	724	2 872	.. c	.. c	.. c	.. c	.. c
Foreign companies (branches)	..	..	..	..	..	.. c	.. c	.. c
All undertakings	2 858	2 939	2 872	3 103	3 179	.. c	.. c	.. c
Composite, all undertakings	..	..	..	..	..	..	..	..
Total								
Domestic undertakings	6 785	6 810	6 829	7 427	7 412	7 170	9 864	6 817
Foreign controlled undertakings	2 140	1 884	3 996	..	..	..	..	..
Foreign companies (branches)	..	..	..	..	..	..	..	..
All undertakings	6 785	6 810	6 829	7 427	7 412	4 632	7 239	4 183
1.3 Commissions								
Life								
Domestic undertakings	90	-83	101	126	121	116	113	79
Foreign controlled undertakings	9	-10	15	.. c	.. c	.. c	.. c	.. c
Foreign companies (branches)	..	..	..	..	..	..	..	..
All undertakings	90	-83	101	126	121	..	..	..
Non-life								
Domestic undertakings	58	-142	113	166	160	131	142	140
Foreign controlled undertakings	21	-18	23	.. c	.. c	.. c	.. c	.. c
Foreign companies (branches)	..	..	..	..	..	..	..	..
All undertakings	58	-142	113	166	160	..	..	..
Composite, all undertakings	..	..	..	..	..	..	..	..
Total								
Domestic undertakings	148	-225	214	292	281	247	255	219
Foreign controlled undertakings	30	-28	38	..	..	..	..	..
Foreign companies (branches)	..	..	..	..	..	..	..	..
All undertakings	148	-225	214	292	281	..	..	..

FINLAND

Table 1. Selected aggregates *(cont.)*

Million EUR

	2013	2014	2015	2016	2017	2018	2019	2020
1.4 Gross operating expenses								
Life								
Domestic undertakings	302	317	316	341	355	359	385	368
Foreign controlled undertakings	34	36	34	.. c	.. c	.. c	.. c	.. c
Foreign companies (branches)	..	..	..	..	..	..	..	..
All undertakings	302	317	316	341	355	359	385	368
Non-life								
Domestic undertakings	827	844	847	876	884	746	832	774
Foreign controlled undertakings	161	158	847	.. c	.. c	.. c	.. c	.. c
Foreign companies (branches)	..	..	..	..	..	..	..	..
All undertakings	827	844	847	876	884	..	..	..
Composite, all undertakings	..	..	..	..	..	..	..	..
Total								
Domestic undertakings	1 129	1 161	1 163	1 217	1 239	1 105	1 217	1 142
Foreign controlled undertakings	195	194	881	..	..	..	..	..
Foreign companies (branches)	..	..	..	..	..	..	..	..
All undertakings	1 129	1 161	1 163	1 217	1 239	359	385	368
1.5 Insurance business written abroad by branches, gross premiums								
Life								
Branches and agencies	162	107	17	..	..	..	..	..
Subsidaries	..	..	..	..	..	..	..	..
Total	162	107	17	..	..	..	..	..
Non-life								
Branches and agencies	..	..	..	..	..	..	..	..
Subsidaries	..	..	..	..	..	..	..	..
Total	..	..	..	..	..	..	..	..
Composite total	..	..	..	..	..	..	..	..
Total								
Branches and agencies	162	107	17	..	..	..	..	..
Subsidaries	..	..	..	..	..	..	..	..
Total	162	107	17	..	..	..	..	..

.. Not available; c Confidential data

Note: Detailed metadata at: *http://metalinks.oecd.org/ins/20220309/059c.*

Source: *OECD Insurance Statistics (database)*

Table 2. Number of companies and employees

	2013	2014	2015	2016	2017	2018	2019	2020
2.1 Number of companies								
Life								
Domestic undertakings	13	13	13	11	10	10	11	9
Foreign controlled undertakings	1	1	1	1	1	1	1	1
Foreign companies (branches)	..	..	..	..	..	10	10	11
All undertakings	13	13	13	11	10	20	21	20
Non-life								
Domestic undertakings	42	38	38	37	37	40	37	32
Foreign controlled undertakings	1	1	1	2	2	1	1	1
Foreign companies (branches)	..	..	..	..	..	8	8	8
All undertakings	42	38	38	37	37	48	46	40
Composite, all undertakings	..	..	..	..	..	0	..	..
Reinsurance								
Domestic undertakings	..	..	..	..	..	0	..	..
Foreign controlled undertakings	..	..	..	..	..	0	..	..
Foreign companies (branches)	..	..	..	..	..	0	..	..
All undertakings	..	..	..	..	..	0	..	..
Total								
Domestic undertakings	55	51	51	48	47	50	48	41
Foreign controlled undertakings	2	2	2	3	3	2	2	2
Foreign companies (branches)	..	..	..	..	..	18	18	19
All undertakings	55	51	51	48	47	68	67	60
2.2 Number of employees								
Insurance undertakings	9 231	8 980	8 750	8 815	7 751	7 866	6 893	9 813
Intermediaries	203	216	221	244	265	265	86	93
Total	9 434	9 196	8 971	9 059	8 016	8 131	6 979	9 906

.. Not available

Note: Detailed metadata at: *http://metalinks.oecd.org/ins/20220309/059c.*

Source: *OECD Insurance Statistics (database)*

FRANCE

Table 1. Selected aggregates

Million EUR

	2013	2014	2015	2016	2017	2018	2019	2020
1.1 Insurance business written in the reporting country								
1.1.1 Insurance business, by ownership								
Gross premiums								
Domestic undertakings	207 521	221 223	226 000	..	..	286 809	296 989	265 041
Foreign controlled undertakings	..	..	..	..	..	..	..	..
Foreign companies (branches)	103	103	111	..	..	..	..	..
All undertakings	207 624	221 327	226 111	283 901	278 237	286 809	296 989	265 041
Premiums ceded								
Domestic undertakings	22 115	19 932	25 840	..	..	35 307	38 657	39 897
Foreign controlled undertakings	..	..	..	..	..	..	..	..
Foreign companies (branches)	19	22	21	..	..	..	..	..
All undertakings	22 135	19 954	25 861	43 153	33 277	35 307	38 657	39 897
Net written premiums								
Domestic undertakings	185 406	201 291	200 160	..	..	251 502	258 332	225 144
Foreign controlled undertakings	..	..	..	..	..	..	..	..
Foreign companies (branches)	84	82	90	..	..	..	..	..
All undertakings	185 490	201 373	200 250	240 747	244 960	251 502	258 332	225 144
1.1.2 Insurance business on foreign risks, gross premiums								
Life	259	73	60	..	..	..	..	..
Non-life	1 735	1 876	2 188	..	..	..	..	..
Composite	636	468	485	..	..	..	..	..
of which:								
Life	167	456	482	..	..	..	..	..
Non-life	469	12	3	..	..	..	..	..
Total	2 631	2 416	2 734	..	..	..	..	..
1.1.3 Life insurance payments, by class, gross premiums								
Annuities	..	..	..	..	..	..	..	..
Unit linked	..	..	..	28 208	38 135	38 569	39 657	39 333
Other life insurance	..	..	..	111 059	102 007	106 170	110 125	81 323
Total life insurance	..	..	..	139 267	140 142	144 740	149 781	120 656
***of which:** Pension contracts*	..	..	..	..	..	..	..	..
1.1.4 Non-life insurance payments, by class, gross premiums								
Motor vehicle insurance	..	..	..	..	..	..	..	..
Marine, aviation and other transport insurance	..	..	..	..	..	..	..	..
Freight insurance	..	..	..	..	..	..	..	..
Fire and other property damage insurance	..	..	..	..	..	..	..	..
Pecuniary loss insurance	..	..	..	..	..	..	..	..
General liability insurance	..	..	..	..	..	..	..	..
Accident and health	..	..	..	..	..	..	..	..
***of which:** Health*	..	..	..	..	..	..	..	..
Other non-life insurance	..	..	..	..	..	..	..	..
Treaty reinsurance	..	..	..	..	..	..	..	..
Total non-life insurance	..	..	..	119 104	124 560	128 064	131 451	133 266
1.2 Gross claims payments								
Life								
Domestic undertakings	25 663	26 144	26 794	..	..	21 986	23 357	23 635
Foreign controlled undertakings	..	..	..	..	..	..	..	..
Foreign companies (branches)	..	..	..	..	..	..	..	..
All undertakings	25 663	26 144	26 794	133 135	145 577	21 986	23 357	23 635
Non-life								
Domestic undertakings	45 317	61 895	63 029	..	..	56 407	60 336	61 799
Foreign controlled undertakings	..	..	..	..	..	..	..	..
Foreign companies (branches)	59	52	51	..	..	..	..	..
All undertakings	45 376	61 947	63 080	95 217	101 007	56 407	60 336	61 799
Composite								
Domestic undertakings	97 287	86 518	91 862	..	..	158 076	158 713	154 653
Foreign controlled undertakings	..	..	..	..	..	..	..	..
Foreign companies (branches)	..	..	..	..	..	..	..	..
All undertakings	97 287	86 518	91 862	..	..	158 076	158 713	154 653
of which:								
Life	88 620	..	..	..	..	111 830	112 716	103 838
Domestic undertakings	88 620	..	..	..	..	111 830	112 716	103 838
Foreign controlled undertakings	..	..	..	..	..	..	..	..
Foreign companies (branches)	..	..	..	..	..	..	..	..
All undertakings	88 620	..	..	..	..	111 830	112 716	103 838
Non-life	8 667	..	..	..	..	46 246	45 996	50 815
Domestic undertakings	8 667	..	..	..	..	46 246	45 996	50 815
Foreign controlled undertakings	..	..	..	..	..	..	..	..
Foreign companies (branches)	..	..	..	..	..	..	..	..
All undertakings	8 667	..	..	..	..	46 246	45 996	50 815
Total								
Domestic undertakings	168 267	174 557	181 685	..	..	236 469	242 406	240 087
Foreign controlled undertakings	..	..	..	..	..	..	..	..
Foreign companies (branches)	59	52	51	..	..	..	..	..
All undertakings	168 326	174 608	181 736	228 352	246 584	236 469	242 406	240 087

FRANCE

Table 1. Selected aggregates *(cont.)*

Million EUR

	2013	2014	2015	2016	2017	2018	2019	2020
1.3 Commissions								
Life								
Domestic undertakings	..	..	..	..	..	..	..	..
Foreign controlled undertakings	..	..	..	..	..	..	..	..
Foreign companies (branches)	..	..	..	..	..	..	..	..
All undertakings	..	..	..	..	..	..	..	..
Non-life								
Domestic undertakings	..	..	..	..	..	..	..	..
Foreign controlled undertakings	..	..	..	..	..	..	..	..
Foreign companies (branches)	..	..	..	..	..	..	..	..
All undertakings	..	..	..	..	..	..	..	..
Composite								
Domestic undertakings	..	..	..	..	..	..	..	..
Foreign controlled undertakings	..	..	..	..	..	..	..	..
Foreign companies (branches)	..	..	..	..	..	..	..	..
All undertakings	..	..	..	..	..	..	..	..
of which:								
Life	..	..	..	..	..	..	..	..
Domestic undertakings	..	..	..	..	..	..	..	..
Foreign controlled undertakings	..	..	..	..	..	..	..	..
Foreign companies (branches)	..	..	..	..	..	..	..	..
All undertakings	..	..	..	..	..	..	..	..
Non-life	..	..	..	..	..	..	..	..
Domestic undertakings	..	..	..	..	..	..	..	..
Foreign controlled undertakings	..	..	..	..	..	..	..	..
Foreign companies (branches)	..	..	..	..	..	..	..	..
All undertakings	..	..	..	..	..	..	..	..
Total								
Domestic undertakings	..	..	..	..	..	..	..	..
Foreign controlled undertakings	..	..	..	..	..	..	..	..
Foreign companies (branches)	..	..	..	..	..	..	..	..
All undertakings	..	..	..	..	..	..	..	..
1.4 Gross operating expenses								
Life								
Domestic undertakings	2 828	2 893	2 914	..	..	2 545	2 697	3 187
Foreign controlled undertakings	..	..	..	..	..	..	..	..
Foreign companies (branches)	..	..	..	..	..	..	..	..
All undertakings	2 828	2 893	2 914	15 848	16 123	2 545	2 697	3 187
Non-life								
Domestic undertakings	15 969	16 156	15 936	..	..	18 654	20 368	22 338
Foreign controlled undertakings	..	..	..	..	..	..	..	..
Foreign companies (branches)	..	8	..	..	..	..	..	..
All undertakings	15 969	16 164	15 936	27 415	27 948	18 654	20 368	22 338
Composite								
Domestic undertakings	12 957	13 439	14 727	..	..	24 734	25 749	28 970
Foreign controlled undertakings	..	..	..	..	..	..	..	..
Foreign companies (branches)	..	..	..	..	..	..	..	..
All undertakings	12 957	13 439	14 727	..	..	24 734	25 749	28 970
of which:								
Life	10 533	10 808	11 414	..	..	13 366	16 771	18 778
Domestic undertakings	10 533	..	..	..	..	13 366	16 771	18 778
Foreign controlled undertakings	..	..	..	..	..	..	..	..
Foreign companies (branches)	..	..	..	..	..	..	..	..
All undertakings	10 533	10 808	11 414	..	..	13 366	16 771	18 778
Non-life	2 424	2 631	3 313	..	..	11 368	8 979	10 192
Domestic undertakings	2 424	..	..	..	..	11 368	8 979	10 192
Foreign controlled undertakings	..	..	..	..	..	..	..	..
Foreign companies (branches)	..	..	..	..	..	..	..	..
All undertakings	2 424	2 631	3 313	..	..	11 368	8 979	10 192
Total								
Domestic undertakings	31 754	32 488	33 578	..	..	45 933	48 814	54 495
Foreign controlled undertakings	..	..	..	..	..	..	..	..
Foreign companies (branches)	..	8	..	..	..	..	..	..
All undertakings	31 754	32 497	33 578	43 263	44 071	45 933	48 814	54 495

Table 1. Selected aggregates *(cont.)*

Million EUR

	2013	2014	2015	2016	2017	2018	2019	2020
1.5 Insurance business written abroad by branches, gross premiums								
Life								
Branches and agencies	2 691	2 860	3 373	4 393	5 050	..	..	4 041
Subsidaries	..	..	..	..	..	..	..	..
Total	2 691	2 860	3 373	4 393	5 050	..	..	4 041
Non-life								
Branches and agencies	4 176	4 960	5 460	8 837	9 719	..	..	12 991
Subsidaries	..	..	..	..	..	..	..	..
Total	4 176	4 960	5 460	8 837	9 719	..	..	12 991
Composite								
Branches and agencies	..	..	..	..	..	..	..	..
Subsidaries	..	..	..	..	..	..	..	..
Total	..	..	..	..	..	..	..	..
of which:								
Life	..	..	..	..	..	..	..	..
Branches and agencies	..	..	..	..	..	..	..	..
Subsidaries	..	..	..	..	..	..	..	..
Total	..	..	..	..	..	..	..	..
Non-life	..	..	..	..	..	..	..	..
Branches and agencies	..	..	..	..	..	..	..	..
Subsidaries	..	..	..	..	..	..	..	..
Total	..	..	..	..	..	..	..	..
Total								
Branches and agencies	6 867	7 820	8 834	13 230	14 769	..	..	17 032
Subsidaries	..	..	..	..	..	..	..	..
Total	6 867	7 820	8 834	13 230	14 769	..	..	17 032

.. Not available

Note: Detailed metadata at: *http://metalinks.oecd.org/ins/20220309/ea17*.

Source: *OECD Insurance Statistics (database)*

Table 2. Number of companies and employees

	2013	2014	2015	2016	2017	2018	2019	2020
2.1 Number of companies								
Life								
Domestic undertakings	59	55	51	..	..	..	..	..
Foreign controlled undertakings	..	..	..	..	..	..	..	..
Foreign companies (branches)	..	..	..	..	..	..	..	..
All undertakings	59	55	51	..	..	..	..	52
Non-life								
Domestic undertakings	212	206	191	..	..	..	..	..
Foreign controlled undertakings	..	..	..	..	..	..	..	..
Foreign companies (branches)	4	4	4	..	..	..	..	..
All undertakings	216	210	195	394	381	364	345	348
Composite								
Domestic undertakings	38	38	39	..	..	..	..	..
Foreign controlled undertakings	..	..	..	..	..	..	..	..
Foreign companies (branches)	..	..	..	..	..	..	..	..
All undertakings	38	38	39	239	236	239	243	177
Reinsurance								
Domestic undertakings	16	15	16	..	..	..	..	..
Foreign controlled undertakings	..	..	..	..	..	..	..	..
Foreign companies (branches)	..	..	..	..	..	..	..	..
All undertakings	16	15	16	14	14	12	10	12
Total								
Domestic undertakings	325	314	297	..	..	..	..	..
Foreign controlled undertakings	..	..	..	..	..	..	..	..
Foreign companies (branches)	4	4	4	..	..	..	..	..
All undertakings	329	318	301	647	631	615	598	589
2.2 Number of employees								
Insurance undertakings	..	..	..	..	..	..	..	..
Intermediaries	..	..	..	..	..	..	..	..
Total	..	..	..	..	..	..	..	..

.. Not available

Note: Detailed metadata at: *http://metalinks.oecd.org/ins/20220309/ea17*.

Source: *OECD Insurance Statistics (database)*

GERMANY

Table 1. Selected aggregates

Million EUR

	2013	2014	2015	2016	2017	2018	2019	2020
1.1 Insurance business written in the reporting country								
1.1.1 Insurance business, by ownership								
Gross premiums								
Domestic undertakings	243 304	246 201	254 407	257 208	264 933	273 036	296 378	307 670
Foreign controlled undertakings	39 396	38 694	39 170	36 978	36 644	39 215	40 551	41 054
Foreign companies (branches)	7 963	8 796	9 751	8 994	10 550	11 199	11 148	12 674
All undertakings	251 267	254 997	264 158	266 203	275 483	284 235	307 527	320 345
Premiums ceded								
Domestic undertakings	25 709	27 853	32 499	31 990	34 336	39 483	41 736	45 657
Foreign controlled undertakings	4 645	4 615	4 593	4 041	4 046	4 482	4 167	4 276
Foreign companies (branches)	108	103	114	112	132	127	83	85
All undertakings	25 817	27 956	32 613	32 102	34 469	39 609	41 819	45 742
Net written premiums								
Domestic undertakings	217 596	218 348	221 907	225 218	230 596	233 553	254 643	262 014
Foreign controlled undertakings	34 751	34 078	34 577	32 937	32 598	34 732	36 383	36 779
Foreign companies (branches)	7 854	8 693	9 637	8 882	10 418	11 073	11 065	12 589
All undertakings	225 450	227 041	231 545	234 100	241 014	244 626	265 707	274 603
1.1.2 Insurance business on foreign risks, gross premiums								
Life	..	..	..	..	..	..	..	..
Non-life	..	..	..	..	..	..	..	..
Composite total	..	..	..	..	..	..	..	..
Total	..	..	..	..	..	..	..	..
1.1.3 Life insurance payments, by class, gross premiums								
Annuities	32 863	34 019	31 782	31 215	30 000	31 730	36 776	35 056
Unit linked	12 919	13 863	13 863	15 351	15 994	17 293	18 685	21 318
Other life insurance	41 934	40 891	41 214	38 845	41 612	40 959	44 755	44 288
Total life insurance	87 716	88 774	86 859	85 411	87 606	89 982	100 217	100 663
***of which:** Pension contracts*	..	..	..	..	..	..	..	..
1.1.4 Non-life insurance payments, by class, gross premiums								
Motor vehicle insurance	28 592	31 425	32 589	36 521	40 579	44 565	46 631	47 107
Marine, aviation and other transport insurance	4 476	4 379	5 116	4 749	4 933	5 050	5 786	6 340
Freight insurance	..	..	..	..	..	..	..	..
Fire and other property damage insurance	36 832	35 422	38 830	42 499	46 541	50 056	55 618	61 518
Pecuniary loss insurance	2 815	2 088	2 197	2 376	3 872	3 857	4 134	4 022
General liability insurance	13 265	14 213	15 425	16 126	17 517	18 440	20 008	21 756
Accident and health	49 395	48 811	49 176	49 721	52 572	52 301	54 040	56 357
***of which:** Health*	41 747	40 924	41 627	37 178	39 328	40 220	41 217	43 011
Other non-life insurance	4 841	4 865	31 030	25 991	21 153	19 528	20 628	21 500
Treaty reinsurance	..	..	..	..	..	..	..	..
Total non-life insurance	140 215	141 203	174 363	177 983	187 167	193 798	206 844	218 600
1.2 Gross claims payments								
Life								
Domestic undertakings	69 267	74 625	73 307	78 596	69 073	70 871	75 975	74 210
Foreign controlled undertakings	17 017	17 510	17 929	17 942	16 501	16 759	17 071	16 996
Foreign companies (branches)	..	..	..	..	..	..	..	..
All undertakings	69 267	74 625	73 307	78 596	69 073	70 871	75 975	74 210
Non-life								
Domestic undertakings	113 293	72 709	77 667	78 086	84 787	87 989	139 877	145 813
Foreign controlled undertakings	12 402	8 955	3 653	9 227	9 500	10 110	13 369	13 934
Foreign companies (branches)	..	..	..	..	..	..	..	..
All undertakings	113 293	72 709	77 667	78 086	84 787	87 989	139 877	145 813
Composite, all undertakings	..	..	..	..	..	..	..	..
Total								
Domestic undertakings	182 560	147 334	150 974	156 682	153 859	158 861	215 852	220 024
Foreign controlled undertakings	29 419	26 465	21 581	27 169	26 001	26 869	30 440	30 930
Foreign companies (branches)	..	..	..	..	..	..	..	..
All undertakings	182 560	147 334	150 974	156 682	153 859	158 861	215 852	220 024
1.3 Commissions								
Life								
Domestic undertakings	5 367	5 583	5 069	4 987	4 794	4 961	5 618	5 628
Foreign controlled undertakings	1 604	1 533	1 488	1 238	1 138	1 211	1 306	1 389
Foreign companies (branches)	..	..	..	..	..	..	..	..
All undertakings	5 367	5 583	5 069	4 987	4 794	4 961	5 618	5 628
Non-life								
Domestic undertakings	10 048	10 221	10 740	11 105	12 173	12 647	13 656	14 022
Foreign controlled undertakings	1 720	1 626	257	1 594	1 623	1 806	1 940	1 988
Foreign companies (branches)	..	..	..	..	..	..	..	..
All undertakings	10 048	10 221	10 740	11 105	12 173	12 647	13 656	14 022
Composite, all undertakings	..	..	..	..	..	..	..	..
Total								
Domestic undertakings	15 416	15 805	15 810	16 092	16 967	17 609	19 273	19 650
Foreign controlled undertakings	3 323	3 159	1 745	2 832	2 760	3 017	3 247	3 377
Foreign companies (branches)	..	..	..	..	..	..	..	..
All undertakings	15 416	15 805	15 810	16 092	16 967	17 609	19 273	19 650

Table 1. Selected aggregates *(cont.)*

Million EUR

	2013	2014	2015	2016	2017	2018	2019	2020
1.4 Gross operating expenses								
Life								
Domestic undertakings	3 954	3 963	4 008	3 902	3 907	3 901	3 769	3 774
Foreign controlled undertakings	921	894	1 036	938	952	1 001	974	949
Foreign companies (branches)	..	..	..	..	..	..	..	..
All undertakings	3 954	3 963	4 008	3 902	3 907	3 901	3 769	3 774
Non-life								
Domestic undertakings	11 599	10 296	10 627	10 807	11 161	11 390	13 638	13 299
Foreign controlled undertakings	1 400	1 187	324	1 183	1 210	1 297	1 448	1 427
Foreign companies (branches)	..	..	..	..	..	..	..	..
All undertakings	11 599	10 296	10 627	10 807	11 161	11 390	13 638	13 299
Composite, all undertakings	..	..	..	..	..	..	..	..
Total								
Domestic undertakings	15 553	14 259	14 635	14 709	15 068	15 291	17 406	17 072
Foreign controlled undertakings	2 321	2 081	1 361	2 121	2 163	2 297	2 421	2 377
Foreign companies (branches)	..	..	..	..	..	..	..	..
All undertakings	15 553	14 259	14 635	14 709	15 068	15 291	17 406	17 072
1.5 Insurance business written abroad by branches, gross premiums								
Life								
Branches and agencies	..	..	..	..	..	200	481	302
Subsidaries	..	..	..	..	..	..	..	..
Total	..	..	..	..	..	200	481	302
Non-life								
Branches and agencies	..	..	..	..	..	22 495	25 723	27 574
Subsidaries	..	..	..	..	..	..	..	..
Total	..	..	..	..	..	22 495	25 723	27 574
Composite total	..	..	..	..	..	..	..	..
Total								
Branches and agencies	..	..	..	..	..	22 695	26 203	27 876
Subsidaries	..	..	..	..	..	..	..	..
Total	..	..	..	..	..	22 695	26 203	27 876

.. Not available

Note: Detailed metadata at: *http://metalinks.oecd.org/ins/20220309/c03f.*

Source: *OECD Insurance Statistics (database)*

Table 2. Number of companies and employees

	2013	2014	2015	2016	2017	2018	2019	2020
2.1 Number of companies								
Life								
Domestic undertakings	91	91	85	85	86	86	84	82
Foreign controlled undertakings	17	17	14	14	15	16	16	16
Foreign companies (branches)	2	2	2	2	1	1	1	1
All undertakings	93	93	87	87	87	87	85	83
Non-life								
Domestic undertakings	259	255	257	252	251	250	254	251
Foreign controlled undertakings	23	21	22	18	17	21	23	20
Foreign companies (branches)	3	3	3	2	2	1	1	1
All undertakings	262	258	260	254	253	251	255	252
Composite, all undertakings	**0**	**0**	**0**	**0**	..	..	..	..
Reinsurance								
Domestic undertakings	29	27	27	27	27	28	29	28
Foreign controlled undertakings	4	3	3	3	3	3	3	3
Foreign companies (branches)	1	1	1	1	1	1	1	0
All undertakings	30	28	28	28	28	29	30	28
Total								
Domestic undertakings	379	373	369	364	364	364	367	361
Foreign controlled undertakings	44	41	39	35	35	40	42	39
Foreign companies (branches)	6	6	6	5	4	3	3	2
All undertakings	385	379	375	369	368	367	370	363
2.2 Number of employees								
Insurance undertakings	128 755	126 755	128 784	..	..	..	..	..
Intermediaries	27 331	26 982	25 917	..	..	..	..	..
Total	156 086	153 737	154 701	156 675	154 262	152 888	150 886	150 547

.. Not available

Note: Detailed metadata at: *http://metalinks.oecd.org/ins/20220309/c03f.*

Source: OECD *Insurance Statistics (database)*

Table 1. Selected aggregates

Million EUR

	2013	2014	2015	2016	2017	2018	2019	2020
1.1 Insurance business written in the reporting country								
1.1.1 Insurance business, by ownership								
Gross premiums								
Domestic undertakings	4 071	3 806	3 573	3 531	3 729	3 798	4 053	4 106
Foreign controlled undertakings	1 730	1 696	1 766	2 350	2 450	2 458	2 487	2 585
Foreign companies (branches)	0	0	0	0	0	0	0	0
All undertakings	4 071	3 806	3 573	3 531	3 729	3 798	4 053	4 106
Premiums ceded								
Domestic undertakings	824	471	459	396	402	429	423	418
Foreign controlled undertakings	214	206	201	244	260	274	270	262
Foreign companies (branches)	0	0	0	0	0	0	0	0
All undertakings	824	471	459	396	402	429	423	418
Net written premiums								
Domestic undertakings	3 247	3 334	3 114	3 135	3 328	3 369	3 631	3 688
Foreign controlled undertakings	1 516	1 490	1 565	2 106	2 190	2 183	2 218	2 322
Foreign companies (branches)	0	0	0	0	0	0	0	0
All undertakings	3 247	3 335	3 114	3 135	3 328	3 369	3 631	3 688
1.1.2 Insurance business on foreign risks, gross premiums								
Life	..	..	..	..	..	..	..	..
Non-life	..	..	..	..	..	..	..	..
Composite	..	..	..	..	..	..	..	..
of which:								
Life	..	..	..	..	..	..	..	..
Non-life	..	..	..	..	..	..	..	..
Total	..	..	..	..	..	..	..	..
1.1.3 Life insurance payments, by class, gross premiums								
Annuities	142	129	125	0	0	0	0	0
Unit linked	240	396	326	250	347	380	363	641
Other life insurance	1 299	1 353	1 348	1 416	1 533	1 499	1 700	1 462
Total life insurance	1 681	1 879	1 799	1 666	1 881	1 879	2 064	2 103
***of which:** Pension contracts*	143	151	156	..	..	..	..	..
1.1.4 Non-life insurance payments, by class, gross premiums								
Motor vehicle insurance	1 417	1 154	1 006	911	938	948	968	946
Marine, aviation and other transport insurance	19	19	20	32	34	38	38	39
Freight insurance	24	21	21	..	0	0	0	0
Fire and other property damage insurance	529	448	440	410	398	409	402	406
Pecuniary loss insurance	69	30	30	40	28	31	36	43
General liability insurance	76	67	68	65	63	75	83	89
Accident and health	64	57	57	300	242	263	298	318
***of which:** Health*	0	0	..	..	0	0	0	0
Other non-life insurance	188	128	129	137	146	153	165	162
Treaty reinsurance	0	0	..	..	0	0	0	0
Total non-life insurance	2 386	1 924	1 770	1 896	1 848	1 918	1 990	2 003
1.2 Gross claims payments								
Life								
Domestic undertakings	1 072	900	744	..	..	..	..	..
Foreign controlled undertakings	707	1	502	..	..	..	..	..
Foreign companies (branches)	0	0	0	..	..	..	..	..
All undertakings	1 072	900	744	..	..	..	..	..
Non-life								
Domestic undertakings	373	355	314	..	..	..	..	..
Foreign controlled undertakings	121	224	109	..	..	..	..	..
Foreign companies (branches)	1	1	0	..	..	..	..	..
All undertakings	375	356	314	..	..	..	..	..
Composite								
Domestic undertakings	1 096	1 018	931	..	..	..	..	..
Foreign controlled undertakings	364	412	347	..	..	..	..	..
Foreign companies (branches)	0	0	0	..	..	..	..	..
All undertakings	1 096	1 018	931	..	..	..	..	..
of which:								
Life	669	613	573	..	..	..	..	..
Domestic undertakings	669	613	573	..	..	..	..	..
Foreign controlled undertakings	226	7	220	..	..	..	..	..
Foreign companies (branches)	0	0	0	..	..	..	..	..
All undertakings	669	613	573	..	..	..	..	..
Non-life	426	405	358	..	..	..	..	..
Domestic undertakings	426	405	358	..	..	..	..	..
Foreign controlled undertakings	138	405	126	..	..	..	..	..
Foreign companies (branches)	0	0	0	..	..	..	..	..
All undertakings	426	405	358	..	..	..	..	..
Total								
Domestic undertakings	2 541	2 273	1 989	..	..	..	..	..
Foreign controlled undertakings	1 192	637	957	..	..	..	..	..
Foreign companies (branches)	1	1	0	..	..	..	..	..
All undertakings	2 542	2 274	1 989	..	..	..	..	..

Table 1. Selected aggregates *(cont.)*

Million EUR

	2013	2014	2015	2016	2017	2018	2019	2020
1.3 Commissions								
Life								
Domestic undertakings	..	95	91	..	..	..	..	..
Foreign controlled undertakings	..	70	70	..	..	..	..	..
Foreign companies (branches)	..	0	0	..	..	..	..	..
All undertakings	..	95	91	..	..	..	..	..
Non-life								
Domestic undertakings	..	161	158	..	..	..	..	..
Foreign controlled undertakings	..	63	66	..	..	..	..	..
Foreign companies (branches)	..	0	0	..	..	..	..	..
All undertakings	..	162	158	..	..	..	..	..
Composite								
Domestic undertakings	..	276	709	..	..	..	..	..
Foreign controlled undertakings	..	115	115	..	..	..	..	..
Foreign companies (branches)	..	0	0	..	..	..	..	..
All undertakings	..	276	709	..	..	..	..	..
of which:								
Life	..	102	544	..	..	..	..	..
Domestic undertakings	..	102	544	..	..	..	..	..
Foreign controlled undertakings	..	39	40	..	..	..	..	..
Foreign companies (branches)	..	0	0	..	..	..	..	..
All undertakings	..	102	544	..	..	..	..	..
Non-life	..	174	164	..	..	..	..	..
Domestic undertakings	..	174	164	..	..	..	..	..
Foreign controlled undertakings	..	76	75	..	..	..	..	..
Foreign companies (branches)	..	0	0	..	..	..	..	..
All undertakings	..	174	164	..	..	..	..	..
Total								
Domestic undertakings	..	532	957	..	..	..	..	..
Foreign controlled undertakings	..	248	251	..	..	..	..	..
Foreign companies (branches)	..	0	0	..	..	..	..	..
All undertakings	..	532	957	..	..	..	..	..
1.4 Gross operating expenses								
Life								
Domestic undertakings	79	176	163	35	38	39	46	49
Foreign controlled undertakings	66	141	132	32	35	35	40	42
Foreign companies (branches)	0	0	..	0	0	0	0	0
All undertakings	79	176	163	35	38	39	46	49
Non-life								
Domestic undertakings	124	264	247	248	301	242	256	253
Foreign controlled undertakings	61	115	116	145	168	104	112	112
Foreign companies (branches)	0	0	0	0	0	0	0	0
All undertakings	124	264	247	248	301	242	256	253
Composite								
Domestic undertakings	169	404	371	700	701	811	774	759
Foreign controlled undertakings	57	154	150	448	438	550	495	489
Foreign companies (branches)	0	0	..	0	0	0	0	0
All undertakings	169	404	371	700	701	811	774	759
of which:								
Life	53	144	145	315	322	312	283	302
Domestic undertakings	53	144	145	315	322	312	283	302
Foreign controlled undertakings	21	53	52	231	223	219	216	209
Foreign companies (branches)	0	0	..	0	0	0	0	0
All undertakings	53	144	145	315	322	312	283	302
Non-life	116	260	226	385	379	499	492	458
Domestic undertakings	116	260	226	385	379	499	492	458
Foreign controlled undertakings	36	101	98	217	215	331	279	279
Foreign companies (branches)	0	0	..	0	0	0	0	0
All undertakings	116	260	226	385	379	499	492	458
Total								
Domestic undertakings	372	844	781	983	1 041	1 092	1 076	1 062
Foreign controlled undertakings	184	410	398	625	641	689	647	643
Foreign companies (branches)	0	0	0	0	0	0	0	0
All undertakings	372	844	781	983	1 041	1 092	1 076	1 062

Table 1. Selected aggregates *(cont.)*

Million EUR

	2013	2014	2015	2016	2017	2018	2019	2020
1.5 Insurance business written abroad by branches, gross premiums								
Life								
Branches and agencies	..	..	..	..	0	0	0	0
Subsidaries	..	..	..	..	0	0	0	0
Total	..	..	..	..	0	0	0	0
Non-life								
Branches and agencies	..	..	..	..	1	3	6	7
Subsidaries	..	..	..	..	0	0	0	0
Total	..	..	..	..	1	3	6	7
Composite								
Branches and agencies	..	..	..	..	0	18	4	5
Subsidaries	..	..	..	..	0	0	0	0
Total	..	..	..	..	0	18	4	5
of which:								
Life	..	..	..	..	0	0	0	0
Branches and agencies	..	..	..	..	0	0	0	0
Subsidaries	..	..	..	..	0	0	0	0
Total	..	..	..	..	0	0	0	0
Non-life	..	..	..	..	0	17	4	5
Branches and agencies	..	..	..	..	0	17	4	5
Subsidaries	..	..	..	..	0	0	0	0
Total	..	..	..	..	0	17	4	5
Total								
Branches and agencies	..	..	..	..	1	21	10	12
Subsidaries	..	..	..	..	0	0	0	0
Total	..	..	..	..	1	21	10	12

.. Not available

Note: Detailed metadata at: *http://metalinks.oecd.org/ins/20220309/cf0c.*

Source: *OECD Insurance Statistics (database)*

Table 2. Number of companies and employees

	2013	2014	2015	2016	2017	2018	2019	2020
2.1 Number of companies								
Life								
Domestic undertakings	11	11	11	4	3	2	2	2
Foreign controlled undertakings	7	7	7	2	2	1	1	1
Foreign companies (branches)	0	0	0	0	0	0	0	0
All undertakings	11	11	11	4	3	2	2	2
Non-life								
Domestic undertakings	28	24	24	24	22	20	19	18
Foreign controlled undertakings	7	6	5	7	6	5	5	4
Foreign companies (branches)	2	2	2	0	0	0	0	0
All undertakings	30	26	26	24	22	20	19	18
Composite								
Domestic undertakings	11	11	11	17	17	17	17	17
Foreign controlled undertakings	4	4	4	10	10	10	10	10
Foreign companies (branches)	0	0	0	0	0	0	0	0
All undertakings	11	11	11	17	17	17	17	17
Reinsurance								
Domestic undertakings	0	0	0	0	0	0	0	0
Foreign controlled undertakings	0	0	0	0	0	0	0	0
Foreign companies (branches)	0	0	0	0	0	0	0	0
All undertakings	0	0	0	0	0	0	0	0
Total								
Domestic undertakings	50	46	46	45	42	39	38	37
Foreign controlled undertakings	18	17	16	19	18	16	16	15
Foreign companies (branches)	2	2	2	0	0	0	0	..
All undertakings	52	48	48	45	42	39	38	37
2.2 Number of employees								
Insurance undertakings	..	..	..	..	..	..	..	..
Intermediaries	..	..	..	..	..	..	..	..
Total	..	..	..	..	..	..	..	..

.. Not available

Note: Detailed metadata at: *http://metalinks.oecd.org/ins/20220309/cf0c.*

Source: *OECD Insurance Statistics (database)*

HUNGARY

Table 1. Selected aggregates

Million HUF

	2013	2014	2015	2016	2017	2018	2019	2020
1.1 Insurance business written in the reporting country								
1.1.1 Insurance business, by ownership								
Gross premiums								
Domestic undertakings	801 210	833 664	835 428	885 781	956 006	1 017 779	1 149 523	1 204 157
Foreign controlled undertakings	763 286	796 332	788 248	835 272	897 699	953 320	1 075 690	1 133 759
Foreign companies (branches)	..	..	..	..	..	..	..	..
All undertakings	801 210	833 664	835 428	885 781	956 006	1 017 779	1 149 523	1 204 157
Premiums ceded								
Domestic undertakings	111 755	116 117	115 801	118 081	120 524	126 479	139 265	144 337
Foreign controlled undertakings	104 254	108 557	104 464	107 021	106 729	113 942	128 554	134 943
Foreign companies (branches)	..	..	..	..	..	..	..	..
All undertakings	111 755	116 117	115 801	118 081	120 524	126 479	139 265	144 337
Net written premiums								
Domestic undertakings	689 455	717 547	719 627	767 700	835 482	891 300	1 010 258	1 059 820
Foreign controlled undertakings	659 032	687 774	683 784	728 251	790 970	839 379	947 137	998 815
Foreign companies (branches)	..	..	..	..	..	..	..	..
All undertakings	689 455	717 547	719 627	767 700	835 482	891 300	1 010 258	1 059 820
1.1.2 Insurance business on foreign risks, gross premiums								
Life	3 358	3 533	4 234	4 317	4 630	5 116	5 343	5 895
Non-life	1 840	1 923	1 052	2 308	2 657	2 100	2 517	191
Composite	4 500	2 829	4 368	8 142	9 004	8 816	7 724	8 213
of which:								
Life	781	228	216	177	172	199	808	1 063
Non-life	3 719	2 602	4 152	7 965	8 832	8 617	6 916	7 150
Total	9 698	8 285	9 654	14 767	16 291	16 033	15 584	14 299
1.1.3 Life insurance payments, by class, gross premiums								
Annuities	2 975	3 147	3 479	..	..	..	..	..
Unit linked	286 919	282 059	266 857	..	..	..	..	..
Other life insurance	146 439	171 738	156 617	..	..	..	..	..
Total life insurance	436 333	456 944	426 953	438 718	460 791	470 685	509 033	530 350
of which: *Pension contracts*	19	..	10	..	..	..	..	..
1.1.4 Non-life insurance payments, by class, gross premiums								
Motor vehicle insurance	144 515	152 283	175 045	203 396	232 622	263 731	332 134	356 761
Marine, aviation and other transport insurance	661	793	879	142	172	201	354	276
Freight insurance	2 552	2 856	3 165	5 733	6 143	6 313	6 159	6 542
Fire and other property damage insurance	159 562	158 219	161 160	168 736	179 697	188 516	203 660	219 757
Pecuniary loss insurance	3 739	3 672	4 822	5 430	5 027	6 051	6 737	5 066
General liability insurance	20 074	21 904	23 585	21 274	24 525	26 379	27 271	28 248
Accident and health	25 922	28 358	29 859	22 389	24 898	31 241	36 837	26 958
of which: *Health*	8 559	9 558	8 668	4 250	5 557	8 909	11 827	10 598
Other non-life insurance	7 781	8 557	9 909	19 916	22 112	24 662	27 338	30 138
Treaty reinsurance	..	..	..	..	..	..	..	..
Total non-life insurance	364 806	376 641	408 424	447 017	495 197	547 094	640 490	673 746
1.2 Gross claims payments								
Life								
Domestic undertakings	139 994	130 633	150 198	155 047	172 359	156 899	185 600	178 105
Foreign controlled undertakings	129 594	121 318	139 595	147 047	160 787	146 733	171 402	165 880
Foreign companies (branches)	..	..	..	..	..	..	..	..
All undertakings	139 994	130 633	150 198	155 047	172 359	156 899	185 600	178 105
Non-life								
Domestic undertakings	25 692	27 416	30 571	34 112	32 258	34 114	32 143	34 180
Foreign controlled undertakings	12 611	13 973	14 605	16 056	12 917	12 308	11 636	12 726
Foreign companies (branches)	..	..	..	..	..	..	..	..
All undertakings	25 692	27 416	30 571	34 112	32 258	34 114	32 143	34 180
Composite								
Domestic undertakings	422 789	379 879	356 926	361 448	389 622	413 120	463 620	454 559
Foreign controlled undertakings	422 789	379 879	356 926	361 448	389 622	413 120	463 620	454 559
Foreign companies (branches)	..	..	..	..	..	..	..	..
All undertakings	422 789	379 879	356 926	361 448	389 622	413 120	463 620	454 559
of which:								
Life	242 802	212 244	180 098	176 820	185 216	205 734	230 696	215 006
Domestic undertakings	242 802	212 244	180 098	176 820	185 216	205 734	230 696	215 006
Foreign controlled undertakings	242 802	212 244	180 098	176 820	185 216	205 734	230 696	215 006
Foreign companies (branches)	..	..	..	..	..	..	..	..
All undertakings	242 802	212 244	180 098	176 820	185 216	205 734	230 696	215 006
Non-life	179 988	167 635	176 829	184 628	204 406	207 386	232 924	239 553
Domestic undertakings	179 988	167 635	176 829	184 628	204 406	207 386	232 924	239 553
Foreign controlled undertakings	179 988	167 635	176 829	184 628	204 406	207 386	232 924	239 553
Foreign companies (branches)	..	..	..	..	..	..	..	..
All undertakings	179 988	167 635	176 829	184 628	204 406	207 386	232 924	239 553
Total								
Domestic undertakings	588 475	537 928	537 695	550 607	594 239	604 133	681 363	666 843
Foreign controlled undertakings	564 995	515 171	511 127	524 551	563 326	572 162	646 658	633 164
Foreign companies (branches)	..	..	..	..	..	..	..	..
All undertakings	588 475	537 928	537 695	550 607	594 239	604 133	681 363	666 843

Table 1. Selected aggregates *(cont.)*

Million HUF

	2013	2014	2015	2016	2017	2018	2019	2020
1.3 Commissions								
Life								
Domestic undertakings	14 900	14 024	13 526	16 531	17 513	15 243	16 536	17 362
Foreign controlled undertakings	11 559	11 559	11 089	14 360	15 017	12 599	13 254	14 687
Foreign companies (branches)	..	..	..	..	..	..	..	..
All undertakings	14 900	14 024	13 526	16 531	17 513	15 243	16 536	17 362
Non-life								
Domestic undertakings	7 349	7 243	9 161	10 325	13 383	14 338	15 392	12 260
Foreign controlled undertakings	4 813	4 948	5 986	5 650	6 550	6 809	7 114	5 650
Foreign companies (branches)	..	..	..	..	..	..	..	..
All undertakings	7 349	7 243	9 161	10 325	13 383	14 338	15 392	12 260
Composite								
Domestic undertakings	75 007	72 592	79 086	108 207	114 286	123 934	138 745	149 512
Foreign controlled undertakings	75 007	72 592	79 086	108 207	114 286	123 934	138 745	149 512
Foreign companies (branches)	..	..	..	..	..	..	..	..
All undertakings	75 007	72 592	79 086	108 207	114 286	123 934	138 745	149 512
of which:								
Life	29 847	30 235	29 116	39 083	38 017	36 194	39 422	42 535
Domestic undertakings	29 847	30 235	29 116	39 083	38 017	36 194	39 422	42 535
Foreign controlled undertakings	29 847	30 235	29 116	39 083	38 017	36 194	39 422	42 535
Foreign companies (branches)	..	..	..	..	..	..	..	..
All undertakings	29 847	30 235	29 116	39 083	38 017	36 194	39 422	42 535
Non-life	45 160	42 357	49 970	69 124	76 269	87 740	99 323	106 977
Domestic undertakings	45 160	42 357	49 970	69 124	76 269	87 740	99 323	106 977
Foreign controlled undertakings	45 160	42 357	49 970	69 124	76 269	87 740	99 323	106 977
Foreign companies (branches)	..	..	..	..	..	..	..	..
All undertakings	45 160	42 357	49 970	69 124	76 269	87 740	99 323	106 977
Total								
Domestic undertakings	97 256	93 859	101 773	135 063	145 182	153 515	170 673	179 134
Foreign controlled undertakings	91 380	89 099	96 162	128 218	135 853	143 341	159 113	169 848
Foreign companies (branches)	..	..	..	..	..	..	..	..
All undertakings	97 256	93 859	101 773	135 063	145 182	153 515	170 673	179 134
1.4 Gross operating expenses								
Life								
Domestic undertakings	32 595	35 399	32 897	34 946	34 955	32 702	34 429	33 133
Foreign controlled undertakings	27 473	30 053	29 279	31 818	30 865	28 684	31 147	30 457
Foreign companies (branches)	..	..	..	..	..	..	..	..
All undertakings	32 595	35 399	32 897	34 946	34 955	32 702	34 429	33 133
Non-life								
Domestic undertakings	17 413	17 638	20 337	21 977	21 528	19 122	24 892	22 813
Foreign controlled undertakings	11 126	11 890	14 690	13 298	10 965	11 520	12 934	12 482
Foreign companies (branches)	..	..	..	..	..	..	..	..
All undertakings	17 413	17 638	20 337	21 977	21 528	19 122	24 892	22 813
Composite								
Domestic undertakings	172 680	181 142	167 842	176 431	185 944	203 460	226 949	239 438
Foreign controlled undertakings	172 680	181 142	167 842	176 431	185 944	203 460	226 949	239 438
Foreign companies (branches)	..	..	..	..	..	..	..	..
All undertakings	172 680	181 142	167 842	176 431	185 944	203 460	226 949	239 438
of which:								
Life	56 633	70 675	55 349	56 859	50 779	55 001	63 365	63 028
Domestic undertakings	56 633	70 675	55 349	56 859	50 779	55 001	63 365	63 028
Foreign controlled undertakings	56 633	70 675	55 349	56 859	50 779	55 001	63 365	63 028
Foreign companies (branches)	..	..	..	..	..	..	..	..
All undertakings	56 633	70 675	55 349	56 859	50 779	55 001	63 365	63 028
Non-life	116 047	110 467	112 493	119 571	135 165	148 459	163 584	176 410
Domestic undertakings	116 047	110 467	112 493	119 571	135 165	148 459	163 584	176 410
Foreign controlled undertakings	116 047	110 467	112 493	119 571	135 165	148 459	163 584	176 410
Foreign companies (branches)	..	..	..	..	..	..	..	..
All undertakings	116 047	110 467	112 493	119 571	135 165	148 459	163 584	176 410
Total								
Domestic undertakings	222 687	234 179	221 076	233 354	242 427	255 284	286 269	295 384
Foreign controlled undertakings	211 279	223 085	211 811	221 547	227 774	243 664	271 030	282 377
Foreign companies (branches)	..	..	..	..	..	..	..	..
All undertakings	222 687	234 179	221 076	233 354	242 427	255 284	286 269	295 384

Table 1. Selected aggregates *(cont.)*

Million HUF

	2013	2014	2015	2016	2017	2018	2019	2020
1.5 Insurance business written abroad by branches, gross premiums								
Life								
Branches and agencies	..	..	..	..	..	..	..	..
Subsidaries	..	..	..	..	..	..	..	..
Total	..	..	..	..	..	..	..	..
Non-life								
Branches and agencies	..	..	..	..	..	..	..	..
Subsidaries	..	..	..	..	..	..	..	..
Total	..	..	..	..	..	..	..	..
Composite								
Branches and agencies	..	..	..	..	..	..	..	..
Subsidaries	..	..	..	..	..	..	..	..
Total	..	..	..	..	..	..	..	..
of which:								
Life	..	..	..	..	..	..	..	..
Branches and agencies	..	..	..	..	..	..	..	..
Subsidaries	..	..	..	..	..	..	..	..
Total	..	..	..	..	..	..	..	..
Non-life	..	..	..	..	..	..	..	..
Branches and agencies	..	..	..	..	..	..	..	..
Subsidaries	..	..	..	..	..	..	..	..
Total	..	..	..	..	..	..	..	..
Total								
Branches and agencies	..	..	..	..	..	..	..	..
Subsidaries	..	..	..	..	..	..	..	..
Total	..	..	..	..	..	..	..	..

.. Not available

Note: Detailed metadata at: *http://metalinks.oecd.org/ins/20220309/a85a.*

Source: *OECD Insurance Statistics (database)*

HUNGARY

Table 2. Number of companies and employees

	2013	2014	2015	2016	2017	2018	2019	2020
2.1 Number of companies								
Life								
Domestic undertakings	10	10	10	8	7	6	5	5
Foreign controlled undertakings	7	7	7	7	6	5	4	4
Foreign companies (branches)	..	..	0	0	0	0	0	0
All undertakings	10	10	10	8	7	6	5	5
Non-life								
Domestic undertakings	12	12	11	10	9	9	9	9
Foreign controlled undertakings	6	6	6	6	5	5	5	5
Foreign companies (branches)	14	14	13	14	13	12	11	12
All undertakings	26	26	24	24	22	21	20	21
Composite								
Domestic undertakings	10	10	9	9	9	8	8	8
Foreign controlled undertakings	10	10	9	9	9	8	8	8
Foreign companies (branches)	1	1	2	2	2	2	1	1
All undertakings	11	11	11	11	11	10	9	9
Reinsurance								
Domestic undertakings	..	..	..	..	..	..	..	..
Foreign controlled undertakings	..	..	..	..	..	..	..	..
Foreign companies (branches)	..	..	..	..	..	..	..	..
All undertakings	..	..	..	..	..	..	..	..
Total								
Domestic undertakings	32	32	30	27	25	23	22	22
Foreign controlled undertakings	23	23	22	22	20	18	17	17
Foreign companies (branches)	15	15	15	16	15	14	12	13
All undertakings	47	47	45	43	40	37	34	35
2.2 Number of employees								
Insurance undertakings	9 363	9 229	8 728	8 542	8 133	11 116	8 858	7 047
Intermediaries	13 083	12 768	11 392	9 822	12 287	7 791	13 186	11 553
Total	22 445	21 997	20 121	18 364	20 420	18 907	22 044	18 600

.. Not available

Note: Detailed metadata at: *http://metalinks.oecd.org/ins/20220309/a85a*.

Source: *OECD Insurance Statistics (database)*

ICELAND

Table 1. Selected aggregates

Million ISK

	2013	2014	2015	2016	2017	2018	2019	2020
1.1 Insurance business written in the reporting country								
1.1.1 Insurance business, by ownership								
Gross premiums								
Domestic undertakings	51 142	51 849	55 346	58 777	65 274	70 561	74 978	73 768
Foreign controlled undertakings	5 088	5 401	6 010	..	..	..	..	..
Foreign companies (branches)	..	..	..	..	..	..	..	..
All undertakings	51 142	51 849	55 346	58 777	65 274	70 561	74 978	73 768
Premiums ceded								
Domestic undertakings	3 136	2 918	2 882	2 725	2 613	2 869	2 802	3 009
Foreign controlled undertakings	310	310	272	..	..	..	..	..
Foreign companies (branches)	..	..	..	..	..	..	..	..
All undertakings	3 136	2 918	2 882	2 725	2 613	2 869	2 802	3 009
Net written premiums								
Domestic undertakings	48 005	48 931	52 465	56 052	62 662	67 693	72 176	70 759
Foreign controlled undertakings	4 779	5 091	5 737	..	..	..	..	..
Foreign companies (branches)	..	..	..	..	..	..	..	..
All undertakings	48 005	48 931	52 465	56 052	62 662	67 693	72 176	70 759
1.1.2 Insurance business on foreign risks, gross premiums								
Life	0	0	0	0	0	0	0	..
Non-life	2 156	2 563	3 018	1 010	1 737	3 444	1 735	..
Composite total	..	..	..	..	..	..	..	..
Total	2 156	2 563	3 018	1 010	1 737	3 444	1 735	..
1.1.3 Life insurance payments, by class, gross premiums								
Annuities	61	111	473	..	..	..	..	..
Unit linked	86	87	91	20	32	23	17	15
Other life insurance	3 913	4 042	4 087	5 141	5 789	5 815	6 199	6 587
Total life insurance	4 061	4 240	4 651	5 161	5 821	5 837	6 217	6 603
of which: *Pension contracts*	0	0	0	0	0	0	0	0
1.1.4 Non-life insurance payments, by class, gross premiums								
Motor vehicle insurance	21 522	22 084	23 952	28 398	33 127	35 842	38 310	36 944
Marine, aviation and other transport insurance	3 372	3 419	3 690	3 631	3 139	3 251	3 130	2 680
Freight insurance	638	646	751	0	0	0	0	0
Fire and other property damage insurance	13 816	13 903	13 911	12 484	13 048	14 472	15 552	15 679
Pecuniary loss insurance	45	23	27	33	26	59	70	106
General liability insurance	2 556	2 565	2 672	3 078	3 561	3 974	4 163	4 222
Accident and health	5 102	4 947	5 646	5 960	6 509	7 093	7 507	7 507
of which: *Health*	..	..	..	..	..	..	..	..
Other non-life insurance	30	22	42	32	42	33	29	28
Treaty reinsurance	0	0	0	0	0	0	0	0
Total non-life insurance	47 081	47 608	50 690	53 616	59 453	64 724	68 761	67 165
1.2 Gross claims payments								
Life								
Domestic undertakings	1 381	1 529	1 325	1 690	1 755	1 752	2 380	2 326
Foreign controlled undertakings	47	30	58	..	..	..	..	..
Foreign companies (branches)	..	..	..	..	..	..	..	..
All undertakings	1 381	1 529	1 325	1 690	1 755	1 752	2 380	2 326
Non-life								
Domestic undertakings	31 417	32 554	36 082	41 655	43 781	51 533	52 944	52 454
Foreign controlled undertakings	3 412	3 520	4 169	..	..	..	..	..
Foreign companies (branches)	..	..	..	..	..	..	..	..
All undertakings	31 417	32 554	36 082	41 655	43 781	51 533	52 944	52 454
Composite, all undertakings	..	..	..	..	..	..	..	..
Total								
Domestic undertakings	32 798	34 083	37 407	43 345	45 536	53 285	55 324	54 780
Foreign controlled undertakings	3 459	3 550	4 227	..	..	..	..	..
Foreign companies (branches)	..	..	..	..	..	..	..	..
All undertakings	32 798	34 083	37 407	43 345	45 536	53 285	55 324	54 780
1.3 Commissions								
Life								
Domestic undertakings	66	118	90	..	..	..	..	..
Foreign controlled undertakings	20	42	3	..	..	..	..	..
Foreign companies (branches)	..	..	..	..	..	..	..	..
All undertakings	66	118	90	..	..	..	..	..
Non-life								
Domestic undertakings	102	39	36	..	..	..	..	..
Foreign controlled undertakings	0	0	0	..	..	..	..	..
Foreign companies (branches)	..	..	..	..	..	..	..	..
All undertakings	102	39	36	..	..	..	..	..
Composite, all undertakings	..	..	..	..	..	..	..	..
Total								
Domestic undertakings	168	157	126	..	..	..	..	..
Foreign controlled undertakings	20	42	3	..	..	..	..	..
Foreign companies (branches)	..	..	..	..	..	..	..	..
All undertakings	168	157	126	..	..	..	..	..

Table 1. Selected aggregates *(cont.)*

Million ISK

	2013	2014	2015	2016	2017	2018	2019	2020
1.4 Gross operating expenses								
Life								
Domestic undertakings	1 384	1 098	1 498	1 231	1 528	1 394	1 411	1 472
Foreign controlled undertakings	90	18	161	..	..	..	..	..
Foreign companies (branches)	..	..	..	..	..	..	..	..
All undertakings	1 384	1 098	1 498	1 231	1 528	1 394	1 411	1 472
Non-life								
Domestic undertakings	9 860	9 680	4 314	6 931	7 422	11 994	12 605	12 414
Foreign controlled undertakings	1 084	1 086	1 225	..	..	..	..	..
Foreign companies (branches)	..	..	..	..	..	..	..	..
All undertakings	9 860	9 680	4 314	6 931	7 422	12 026	12 605	12 414
Composite, all undertakings	..	..	..	..	..	..	..	..
Total								
Domestic undertakings	11 244	10 778	5 812	8 162	8 950	13 389	14 016	13 886
Foreign controlled undertakings	1 173	1 104	1 387	..	..	..	..	..
Foreign companies (branches)	..	..	..	..	..	..	..	..
All undertakings	11 244	10 778	5 812	8 162	8 950	13 421	14 016	13 886
1.5 Insurance business written abroad by branches, gross premiums								
Life								
Branches and agencies	..	..	..	..	..	..	..	..
Subsidaries	..	..	..	..	..	..	..	..
Total	..	..	..	..	..	..	..	..
Non-life								
Branches and agencies	..	..	..	..	..	..	..	..
Subsidaries	..	..	..	..	..	..	..	..
Total	..	..	..	..	..	..	..	..
Composite total	..	..	..	..	..	..	..	..
Total								
Branches and agencies	..	..	..	..	..	..	..	..
Subsidaries	..	..	..	..	..	..	..	..
Total	..	..	..	..	..	..	..	..

.. Not available

Note: Detailed metadata at: *http://metalinks.oecd.org/ins/20220309/ba93.*

Source: *OECD Insurance Statistics (database)*

Table 2. Number of companies and employees

	2013	2014	2015	2016	2017	2018	2019	2020
2.1 Number of companies								
Life								
Domestic undertakings	5	5	5	4	4	4	4	4
Foreign controlled undertakings	1	1	1	..	..	..	..	0
Foreign companies (branches)	1	1	1	..	..	..	..	0
All undertakings	6	6	6	4	4	4	4	4
Non-life								
Domestic undertakings	5	5	5	4	4	4	4	4
Foreign controlled undertakings	1	1	1	..	..	..	..	0
Foreign companies (branches)	1	1	1	..	..	..	..	0
All undertakings	6	6	6	4	4	4	4	4
Composite, all undertakings	**0**	**0**	**0**	**0**	**0**	**0**	**0**	**0**
Reinsurance								
Domestic undertakings	2	2	2	0	0	0	0	0
Foreign controlled undertakings	..	..	..	..	..	..	..	0
Foreign companies (branches)	..	..	..	..	..	..	..	0
All undertakings	2	2	2	0	0	0	0	0
Total								
Domestic undertakings	12	12	12	8	8	8	8	8
Foreign controlled undertakings	2	2	2	0	0	0	0	0
Foreign companies (branches)	2	2	2	0	0	0	0	0
All undertakings	14	14	14	8	8	8	8	8
2.2 Number of employees								
Insurance undertakings	614	..	582	..	..	..	..	..
Intermediaries	..	592	..	..	..	..	..	..
Total	614	592	582	..	..	..	..	..

.. Not available

Note: Detailed metadata at: *http://metalinks.oecd.org/ins/20220309/ba93*.

Source: *OECD Insurance Statistics (database)*

IRELAND

Table 1. Selected aggregates

Million EUR

	2013	2014	2015	2016	2017	2018	2019	2020
1.1 Insurance business written in the reporting country								
1.1.1 Insurance business, by ownership								
Gross premiums								
Domestic undertakings	31 818	36 377	40 340	48 949	40 281	36 998	40 282	39 402
Foreign controlled undertakings	..	..	..	..	..	..	..	..
Foreign companies (branches)	2 301	3 184	3 645	..	3 821	3 756	4 283	..
All undertakings	34 119	39 561	43 985	48 949	44 102	40 754	44 565	39 402
Premiums ceded								
Domestic undertakings	3 908	3 891	4 933	9 985	..	..	..	..
Foreign controlled undertakings	..	..	..	..	..	..	..	..
Foreign companies (branches)	268	371	359	..	..	..	..	..
All undertakings	4 176	4 262	5 292	9 985	..	..	..	..
Net written premiums								
Domestic undertakings	27 910	32 486	35 407	38 964	..	..	..	..
Foreign controlled undertakings	..	..	..	..	..	..	..	..
Foreign companies (branches)	2 033	2 813	3 286	..	..	..	..	..
All undertakings	29 943	35 299	38 693	38 964	..	..	..	..
1.1.2 Insurance business on foreign risks, gross premiums								
Life	16 125	21 410	23 192	..	19 774	16 644	16 606	15 156
Non-life	3 826	3 960	4 263	..	2 277	2 671	3 032	3 002
Composite	..	..	..	..	6	191	180	..
of which:								
Life	..	..	..	..	..	..	..	..
Non-life	..	..	..	..	..	..	..	..
Total	19 951	25 370	27 455	..	22 057	19 506	19 818	18 158
1.1.3 Life insurance payments, by class, gross premiums								
Annuities	..	..	..	0	0	0	0	..
Unit linked	..	..	..	28 838	30 737	26 568	27 840	26 638
Other life insurance	..	..	..	4 477	4 279	4 102	4 135	3 469
Total life insurance	27 207	32 171	34 587	33 315	35 016	30 670	31 975	30 107
of which: *Pension contracts*	..	..	..	..	..	..	..	..
1.1.4 Non-life insurance payments, by class, gross premiums								
Motor vehicle insurance	1 435	1 599	1 795	3 905	2 086	2 067	2 900	2 072
Marine, aviation and other transport insurance	183	143	163	421	144	219	292	549
Freight insurance	..	..	..	0	0	..	0	..
Fire and other property damage insurance	1 763	1 758	1 768	4 023	1 401	1 503	2 156	1 817
Pecuniary loss insurance	105	124	92	332	830	848	1 152	826
General liability insurance	1 127	1 301	1 400	2 887	1 288	1 296	1 967	1 379
Accident and health	1 171	1 235	2 750	1 935	2 396	2 323	2 575	2 563
of which: *Health*	..	..	..	..	..	..	..	..
Other non-life insurance	504	494	585	1 159	158	217	139	22
Treaty reinsurance	330	373	414	746	217	..	0	0
Total non-life insurance	6 618	7 027	8 967	15 408	8 520	8 473	11 181	9 228
1.2 Gross claims payments								
Life								
Domestic undertakings	28 263	27 434	28 474	32 280	26 726	25 196	26 254	27 596
Foreign controlled undertakings	..	..	..	..	..	..	..	..
Foreign companies (branches)	1 235	1 114	1 356	..	2 435	2 052	836	..
All undertakings	29 498	28 548	29 830	32 280	29 161	27 248	27 090	27 596
Non-life								
Domestic undertakings	4 369	3 853	5 343	15 941	8 482	8 283	9 604	11 850
Foreign controlled undertakings	..	..	..	..	..	..	..	..
Foreign companies (branches)	677	1 177	1 179	..	725	871	1 714	..
All undertakings	5 046	5 030	6 522	15 941	9 207	9 154	11 318	11 850
Composite								
Domestic undertakings	..	..	..	..	..	..	..	..
Foreign controlled undertakings	..	..	..	..	..	..	..	..
Foreign companies (branches)	..	..	..	..	357	983	974	..
All undertakings	..	..	..	..	357	983	974	..
of which:								
Life	..	..	..	..	..	..	..	..
Domestic undertakings	..	..	..	..	..	..	..	..
Foreign controlled undertakings	..	..	..	..	..	..	..	..
Foreign companies (branches)	..	..	..	..	..	..	..	..
All undertakings	..	..	..	..	..	..	..	..
Non-life	..	..	..	..	..	..	..	..
Domestic undertakings	..	..	..	..	..	..	..	..
Foreign controlled undertakings	..	..	..	..	..	..	..	..
Foreign companies (branches)	..	..	..	..	..	..	..	..
All undertakings	..	..	..	..	..	..	..	..
Total								
Domestic undertakings	32 632	31 287	33 817	48 221	35 208	33 479	35 858	39 446
Foreign controlled undertakings	..	..	..	..	..	..	..	..
Foreign companies (branches)	1 912	2 291	2 535	..	3 517	3 906	3 524	..
All undertakings	34 544	33 578	36 352	48 221	38 725	37 385	39 382	39 446

Table 1. Selected aggregates *(cont.)*

Million EUR

	2013	2014	2015	2016	2017	2018	2019	2020
1.3 Commissions								
Life								
Domestic undertakings	1 844	2 051	2 281	2 198	1 517	1 625	1 497	1 526
Foreign controlled undertakings	..	..	..	..	..	..	..	..
Foreign companies (branches)	43	64	59	..	94	44	-10	..
All undertakings	1 887	2 115	2 340	2 198	1 611	1 669	1 487	1 526
Non-life								
Domestic undertakings	737	764	896	2 292	957	1 012	1 187	1 343
Foreign controlled undertakings	..	..	..	..	..	..	..	..
Foreign companies (branches)	130	248	299	..	194	221	227	..
All undertakings	867	1 012	1 195	2 292	1 511	1 233	1 414	1 343
Composite								
Domestic undertakings	..	..	..	..	..	..	..	..
Foreign controlled undertakings	..	..	..	..	..	..	..	..
Foreign companies (branches)	..	..	..	..	80	110	94	..
All undertakings	..	..	..	..	80	110	94	..
of which:								
Life	..	..	..	..	..	..	..	..
Domestic undertakings	..	..	..	..	..	..	..	..
Foreign controlled undertakings	..	..	..	..	..	..	..	..
Foreign companies (branches)	..	..	..	..	..	..	..	..
All undertakings	..	..	..	..	..	..	..	..
Non-life	..	..	..	..	..	..	..	..
Domestic undertakings	..	..	..	..	..	..	..	..
Foreign controlled undertakings	..	..	..	..	..	..	..	..
Foreign companies (branches)	..	..	..	..	..	..	..	..
All undertakings	..	..	..	..	..	..	..	..
Total								
Domestic undertakings	2 581	2 815	3 177	4 490	2 474	2 637	2 684	2 869
Foreign controlled undertakings	..	..	..	..	..	..	..	..
Foreign companies (branches)	173	312	358	..	368	375	311	..
All undertakings	2 754	3 127	3 535	4 490	3 202	3 012	2 995	2 869
1.4 Gross operating expenses								
Life								
Domestic undertakings	1 346	1 429	1 437	1 319	444	..	..	..
Foreign controlled undertakings	..	..	..	..	..	..	..	..
Foreign companies (branches)	154	657	158	..	..	..	..	..
All undertakings	1 500	2 086	1 595	1 319	444	..	..	..
Non-life								
Domestic undertakings	650	589	484	1 873	932	..	..	..
Foreign controlled undertakings	..	..	..	..	..	..	..	..
Foreign companies (branches)	159	223	224	..	..	..	..	..
All undertakings	809	812	708	1 873	932	..	..	..
Composite								
Domestic undertakings	..	..	..	..	..	..	..	..
Foreign controlled undertakings	..	..	..	..	..	..	..	..
Foreign companies (branches)	..	..	..	..	..	..	..	..
All undertakings	..	..	..	..	..	..	..	..
of which:								
Life	..	..	..	..	..	..	..	..
Domestic undertakings	..	..	..	..	..	..	..	..
Foreign controlled undertakings	..	..	..	..	..	..	..	..
Foreign companies (branches)	..	..	..	..	..	..	..	..
All undertakings	..	..	..	..	..	..	..	..
Non-life	..	..	..	..	..	..	..	..
Domestic undertakings	..	..	..	..	..	..	..	..
Foreign controlled undertakings	..	..	..	..	..	..	..	..
Foreign companies (branches)	..	..	..	..	..	..	..	..
All undertakings	..	..	..	..	..	..	..	..
Total								
Domestic undertakings	1 996	2 018	1 921	3 192	1 376	..	..	..
Foreign controlled undertakings	..	..	..	..	..	..	..	..
Foreign companies (branches)	313	880	382	..	..	..	..	..
All undertakings	2 309	2 898	2 303	3 192	1 376	..	..	..

Table 1. Selected aggregates *(cont.)*

Million EUR

	2013	2014	2015	2016	2017	2018	2019	2020
1.5 Insurance business written abroad by branches, gross premiums								
Life								
Branches and agencies	5 563	5 970	6 234	..	6 438	5 266	6 513	7 182
Subsidaries	..	..	..	..	..	..	..	..
Total	5 563	5 970	6 234	..	6 438	5 266	6 513	7 182
Non-life								
Branches and agencies	9 228	9 640	9 835	..	8 739	9 029	11 204	15 553
Subsidaries	..	..	..	..	..	..	..	..
Total	9 228	9 640	9 835	..	8 739	9 029	11 204	15 553
Composite								
Branches and agencies	..	..	..	..	..	..	..	..
Subsidaries	..	..	..	..	..	..	..	..
Total	..	..	..	..	..	..	..	..
of which:								
Life	..	..	..	..	..	..	..	..
Branches and agencies	..	..	..	..	..	..	..	..
Subsidaries	..	..	..	..	..	..	..	..
Total	..	..	..	..	..	..	..	..
Non-life	..	..	..	..	..	..	..	..
Branches and agencies	..	..	..	..	..	..	..	..
Subsidaries	..	..	..	..	..	..	..	..
Total	..	..	..	..	..	..	..	..
Total								
Branches and agencies	14 791	15 610	16 069	..	15 177	14 295	17 717	22 735
Subsidaries	..	..	..	..	..	..	..	..
Total	14 791	15 610	16 069	..	15 177	14 295	17 717	22 735

.. Not available

Note: Detailed metadata at: *http://metalinks.oecd.org/ins/20220309/1845.*

Source: *OECD Insurance Statistics (database)*

Table 2. Number of companies and employees

	2013	2014	2015	2016	2017	2018	2019	2020
2.1 Number of companies								
Life								
Domestic undertakings	53	51	48	44	45	42	43	40
Foreign controlled undertakings	..	..	..	0	0	..	..	..
Foreign companies (branches)	8	8	11	11	12	13	15	..
All undertakings	61	59	59	55	57	55	58	..
Non-life								
Domestic undertakings	104	102	101	90	99	95	95	92
Foreign controlled undertakings	..	..	..	0	0	..	..	..
Foreign companies (branches)	27	30	32	31	30	38	33	..
All undertakings	131	132	133	121	129	133	128	..
Composite								
Domestic undertakings	0	0	0	0	1	0	..	..
Foreign controlled undertakings	0	0	0	0	0	..	..	..
Foreign companies (branches)	0	0	0	0	0	0	..	..
All undertakings	0	0	0	0	1	0	..	..
Reinsurance								
Domestic undertakings	77	75	67	61	64	63	59	59
Foreign controlled undertakings	..	..	..	0	0	..	..	..
Foreign companies (branches)	0	0	0	0	0	0	..	..
All undertakings	77	75	67	61	64	63	59	..
Total								
Domestic undertakings	234	228	216	196	209	200	197	..
Foreign controlled undertakings	..	..	..	0	0	..	..	..
Foreign companies (branches)	35	38	43	42	42	51	48	..
All undertakings	269	266	259	238	251	251	245	..
2.2 Number of employees								
Insurance undertakings	8 887	8 095	9 404	..	..	..	..	..
Intermediaries	..	..	..	..	..	..	..	..
Total	8 887	..	..	..	..	..	..	..

.. Not available

Note: Detailed metadata at: *http://metalinks.oecd.org/ins/20220309/1845*.

Source: *OECD Insurance Statistics (database)*

ISRAEL

Table 1. Selected aggregates

Million ILS

	2013	2014	2015	2016	2017	2018	2019	2020
1.1 Insurance business written in the reporting country								
1.1.1 Insurance business, by ownership								
Gross premiums								
Domestic undertakings	50 339	51 400	54 869	58 153	62 730	66 640	68 881	67 171
Foreign controlled undertakings	889	953	1 135	1 165	1 234	1 296	12 576	11 659
Foreign companies (branches)	..	..	..	..	..	..	..	..
All undertakings	50 339	51 400	54 869	58 153	62 730	66 640	68 881	67 171
Premiums ceded								
Domestic undertakings	6 418	5 934	6 356	8 756	8 468	9 454	10 098	10 693
Foreign controlled undertakings	164	162	232	225	228	249	1 646	1 595
Foreign companies (branches)	..	..	..	..	..	..	..	..
All undertakings	6 418	5 934	6 356	8 756	8 468	9 454	10 098	10 693
Net written premiums								
Domestic undertakings	43 921	45 466	48 512	49 398	54 263	57 186	58 782	56 479
Foreign controlled undertakings	726	791	903	940	1 006	1 047	10 930	10 064
Foreign companies (branches)	..	..	..	..	..	..	..	..
All undertakings	43 921	45 466	48 512	49 398	54 263	57 186	58 782	56 479
1.1.2 Insurance business on foreign risks, gross premiums								
Life	..	..	..	..	..	..	..	..
Non-life	..	..	..	..	..	..	..	..
Composite	..	..	..	..	..	..	..	..
of which:								
Life	..	..	..	..	..	..	..	..
Non-life	..	..	..	..	..	..	..	..
Total	..	..	..	..	..	..	..	..
1.1.3 Life insurance payments, by class, gross premiums								
Annuities	1 361	1 194	1 084	1 273	1 125	1 118	1 108	891
Unit linked	18 557	18 236	20 266	20 897	23 867	25 433	26 378	24 759
Other life insurance	6 709	7 141	8 066	8 492	8 730	9 412	10 352	10 654
Total life insurance	26 627	26 571	29 416	30 662	33 722	35 963	37 838	36 304
of which: *Pension contracts*	..	..	..	..	..	..	..	..
1.1.4 Non-life insurance payments, by class, gross premiums								
Motor vehicle insurance	11 040	11 439	11 775	13 053	13 396	14 129	13 976	13 708
Marine, aviation and other transport insurance	38	38	39	38	36	40	43	45
Freight insurance	169	170	174	176	187	174	173	174
Fire and other property damage insurance	4 283	4 292	4 238	4 375	4 481	4 549	4 720	4 914
Pecuniary loss insurance	284	278	307	335	348	480	359	390
General liability insurance	2 575	2 697	2 814	2 917	3 094	3 250	3 402	3 627
Accident and health	4 869	5 425	5 678	6 086	6 961	7 548	7 826	7 482
of which: *Health*	3 859	4 189	4 203	4 448	5 144	5 614	5 908	5 587
Other non-life insurance	452	492	426	502	506	506	545	527
Treaty reinsurance	..	0	0	0	..	0	0	0
Total non-life insurance	23 712	24 830	25 452	27 483	29 009	30 676	31 043	30 867
1.2 Gross claims payments								
Life								
Domestic undertakings	0	3	6	8	.. c	..	..	..
Foreign controlled undertakings	..	..	..	0	..	..	..	..
Foreign companies (branches)	..	..	..	..	..	..	..	..
All undertakings	0	3	6	8	.. c	..	..	..
Non-life								
Domestic undertakings	2 013	2 470	2 589	2 180	2 124	2 189	2 368	2 835
Foreign controlled undertakings	..	..	39	72	22	30	36	60
Foreign companies (branches)	..	..	..	..	..	..	..	..
All undertakings	2 013	2 470	2 589	2 180	2 124	2 189	2 368	2 835
Composite								
Domestic undertakings	24 594	27 644	30 828	31 879	35 461	36 580	40 374	43 454
Foreign controlled undertakings	280	462	640	538	0	578	6 432	7 179
Foreign companies (branches)	..	..	..	..	..	..	..	..
All undertakings	24 594	27 644	30 828	31 879	35 461	36 580	40 374	43 454
of which:								
Life	12 644	13 825	15 363	16 243	18 411	19 489	23 113	26 215
Domestic undertakings	12 644	13 825	15 363	16 243	18 411	19 489	23 113	26 215
Foreign controlled undertakings	18	26	39	36	42	50	3 257	4 035
Foreign companies (branches)	..	..	..	..	..	..	..	..
All undertakings	12 644	13 825	15 363	16 243	18 411	19 489	23 113	26 215
Non-life	11 949	13 819	15 465	15 636	17 051	17 091	17 261	17 239
Domestic undertakings	11 949	13 819	15 465	15 636	17 051	17 091	17 261	17 239
Foreign controlled undertakings	262	436	600	502	575	528	3 175	3 144
Foreign companies (branches)	..	..	..	..	..	..	..	..
All undertakings	11 949	13 819	15 465	15 636	17 051	17 091	17 261	17 239
Total								
Domestic undertakings	26 607	30 117	33 422	34 067	37 598	38 769	42 742	46 289
Foreign controlled undertakings	280	462	679	609	22	608	6 469	7 239
Foreign companies (branches)	..	..	..	..	..	..	..	..
All undertakings	26 607	30 117	33 422	34 067	37 598	38 769	42 742	46 289

Table 1. Selected aggregates *(cont.)*

Million ILS

	2013	2014	2015	2016	2017	2018	2019	2020
1.3 Commissions								
Life								
Domestic undertakings	0	6	15	19	.. c	..	..	..
Foreign controlled undertakings	..	..	..	0	..	..	..	..
Foreign companies (branches)	..	..	..	..	..	..	..	..
All undertakings	0	6	15	19	.. c	..	..	..
Non-life								
Domestic undertakings	248	281	317	291	341	358	347	389
Foreign controlled undertakings	..	..	0	0	0	0	0	0
Foreign companies (branches)	..	..	..	..	..	..	..	..
All undertakings	248	281	317	291	341	358	347	389
Composite								
Domestic undertakings	5 688	5 940	6 296	6 709	7 109	7 592	7 630	7 109
Foreign controlled undertakings	39	..	42	40	..	38	1 429	1 211
Foreign companies (branches)	..	..	..	..	..	..	..	..
All undertakings	5 688	5 940	6 296	6 709	7 109	7 592	7 630	7 109
of which:								
Life	2 571	2 639	2 912	3 097	3 215	3 531	3 507	3 283
Domestic undertakings	2 571	2 639	2 912	3 097	3 215	3 531	3 507	3 283
Foreign controlled undertakings	1	1	1	1	1	1	461	429
Foreign companies (branches)	..	..	..	..	..	..	..	..
All undertakings	2 571	2 639	2 912	3 097	3 215	3 531	3 507	3 283
Non-life	3 118	3 300	3 384	3 612	3 893	4 061	4 123	3 826
Domestic undertakings	3 118	3 300	3 384	3 612	3 893	4 061	4 123	3 826
Foreign controlled undertakings	38	38	41	39	37	37	968	782
Foreign companies (branches)	..	..	..	..	..	..	..	..
All undertakings	3 118	3 300	3 384	3 612	3 893	4 061	4 123	3 826
Total								
Domestic undertakings	5 936	6 226	6 628	7 019	7 464	7 950	7 976	7 498
Foreign controlled undertakings	39	..	42	40	0	38	1 429	1 211
Foreign companies (branches)	..	..	..	..	..	..	..	..
All undertakings	5 936	6 226	6 628	7 019	7 464	7 950	7 976	7 498
1.4 Gross operating expenses								
Life								
Domestic undertakings	1	10	32	32	.. c	..	..	..
Foreign controlled undertakings	..	..	..	0	..	..	..	..
Foreign companies (branches)	..	..	..	..	..	..	..	..
All undertakings	1	10	32	32	.. c	..	..	..
Non-life								
Domestic undertakings	449	322	402	380	417	32	33	647
Foreign controlled undertakings	..	..	30	29	33	36	37	36
Foreign companies (branches)	..	..	..	..	..	..	..	..
All undertakings	449	322	402	380	417	32	33	647
Composite								
Domestic undertakings	5 285	5 169	5 719	6 033	6 504	13 992	6 773	6 816
Foreign controlled undertakings	272	276	282	275	278	289	1 365	1 443
Foreign companies (branches)	..	..	..	..	..	..	..	..
All undertakings	5 285	5 169	5 719	6 033	6 504	13 992	6 773	6 816
of which:								
Life	2 542	2 608	2 790	2 707	2 849	2 946	3 041	3 065
Domestic undertakings	2 542	2 608	2 790	2 707	2 849	2 946	3 041	3 065
Foreign controlled undertakings	61	56	54	55	51	51	641	629
Foreign companies (branches)	..	..	..	..	..	..	..	..
All undertakings	2 542	2 608	2 790	2 707	2 849	2 946	3 041	3 065
Non-life	2 502	2 561	2 721	2 785	3 002	3 185	3 297	3 314
Domestic undertakings	2 502	2 561	2 721	2 785	3 002	3 185	3 297	3 314
Foreign controlled undertakings	212	220	228	220	227	239	724	756
Foreign companies (branches)	..	..	..	..	..	..	..	..
All undertakings	2 502	2 561	2 721	2 785	3 002	3 185	3 297	3 314
Total								
Domestic undertakings	5 736	5 501	6 153	6 445	6 940	14 024	6 806	7 462
Foreign controlled undertakings	272	276	312	304	311	325	1 402	1 478
Foreign companies (branches)	..	..	..	..	..	..	..	..
All undertakings	5 736	5 501	6 153	6 445	6 940	14 024	6 806	7 462

Table 1. Selected aggregates *(cont.)*

Million ILS

	2013	2014	2015	2016	2017	2018	2019	2020
1.5 Insurance business written abroad by branches, gross premiums								
Life								
Branches and agencies	..	..	..	..	..	..	..	..
Subsidaries	..	..	..	..	..	..	..	..
Total	..	..	..	..	..	..	..	..
Non-life								
Branches and agencies	..	..	..	..	..	..	..	..
Subsidaries	..	..	..	..	..	..	..	..
Total	..	..	..	..	..	..	..	..
Composite								
Branches and agencies	..	..	..	..	..	..	..	..
Subsidaries	..	..	..	..	..	..	..	..
Total	..	..	..	..	..	..	..	..
of which:								
Life	..	..	..	..	..	..	..	..
Branches and agencies	..	..	..	..	..	..	..	..
Subsidaries	..	..	..	..	..	..	..	..
Total	..	..	..	..	..	..	..	..
Non-life	..	..	..	..	..	..	..	..
Branches and agencies	..	..	..	..	..	..	..	..
Subsidaries	..	..	..	..	..	..	..	..
Total	..	..	..	..	..	..	..	..
Total								
Branches and agencies	..	..	..	..	..	..	..	..
Subsidaries	..	..	..	..	..	..	..	..
Total	..	..	..	..	..	..	..	..

.. Not available; c Confidential data

Note: Detailed metadata at: *http://metalinks.oecd.org/ins/20220309/4a9f.*

The statistical data for Israel are supplied by and under the responsibility of the relevant Israeli authorities. The use of such data by the OECD is without prejudice to the status of the Golan Heights, East Jerusalem and Israeli settlements in the West Bank under the terms of international law.

Source: *OECD Insurance Statistics (database)*

Table 2. Number of companies and employees

	2013	2014	2015	2016	2017	2018	2019	2020
2.1 Number of companies								
Life								
Domestic undertakings	1	1	2	2	1	0	0	..
Foreign controlled undertakings	..	..	0	..	..	0	0	..
Foreign companies (branches)	..	..	0	..	..	0	0	..
All undertakings	1	1	2	2	1	0	0	..
Non-life								
Domestic undertakings	12	12	10	10	10	12	12	14
Foreign controlled undertakings	..	..	1	1	1	1	1	1
Foreign companies (branches)	2	3	3	3	3	3	3	3
All undertakings	14	15	13	13	13	15	15	17
Composite								
Domestic undertakings	10	10	11	10	10	10	10	9
Foreign controlled undertakings	1	1	1	1	1	1	2	2
Foreign companies (branches)	..	..	0	..	..	0	0	..
All undertakings	10	10	11	10	10	10	10	9
Reinsurance								
Domestic undertakings	..	..	0	..	..	0	0	..
Foreign controlled undertakings	..	..	0	..	..	0	0	..
Foreign companies (branches)	..	..	0	..	..	0	0	..
All undertakings	..	0	0	0	..	0	0	..
Total								
Domestic undertakings	23	23	23	22	21	22	22	23
Foreign controlled undertakings	1	1	2	..	2	2	3	3
Foreign companies (branches)	2	3	3	3	3	3	3	..
All undertakings	25	26	26	25	24	25	25	26
2.2 Number of employees								
Insurance undertakings	..	..	..	..	..	..	..	..
Intermediaries	..	..	..	..	..	..	..	..
Total	..	..	..	..	..	..	..	..

.. Not available

Note: Detailed metadata at: *http://metalinks.oecd.org/ins/20220309/4a9f.*

The statistical data for Israel are supplied by and under the responsibility of the relevant Israeli authorities. The use of such data by the OECD is without prejudice to the status of the Golan Heights, East Jerusalem and Israeli settlements in the West Bank under the terms of international law.

Source: *OECD Insurance Statistics (database)*

ITALY

Table 1. Selected aggregates

Million EUR

	2013	2014	2015	2016	2017	2018	2019	2020
1.1 Insurance business written in the reporting country								
1.1.1 Insurance business, by ownership								
Gross premiums								
Domestic undertakings	120 973	145 244	149 011	136 278	132 924	138 120	140 752	135 774
Foreign controlled undertakings	34 302	44 419	45 694	44 287	41 990	48 367	49 764	46 241
Foreign companies (branches)	373	375	473	521	504	565	601	588
All undertakings	121 345	145 619	149 484	136 799	133 429	138 685	141 353	136 362
Premiums ceded								
Domestic undertakings	4 513	4 203	4 079	4 914	4 939	5 213	4 904	4 958
Foreign controlled undertakings	1 116	991	983	1 822	1 829	1 867	1 940	1 748
Foreign companies (branches)	49	58	53	62	57	67	74	75
All undertakings	4 563	4 262	4 132	4 976	4 996	5 281	4 979	5 033
Net written premiums								
Domestic undertakings	116 459	141 041	144 932	131 364	127 986	132 907	135 847	130 815
Foreign controlled undertakings	33 186	43 428	44 711	42 465	40 160	46 500	47 824	44 493
Foreign companies (branches)	323	317	420	459	447	497	527	513
All undertakings	116 782	141 358	145 352	131 823	128 433	133 404	136 374	131 328
1.1.2 Insurance business on foreign risks, gross premiums								
Life	1	1	1	1	1	3	10	4
Non-life	53	59	54	59	57	72	85	73
Composite	2 044	1 904	2 016	2 070	2 037	2 008	3 652	1 230
of which:								
Life	1 232	1 073	1 166	1 255	1 252	1 215	1 538	140
Non-life	811	831	849	814	784	792	2 114	1 090
Total	2 098	1 963	2 071	2 130	2 095	2 082	3 747	1 307
1.1.3 Life insurance payments, by class, gross premiums								
Annuities	1 012	956	737	710	716	701	705	683
Unit linked	15 497	21 829	31 884	23 848	31 305	29 887	27 928	29 609
Other life insurance	68 501	87 639	82 220	77 596	66 709	71 545	77 445	71 036
Total life insurance	85 010	110 424	114 842	102 154	98 730	102 133	106 077	101 329
***of which:** Pension contracts*	3 825	4 873	5 492	5 848	6 308	6 631	7 536	8 735
1.1.4 Non-life insurance payments, by class, gross premiums								
Motor vehicle insurance	18 661	17 468	16 590	16 260	16 097	16 262	16 393	15 621
Marine, aviation and other transport insurance	327	334	326	417	387	288	349	314
Freight insurance	208	212	204	198	202	209	226	174
Fire and other property damage insurance	5 269	5 611	5 544	5 863	5 851	6 116	6 373	5 847
Pecuniary loss insurance	967	1 018	1 034	1 119	1 204	1 203	1 309	1 079
General liability insurance	2 905	2 879	2 952	3 073	3 094	3 198	3 427	3 314
Accident and health	5 144	5 221	5 415	5 868	6 200	6 471	7 004	6 516
***of which:** Health*	2 114	2 149	2 323	2 655	2 909	3 142	3 534	3 290
Other non-life insurance	1 163	988	1 082	1 217	1 293	1 373	1 528	1 425
Treaty reinsurance	0	0	0	0	0	0	..	0
Total non-life insurance	34 646	33 730	33 147	34 015	34 326	35 121	36 607	34 289
1.2 Gross claims payments								
Life								
Domestic undertakings	23 754	22 852	22 955	21 169	21 166	21 382	22 878	21 687
Foreign controlled undertakings	11 058	10 413	12 229	10 866	10 142	10 653	12 066	11 516
Foreign companies (branches)	0	0	0	0	0	0	0	..
All undertakings	23 754	22 852	22 955	21 169	21 166	21 382	22 878	21 687
Non-life								
Domestic undertakings	5 061	5 016	4 931	4 776	5 209	5 170	5 458	4 744
Foreign controlled undertakings	1 758	1 853	2 005	2 008	2 021	1 920	1 994	1 699
Foreign companies (branches)	231	257	308	369	364	357	394	363
All undertakings	5 292	5 273	5 240	5 144	5 574	5 527	5 852	5 107
Composite								
Domestic undertakings	64 138	61 204	65 892	59 690	68 163	69 576	71 806	72 016
Foreign controlled undertakings	16 899	14 972	16 842	16 097	17 146	17 740	18 704	18 921
Foreign companies (branches)	0	0	0	0	0	0	0	..
All undertakings	64 138	61 204	65 892	59 690	68 163	69 576	71 806	72 016
of which:								
Life	44 754	43 279	48 546	43 755	52 096	53 576	55 052	56 549
Domestic undertakings	44 754	43 279	48 546	43 755	52 096	53 576	55 052	56 549
Foreign controlled undertakings	12 685	11 217	12 693	12 061	13 358	13 790	14 438	14 915
Foreign companies (branches)	0	0	0	0	0	0	0	..
All undertakings	44 754	43 279	48 546	43 755	52 096	53 576	55 052	56 549
Non-life	19 384	17 925	17 346	15 935	16 067	16 000	16 754	15 467
Domestic undertakings	19 384	17 925	17 346	15 935	16 067	16 000	16 754	15 467
Foreign controlled undertakings	4 215	3 754	4 149	4 037	3 788	3 950	4 266	4 006
Foreign companies (branches)	0	0	0	0	0	0	0	..
All undertakings	19 384	17 925	17 346	15 935	16 067	16 000	16 754	15 467
Total								
Domestic undertakings	92 953	89 071	93 778	85 635	94 539	96 128	100 143	98 447
Foreign controlled undertakings	29 715	27 238	31 075	28 972	29 309	30 313	32 763	32 135
Foreign companies (branches)	231	257	308	369	364	357	394	363
All undertakings	93 185	89 328	94 087	86 003	94 904	96 485	100 536	98 810

Table 1. Selected aggregates *(cont.)*

Million EUR

	2013	2014	2015	2016	2017	2018	2019	2020
1.3 Commissions								
Life								
Domestic undertakings	576	650	641	626	620	590	669	592
Foreign controlled undertakings	384	430	436	449	434	432	465	405
Foreign companies (branches)	0	0	0	0	0	..	..	..
All undertakings	576	650	641	626	620	590	1 134	592
Non-life								
Domestic undertakings	1 576	1 656	1 706	1 748	1 829	1 915	2 087	1 946
Foreign controlled undertakings	548	608	734	767	752	777	828	741
Foreign companies (branches)	73	72	93	107	108	123	136	133
All undertakings	1 649	1 729	1 799	1 855	1 937	2 038	3 051	2 079
Composite								
Domestic undertakings	7 278	7 573	7 699	7 571	7 600	7 673	7 791	7 704
Foreign controlled undertakings	1 830	1 978	2 106	2 006	2 073	2 139	2 153	2 081
Foreign companies (branches)	0	0	0	0	0	..	..	..
All undertakings	7 278	7 573	7 699	7 571	7 600	7 673	9 944	7 704
of which:								
Life	2 088	2 273	2 447	2 306	2 317	2 300	2 804	2 187
Domestic undertakings	2 088	2 273	2 447	2 306	2 317	2 300	2 253	2 187
Foreign controlled undertakings	450	510	542	504	550	608	550	581
Foreign companies (branches)	0	0	0	0	0	..	..	..
All undertakings	2 088	2 273	2 447	2 306	2 317	2 300	2 804	2 187
Non-life	5 190	5 300	5 251	5 265	5 283	5 372	7 141	5 516
Domestic undertakings	5 190	5 300	5 251	5 265	5 283	5 372	5 538	5 516
Foreign controlled undertakings	1 380	1 468	1 564	1 502	1 523	1 531	1 603	1 499
Foreign companies (branches)	0	0	0	0	0	..	..	..
All undertakings	5 190	5 300	5 251	5 265	5 283	5 372	7 141	5 516
Total								
Domestic undertakings	9 431	9 879	10 046	9 945	10 049	10 177	10 546	10 242
Foreign controlled undertakings	2 763	3 015	3 277	3 222	3 259	3 349	3 446	3 227
Foreign companies (branches)	73	72	93	107	108	123	136	133
All undertakings	9 504	9 952	10 139	10 052	10 157	10 300	14 129	10 375
1.4 Gross operating expenses								
Life								
Domestic undertakings	876	953	948	963	970	925	1 008	957
Foreign controlled undertakings	570	622	634	673	658	649	681	643
Foreign companies (branches)	0	0	0	0	0	..	..	..
All undertakings	876	953	948	963	970	925	1 689	957
Non-life								
Domestic undertakings	2 154	2 252	2 332	2 390	2 501	2 634	2 869	2 675
Foreign controlled undertakings	794	818	968	1 012	992	1 022	1 106	1 016
Foreign companies (branches)	112	110	144	176	174	183	197	192
All undertakings	2 266	2 362	2 476	2 565	2 676	2 817	4 172	2 868
Composite								
Domestic undertakings	9 490	9 686	9 829	9 860	9 929	10 069	10 269	10 218
Foreign controlled undertakings	2 294	2 443	2 632	2 566	2 658	2 742	2 707	2 633
Foreign companies (branches)	0	0	0	0	0	..	..	..
All undertakings	9 490	9 686	9 829	9 860	9 929	10 069	12 976	10 218
of which:								
Life	2 970	3 109	3 292	3 196	3 223	3 244	3 991	3 101
Domestic undertakings	2 970	3 109	3 292	3 196	3 223	3 244	3 213	3 101
Foreign controlled undertakings	628	696	743	708	773	833	778	814
Foreign companies (branches)	0	0	0	0	0	..	..	..
All undertakings	2 970	3 109	3 292	3 196	3 223	3 244	3 991	3 101
Non-life	6 520	6 577	6 537	6 664	6 706	6 825	8 985	7 117
Domestic undertakings	6 520	6 577	6 537	6 664	6 706	6 825	7 056	7 117
Foreign controlled undertakings	1 667	1 747	1 889	1 858	1 885	1 909	1 929	1 819
Foreign companies (branches)	0	0	0	0	0	..	..	..
All undertakings	6 520	6 577	6 537	6 664	6 706	6 825	8 985	7 117
Total								
Domestic undertakings	12 520	12 891	13 109	13 213	13 400	13 629	14 146	13 850
Foreign controlled undertakings	3 658	3 883	4 234	4 251	4 307	4 413	4 494	4 291
Foreign companies (branches)	112	110	144	176	174	183	197	192
All undertakings	12 633	13 001	13 253	13 388	13 574	13 812	18 837	14 042

Table 1. Selected aggregates *(cont.)*

Million EUR

	2013	2014	2015	2016	2017	2018	2019	2020
1.5 Insurance business written abroad by branches, gross premiums								
Life								
Branches and agencies	0	1	1	3	1	2	0	0
Subsidaries	3 333	3 469	4 224	1 339	1 712	1 403	1 529	1 308
Total	3 333	3 469	4 226	1 342	1 713	1 404	1 529	1 308
Non-life								
Branches and agencies	12	12	9	10	13	7	15	9
Subsidaries	0	0	0	0	0	..	..	0
Total	12	12	9	10	13	7	15	9
Composite								
Branches and agencies	823	892	868	1 376	1 114	1 138	2 791	2 380
Subsidaries	56 340	54 902	58 541	57 863	60 367	56 485	56 132	54 047
Total	57 163	55 795	59 409	59 239	61 482	57 623	58 923	56 426
of which:								
Life	39 445	39 878	42 059	41 554	43 469	40 058	40 286	37 604
Branches and agencies	154	175	235	477	215	208	1 366	1 263
Subsidaries	39 291	39 703	41 824	41 077	43 254	39 850	38 920	36 341
Total	39 445	39 878	42 059	41 554	43 469	40 058	40 286	37 604
Non-life	17 718	15 917	17 350	17 685	18 012	17 565	18 637	18 823
Branches and agencies	668	718	633	899	899	930	1 425	1 116
Subsidaries	17 049	15 199	16 717	16 785	17 113	16 635	17 212	17 706
Total	17 718	15 917	17 350	17 685	18 012	17 565	18 637	18 823
Total								
Branches and agencies	835	905	878	1 390	1 128	1 147	2 806	2 389
Subsidaries	59 673	58 371	62 765	59 202	62 079	57 887	57 661	55 355
Total	60 508	59 276	63 643	60 592	63 207	59 034	60 467	57 743

.. Not available

Note: Detailed metadata at: *http://metalinks.oecd.org/ins/20220309/e92e.*

Source: *OECD Insurance Statistics (database)*

Table 2. Number of companies and employees

	2013	2014	2015	2016	2017	2018	2019	2020
2.1 Number of companies								
Life								
Domestic undertakings	41	38	35	32	30	26	26	26
Foreign controlled undertakings	23	20	19	17	13	11	11	11
Foreign companies (branches)	17	19	20	22	19	20	20	20
All undertakings	58	57	55	54	49	46	46	46
Non-life								
Domestic undertakings	67	63	58	54	50	51	52	50
Foreign controlled undertakings	20	18	19	18	16	16	17	16
Foreign companies (branches)	65	60	65	65	73	81	77	74
All undertakings	132	123	123	119	123	132	129	124
Composite								
Domestic undertakings	23	21	21	21	20	20	20	20
Foreign controlled undertakings	8	8	9	10	9	9	9	9
Foreign companies (branches)	13	14	14	13	14	13	13	12
All undertakings	36	35	35	34	34	33	33	32
Reinsurance								
Domestic undertakings	0	0	0	0	0	..	..	..
Foreign controlled undertakings	0	0	0	0	0	..	..	..
Foreign companies (branches)	7	7	7	7	7	7	6	6
All undertakings	7	7	7	7	7	7	6	6
Total								
Domestic undertakings	131	122	114	107	100	97	98	96
Foreign controlled undertakings	51	46	47	45	38	36	37	36
Foreign companies (branches)	102	100	106	107	113	121	116	112
All undertakings	233	222	220	214	213	218	214	208
2.2 Number of employees								
Insurance undertakings	39 887	40 259	40 588	40 872	40 386	40 028	39 733	40 192
Intermediaries	227 444	220 288	220 850	212 596	..	..	..	..
Total	267 331	260 547	261 438	253 468	..	..	..	..

.. Not available

Note: Detailed metadata at: *http://metalinks.oecd.org/ins/20220309/e92e.*

Source: *OECD Insurance Statistics (database)*

JAPAN

Table 1. Selected aggregates

Million JPY

	2013	2014	2015	2016	2017	2018	2019	2020
1.1 Insurance business written in the reporting country								
1.1.1 Insurance business, by ownership								
Gross premiums								
Domestic undertakings	42 971 395	46 031 579	46 908 456	42 615 488	41 452 663	44 740 881	42 580 813	40 267 595
Foreign controlled undertakings	6 184 716	6 724 592	7 046 820	6 617 836	6 432 494	8 315 056	7 768 028	7 364 989
Foreign companies (branches)	1 699 621	1 548 143	1 537 624	1 703 444	1 739 958	348 167	314 078	426 961
All undertakings	34 738 150	37 222 352	37 748 110	44 318 932	43 192 621	45 089 048	42 894 891	40 694 556
Premiums ceded								
Domestic undertakings	3 823 919	4 207 229	4 127 260	4 449 638	4 176 204	4 817 685	6 191 736	5 616 176
Foreign controlled undertakings	1 802 239	2 084 233	1 890 218	2 143 727	1 733 566	2 285 450	2 793 927	2 286 106
Foreign companies (branches)	38 391	47 768	75 917	214 477	239 041	223 967	206 605	293 419
All undertakings	1 780 848	2 129 106	2 022 086	4 664 115	4 415 245	5 041 652	6 398 341	5 909 595
Net written premiums								
Domestic undertakings	39 147 476	41 824 350	42 781 196	38 165 836	37 276 448	39 923 181	36 388 692	34 651 403
Foreign controlled undertakings	4 382 477	4 640 359	5 156 602	4 474 105	4 698 925	6 029 602	4 974 097	5 078 879
Foreign companies (branches)	1 661 230	1 500 375	1 461 707	1 488 976	1 499 865	124 190	107 464	133 553
All undertakings	32 957 302	35 093 246	35 726 024	39 654 812	38 776 313	40 047 371	36 496 156	34 784 956
1.1.2 Insurance business on foreign risks, gross premiums								
Life	..	..	..	..	..	..	..	..
Non-life	..	..	..	..	..	..	..	..
Composite total	..	..	..	..	..	..	..	..
Total	..	..	..	..	..	..	..	..
1.1.3 Life insurance payments, by class, gross premiums								
Annuities	4 312 468	5 154 122	4 729 892	4 340 846	3 607 407	3 875 104	3 300 278	3 087 609
Unit linked	..	..	..	..	..	..	..	..
Other life insurance	27 864 772	30 015 418	31 464 495	27 968 949	27 990 703	29 370 822	27 589 307	25 659 381
Total life insurance	32 177 240	35 169 540	36 194 387	32 309 795	31 598 110	33 245 926	30 889 585	28 746 990
***of which:** Pension contracts*	3 851 878	4 175 622	4 562 867	3 057 696	2 953 431	2 861 906	2 833 705	2 549 060
1.1.4 Non-life insurance payments, by class, gross premiums								
Motor vehicle insurance	5 632 807	5 786 949	5 916 489	6 026 253	5 814 388	5 905 312	5 988 484	5 781 766
Marine, aviation and other transport insurance	170 502	170 115	186 542	159 142	152 632	150 286	177 296	170 320
Freight insurance	242 939	248 817	242 488	230 397	239 546	253 139	250 516	243 978
Fire and other property damage insurance	1 983 049	2 104 111	2 228 178	..	..	..	..	..
Pecuniary loss insurance	266 835	299 082	342 570	..	..	..	..	..
General liability insurance	584 318	598 945	615 167	633 290	657 637	692 945	713 193	725 688
Accident and health	897 507	979 477	982 614	..	..	..	..	..
***of which:** Health*	76	214	-152	..	..	..	..	..
Other non-life insurance	154 909	169 874	183 922	..	..	..	..	..
Treaty reinsurance	..	..	..	..	..	..	..	..
Total non-life insurance	9 932 866	10 357 370	10 697 970	10 859 799	10 750 127	11 173 102	11 483 495	11 496 729
1.2 Gross claims payments								
Life								
Domestic undertakings	33 069 327	34 214 304	31 685 988	28 227 418	28 115 903	28 748 864	29 502 430	30 087 116
Foreign controlled undertakings	6 584 738	6 428 288	5 559 928	5 107 453	5 198 975	5 980 013	6 200 318	5 696 378
Foreign companies (branches)	709 471	738 243	768 206	786 644	827 193	37 839	45 369	51 496
All undertakings	33 778 798	34 952 547	32 454 194	29 014 062	28 943 096	28 786 703	29 547 799	30 138 612
Non-life								
Domestic undertakings	5 904 278	5 953 809	5 917 050	6 694 135	5 856 017	7 585 094	7 135 164	6 214 759
Foreign controlled undertakings	341 353	373 601	366 795	383 518	237 359	480 088	411 562	332 483
Foreign companies (branches)	..	..	..	104 648	98 935	222 146	200 874	291 564
All undertakings	..	..	..	6 798 783	5 954 952	7 807 240	7 336 038	6 506 323
Composite, all undertakings	..	..	..	..	..	..	..	..
Total								
Domestic undertakings	38 973 605	40 168 113	37 603 038	34 921 553	33 971 920	36 333 958	36 637 594	36 301 875
Foreign controlled undertakings	6 926 091	6 801 889	5 926 723	5 490 971	5 436 334	6 460 101	6 611 880	6 028 861
Foreign companies (branches)	709 471	738 243	768 206	891 292	926 128	259 985	246 243	343 060
All undertakings	33 778 798	34 952 547	32 454 194	35 812 845	34 898 048	36 593 943	36 883 837	36 644 935
1.3 Commissions								
Life								
Domestic undertakings	..	..	..	..	..	..	..	..
Foreign controlled undertakings	..	..	..	..	..	..	..	..
Foreign companies (branches)	..	..	..	..	..	..	..	..
All undertakings	..	..	..	..	..	..	..	..
Non-life								
Domestic undertakings	1 149 357	1 229 205	1 273 631	1 240 454	1 221 324	1 241 826	1 296 198	1 335 507
Foreign controlled undertakings	25 883	33 975	37 223	20 067	-15 311	-19 855	-27 941	-31 429
Foreign companies (branches)	..	..	..	-19 897	-29 330	-33 799	-1 094	-43 029
All undertakings	..	..	..	1 220 557	1 191 994	1 208 027	1 295 104	1 292 478
Composite, all undertakings	..	..	..	..	..	..	..	..
Total								
Domestic undertakings	1 149 357	1 229 205	1 273 631	1 240 454	1 221 324	1 241 826	1 296 198	1 335 507
Foreign controlled undertakings	25 883	33 975	37 223	20 067	-15 311	-19 855	-27 941	-31 429
Foreign companies (branches)	..	..	..	-19 897	-29 330	-33 799	-1 094	-43 029
All undertakings	..	..	..	1 220 557	1 191 994	1 208 027	1 295 104	1 292 478

Table 1. Selected aggregates *(cont.)*

Million JPY

	2013	2014	2015	2016	2017	2018	2019	2020
1.4 Gross operating expenses								
Life								
Domestic undertakings	4 068 896	4 178 568	4 356 425	4 369 595	4 385 030	4 856 591	4 691 017	4 580 593
Foreign controlled undertakings	862 622	893 811	945 921	948 132	965 055	1 353 249	1 282 164	1 237 324
Foreign companies (branches)	320 576	320 518	349 858	357 069	366 406	22 814	23 341	21 191
All undertakings	4 389 472	4 499 086	4 706 283	4 726 664	4 751 436	4 879 405	4 714 358	4 601 784
Non-life								
Domestic undertakings	3 034 716	3 189 416	3 275 358	3 247 478	3 206 606	3 318 518	3 389 286	3 429 411
Foreign controlled undertakings	176 725	238 092	249 835	207 689	125 459	185 822	158 127	136 824
Foreign companies (branches)	..	..	..	34 405	37 023	34 772	61 577	34 791
All undertakings	..	..	..	3 281 883	3 243 629	3 353 290	3 450 863	3 464 202
Composite, all undertakings	..	..	..	..	..	..	..	..
Total								
Domestic undertakings	7 103 612	7 367 984	7 631 783	7 617 073	7 591 636	8 175 109	8 080 303	8 010 004
Foreign controlled undertakings	1 039 347	1 131 903	1 195 756	1 155 821	1 090 514	1 539 071	1 440 291	1 374 148
Foreign companies (branches)	320 576	320 518	349 858	391 474	403 429	57 586	84 918	55 982
All undertakings	4 389 472	4 499 086	4 706 283	8 008 547	7 995 065	8 232 695	8 165 221	8 065 986
1.5 Insurance business written abroad by branches, gross premiums								
Life								
Branches and agencies	..	..	..	..	..	..	..	..
Subsidaries	..	..	..	..	..	..	..	..
Total	..	..	..	..	..	..	..	..
Non-life								
Branches and agencies	..	..	..	..	..	..	..	..
Subsidaries	..	..	..	..	..	..	..	..
Total	..	..	..	..	..	..	..	..
Composite total	..	..	..	..	..	..	..	..
Total								
Branches and agencies	..	..	..	..	..	..	..	..
Subsidaries	..	..	..	..	..	..	..	..
Total	..	..	..	..	..	..	..	..

.. Not available

Note: Detailed metadata at: *http://metalinks.oecd.org/ins/20220309/8153.*

Source: *OECD Insurance Statistics (database)*

Table 2. Number of companies and employees

	2013	2014	2015	2016	2017	2018	2019	2020
2.1 Number of companies								
Life								
Domestic undertakings	40	39	38	38	38	40	41	41
Foreign controlled undertakings	15	13	13	13	13	14	14	12
Foreign companies (branches)	3	3	3	3	3	1	1	1
All undertakings	43	42	41	41	41	41	42	42
Non-life								
Domestic undertakings	30	30	30	30	29	30	32	32
Foreign controlled undertakings	6	7	7	7	6	7	7	7
Foreign companies (branches)	22	22	22	21	23	21	21	21
All undertakings	52	52	52	51	52	51	53	53
Composite, all undertakings	**0**	**0**	**0**	**0**	..	..	..	..
Reinsurance								
Domestic undertakings	..	..	..	..	..	..	..	..
Foreign controlled undertakings	..	..	..	..	..	..	..	..
Foreign companies (branches)	..	..	..	..	..	..	..	..
All undertakings	..	..	..	..	..	..	..	..
Total								
Domestic undertakings	..	..	68	68	67	70	..	73
Foreign controlled undertakings	..	..	20	20	19	21	..	19
Foreign companies (branches)	..	..	25	24	26	22	..	22
All undertakings	..	..	93	92	93	92	..	95
2.2 Number of employees								
Insurance undertakings	221 675	226 043	120 353	..	..	..	..	..
Intermediaries	2 283 335	2 293 863	2 059 743	..	..	..	..	..
Total	2 505 010	2 519 906	2 080 096	..	345 582	..	..	..

.. Not available

Note: Detailed metadata at: *http://metalinks.oecd.org/ins/20220309/8153*.

Source: *OECD Insurance Statistics (database)*

Table 1. Selected aggregates

Million KRW

	2013	2014	2015	2016	2017	2018	2019	2020
1.1 Insurance business written in the reporting country								
1.1.1 Insurance business, by ownership								
Gross premiums								
Domestic undertakings	180 479 019	192 380 611	205 460 047	210 800 275	209 464 937	206 866 894	..	231 158 909
Foreign controlled undertakings	15 928 630	13 324 532	15 765 302	16 670 208	17 513 911	14 930 441	..	26 652 331
Foreign companies (branches)	4 755 050	4 594 745	2 267 929	4 629 847	4 849 409	5 320 101	..	3 453 833
All undertakings	185 234 069	196 975 356	207 727 976	215 430 122	214 314 346	212 186 995	..	234 612 743
Premiums ceded								
Domestic undertakings	9 411 425	9 694 294	10 255 858	10 505 959	11 215 981	11 733 647	..	13 990 016
Foreign controlled undertakings	538 227	478 174	638 961	599 183	611 390	584 975	..	1 057 754
Foreign companies (branches)	456 049	651 726	732 347	817 712	990 510	1 035 820	..	1 183 597
All undertakings	9 867 474	10 346 020	10 988 205	11 323 671	12 206 491	12 769 467	..	15 173 613
Net written premiums								
Domestic undertakings	171 067 594	182 686 317	195 204 189	200 294 316	198 248 956	195 133 247	..	217 168 894
Foreign controlled undertakings	15 390 403	12 846 358	15 126 341	16 071 025	16 902 521	14 345 466	..	25 594 577
Foreign companies (branches)	4 299 001	3 943 019	1 535 582	3 812 135	3 858 899	4 284 281	..	2 270 236
All undertakings	175 366 595	186 629 336	196 739 771	204 106 451	202 107 855	199 417 528	..	219 439 130
1.1.2 Insurance business on foreign risks, gross premiums								
Life	..	..	..	..	..	..	..	..
Non-life	..	..	..	..	..	..	..	..
Composite total	..	..	..	..	..	..	..	..
Total	..	..	..	..	..	..	..	..
1.1.3 Life insurance payments, by class, gross premiums								
Annuities	25 867 249	23 905 884	24 586 649	21 347 503	19 558 128	17 605 227	..	17 041 847
Unit linked	21 073 957	20 670 949	20 643 073	19 406 180	19 623 687	18 834 528	..	17 224 130
Other life insurance	61 618 265	65 998 453	71 983 930	79 057 566	74 791 666	74 403 374	..	85 321 224
Total life insurance	108 559 471	110 575 286	117 213 652	119 811 249	113 973 481	110 843 129	..	119 587 220
***of which:** Pension contracts*	8 103 216	11 817 288	13 694 337	16 718 996	14 905 838	16 869 826	..	22 552 785
1.1.4 Non-life insurance payments, by class, gross premiums								
Motor vehicle insurance	13 692 186	14 188 378	15 635 198	16 975 333	17 426 917	17 276 192	..	20 157 896
Marine, aviation and other transport insurance	1 062 919	1 006 367	971 854	854 536	917 229	832 470	..	1 026 829
Freight insurance	0	0	..	..	..	..	..	..
Fire and other property damage insurance	515 217	484 799	472 624	471 017	428 560	373 175	..	374 725
Pecuniary loss insurance	1 637 782	1 601 517	1 672 799	1 693 861	1 858 689	2 133 544	..	2 322 178
General liability insurance	947 583	910 341	967 362	1 100 438	1 182 101	1 233 606	..	1 616 339
Accident and health	49 501 658	24 196 315	39 104 233	30 297 640	33 024 528	36 093 627	..	42 228 583
***of which:** Health*	83 983	10 090 810	11 740 294	13 406 917	14 799 985	16 444 106	..	20 528 740
Other non-life insurance	8 105 434	32 685 216	30 357 048	42 702 138	43 864 781	41 435 506	..	47 294 397
Treaty reinsurance	0	0	..	..	..	..	..	..
Total non-life insurance	75 462 779	85 163 744	89 181 118	94 094 963	98 702 805	99 378 120	..	115 020 946
1.2 Gross claims payments								
Life								
Domestic undertakings	51 098 146	61 070 702	65 751 692	77 155 805	78 055 802	77 155 805	..	95 341 531
Foreign controlled undertakings	8 103 569	69 035 817	6 945 034	9 505 582	10 803 105	9 505 582	..	18 268 575
Foreign companies (branches)	1 252 924	1 292 842	1 333 124	1 410 493	1 457 100	1 410 493	..	..
All undertakings	52 351 070	62 363 544	67 084 816	78 566 298	79 512 902	78 566 298	..	95 341 531
Non-life								
Domestic undertakings	22 119 519	30 233 735	30 895 053	32 747 964	35 060 020	40 091 995	..	48 381 362
Foreign controlled undertakings	516 770	844 722	843 763	802 729	767 651	824 571	..	910 807
Foreign companies (branches)	7 033 799	1 098 087	1 264 227	1 282 459	1 285 551	1 554 862	..	2 212 454
All undertakings	29 153 318	31 331 823	32 159 280	34 030 423	36 345 571	41 646 857	..	50 593 816
Composite, all undertakings	..	..	..	..	..	..	..	..
Total								
Domestic undertakings	73 217 665	91 304 438	96 646 745	109 903 769	113 115 822	117 247 800	..	143 722 893
Foreign controlled undertakings	8 620 339	69 880 539	7 788 797	10 308 311	11 570 756	10 330 153	..	19 179 382
Foreign companies (branches)	8 286 723	2 390 929	2 597 351	2 692 952	2 742 651	2 965 355	..	2 212 454
All undertakings	81 504 388	93 695 367	99 244 096	112 596 721	115 858 473	120 213 155	..	145 935 347
1.3 Commissions								
Life								
Domestic undertakings	..	..	..	..	..	..	..	..
Foreign controlled undertakings	..	..	..	..	..	..	..	..
Foreign companies (branches)	..	..	..	..	..	..	..	..
All undertakings	..	..	..	..	..	..	..	..
Non-life								
Domestic undertakings	..	..	..	..	..	..	..	..
Foreign controlled undertakings	..	..	..	..	..	..	..	..
Foreign companies (branches)	..	..	..	..	..	..	..	..
All undertakings	..	..	..	..	..	..	..	..
Composite, all undertakings	..	..	..	..	..	..	..	..
Total								
Domestic undertakings	..	..	..	..	..	..	..	..
Foreign controlled undertakings	..	..	..	..	..	..	..	..
Foreign companies (branches)	..	..	..	..	..	..	..	..
All undertakings	..	..	..	..	..	..	..	..

Table 1. Selected aggregates *(cont.)*

Million KRW

	2013	2014	2015	2016	2017	2018	2019	2020
1.4 Gross operating expenses								
Life								
Domestic undertakings	25 608 456	27 511 983	28 987 407	28 236 989	28 574 504	36 539 562	..	15 375 567
Foreign controlled undertakings	5 278 175	806 034	756 903	5 074 779	5 675 330	5 878 573	..	3 667 962
Foreign companies (branches)	770 753	4 595 483	5 009 714	760 976	619 584	790 806	..	..
All undertakings	26 379 209	32 107 466	33 997 121	28 997 965	29 194 088	37 330 368	..	15 375 567
Non-life								
Domestic undertakings	11 294 192	16 760 436	13 511 865	14 238 364	15 685 551	16 637 805	..	18 024 767
Foreign controlled undertakings	129 781	245 017	182 669	163 724	225 860	254 141	..	336 057
Foreign companies (branches)	1 592 503	1 116 586	405 386	411 714	434 676	510 688	..	566 518
All undertakings	12 886 695	17 877 022	13 917 251	14 650 078	16 120 227	17 148 493	..	18 591 285
Composite, all undertakings	..	..	..	..	..	..	..	..
Total								
Domestic undertakings	36 902 648	44 272 419	42 499 272	42 475 353	44 260 055	53 177 367	..	33 400 334
Foreign controlled undertakings	5 407 956	1 051 051	939 572	5 238 503	5 901 190	6 132 714	..	4 004 019
Foreign companies (branches)	2 363 256	5 712 069	5 415 100	1 172 690	1 054 260	1 301 494	..	566 518
All undertakings	39 265 904	49 984 488	47 914 372	43 648 043	45 314 315	54 478 861	..	33 966 852
1.5 Insurance business written abroad by branches, gross premiums								
Life								
Branches and agencies	..	..	..	..	..	..	..	..
Subsidaries	..	..	..	..	..	..	..	..
Total	..	..	..	..	..	..	..	..
Non-life								
Branches and agencies	..	..	..	..	..	..	..	..
Subsidaries	..	..	..	..	..	..	..	..
Total	..	..	..	..	..	..	..	..
Composite total	..	..	..	..	..	..	..	..
Total								
Branches and agencies	..	..	..	..	..	..	..	..
Subsidaries	..	..	..	..	..	..	..	..
Total	..	..	..	..	..	..	..	..

.. Not available

Note: Detailed metadata at: *http://metalinks.oecd.org/ins/20220309/52a9.*

Source: *OECD Insurance Statistics (database)*

Table 2. Number of companies and employees

	2013	2014	2015	2016	2017	2018	2019	2020
2.1 Number of companies								
Life								
Domestic undertakings	24	24	24	24	24	24	..	24
Foreign controlled undertakings	8	7	7	8	8	8	..	9
Foreign companies (branches)	1	1	1	1	1	1	..	0
All undertakings	25	25	25	25	25	25	..	24
Non-life								
Domestic undertakings	16	17	17	17	18	17	..	17
Foreign controlled undertakings	3	4	4	4	5	4	..	4
Foreign companies (branches)	8	5	5	5	6	5	..	4
All undertakings	24	22	22	22	24	22	..	21
Composite, all undertakings	**0**	**0**	**0**	**0**	..	..	..	..
Reinsurance								
Domestic undertakings	1	1	1	1	1	1	..	1
Foreign controlled undertakings	..	0	0	0	0	0	..	0
Foreign companies (branches)	6	8	8	9	9	9	..	9
All undertakings	7	9	9	10	10	10	..	10
Total								
Domestic undertakings	41	42	42	42	43	42	..	42
Foreign controlled undertakings	11	11	11	12	13	12	..	13
Foreign companies (branches)	15	14	14	15	16	15	..	13
All undertakings	56	56	56	57	59	57	..	55
2.2 Number of employees								
Insurance undertakings	63 859	61 158	59 685	58 833	57 854	58 833	..	58 617
Intermediaries	280 087	245 127	235 319	229 292	222 411	229 292	..	197 418
Total	343 946	306 285	295 004	288 125	280 265	288 125	..	256 035

.. Not available

Note: Detailed metadata at: *http://metalinks.oecd.org/ins/20220309/52a9*.

Source: *OECD Insurance Statistics (database)*

LATVIA

Table 1. Selected aggregates

Million EUR

	2013	2014	2015	2016	2017	2018	2019	2020
1.1 Insurance business written in the reporting country								
1.1.1 Insurance business, by ownership								
Gross premiums								
Domestic undertakings	350	371	379	364	419	489	569	517
Foreign controlled undertakings	150	151	188	267	293	352	446	419
Foreign companies (branches)	121	146	152	168	227	267	289	281
All undertakings	471	517	531	532	646	756	857	798
Premiums ceded								
Domestic undertakings	17	19	22	25	44	77	83	67
Foreign controlled undertakings	4	4	7	18	27	54	58	58
Foreign companies (branches)	..	..	..	..	..	..	..	..
All undertakings	17	19	22	25	44	77	83	67
Net written premiums								
Domestic undertakings	333	352	357	339	375	412	486	449
Foreign controlled undertakings	146	147	182	249	266	298	388	360
Foreign companies (branches)	121	146	152	168	227	267	289	281
All undertakings	454	498	509	507	602	679	774	731
1.1.2 Insurance business on foreign risks, gross premiums								
Life	..	..	..	0	0	..	..	..
Non-life	..	..	..	160	204	234	226	189
Composite	..	..	..	0	0	0	69	70
of which:								
Life	..	..	..	0	0	0	69	70
Non-life	..	..	..	..	0	..	..	..
Total	..	..	..	160	204	234	296	259
1.1.3 Life insurance payments, by class, gross premiums								
Annuities	0	0	0	11	18	25	41	59
Unit linked	23	34	43	45	57	55	102	97
Other life insurance	66	73	72	68	70	65	85	85
Total life insurance	89	107	115	124	145	145	228	241
***of which:** Pension contracts*	0	0	0	..	..	..	..	37
1.1.4 Non-life insurance payments, by class, gross premiums								
Motor vehicle insurance	221	222	221	229	301	381	370	319
Marine, aviation and other transport insurance	2	2	2	2	5	4	4	3
Freight insurance	5	3	3	3	1	3	3	3
Fire and other property damage insurance	67	86	84	76	84	90	104	95
Pecuniary loss insurance	11	13	14	12	11	16	20	21
General liability insurance	17	21	21	19	19	21	23	21
Accident and health	46	52	58	55	63	78	85	84
***of which:** Health*	38	42	48	45	54	64	71	71
Other non-life insurance	12	12	13	13	16	18	20	11
Treaty reinsurance	0	0	0	0	0	0	0	0
Total non-life insurance	382	411	416	409	501	611	629	557
1.2 Gross claims payments								
Life								
Domestic undertakings	31	26	29	0	0	..	..	..
Foreign controlled undertakings	26	24	27	0	0	0	..	..
Foreign companies (branches)	31	31	34	0	0	..	..	..
All undertakings	62	57	63	0	0	..	..	..
Non-life								
Domestic undertakings	165	184	198	180	193	229	303	245
Foreign controlled undertakings	68	77	92	139	126	170	231	186
Foreign companies (branches)	38	43	50	60	78	86	101	105
All undertakings	204	226	248	240	271	315	404	350
Composite								
Domestic undertakings	..	..	..	33	43	43	86	81
Foreign controlled undertakings	..	..	..	27	31	34	77	70
Foreign companies (branches)	..	..	..	40	47	48	59	71
All undertakings	..	..	..	72	90	91	145	152
of which:								
Life	..	..	..	72	90	91	145	152
Domestic undertakings	..	..	..	33	43	43	86	81
Foreign controlled undertakings	..	..	..	27	31	34	77	70
Foreign companies (branches)	..	..	..	40	47	48	59	71
All undertakings	..	..	..	72	90	91	145	152
Non-life	..	..	..	..	0	..	..	..
Domestic undertakings	..	..	..	..	0	..	..	..
Foreign controlled undertakings	..	..	..	..	0	..	..	..
Foreign companies (branches)	..	..	..	..	0	..	..	..
All undertakings	..	..	..	..	0	..	..	..
Total								
Domestic undertakings	196	209	227	213	236	272	388	325
Foreign controlled undertakings	94	102	119	166	158	203	308	256
Foreign companies (branches)	69	73	83	99	125	134	161	176
All undertakings	265	283	311	312	361	406	549	501

Table 1. Selected aggregates *(cont.)*

Million EUR

	2013	2014	2015	2016	2017	2018	2019	2020
1.3 Commissions								
Life								
Domestic undertakings	1	1	0	0	0	0	..	..
Foreign controlled undertakings	1	1	1	0	0	0	..	..
Foreign companies (branches)	5	5	6	..	..	..	..	..
All undertakings	5	6	6	0	0	0	..	..
Non-life								
Domestic undertakings	32	45	34	32	40	65	60	51
Foreign controlled undertakings	..	7	11	16	13	37	38	37
Foreign companies (branches)	10	12	13	..	..	..	..	..
All undertakings	42	58	47	32	40	65	60	51
Composite								
Domestic undertakings	..	..	..	0	1	1	6	7
Foreign controlled undertakings	..	..	..	0	0	1	6	7
Foreign companies (branches)	..	..	..	..	..	..	..	..
All undertakings	..	..	..	0	1	1	6	7
of which:								
Life	..	..	..	0	1	1	6	7
Domestic undertakings	..	..	..	0	1	1	6	7
Foreign controlled undertakings	..	..	..	0	0	1	6	7
Foreign companies (branches)	..	..	..	..	..	..	..	..
All undertakings	..	..	..	0	1	1	6	7
Non-life	..	..	..	..	0	..	..	..
Domestic undertakings	..	..	..	..	0	..	..	..
Foreign controlled undertakings	..	..	..	..	0	..	..	..
Foreign companies (branches)	..	..	..	..	..	..	..	..
All undertakings	..	..	..	..	0	..	..	..
Total								
Domestic undertakings	33	46	34	33	41	65	66	59
Foreign controlled undertakings	1	8	11	16	14	37	44	44
Foreign companies (branches)	15	17	19	..	..	..	..	..
All undertakings	48	64	53	33	41	65	66	59
1.4 Gross operating expenses								
Life								
Domestic undertakings	4	4	4	0	0	0	..	..
Foreign controlled undertakings	4	4	4	0	0	0	..	..
Foreign companies (branches)	..	..	..	..	..	..	..	..
All undertakings	4	4	4	0	0	0	..	..
Non-life								
Domestic undertakings	102	108	109	56	87	119	118	111
Foreign controlled undertakings	40	40	51	30	51	81	87	88
Foreign companies (branches)	..	..	..	..	..	..	..	..
All undertakings	102	108	109	56	87	119	118	111
Composite								
Domestic undertakings	..	..	..	4	5	5	17	18
Foreign controlled undertakings	..	..	..	4	4	5	16	18
Foreign companies (branches)	..	..	..	..	..	..	..	..
All undertakings	..	..	..	4	5	5	17	18
of which:								
Life	..	..	..	4	5	5	17	18
Domestic undertakings	..	..	..	4	5	5	17	18
Foreign controlled undertakings	..	..	..	4	4	5	16	18
Foreign companies (branches)	..	..	..	..	..	..	..	..
All undertakings	..	..	..	4	5	5	17	18
Non-life	..	..	..	..	0	..	..	..
Domestic undertakings	..	..	..	..	0	..	..	..
Foreign controlled undertakings	..	..	..	..	0	..	..	..
Foreign companies (branches)	..	..	..	..	..	..	..	..
All undertakings	..	..	..	..	0	..	..	..
Total								
Domestic undertakings	106	112	113	60	92	124	135	129
Foreign controlled undertakings	44	44	55	34	55	86	104	105
Foreign companies (branches)	..	..	..	..	..	..	..	..
All undertakings	106	112	113	60	92	124	135	129

Table 1. Selected aggregates *(cont.)*

Million EUR

	2013	2014	2015	2016	2017	2018	2019	2020
1.5 Insurance business written abroad by branches, gross premiums								
Life								
Branches and agencies	0	0	0	0	0	..	..	..
Subsidaries	..	..	..	..	..	..	..	..
Total	0	0	0	0	0	..	..	..
Non-life								
Branches and agencies	158	168	157	158	203	233	226	189
Subsidaries	..	..	..	..	..	..	..	..
Total	158	168	157	158	203	233	226	189
Composite								
Branches and agencies	..	..	..	0	0	..	69	70
Subsidaries	..	..	..	..	..	..	..	..
Total	..	..	..	0	0	..	69	70
of which:								
Life	..	..	..	0	0	..	69	70
Branches and agencies	..	..	..	0	0	..	69	70
Subsidaries	..	..	..	..	..	..	..	..
Total	..	..	..	0	0	..	69	70
Non-life	..	..	..	..	0	..	..	..
Branches and agencies	..	..	..	..	0	..	..	..
Subsidaries	..	..	..	..	..	..	..	..
Total	..	..	..	..	0	..	..	..
Total								
Branches and agencies	158	168	157	158	203	233	296	259
Subsidaries	..	..	..	..	..	..	..	..
Total	158	168	157	158	203	233	296	259

.. Not available

Note: Detailed metadata at: *http://metalinks.oecd.org/ins/20220309/b74f.*

Source: *OECD Insurance Statistics (database)*

LATVIA

Table 2. Number of companies and employees

	2013	2014	2015	2016	2017	2018	2019	2020
2.1 Number of companies								
Life								
Domestic undertakings	2	2	2	..	0	0	0	..
Foreign controlled undertakings	1	1	1	..	0	0	0	..
Foreign companies (branches)	5	5	4	..	0	0	0	..
All undertakings	7	7	6	..	0	0	..	..
Non-life								
Domestic undertakings	5	5	6	5	4	4	4	4
Foreign controlled undertakings	2	2	3	3	2	2	2	2
Foreign companies (branches)	7	9	10	8	7	7	8	7
All undertakings	12	14	16	13	11	11	12	11
Composite								
Domestic undertakings	0	0	0	2	2	2	2	2
Foreign controlled undertakings	0	0	0	1	1	1	1	1
Foreign companies (branches)	0	0	0	4	4	4	4	4
All undertakings	0	0	0	6	6	6	6	6
Reinsurance								
Domestic undertakings	0	0	0	..	0	..	..	..
Foreign controlled undertakings	0	0	0	..	0	..	..	..
Foreign companies (branches)	0	0	0	..	0	..	..	..
All undertakings	0	0	0	..	0	..	..	..
Total								
Domestic undertakings	7	7	8	7	6	6	6	6
Foreign controlled undertakings	3	3	4	4	3	3	3	3
Foreign companies (branches)	12	14	14	12	11	11	12	11
All undertakings	19	21	22	19	17	17	18	17
2.2 Number of employees								
Insurance undertakings	2 300	2 121	1 047	..	..	..	..	..
Intermediaries	846	773	905	..	..	..	..	..
Total	3 146	2 894	1 952	..	..	..	..	..

.. Not available

Note: Detailed metadata at: *http://metalinks.oecd.org/ins/20220309/b74f.*

Source: *OECD Insurance Statistics (database)*

LITHUANIA

Table 1. Selected aggregates

Million EUR

	2013	2014	2015	2016	2017	2018	2019	2020
1.1 Insurance business written in the reporting country								
1.1.1 Insurance business, by ownership								
Gross premiums								
Domestic undertakings	288	303	326	393	425	447	430	435
Foreign controlled undertakings	278	294	316	383	416	437	419	425
Foreign companies (branches)	280	298	319	317	367	432	516	520
All undertakings	567	601	645	710	793	878	946	955
Premiums ceded								
Domestic undertakings	10	8	8	21	27	29	23	22
Foreign controlled undertakings	10	8	8	21	27	29	23	22
Foreign companies (branches)	..	21	24	15	40	55	63	46
All undertakings	..	29	32	36	68	84	86	69
Net written premiums								
Domestic undertakings	277	295	318	372	398	418	407	413
Foreign controlled undertakings	268	285	308	362	388	408	397	403
Foreign companies (branches)	..	277	295	302	327	376	453	473
All undertakings	..	572	613	674	725	794	860	886
1.1.2 Insurance business on foreign risks, gross premiums								
Life	..	..	..	..	..	..	..	..
Non-life	..	..	..	..	..	..	..	..
Composite	..	..	..	..	..	..	..	..
of which:								
Life	..	..	..	..	..	..	..	..
Non-life	..	..	..	..	..	..	..	..
Total	..	..	..	..	..	..	..	..
1.1.3 Life insurance payments, by class, gross premiums								
Annuities	3	4	5	6	7	7	6	5
Unit linked	126	152	170	157	137	151	170	189
Other life insurance	52	59	60	84	88	90	94	96
Total life insurance	181	215	236	247	231	248	270	291
***of which:** Pension contracts*	..	..	..	1	..	..	..	..
1.1.4 Non-life insurance payments, by class, gross premiums								
Motor vehicle insurance	228	227	236	273	353	403	420	396
Marine, aviation and other transport insurance	2	2	2	2	2	2	1	1
Freight insurance	2	2	2	2	3	3	3	3
Fire and other property damage insurance	74	79	89	98	103	109	120	130
Pecuniary loss insurance	20	18	17	17	20	23	25	27
General liability insurance	19	20	20	20	21	22	24	24
Accident and health	40	37	42	49	56	65	78	79
***of which:** Health*	25	21	24	30	35	42	51	51
Other non-life insurance	1	1	1	2	3	3	4	4
Treaty reinsurance	..	..	..	..	0	0	0	0
Total non-life insurance	386	386	409	463	561	630	675	664
1.2 Gross claims payments								
Life								
Domestic undertakings	15	13	15	26	29	32	34	30
Foreign controlled undertakings	15	13	15	23	26	29	30	27
Foreign companies (branches)	41	47	42	45	56	48	45	68
All undertakings	57	60	57	71	85	80	79	98
Non-life								
Domestic undertakings	105	105	116	134	169	153	168	172
Foreign controlled undertakings	85	92	102	134	169	153	168	172
Foreign companies (branches)	104	111	113	117	126	158	184	187
All undertakings	209	216	229	251	295	311	353	360
Composite								
Domestic undertakings	40	35	40	43	65	46	20	21
Foreign controlled undertakings	38	33	38	43	65	46	20	21
Foreign companies (branches)	4	4	6	8	11	15	47	22
All undertakings	44	40	46	51	75	62	67	43
of which:								
Life	39	35	40	43	66	49	51	28
Domestic undertakings	37	32	36	39	60	42	15	18
Foreign controlled undertakings	35	30	34	39	60	42	15	18
Foreign companies (branches)	2	2	3	4	6	7	36	11
All undertakings	39	35	40	43	66	49	51	28
Non-life	5	5	6	8	9	13	16	14
Domestic undertakings	3	3	4	4	4	4	5	3
Foreign controlled undertakings	3	3	4	4	4	4	5	3
Foreign companies (branches)	2	2	2	4	5	9	11	11
All undertakings	5	5	6	8	9	13	16	14
Total								
Domestic undertakings	161	154	171	203	263	231	222	223
Foreign controlled undertakings	138	138	155	200	260	228	219	220
Foreign companies (branches)	149	163	161	170	193	221	277	278
All undertakings	310	316	332	373	456	453	499	501

Table 1. Selected aggregates *(cont.)*

Million EUR

	2013	2014	2015	2016	2017	2018	2019	2020
1.3 Commissions								
Life								
Domestic undertakings	0	0	0	0	0	0	0	0
Foreign controlled undertakings	0	0	0	0	0	0	0	0
Foreign companies (branches)	..	0	0	0	0	0	0	0
All undertakings	..	0	0	0	0	0	0	0
Non-life								
Domestic undertakings	0	1	0	2	5	7	5	5
Foreign controlled undertakings	0	1	0	2	5	7	5	5
Foreign companies (branches)	..	3	3	2	7	12	11	11
All undertakings	..	3	3	4	12	19	16	16
Composite								
Domestic undertakings	3	1	1	0	0	0	0	0
Foreign controlled undertakings	3	1	1	0	0	0	0	0
Foreign companies (branches)	..	0	1	1	1	1	1	1
All undertakings	..	1	1	1	1	2	2	2
of which:								
Life	..	..	1	1	1	2	2	2
Domestic undertakings	1	..	1	0	0	0	0	0
Foreign controlled undertakings	1	..	1	0	0	0	0	0
Foreign companies (branches)	..	..	1	1	1	1	1	1
All undertakings	..	..	1	1	1	2	2	2
Non-life	..	..	0	0	0	0	0	0
Domestic undertakings	2	..	0	0	0	0	0	0
Foreign controlled undertakings	2	..	0	0	0	0	0	0
Foreign companies (branches)	..	..	0	0	0	0	0	0
All undertakings	..	..	0	0	0	0	0	0
Total								
Domestic undertakings	3	1	1	3	5	7	6	6
Foreign controlled undertakings	3	1	1	3	5	7	6	6
Foreign companies (branches)	..	3	4	3	8	13	12	12
All undertakings	..	4	5	6	13	21	18	18
1.4 Gross operating expenses								
Life								
Domestic undertakings	9	9	12	16	16	16	17	18
Foreign controlled undertakings	9	9	12	14	14	15	15	15
Foreign companies (branches)	..	8	6	7	6	6	7	8
All undertakings	..	17	18	22	21	22	24	25
Non-life								
Domestic undertakings	72	71	97	87	90	94	98	101
Foreign controlled undertakings	68	68	94	85	89	92	96	99
Foreign companies (branches)	..	63	95	63	65	76	81	80
All undertakings	..	134	192	150	155	170	179	181
Composite								
Domestic undertakings	22	17	28	9	14	14	7	7
Foreign controlled undertakings	21	16	25	9	14	14	7	7
Foreign companies (branches)	..	9	29	12	13	14	23	23
All undertakings	..	27	56	22	26	28	30	30
of which:								
Life	..	26	55	20	24	25	27	27
Domestic undertakings	19	17	27	8	13	13	6	6
Foreign controlled undertakings	17	15	24	8	13	13	6	6
Foreign companies (branches)	..	9	28	12	11	12	21	21
All undertakings	..	26	55	20	24	25	27	27
Non-life	..	1	2	2	2	3	3	3
Domestic undertakings	3	1	1	1	1	1	1	1
Foreign controlled undertakings	3	1	1	1	1	1	1	1
Foreign companies (branches)	..	0	1	1	1	2	2	2
All undertakings	..	1	2	2	2	3	3	3
Total								
Domestic undertakings	102	97	137	111	120	124	122	125
Foreign controlled undertakings	98	93	131	108	116	121	118	121
Foreign companies (branches)	..	81	130	82	83	96	111	111
All undertakings	..	178	267	194	203	220	234	236

Table 1. Selected aggregates *(cont.)*

Million EUR

	2013	2014	2015	2016	2017	2018	2019	2020
1.5 Insurance business written abroad by branches, gross premiums								
Life								
Branches and agencies	0	0	0	0	0	0	0	0
Subsidaries	..	..	..	..	..	..	..	..
Total	0	0	0	0	0	0	0	0
Non-life								
Branches and agencies	1	17	40	65	115	142	150	167
Subsidaries	..	..	..	..	..	..	..	..
Total	1	17	40	65	115	142	150	167
Composite								
Branches and agencies	26	31	37	40	46	46	46	50
Subsidaries	..	..	..	..	..	..	..	..
Total	26	31	37	40	46	46	46	50
of which:								
Life	11	14	18	19	22	22	21	23
Branches and agencies	11	14	18	19	22	22	21	23
Subsidaries	..	..	..	..	..	..	..	..
Total	11	14	18	19	22	22	21	23
Non-life	15	17	20	21	24	24	25	26
Branches and agencies	15	17	20	21	24	24	25	26
Subsidaries	..	..	..	..	..	..	..	..
Total	15	17	20	21	24	24	25	26
Total								
Branches and agencies	27	48	77	105	161	188	196	217
Subsidaries	..	..	..	..	..	..	..	..
Total	27	48	77	105	161	188	196	217

.. Not available

Note: Detailed metadata at: *http://metalinks.oecd.org/ins/20220309/87d7.*

Source: *OECD Insurance Statistics (database)*

Table 2. Number of companies and employees

	2013	2014	2015	2016	2017	2018	2019	2020
2.1 Number of companies								
Life								
Domestic undertakings	1	1	1	3	3	3	3	3
Foreign controlled undertakings	1	1	1	2	2	2	2	2
Foreign companies (branches)	3	3	3	2	2	2	2	3
All undertakings	4	4	4	5	5	5	5	6
Non-life								
Domestic undertakings	5	5	5	4	4	4	4	4
Foreign controlled undertakings	2	2	3	3	3	3	3	3
Foreign companies (branches)	10	10	10	9	9	8	8	8
All undertakings	15	15	15	13	13	12	12	12
Composite								
Domestic undertakings	4	4	4	2	2	2	1	1
Foreign controlled undertakings	3	3	3	2	2	2	1	1
Foreign companies (branches)	1	1	1	1	1	1	2	1
All undertakings	5	5	5	3	3	3	3	2
Reinsurance								
Domestic undertakings	..	..	..	..	..	..	..	0
Foreign controlled undertakings	..	..	..	..	..	..	..	0
Foreign companies (branches)	..	..	..	..	..	..	..	0
All undertakings	..	..	..	..	..	..	..	0
Total								
Domestic undertakings	10	10	10	9	9	9	8	8
Foreign controlled undertakings	6	6	7	7	7	7	6	6
Foreign companies (branches)	14	14	14	12	12	11	12	12
All undertakings	24	24	24	21	21	20	20	20
2.2 Number of employees								
Insurance undertakings	4 519	4 414	4 482	4 562	4 599	4 569	4 409	3 850
Intermediaries	1 320	1 433	1 441	1 480	1 463	1 459	1 480	1 429
Total	5 839	5 847	5 923	6 042	6 062	6 028	5 889	5 279

.. Not available

Note: Detailed metadata at: *http://metalinks.oecd.org/ins/20220309/87d7*.

Source: *OECD Insurance Statistics (database)*

Table 1. Selected aggregates

Million EUR

	2013	2014	2015	2016	2017	2018	2019	2020
1.1 Insurance business written in the reporting country								
1.1.1 Insurance business, by ownership								
Gross premiums								
Domestic undertakings	18 410	21 712	19 100	18 259	21 446	20 702	23 692	19 810
Foreign controlled undertakings	17 036	20 356	17 075	13 690	18 728	18 360	21 280	14 361
Foreign companies (branches)	191	76	78	70	77	77	1 435	1 355
All undertakings	18 601	21 788	19 178	18 329	21 523	20 779	25 128	21 165
Premiums ceded								
Domestic undertakings	4 624	6 122	3 030	3 235	3 026	4 794	6 325	3 574
Foreign controlled undertakings	4 246	5 863	2 770	2 943	2 657	4 452	6 126	3 288
Foreign companies (branches)	37	33	26	31	27	33	456	475
All undertakings	4 661	6 155	3 056	3 267	3 053	4 827	6 781	4 050
Net written premiums								
Domestic undertakings	13 787	15 590	16 070	15 024	18 421	15 908	17 367	16 235
Foreign controlled undertakings	12 790	14 493	14 305	10 747	16 070	13 907	15 155	11 073
Foreign companies (branches)	153	43	52	39	50	44	980	880
All undertakings	13 940	15 633	16 122	15 063	18 470	15 952	18 347	17 115
1.1.2 Insurance business on foreign risks, gross premiums								
Life	15 837	18 455	16 383	15 071	18 182	17 356	19 705	16 131
Non-life	572	438	587	621	784	658	1 014	1 148
Composite	0	0	0	0	0	0	1 344	1 295
of which:								
Life	0	0	0	0	0	0	1 133	1 073
Non-life	0	0	0	0	0	0	211	222
Total	16 408	18 893	16 969	15 692	18 967	18 014	22 063	18 574
1.1.3 Life insurance payments, by class, gross premiums								
Annuities	..	..	..	..	..	..	..	..
Unit linked	10 516	11 086	12 874	11 949	15 426	12 966	14 616	13 063
Other life insurance	6 413	9 103	4 685	4 767	4 283	6 064	6 994	4 532
Total life insurance	16 929	20 190	17 559	16 716	19 709	19 030	21 610	17 595
***of which:** Pension contracts*	..	..	..	..	..	..	..	..
1.1.4 Non-life insurance payments, by class, gross premiums								
Motor vehicle insurance	..	..	..	..	..	..	..	..
Marine, aviation and other transport insurance	..	..	..	..	..	..	..	..
Freight insurance	..	..	..	..	..	..	..	..
Fire and other property damage insurance	..	..	..	..	..	..	..	..
Pecuniary loss insurance	..	..	..	..	..	..	..	..
General liability insurance	..	..	..	..	..	..	..	..
Accident and health	..	..	..	..	..	..	..	..
***of which:** Health*	..	..	..	..	..	..	..	..
Other non-life insurance	..	..	..	..	..	..	..	..
Treaty reinsurance	..	..	..	..	..	..	..	..
Total non-life insurance	1 501	1 339	1 476	1 554	1 767	1 707	2 339	2 462
1.2 Gross claims payments								
Life								
Domestic undertakings	11 696	10 597	9 995	11 802	12 002	11 103	11 861	13 703
Foreign controlled undertakings	11 179	10 214	9 032	11 035	11 291	10 262	10 534	10 591
Foreign companies (branches)	25	25	27	28	27	26	60	841
All undertakings	11 721	10 622	10 023	11 829	12 029	11 129	11 921	14 544
Non-life								
Domestic undertakings	1 105	809	900	860	961	987	1 192	1 363
Foreign controlled undertakings	691	428	512	766	500	488	552	843
Foreign companies (branches)	39	36	18	31	37	26	34	28
All undertakings	1 143	845	918	891	999	1 014	1 225	1 391
Composite								
Domestic undertakings	0	0	0	0	0	0	0	0
Foreign controlled undertakings	0	0	0	0	0	0	0	0
Foreign companies (branches)	27	133	17	8	8	9	754	158
All undertakings	27	133	17	8	8	9	754	158
of which:								
Life	15	130	17	8	8	9	624	4
Domestic undertakings	0	0	0	0	0	0	0	0
Foreign controlled undertakings	0	0	0	0	0	0	0	0
Foreign companies (branches)	15	130	17	8	8	9	624	4
All undertakings	15	130	17	8	8	9	624	4
Non-life	12	3	0	0	0	0	130	154
Domestic undertakings	0	0	0	0	0	0	0	0
Foreign controlled undertakings	0	0	0	0	0	0	0	0
Foreign companies (branches)	12	3	0	0	0	0	130	154
All undertakings	12	3	0	0	0	0	130	154
Total								
Domestic undertakings	12 801	11 406	10 896	12 661	12 964	12 091	13 053	15 066
Foreign controlled undertakings	11 869	10 642	9 544	11 802	11 791	10 751	11 086	11 433
Foreign companies (branches)	90	195	62	66	72	61	848	1 027
All undertakings	12 891	11 600	10 958	12 728	13 036	12 152	13 900	16 093

Table 1. Selected aggregates *(cont.)*

Million EUR

	2013	2014	2015	2016	2017	2018	2019	2020
1.3 Commissions								
Life								
Domestic undertakings	327	317	326	291	320	312	319	306
Foreign controlled undertakings	309	297	289	186	283	276	273	226
Foreign companies (branches)	0	0	0	0	0	0	0	0
All undertakings	328	317	326	292	320	312	319	306
Non-life								
Domestic undertakings	217	211	237	251	284	283	344	343
Foreign controlled undertakings	119	109	122	143	151	140	194	188
Foreign companies (branches)	12	9	9	9	8	7	9	8
All undertakings	229	221	246	260	292	290	353	351
Composite								
Domestic undertakings	0	0	0	0	0	0	0	0
Foreign controlled undertakings	0	0	0	0	0	0	0	0
Foreign companies (branches)	12	3	4	4	3	0	0	0
All undertakings	12	3	4	4	3	0	0	0
of which:								
Life	5	3	4	4	3	0	0	0
Domestic undertakings	0	0	0	0	0	0	0	0
Foreign controlled undertakings	0	0	0	0	0	0	0	0
Foreign companies (branches)	5	3	4	4	3	0	0	0
All undertakings	5	3	4	4	3	0	0	0
Non-life	7	0	0	0	0	0	0	0
Domestic undertakings	0	0	0	0	0	0	0	0
Foreign controlled undertakings	0	0	0	0	0	0	0	0
Foreign companies (branches)	7	0	0	0	0	0	0	0
All undertakings	7	0	0	0	0	0	0	0
Total								
Domestic undertakings	544	528	563	542	604	595	662	649
Foreign controlled undertakings	428	406	411	329	435	416	467	413
Foreign companies (branches)	25	13	14	14	11	7	9	8
All undertakings	569	541	576	556	615	602	672	657
1.4 Gross operating expenses								
Life								
Domestic undertakings	362	376	406	417	433	450	470	483
Foreign controlled undertakings	347	358	374	352	392	411	422	403
Foreign companies (branches)	0	1	0	1	1	1	0	30
All undertakings	362	376	406	418	433	450	470	513
Non-life								
Domestic undertakings	66	72	82	81	96	59	125	111
Foreign controlled undertakings	34	41	46	78	58	17	82	67
Foreign companies (branches)	3	2	2	3	3	5	6	4
All undertakings	69	74	84	84	99	64	131	116
Composite								
Domestic undertakings	0	0	0	0	0	0	0	0
Foreign controlled undertakings	0	0	0	0	0	0	0	..
Foreign companies (branches)	7	1	1	1	1	1	17	4
All undertakings	7	1	1	1	1	1	17	4
of which:								
Life	3	1	1	1	1	1	16	0
Domestic undertakings	0	0	0	0	0	0	0	0
Foreign controlled undertakings	0	0	0	0	0	0	0	..
Foreign companies (branches)	3	1	1	1	1	1	16	0
All undertakings	3	1	1	1	1	1	16	0
Non-life	4	0	0	0	0	0	1	3
Domestic undertakings	0	0	0	0	0	0	0	0
Foreign controlled undertakings	0	0	0	0	0	0	0	..
Foreign companies (branches)	4	0	0	0	0	0	1	3
All undertakings	4	0	0	0	0	0	1	3
Total								
Domestic undertakings	429	448	488	498	529	509	595	594
Foreign controlled undertakings	381	399	421	430	450	428	504	471
Foreign companies (branches)	9	4	3	4	5	6	23	38
All undertakings	438	451	491	502	534	515	618	632

Table 1. Selected aggregates (*cont.*)

Million EUR

	2013	2014	2015	2016	2017	2018	2019	2020
1.5 Insurance business written abroad by branches, gross premiums								
Life								
Branches and agencies	2 648	3 250	3 552	4 622	3 492	4 746	3 999	3 354
Subsidaries	..	..	..	..	..	..	..	..
Total	2 648	3 250	3 552	4 622	3 492	4 746	3 999	3 354
Non-life								
Branches and agencies	1 546	1 831	1 965	2 022	1 957	2 847	10 306	10 799
Subsidaries	..	..	..	..	..	..	..	..
Total	1 546	1 831	1 965	2 022	1 957	2 847	10 306	10 799
Composite								
Branches and agencies	0	0	0	0	0	0	0	0
Subsidaries	..	..	..	..	..	..	..	..
Total	0	0	0	0	0	0	0	0
of which:								
Life	0	0	0	0	0	0	0	0
Branches and agencies	0	0	0	0	0	0	0	0
Subsidaries	..	..	..	..	..	..	..	..
Total	0	0	0	0	0	0	0	0
Non-life	0	0	0	0	0	0	0	0
Branches and agencies	0	0	0	0	0	0	0	0
Subsidaries	..	..	..	..	..	..	..	..
Total	0	0	0	0	0	0	0	0
Total								
Branches and agencies	4 194	5 082	5 516	6 644	5 449	7 593	14 305	14 153
Subsidaries	..	..	..	..	..	..	..	..
Total	4 194	5 082	5 516	6 644	5 449	7 593	14 305	14 153

.. Not available
Note: Detailed metadata at: *http://metalinks.oecd.org/ins/20220309/7a18.*
Source: OECD *Insurance Statistics (database)*

Table 2. Number of companies and employees

	2013	2014	2015	2016	2017	2018	2019	2020
2.1 Number of companies								
Life								
Domestic undertakings	42	44	43	40	39	38	36	33
Foreign controlled undertakings	34	39	38	34	35	30	30	28
Foreign companies (branches)	2	2	2	3	3	3	2	2
All undertakings	44	46	45	43	42	41	38	35
Non-life								
Domestic undertakings	34	34	32	33	34	41	42	40
Foreign controlled undertakings	27	8	21	24	25	33	31	30
Foreign companies (branches)	10	10	10	10	9	8	9	6
All undertakings	44	44	42	43	43	49	51	46
Composite								
Domestic undertakings	0	0	0	0	0	0	0	0
Foreign controlled undertakings	0	0	0	0	0	0	0	0
Foreign companies (branches)	3	3	3	3	2	3	3	3
All undertakings	3	3	3	3	2	3	3	3
Reinsurance								
Domestic undertakings	226	224	217	208	204	198	196	199
Foreign controlled undertakings	207	205	204	191	187	181	179	182
Foreign companies (branches)	0	0	0	0	0	0	0	0
All undertakings	226	224	217	208	204	198	196	199
Total								
Domestic undertakings	302	302	292	281	277	277	274	272
Foreign controlled undertakings	268	252	263	249	247	244	240	240
Foreign companies (branches)	15	15	15	16	14	14	14	11
All undertakings	317	317	307	297	291	291	288	283
2.2 Number of employees								
Insurance undertakings	5 692	6 057	6 484	6 484	7 446	8 034	10 295	13 113
Intermediaries	10 030	550	561	522	586	637	578	607
Total	15 722	6 607	7 045	7 006	8 032	8 671	10 873	13 720

Note: Detailed metadata at: *http://metalinks.oecd.org/ins/20220309/7a18*.
Source: *OECD Insurance Statistics (database)*

MEXICO

Table 1. Selected aggregates

Million MXN

	2013	2014	2015	2016	2017	2018	2019	2020
1.1 Insurance business written in the reporting country								
1.1.1 Insurance business, by ownership								
Gross premiums								
Domestic undertakings	347 196	363 530	395 083	450 740	502 856	543 652	603 832	608 067
Foreign controlled undertakings	207 890	220 225	242 872	265 159	290 985	312 037	350 508	336 659
Foreign companies (branches)	..	..	..	..	..	..	..	..
All undertakings	347 196	363 530	395 083	450 740	502 856	543 652	603 832	608 067
Premiums ceded								
Domestic undertakings	60 551	58 378	67 135	70 420	93 577	91 472	112 667	109 313
Foreign controlled undertakings	26 822	29 932	40 217	40 674	58 977	51 768	68 212	58 064
Foreign companies (branches)	..	..	..	..	..	..	..	..
All undertakings	60 551	58 378	67 135	70 420	93 577	91 472	112 667	109 313
Net written premiums								
Domestic undertakings	286 645	305 152	327 947	380 320	409 279	452 180	491 165	498 754
Foreign controlled undertakings	181 068	190 293	202 655	224 485	232 008	260 270	282 295	278 595
Foreign companies (branches)	..	..	..	..	..	..	..	..
All undertakings	286 645	305 152	327 947	380 320	409 279	452 180	491 165	498 754
1.1.2 Insurance business on foreign risks, gross premiums								
Life	..	..	..	..	..	..	..	..
Non-life	402	..	..	..	..	..	..	..
Composite	1 692	..	..	..	..	..	..	..
of which:								
Life	..	..	..	..	..	..	..	..
Non-life	..	..	..	..	..	..	..	..
Total	2 093	..	..	..	..	..	..	..
1.1.3 Life insurance payments, by class, gross premiums								
Annuities	20 099	20 521	19 719	19 286	21 310	24 176	27 278	29 183
Unit linked	..	..	..	..	..	0	0	0
Other life insurance	138 959	148 624	162 199	189 860	193 587	218 641	243 178	245 057
Total life insurance	159 058	169 145	181 918	209 146	214 897	242 817	270 456	274 240
***of which:** Pension contracts*	..	..	..	..	..	..	..	..
1.1.4 Non-life insurance payments, by class, gross premiums								
Motor vehicle insurance	66 562	68 735	75 858	91 375	103 014	110 405	115 377	102 231
Marine, aviation and other transport insurance	7 851	9 356	11 007	11 312	16 558	12 811	18 850	49 955
Freight insurance	..	..	..	..	..	..	..	..
Fire and other property damage insurance	16 520	12 232	13 815	14 497	18 115	37 929	46 830	5 591
Pecuniary loss insurance	5 210	501	947	1 131	12 278	1 774	1 933	14 643
General liability insurance	7 341	7 201	9 099	9 668	12 005	11 757	13 878	13 917
Accident and health	51 189	56 686	59 550	66 512	76 720	85 417	92 322	106 204
***of which:** Health*	2 682	2 719	2 622	3 218	3 518	4 279	4 910	1 589
Other non-life insurance	32 581	38 511	42 081	45 976	48 006	39 687	42 678	39 316
Treaty reinsurance	..	..	..	..	..	..	..	..
Total non-life insurance	187 253	193 221	212 357	240 470	286 696	299 780	331 868	331 858
1.2 Gross claims payments								
Life								
Domestic undertakings	11 800	12 325	13 760	14 829	16 234	18 272	20 554	22 871
Foreign controlled undertakings	..	5 875	6 443	6 971	7 390	8 005	8 593	8 413
Foreign companies (branches)	..	..	..	..	..	..	..	..
All undertakings	11 800	12 325	13 760	14 829	16 234	18 272	20 554	22 871
Non-life								
Domestic undertakings	21 716	17 912	19 552	23 827	32 868	32 866	32 639	28 515
Foreign controlled undertakings	..	4 093	4 923	5 515	7 449	5 433	5 012	4 090
Foreign companies (branches)	..	..	..	..	..	..	..	..
All undertakings	21 716	17 912	19 552	23 827	32 868	32 866	32 639	28 515
Composite								
Domestic undertakings	159 315	148 932	162 803	185 481	204 354	224 193	256 776	258 111
Foreign controlled undertakings	..	104 822	109 465	125 575	136 316	151 138	179 902	169 907
Foreign companies (branches)	..	..	..	..	..	..	..	..
All undertakings	159 315	148 932	162 803	185 481	204 354	224 193	256 776	258 111
of which:								
Life	76 467	81 643	88 136	101 700	115 199	124 902	152 184	151 052
Domestic undertakings	76 467	81 643	88 136	101 700	115 199	124 902	152 184	151 052
Foreign controlled undertakings	..	67 855	70 802	81 029	89 726	97 155	122 938	111 557
Foreign companies (branches)	..	..	..	..	..	..	..	..
All undertakings	76 467	81 643	88 136	101 700	115 199	124 902	152 184	151 052
Non-life	82 848	67 289	74 667	83 781	89 154	99 291	104 592	107 060
Domestic undertakings	82 848	67 289	74 667	83 781	89 154	99 291	104 592	107 060
Foreign controlled undertakings	..	36 968	38 662	44 546	46 591	53 983	56 964	58 349
Foreign companies (branches)	..	..	..	..	..	..	..	..
All undertakings	82 848	67 289	74 667	83 781	89 154	99 291	104 592	107 060
Total								
Domestic undertakings	192 832	179 169	196 115	224 138	253 455	275 331	309 969	309 497
Foreign controlled undertakings	..	114 791	120 830	138 061	151 155	164 576	193 507	182 410
Foreign companies (branches)	..	..	..	..	..	..	..	..
All undertakings	192 832	179 169	196 115	224 138	253 455	275 331	309 969	309 497

Table 1. Selected aggregates *(cont.)*

Million MXN

	2013	2014	2015	2016	2017	2018	2019	2020
1.3 Commissions								
Life								
Domestic undertakings	1 075	749	1 045	1 155	..	..	..	..
Foreign controlled undertakings	251	74	192	247	..	..	..	..
Foreign companies (branches)	..	..	..	..	..	..	..	..
All undertakings	1 075	749	1 045	1 155	..	..	..	..
Non-life								
Domestic undertakings	8 410	9 458	7 257	9 473	..	..	..	..
Foreign controlled undertakings	3 523	3 808	1 888	1 618	..	..	..	..
Foreign companies (branches)	..	..	..	..	..	..	..	..
All undertakings	8 410	9 458	7 257	9 473	..	..	..	..
Composite								
Domestic undertakings	46 777	49 973	48 713	56 225	..	..	..	..
Foreign controlled undertakings	29 464	31 616	30 146	33 073	..	..	..	..
Foreign companies (branches)	..	..	..	..	..	..	..	..
All undertakings	46 777	49 973	48 713	56 225	..	..	..	..
of which:								
Life	19 316	21 023	22 507	26 955	..	..	..	..
Domestic undertakings	19 316	21 023	22 507	26 955	..	..	..	..
Foreign controlled undertakings	12 940	17 514	14 838	17 151	..	..	..	..
Foreign companies (branches)	..	..	..	..	..	..	..	..
All undertakings	19 316	21 023	22 507	26 955	..	..	..	..
Non-life	27 462	28 950	26 206	29 270	..	..	..	..
Domestic undertakings	27 462	28 950	26 206	29 270	..	..	..	..
Foreign controlled undertakings	16 524	14 103	15 308	15 922	..	..	..	..
Foreign companies (branches)	..	..	..	..	..	..	..	..
All undertakings	27 462	28 950	26 206	29 270	..	..	..	..
Total								
Domestic undertakings	56 263	60 180	57 016	66 853	..	..	..	..
Foreign controlled undertakings	33 239	35 498	32 226	34 937	..	..	..	..
Foreign companies (branches)	..	..	..	..	..	..	..	..
All undertakings	56 263	60 180	57 016	66 853	..	..	..	..
1.4 Gross operating expenses								
Life								
Domestic undertakings	1 486	1 156	1 336	1 705	1 617	1 480	1 699	1 551
Foreign controlled undertakings	..	570	661	723	759	734	704	718
Foreign companies (branches)	..	..	..	..	..	..	..	..
All undertakings	1 486	1 156	1 336	1 705	1 617	1 480	1 699	1 551
Non-life								
Domestic undertakings	3 545	4 198	4 924	5 852	7 490	8 280	9 060	10 304
Foreign controlled undertakings	..	2 010	3 137	3 249	4 041	3 412	4 004	4 934
Foreign companies (branches)	..	..	..	..	..	..	..	..
All undertakings	3 545	4 198	4 924	5 852	7 490	8 280	9 060	10 304
Composite								
Domestic undertakings	16 389	16 621	18 736	21 447	23 147	25 162	24 951	27 589
Foreign controlled undertakings	..	10 470	12 270	13 297	13 037	15 216	14 640	17 031
Foreign companies (branches)	..	..	..	..	..	..	..	..
All undertakings	16 389	16 621	18 736	21 447	23 147	25 162	24 951	27 589
of which:								
Life	8 530	8 486	9 990	11 792	11 674	12 701	12 400	13 701
Domestic undertakings	8 530	8 486	9 990	11 792	11 674	12 701	12 400	13 701
Foreign controlled undertakings	..	6 273	7 388	8 480	7 981	8 964	8 466	9 798
Foreign companies (branches)	..	..	..	..	..	..	..	..
All undertakings	8 530	8 486	9 990	11 792	11 674	12 701	12 400	13 701
Non-life	7 859	8 135	8 746	9 655	11 473	12 461	12 551	13 887
Domestic undertakings	7 859	8 135	8 746	9 655	11 473	12 461	12 551	13 887
Foreign controlled undertakings	..	4 198	4 882	4 818	5 055	6 252	6 174	7 233
Foreign companies (branches)	..	..	..	..	..	..	..	..
All undertakings	7 859	8 135	8 746	9 655	11 473	12 461	12 551	13 887
Total								
Domestic undertakings	21 420	21 974	24 996	29 004	32 254	34 923	35 709	39 443
Foreign controlled undertakings	..	13 050	16 068	17 270	17 837	19 363	19 349	22 683
Foreign companies (branches)	..	..	..	..	..	..	..	..
All undertakings	21 420	21 974	24 996	29 004	32 254	34 923	35 709	39 443

Table 1. Selected aggregates *(cont.)*

Million MXN

	2013	2014	2015	2016	2017	2018	2019	2020
1.5 Insurance business written abroad by branches, gross premiums								
Life								
Branches and agencies	..	..	..	..	..	..	..	..
Subsidaries	..	..	..	..	..	..	..	..
Total	..	..	..	..	..	..	..	..
Non-life								
Branches and agencies	..	..	..	..	..	..	..	..
Subsidaries	..	..	..	..	..	..	..	..
Total	..	..	..	..	..	..	..	..
Composite								
Branches and agencies	..	..	..	..	..	..	..	..
Subsidaries	..	..	..	..	..	..	..	..
Total	..	..	..	..	..	..	..	..
of which:								
Life	..	..	..	..	..	..	..	..
Branches and agencies	..	..	..	..	..	..	..	..
Subsidaries	..	..	..	..	..	..	..	..
Total	..	..	..	..	..	..	..	..
Non-life	..	..	..	..	..	..	..	..
Branches and agencies	..	..	..	..	..	..	..	..
Subsidaries	..	..	..	..	..	..	..	..
Total	..	..	..	..	..	..	..	..
Total								
Branches and agencies	..	..	..	..	..	..	..	..
Subsidaries	..	..	..	..	..	..	..	..
Total	..	..	..	..	..	..	..	..

.. Not available

Note: Detailed metadata at: *http://metalinks.oecd.org/ins/20220309/ed5b*.

Source: *OECD Insurance Statistics (database)*

Table 2. Number of companies and employees

	2013	2014	2015	2016	2017	2018	2019	2020
2.1 Number of companies								
Life								
Domestic undertakings	20	16	16	17	15	15	14	13
Foreign controlled undertakings	11	9	9	10	8	8	7	6
Foreign companies (branches)	..	..	..	..	..	..	..	..
All undertakings	20	16	16	17	15	15	14	13
Non-life								
Domestic undertakings	45	49	46	44	60	58	61	62
Foreign controlled undertakings	27	26	23	22	31	28	31	31
Foreign companies (branches)	..	..	..	..	..	..	..	..
All undertakings	45	49	46	44	60	58	61	62
Composite								
Domestic undertakings	37	38	37	37	38	36	35	35
Foreign controlled undertakings	21	22	21	20	21	20	19	19
Foreign companies (branches)	..	..	..	..	..	..	..	..
All undertakings	37	38	37	37	38	36	35	35
Reinsurance								
Domestic undertakings	2	2	3	2	2	2	2	2
Foreign controlled undertakings	0	0	0	0	0	..	..	..
Foreign companies (branches)	..	..	..	..	..	..	..	..
All undertakings	2	2	3	2	2	2	2	2
Total								
Domestic undertakings	104	105	102	100	115	111	112	112
Foreign controlled undertakings	59	57	53	52	60	56	57	56
Foreign companies (branches)	..	..	..	..	..	..	..	..
All undertakings	104	105	102	100	115	111	112	112
2.2 Number of employees								
Insurance undertakings	14 500	14 799	19 168	..	..	..	..	..
Intermediaries	46 712	51 780	55 005	57 900	61 695	..	..	..
Total	61 212	66 579	74 173	57 900	61 695	..	..	..

.. Not available

Note: Detailed metadata at: *http://metalinks.oecd.org/ins/20220309/ed5b.*

Source: *OECD Insurance Statistics (database)*

NETHERLANDS

Table 1. Selected aggregates

Million EUR

	2013	2014	2015	2016	2017	2018	2019	2020
1.1 Insurance business written in the reporting country								
1.1.1 Insurance business, by ownership								
Gross premiums								
Domestic undertakings	38 077	36 523	33 708	69 887	71 228	73 667	..	..
Foreign controlled undertakings	7 674	2 969	5 812	4 102	4 371	3 429	..	..
Foreign companies (branches)	430	62	0	..	..	..	..	..
All undertakings	38 507	36 585	33 708	69 887	71 228	73 667	..	..
Premiums ceded								
Domestic undertakings	2 951	3 880	2 814	1 198	1 698	1 460	..	..
Foreign controlled undertakings	1 484	1 615	1 365	287	353	84	..	..
Foreign companies (branches)	20	0	0	..	..	..	..	..
All undertakings	2 971	3 880	2 814	1 198	1 698	1 460	..	..
Net written premiums								
Domestic undertakings	35 126	32 643	30 894	68 689	69 530	72 207	..	..
Foreign controlled undertakings	6 190	1 354	4 447	3 815	4 018	3 345	..	..
Foreign companies (branches)	410	62	0	..	..	..	..	..
All undertakings	35 536	32 705	30 894	68 689	69 530	72 207	..	..
1.1.2 Insurance business on foreign risks, gross premiums								
Life	..	..	..	269	273	300	..	..
Non-life	..	..	..	534	452	1 102	..	..
Composite total	..	..	..	..	252	501	..	..
Total	..	..	..	803	977	1 903	..	..
1.1.3 Life insurance payments, by class, gross premiums								
Annuities	10 998	10 806	9 035	0	0	0	..	..
Unit linked	7 086	6 504	5 533	5 262	4 553	4 296	..	..
Other life insurance	188	150	122	8 465	8 411	7 674	..	..
Total life insurance	18 272	17 460	14 690	13 727	12 964	11 970	..	..
***of which:** Pension contracts*	5 810	5 552	5 208	334	157	38	..	..
1.1.4 Non-life insurance payments, by class, gross premiums								
Motor vehicle insurance	4 376	3 934	3 884	3 892	4 051	4 312	..	..
Marine, aviation and other transport insurance	525	435	404	361	283	273	..	..
Freight insurance	256	231	191	..	0	0	..	..
Fire and other property damage insurance	3 664	3 449	3 456	3 256	3 290	3 380	..	..
Pecuniary loss insurance	206	164	176	258	206	271	..	..
General liability insurance	1 125	1 064	1 033	882	883	919	..	..
Accident and health	8 167	7 867	7 851	46 459	47 499	50 393	..	..
***of which:** Health*	..	..	..	45 064	46 044	48 900	..	..
Other non-life insurance	1 919	1 976	2 016	1 049	1 165	1 099	..	..
Treaty reinsurance	..	..	..	..	0	0	..	..
Total non-life insurance	20 238	19 120	19 011	56 157	57 377	60 647	..	..
1.2 Gross claims payments								
Life								
Domestic undertakings	24 085	25 487	22 576	20 919	25 124	20 129	..	..
Foreign controlled undertakings	3 205	1 136	4 504	4 203	4 286	3 640	..	..
Foreign companies (branches)	420	0	0	..	..	..	..	..
All undertakings	24 505	25 487	22 576	20 919	25 124	20 129	..	..
Non-life								
Domestic undertakings	14 304	13 666	13 806	50 966	51 936	53 872	..	..
Foreign controlled undertakings	2 915	867	1 937	1 053	844	693	..	..
Foreign companies (branches)	41	149	0	..	..	..	..	..
All undertakings	14 345	13 815	13 806	50 966	51 936	53 872	..	..
Composite, all undertakings	**..**	**..**	**..**	**..**	**473**	**481**	**..**	**..**
Total								
Domestic undertakings	38 389	39 153	36 382	71 885	77 533	74 482	..	..
Foreign controlled undertakings	6 120	2 003	6 441	5 256	5 130	4 333	..	..
Foreign companies (branches)	461	149	0	..	..	..	..	..
All undertakings	38 850	39 302	36 382	71 885	77 533	74 482	..	..
1.3 Commissions								
Life								
Domestic undertakings	243	190	158	..	..	..	..	..
Foreign controlled undertakings	64	17	49	..	..	..	..	..
Foreign companies (branches)	12	0	0	..	..	..	..	..
All undertakings	255	190	158	..	..	..	..	..
Non-life								
Domestic undertakings	2 891	2 713	2 663	..	..	..	..	..
Foreign controlled undertakings	734	282	464	..	..	..	..	..
Foreign companies (branches)	22	21	0	..	..	..	..	..
All undertakings	2 913	2 734	2 663	..	..	..	..	..
Composite, all undertakings	**..**	**..**	**..**	**..**	**..**	**..**	**..**	**..**
Total								
Domestic undertakings	3 134	2 903	2 821	..	..	..	..	..
Foreign controlled undertakings	798	299	513	..	..	..	..	..
Foreign companies (branches)	34	21	0	..	..	..	..	..
All undertakings	3 168	2 924	2 821	..	..	..	..	..

Table 1. Selected aggregates *(cont.)*

Million EUR

	2013	2014	2015	2016	2017	2018	2019	2020
1.4 Gross operating expenses								
Life								
Domestic undertakings	2 266	2 497	2 072	2 183	2 002	1 839	..	..
Foreign controlled undertakings	297	113	378	417	356	274	..	..
Foreign companies (branches)	44	0	0	..	..	..	..	..
All undertakings	2 310	2 497	2 072	2 183	2 002	1 839	..	..
Non-life								
Domestic undertakings	4 809	4 635	4 485	6 219	6 156	6 235	..	..
Foreign controlled undertakings	1 136	373	771	525	550	461	..	..
Foreign companies (branches)	25	23	0	..	..	..	..	..
All undertakings	4 834	4 658	4 485	6 219	6 156	6 235	..	..
Composite, all undertakings	**..**	**..**	**..**	**..**	**115**	**71**	**..**	**..**
Total								
Domestic undertakings	7 075	7 132	6 557	8 402	8 273	8 145	..	..
Foreign controlled undertakings	1 433	486	1 149	942	906	735	..	..
Foreign companies (branches)	69	23	0	..	..	..	..	..
All undertakings	7 144	7 155	6 557	8 402	8 273	8 145	..	..
1.5 Insurance business written abroad by branches, gross premiums								
Life								
Branches and agencies	370	276	..	253	260	291	..	..
Subsidaries	..	..	..	..	..	..	..	..
Total	370	276	267	253	260	291	..	..
Non-life								
Branches and agencies	1 132	1 289	..	175	163	153	..	..
Subsidaries	..	..	..	..	..	..	..	..
Total	1 132	1 289	1 487	175	163	153	..	..
Composite total	**..**	**..**	**..**	**..**	**0**	**477**	**..**	**..**
Total								
Branches and agencies	1 502	1 565	..	428	423	921	..	..
Subsidaries	..	..	..	..	..	..	..	..
Total	1 502	1 565	1 754	428	423	921	..	..

.. Not available

Note: Detailed metadata at: *http://metalinks.oecd.org/ins/20220309/07de*.

Source: *OECD Insurance Statistics (database)*

Table 2. Number of companies and employees

	2013	2014	2015	2016	2017	2018	2019	2020
2.1 Number of companies								
Life								
Domestic undertakings	36	38	..	31	30	27	..	..
Foreign controlled undertakings	6	7	..	11	10	6	..	..
Foreign companies (branches)	4	0	..	..	..	..	..	..
All undertakings	40	38	..	31	30	27	..	..
Non-life								
Domestic undertakings	316	136	..	107	101	96	..	..
Foreign controlled undertakings	14	8	..	9	8	7	..	..
Foreign companies (branches)	1	2	..	..	..	..	..	..
All undertakings	317	138	..	107	101	96	..	..
Composite, all undertakings	**0**	**0**	**0**	**0**	**0**	**..**	**..**	**..**
Reinsurance								
Domestic undertakings	11	10	..	9	9	8	..	..
Foreign controlled undertakings	0	0	..	0	0	0	..	..
Foreign companies (branches)	0	0	..	..	..	..	..	..
All undertakings	11	10	..	9	9	8	..	..
Total								
Domestic undertakings	363	184	..	147	140	131	..	..
Foreign controlled undertakings	20	15	..	20	18	13	..	..
Foreign companies (branches)	5	2	..	..	..	..	..	..
All undertakings	368	186	..	147	140	131	..	..
2.2 Number of employees								
Insurance undertakings	..	..	..	..	..	..	..	..
Intermediaries	..	..	..	..	..	..	..	..
Total	..	..	..	..	..	..	..	..

.. Not available

Note: Detailed metadata at: *http://metalinks.oecd.org/ins/20220309/07de.*

Source: OECD *Insurance Statistics (database)*

NEW ZEALAND

Table 1. Selected aggregates

Million NZD

	2013	2014	2015	2016	2017	2018	2019	2020
1.1 Insurance business written in the reporting country								
1.1.1 Insurance business, by ownership								
Gross premiums								
Domestic undertakings	..	..	..	..	..	..	9 384	..
Foreign controlled undertakings	..	..	..	..	..	..	6 678	..
Foreign companies (branches)	..	..	..	..	..	..	1 634	..
All undertakings	6 266	6 460	6 678	6 828	7 240	..	11 017	..
Premiums ceded								
Domestic undertakings	..	..	..	..	..	..	2 548	..
Foreign controlled undertakings	..	..	..	..	..	..	2 148	..
Foreign companies (branches)	..	..	..	..	..	..	721	..
All undertakings	1 412	1 292	1 305	1 789	1 852	..	3 269	..
Net written premiums								
Domestic undertakings	..	..	..	..	..	..	6 836	..
Foreign controlled undertakings	..	..	..	..	..	..	4 530	..
Foreign companies (branches)	..	..	..	..	..	..	912	..
All undertakings	6 758	7 186	7 523	7 303	7 729	..	7 748	..
1.1.2 Insurance business on foreign risks, gross premiums								
Life	..	..	..	..	..	..	0	..
Non-life	..	..	..	..	..	..	0	..
Composite	..	..	..	..	..	..	0	..
of which:								
Life	..	..	..	..	..	..	0	..
Non-life	..	..	..	..	..	..	0	..
Total	..	..	..	..	..	..	0	..
1.1.3 Life insurance payments, by class, gross premiums								
Annuities	..	..	..	..	..	..	1	..
Unit linked	..	..	..	..	..	..	9	..
Other life insurance	..	..	..	..	..	..	2 587	..
Total life insurance	..	..	..	..	..	..	2 597	..
***of which:** Pension contracts*	..	..	..	..	..	..	0	..
1.1.4 Non-life insurance payments, by class, gross premiums								
Motor vehicle insurance	..	..	..	..	..	..	2 154	..
Marine, aviation and other transport insurance	..	..	..	..	..	..	149	..
Freight insurance	..	..	..	..	..	..	..	..
Fire and other property damage insurance	..	..	..	..	..	..	3 388	..
Pecuniary loss insurance	..	..	..	..	..	..	..	..
General liability insurance	..	..	..	..	..	..	593	..
Accident and health	..	..	..	..	..	..	1 678	..
***of which:** Health*	..	..	..	..	..	..	1 633	..
Other non-life insurance	..	..	..	..	..	..	455	..
Treaty reinsurance	..	..	..	..	..	..	..	..
Total non-life insurance	6 266	6 460	6 678	6 828	7 240	..	8 415	..
1.2 Gross claims payments								
Life								
Domestic undertakings	..	..	..	..	..	..	556	..
Foreign controlled undertakings	..	..	..	..	..	..	388	..
Foreign companies (branches)	..	..	..	..	..	..	355	..
All undertakings	1 303	1 399	1 544	1 598	1 579	..	911	..
Non-life								
Domestic undertakings	..	..	..	..	..	..	4 730	..
Foreign controlled undertakings	..	..	..	..	..	..	3 119	..
Foreign companies (branches)	..	..	..	..	..	..	588	..
All undertakings	4 539	5 642	6 302	4 864	6 662	..	5 318	..
Composite								
Domestic undertakings	..	..	..	..	..	..	755	..
Foreign controlled undertakings	..	..	..	..	..	..	590	..
Foreign companies (branches)	..	..	..	..	..	..	84	..
All undertakings	..	..	..	..	..	..	839	..
of which:								
Life	..	..	..	..	..	..	549	..
Domestic undertakings	..	..	..	..	..	..	478	..
Foreign controlled undertakings	..	..	..	..	..	..	372	..
Foreign companies (branches)	..	..	..	..	..	..	71	..
All undertakings	..	..	..	..	..	..	549	..
Non-life	..	..	..	..	..	..	291	..
Domestic undertakings	..	..	..	..	..	..	277	..
Foreign controlled undertakings	..	..	..	..	..	..	218	..
Foreign companies (branches)	..	..	..	..	..	..	13	..
All undertakings	..	..	..	..	..	..	291	..
Total								
Domestic undertakings	..	..	..	..	..	..	6 041	..
Foreign controlled undertakings	..	..	..	..	..	..	4 097	..
Foreign companies (branches)	..	..	..	..	..	..	1 027	..
All undertakings	5 842	7 041	7 846	6 462	8 241	..	7 068	..

Table 1. Selected aggregates *(cont.)*

Million NZD

	2013	2014	2015	2016	2017	2018	2019	2020
1.3 Commissions								
Life								
Domestic undertakings	..	..	..	..	..	..	169	..
Foreign controlled undertakings	..	..	..	..	..	..	105	..
Foreign companies (branches)	..	..	..	..	..	..	35	..
All undertakings	..	..	..	..	..	..	204	..
Non-life								
Domestic undertakings	..	..	..	..	..	..	659	..
Foreign controlled undertakings	..	..	..	..	..	..	618	..
Foreign companies (branches)	..	..	..	..	..	..	190	..
All undertakings	..	..	..	..	..	..	849	..
Composite								
Domestic undertakings	..	..	..	..	..	..	313	..
Foreign controlled undertakings	..	..	..	..	..	..	196	..
Foreign companies (branches)	..	..	..	..	..	..	31	..
All undertakings	..	..	..	..	..	..	343	..
of which:								
Life	..	..	..	..	..	..	267	..
Domestic undertakings	..	..	..	..	..	..	240	..
Foreign controlled undertakings	..	..	..	..	..	..	144	..
Foreign companies (branches)	..	..	..	..	..	..	27	..
All undertakings	..	..	..	..	..	..	267	..
Non-life	..	..	..	..	..	..	76	..
Domestic undertakings	..	..	..	..	..	..	73	..
Foreign controlled undertakings	..	..	..	..	..	..	52	..
Foreign companies (branches)	..	..	..	..	..	..	3	..
All undertakings	..	..	..	..	..	..	76	..
Total								
Domestic undertakings	..	..	..	..	..	..	1 140	..
Foreign controlled undertakings	..	..	..	..	..	..	918	..
Foreign companies (branches)	..	..	..	..	..	..	256	..
All undertakings	..	..	..	..	..	..	1 396	..
1.4 Gross operating expenses								
Life								
Domestic undertakings	..	..	..	..	..	..	291	..
Foreign controlled undertakings	..	..	..	..	..	..	206	..
Foreign companies (branches)	..	..	..	..	..	..	70	..
All undertakings	2 151	2 384	2 323	2 489	2 476	..	360	..
Non-life								
Domestic undertakings	..	..	..	..	..	..	989	..
Foreign controlled undertakings	..	..	..	..	..	..	655	..
Foreign companies (branches)	..	..	..	..	..	..	153	..
All undertakings	6 102	7 490	8 472	6 875	8 884	..	1 142	..
Composite								
Domestic undertakings	..	..	..	..	..	..	342	..
Foreign controlled undertakings	..	..	..	..	..	..	258	..
Foreign companies (branches)	..	..	..	..	..	..	38	..
All undertakings	..	..	..	..	..	..	380	..
of which:								
Life	..	..	..	..	..	..	294	..
Domestic undertakings	..	..	..	..	..	..	261	..
Foreign controlled undertakings	..	..	..	..	..	..	200	..
Foreign companies (branches)	..	..	..	..	..	..	33	..
All undertakings	..	..	..	..	..	..	294	..
Non-life	..	..	..	..	..	..	86	..
Domestic undertakings	..	..	..	..	..	..	81	..
Foreign controlled undertakings	..	..	..	..	..	..	58	..
Foreign companies (branches)	..	..	..	..	..	..	5	..
All undertakings	..	..	..	..	..	..	86	..
Total								
Domestic undertakings	..	..	..	..	..	..	1 622	..
Foreign controlled undertakings	..	..	..	..	..	..	1 119	..
Foreign companies (branches)	..	..	..	..	..	..	261	..
All undertakings	8 253	9 874	10 795	9 364	11 360	..	1 882	..

Table 1. Selected aggregates *(cont.)*

Million NZD

	2013	2014	2015	2016	2017	2018	2019	2020
1.5 Insurance business written abroad by branches, gross premiums								
Life								
Branches and agencies	..	..	..	..	..	..	0	..
Subsidaries	..	..	..	..	..	..	..	..
Total	..	..	..	..	..	..	0	..
Non-life								
Branches and agencies	..	..	..	..	..	..	22	..
Subsidaries	..	..	..	..	..	..	..	..
Total	..	..	..	..	..	..	22	..
Composite								
Branches and agencies	..	..	..	..	..	..	0	..
Subsidaries	..	..	..	..	..	..	..	..
Total	..	..	..	..	..	..	0	..
of which:								
Life	..	..	..	..	..	..	0	..
Branches and agencies	..	..	..	..	..	..	0	..
Subsidaries	..	..	..	..	..	..	..	..
Total	..	..	..	..	..	..	0	..
Non-life	..	..	..	..	..	..	0	..
Branches and agencies	..	..	..	..	..	..	0	..
Subsidaries	..	..	..	..	..	..	..	..
Total	..	..	..	..	..	..	0	..
Total								
Branches and agencies	..	..	..	..	..	..	22	..
Subsidaries	..	..	..	..	..	..	..	..
Total	..	..	..	..	..	..	22	..

.. Not available

Note: Detailed metadata at: *http://metalinks.oecd.org/ins/20220309/3c97*.

Source: *OECD Insurance Statistics (database)*

Table 2. Number of companies and employees

	2013	2014	2015	2016	2017	2018	2019	2020
2.1 Number of companies								
Life								
Domestic undertakings	..	..	..	..	..	..	14	..
Foreign controlled undertakings	..	..	..	..	..	..	6	..
Foreign companies (branches)	..	..	..	..	..	..	3	..
All undertakings	37	43	30	30	30	..	17	..
Non-life								
Domestic undertakings	..	..	..	..	..	..	31	..
Foreign controlled undertakings	..	..	..	..	..	..	9	..
Foreign companies (branches)	..	..	..	..	..	..	20	..
All undertakings	130	145	102	90	87	..	51	..
Composite								
Domestic undertakings	..	..	..	..	..	..	10	..
Foreign controlled undertakings	..	..	..	..	..	..	3	..
Foreign companies (branches)	..	..	..	..	..	..	1	..
All undertakings	..	..	..	..	..	..	11	..
Reinsurance								
Domestic undertakings	..	..	..	..	..	..	0	..
Foreign controlled undertakings	..	..	..	..	..	..	0	..
Foreign companies (branches)	..	..	..	..	..	..	9	..
All undertakings	..	..	..	..	..	..	9	..
Total								
Domestic undertakings	..	..	..	..	..	..	55	..
Foreign controlled undertakings	..	..	..	..	..	..	18	..
Foreign companies (branches)	..	..	..	..	..	..	32	..
All undertakings	167	188	132	120	117	..	87	..
2.2 Number of employees								
Insurance undertakings	10 780	10 720	10 680	..	..	..	..	..
Intermediaries	..	..	..	..	..	..	..	..
Total	10 780	..	..	..	..	..	..	..

.. Not available

Note: Detailed metadata at: *http://metalinks.oecd.org/ins/20220309/3c97.*

Source: *OECD Insurance Statistics (database)*

NORWAY

Table 1. Selected aggregates

Million NOK

	2013	2014	2015	2016	2017	2018	2019	2020
1.1 Insurance business written in the reporting country								
1.1.1 Insurance business, by ownership								
Gross premiums								
Domestic undertakings	119 149	134 884	135 864	138 612	139 748	148 945	161 842	166 238
Foreign controlled undertakings	8 948	11 029	13 195	..	..	..	..	..
Foreign companies (branches)	30 872	31 867	30 638	31 150	29 049	29 917	32 324	34 607
All undertakings	150 021	166 751	166 502	169 762	168 797	178 862	194 166	200 845
Premiums ceded								
Domestic undertakings	6 396	6 891	7 973	7 053	7 061	7 109	6 671	7 364
Foreign controlled undertakings	173	198	218	..	..	..	..	..
Foreign companies (branches)	4 219	4 653	4 976	5 362	4 814	4 868	5 613	6 664
All undertakings	10 614	11 544	12 950	12 415	11 876	11 976	12 284	14 028
Net written premiums								
Domestic undertakings	112 754	127 993	127 890	131 559	132 686	141 836	155 171	158 874
Foreign controlled undertakings	8 775	10 832	12 978	..	..	..	..	..
Foreign companies (branches)	26 653	27 213	25 662	25 788	24 235	25 049	26 711	27 943
All undertakings	139 407	155 206	153 552	157 347	156 921	166 885	181 882	186 817
1.1.2 Insurance business on foreign risks, gross premiums								
Life	..	..	9	7	6	4 144	2	3
Non-life	6 202	11 468	11 250	10 855	10 417	10 989	12 310	16 571
Composite total	..	..	..	..	..	..	..	..
Total	6 202	11 468	11 260	10 862	10 422	15 133	12 313	16 573
1.1.3 Life insurance payments, by class, gross premiums								
Annuities	..	..	..	..	..	..	..	..
Unit linked	..	..	..	..	..	..	..	..
Other life insurance	..	..	..	..	..	..	..	..
Total life insurance	81 299	92 185	91 794	94 093	93 577	99 961	108 693	106 179
***of which:** Pension contracts*	66 873	..	..	..	..	..	..	..
1.1.4 Non-life insurance payments, by class, gross premiums								
Motor vehicle insurance	..	20 378	20 706	20 897	21 029	22 316	24 811	26 390
Marine, aviation and other transport insurance	..	6 574	5 201	15 291	5 292	5 203	11 270	16 064
Freight insurance	..	..	..	0	..	..	..	..
Fire and other property damage insurance	..	18 195	19 041	23 135	22 553	23 487	25 120	26 456
Pecuniary loss insurance	..	127	97	432	92	98	..	375
General liability insurance	..	1 695	1 637	2 000	1 774	1 980	3 276	3 663
Accident and health	..	5 608	5 553	10 526	10 288	11 075	12 004	11 951
***of which:** Health*	..	..	..	0	..	..	..	..
Other non-life insurance	..	21 989	13 048	7 085	6 088	12 644	8 992	9 766
Treaty reinsurance	..	..	..	0	..	2 099	..	..
Total non-life insurance	..	74 566	65 283	79 366	67 116	78 901	85 472	94 666
1.2 Gross claims payments								
Life								
Domestic undertakings	45 143	45 742	49 007	51 548	54 419	58 887	60 593	64 574
Foreign controlled undertakings	3 186	3 150	4 796	.. c	..	..	.. c	..
Foreign companies (branches)	692	476	235	288	281	298	288	261
All undertakings	45 835	46 218	49 242	51 836	54 700	59 185	60 881	64 836
Non-life								
Domestic undertakings	23 486	30 742	34 587	32 537	31 896	34 370	37 564	38 993
Foreign controlled undertakings	.. c	.. c	.. c	.. c	..	..	.. c	..
Foreign companies (branches)	20 026	22 287	21 584	21 146	20 655	20 427	23 006	24 786
All undertakings	43 512	53 030	56 170	53 683	52 550	54 797	60 569	63 779
Composite, all undertakings	..	..	..	..	..	..	..	..
Total								
Domestic undertakings	68 629	76 485	83 593	84 085	86 315	93 257	98 157	103 567
Foreign controlled undertakings	3 186	3 150	4 796	..	..	..	..	..
Foreign companies (branches)	20 718	22 763	21 819	21 434	20 935	20 725	23 294	25 047
All undertakings	89 347	99 248	105 413	105 519	107 250	113 983	121 451	128 615
1.3 Commissions								
Life								
Domestic undertakings	774	839	916	890	783	737	913	990
Foreign controlled undertakings	179	202	227	.. c	.. c	.. c	.. c	.. c
Foreign companies (branches)	0	0	..	..	..	..	..	..
All undertakings	774	839	916	890	783	737	913	990
Non-life								
Domestic undertakings	1 536	2 204	2 119	1 956	2 105	2 309	2 684	3 248
Foreign controlled undertakings	.. c	.. c	..	.. c	.. c	.. c	.. c	.. c
Foreign companies (branches)	1 084	1 099	1 107	950	915	916	952	1 013
All undertakings	2 619	3 303	3 226	2 906	3 020	3 224	3 636	4 260
Composite, all undertakings	..	..	..	..	..	..	..	..
Total								
Domestic undertakings	2 310	3 043	3 035	2 846	2 889	3 046	3 597	4 238
Foreign controlled undertakings	179	202	227	..	..	..	..	..
Foreign companies (branches)	1 084	1 099	1 107	950	915	916	952	1 013
All undertakings	3 393	4 142	4 142	3 797	3 804	3 961	4 549	5 250

NORWAY

Table 1. Selected aggregates (cont.)

Million NOK

	2013	2014	2015	2016	2017	2018	2019	2020
1.4 Gross operating expenses								
Life								
Domestic undertakings	6 688	7 205	7 383	7 750	7 380	7 817	8 313	8 492
Foreign controlled undertakings	185	807	765	.. c	..	..	..	.. c
Foreign companies (branches)	126	162	..	157	143	126	83	85
All undertakings	6 814	7 367	7 383	7 907	7 523	7 943	8 396	8 577
Non-life								
Domestic undertakings	5 925	6 585	6 138	6 139	6 956	11 045	8 474	9 700
Foreign controlled undertakings	.. c	.. c	.. c	.. c	..	..	..	.. c
Foreign companies (branches)	4 203	5 318	5 574	5 465	4 732	5 207	4 862	5 206
All undertakings	10 128	11 903	11 712	11 605	11 688	16 252	13 336	14 907
Composite, all undertakings	..	..	..	..	..	..	..	..
Total								
Domestic undertakings	12 613	13 790	13 521	13 889	14 336	18 862	16 787	18 192
Foreign controlled undertakings	185	807	765	..	..	..	..	..
Foreign companies (branches)	4 329	5 480	5 574	5 623	4 875	5 333	4 945	5 292
All undertakings	16 942	19 270	19 095	19 512	19 211	24 195	21 732	23 484
1.5 Insurance business written abroad by branches, gross premiums								
Life								
Branches and agencies	.. c	..	..	..	..	..	..	..
Subsidaries	..	..	..	..	..	..	..	..
Total	.. c	..	..	..	..	..	..	..
Non-life								
Branches and agencies	1 134	4 636	1 569	7 141	2 493	2 431	4 073	6 351
Subsidaries	.. c	.. c	..	..	..	..	..	..
Total	1 134	4 636	1 569	7 141	2 493	2 431	4 073	6 351
Composite total	..	..	..	..	..	..	..	..
Total								
Branches and agencies	1 134	4 636	1 569	7 141	2 493	2 431	4 073	6 351
Subsidaries	..	..	..	..	..	..	..	..
Total	1 134	4 636	1 569	7 141	2 493	2 431	4 073	6 351

.. Not available; c Confidential data

Note: Detailed metadata at: *http://metalinks.oecd.org/ins/20220309/0be1*.

Source: *OECD Insurance Statistics (database)*

Table 2. Number of companies and employees

	2013	2014	2015	2016	2017	2018	2019	2020
2.1 Number of companies								
Life								
Domestic undertakings	12	10	10	10	13	12	11	12
Foreign controlled undertakings	2	2	2	2	3	3	3	3
Foreign companies (branches)	9	7	7	7	6	6	6	6
All undertakings	21	17	17	17	19	18	17	18
Non-life								
Domestic undertakings	59	59	58	59	58	56	55	52
Foreign controlled undertakings	1	1	2	2	2	1	1	2
Foreign companies (branches)	25	22	21	23	23	21	24	24
All undertakings	84	81	79	82	81	77	79	76
Composite, all undertakings	**0**	**0**	**0**	..	..	..	..	..
Reinsurance								
Domestic undertakings	..	..	..	..	..	..	..	..
Foreign controlled undertakings	..	..	..	..	..	..	..	..
Foreign companies (branches)	..	..	..	..	..	..	..	..
All undertakings	..	..	..	..	..	..	..	..
Total								
Domestic undertakings	71	69	68	69	71	68	66	64
Foreign controlled undertakings	3	3	4	4	5	4	4	5
Foreign companies (branches)	34	29	28	30	29	27	30	30
All undertakings	105	98	96	99	100	95	96	94
2.2 Number of employees								
Insurance undertakings	..	..	..	..	..	..	..	..
Intermediaries	..	..	..	..	..	..	..	..
Total	..	..	..	..	..	..	..	..

.. Not available
Note: Detailed metadata at: *http://metalinks.oecd.org/ins/20220309/0be1*.
Source: *OECD Insurance Statistics (database)*

POLAND

Table 1. Selected aggregates

Million PLN

	2013	2014	2015	2016	2017	2018	2019	2020
1.1 Insurance business written in the reporting country								
1.1.1 Insurance business, by ownership								
Gross premiums								
Domestic undertakings	57 863	54 927	54 804	56 039	62 339	62 161	63 838	63 432
Foreign controlled undertakings	31 562	30 425	30 801	31 961	33 189	33 452	35 129	35 375
Foreign companies (branches)	..	..	..	..	..	..	..	..
All undertakings	57 863	54 927	54 804	56 039	62 339	62 161	63 838	63 432
Premiums ceded								
Domestic undertakings	4 214	4 170	5 197	6 765	7 216	7 235	7 940	8 332
Foreign controlled undertakings	3 664	3 533	4 355	4 798	4 664	4 396	4 768	5 171
Foreign companies (branches)	..	..	..	..	..	..	..	..
All undertakings	4 214	4 170	5 197	6 765	7 216	7 235	7 940	8 332
Net written premiums								
Domestic undertakings	53 649	50 757	49 606	49 274	55 123	54 927	55 898	55 100
Foreign controlled undertakings	27 898	26 892	26 446	27 163	28 525	29 057	30 361	30 204
Foreign companies (branches)	..	..	..	..	..	..	..	..
All undertakings	53 649	50 757	49 606	49 274	55 123	54 927	55 898	55 100
1.1.2 Insurance business on foreign risks, gross premiums								
Life	..	..	..	..	118	100	215	255
Non-life	..	..	..	..	181	255	422	445
Composite total	..	..	..	..	..	..	..	..
Total	..	..	..	..	299	355	637	699
1.1.3 Life insurance payments, by class, gross premiums								
Annuities	107	114	131	138	0	0	0	0
Unit linked	13 052	12 600	12 996	10 325	10 955	7 487	6 440	5 589
Other life insurance	18 082	15 933	14 377	13 370	13 583	14 216	14 187	14 380
Total life insurance	31 241	28 646	27 505	23 833	24 539	21 702	20 627	19 970
***of which:** Pension contracts*	396	356	356	..	243	230	962	945
1.1.4 Non-life insurance payments, by class, gross premiums								
Motor vehicle insurance	13 945	13 397	13 910	18 744	23 249	24 295	24 638	24 483
Marine, aviation and other transport insurance	267	275	210	185	271	319	435	396
Freight insurance	117	126	116	120	..	..	0	0
Fire and other property damage insurance	5 973	5 715	5 938	6 246	6 877	7 618	8 249	8 748
Pecuniary loss insurance	1 858	2 149	1 893	1 805	1 713	1 812	2 203	2 036
General liability insurance	1 891	1 964	2 134	1 915	2 064	2 297	2 518	2 685
Accident and health	1 926	2 007	2 273	2 222	2 347	2 715	2 972	3 478
***of which:** Health*	612	656	613	618	561	872	942	671
Other non-life insurance	622	627	804	947	1 256	1 403	2 197	1 634
Treaty reinsurance	..	..	..	..	..	..	0	0
Total non-life insurance	26 599	26 260	27 278	32 182	37 777	40 459	43 211	43 461
1.2 Gross claims payments								
Life								
Domestic undertakings	23 087	20 360	19 358	18 284	20 315	21 401	18 306	17 198
Foreign controlled undertakings	10 927	9 783	8 795	9 543	9 295	10 029	8 825	7 764
Foreign companies (branches)	..	..	..	..	..	..	..	..
All undertakings	23 087	20 360	19 358	18 284	20 315	21 401	18 306	17 198
Non-life								
Domestic undertakings	13 711	13 811	15 488	18 393	19 931	21 011	22 605	22 951
Foreign controlled undertakings	8 434	8 579	9 515	10 911	11 453	12 435	13 797	13 833
Foreign companies (branches)	..	..	..	..	..	..	..	..
All undertakings	13 711	13 811	15 488	18 393	19 931	21 011	22 605	22 951
Composite, all undertakings	..	..	..	..	..	..	..	..
Total								
Domestic undertakings	36 798	34 171	34 846	36 677	40 246	42 412	40 911	40 149
Foreign controlled undertakings	19 362	18 363	18 310	20 454	20 748	22 464	22 622	21 597
Foreign companies (branches)	..	..	..	..	..	..	..	..
All undertakings	36 798	34 171	34 846	36 677	40 246	42 412	40 911	40 149
1.3 Commissions								
Life								
Domestic undertakings	93	203	231	222	183	2 854	2 719	2 674
Foreign controlled undertakings	70	191	223	218	179	1 754	1 594	1 594
Foreign companies (branches)	..	..	..	..	..	..	..	..
All undertakings	93	203	231	222	183	2 854	2 719	2 674
Non-life								
Domestic undertakings	740	651	719	1 115	1 545	6 720	7 131	7 416
Foreign controlled undertakings	606	594	657	929	1 122	4 641	4 826	4 887
Foreign companies (branches)	..	..	..	..	..	..	..	..
All undertakings	740	651	719	1 115	1 545	6 720	7 131	7 416
Composite, all undertakings	..	..	..	..	..	..	..	..
Total								
Domestic undertakings	833	854	950	1 337	1 727	9 574	9 850	10 090
Foreign controlled undertakings	676	785	880	1 147	1 301	6 396	6 420	6 481
Foreign companies (branches)	..	..	..	..	..	..	..	..
All undertakings	833	854	950	1 337	1 727	9 574	9 850	10 090

Table 1. Selected aggregates *(cont.)*

Million PLN

	2013	2014	2015	2016	2017	2018	2019	2020
1.4 Gross operating expenses								
Life								
Domestic undertakings	6 146	6 588	6 476	5 647	5 963	5 697	5 615	5 682
Foreign controlled undertakings	3 831	4 369	4 182	3 797	3 491	3 276	3 093	3 221
Foreign companies (branches)	..	..	..	..	..	..	..	..
All undertakings	6 146	6 588	6 476	5 647	5 963	5 697	5 615	5 682
Non-life								
Domestic undertakings	7 775	8 018	8 335	9 104	12 793	14 073	14 974	15 194
Foreign controlled undertakings	5 090	5 135	5 569	5 978	7 938	8 744	9 193	9 111
Foreign companies (branches)	..	..	..	..	..	..	..	..
All undertakings	7 775	8 018	8 335	9 104	12 793	14 073	14 974	15 194
Composite, all undertakings	..	..	..	..	..	..	..	..
Total								
Domestic undertakings	13 921	14 606	14 811	14 751	18 756	19 770	20 589	20 876
Foreign controlled undertakings	8 921	9 504	9 751	9 776	11 429	12 021	12 286	12 332
Foreign companies (branches)	..	..	..	..	..	..	..	..
All undertakings	13 921	14 606	14 811	14 751	18 756	19 770	20 589	20 876
1.5 Insurance business written abroad by branches, gross premiums								
Life								
Branches and agencies	..	79	92	..	95	80	99	118
Subsidaries	..	..	..	..	..	..	..	..
Total	..	79	92	..	95	80	99	118
Non-life								
Branches and agencies	..	98	116	..	..	0	0	0
Subsidaries	..	..	..	..	..	..	..	..
Total	..	98	116	..	..	0	0	0
Composite total	..	..	..	..	..	..	..	..
Total								
Branches and agencies	..	177	208	..	95	80	99	118
Subsidaries	..	..	..	..	..	..	..	..
Total	..	177	208	..	95	80	99	118

.. Not available

Note: Detailed metadata at: *http://metalinks.oecd.org/ins/20220309/73c9*.

Source: *OECD Insurance Statistics (database)*

Table 2. Number of companies and employees

	2013	2014	2015	2016	2017	2018	2019	2020
2.1 Number of companies								
Life								
Domestic undertakings	27	26	28	27	27	26	25	27
Foreign controlled undertakings	21	19	21	21	20	18	17	18
Foreign companies (branches)	..	..	..	..	..	..	..	..
All undertakings	27	26	28	27	27	26	25	27
Non-life								
Domestic undertakings	30	30	32	33	33	33	33	32
Foreign controlled undertakings	19	19	22	20	19	19	19	18
Foreign companies (branches)	..	..	..	..	..	..	..	..
All undertakings	30	30	32	33	33	33	33	32
Composite, all undertakings	**0**	**0**	**0**	**0**	..	..	..	..
Reinsurance								
Domestic undertakings	1	1	1	1	1	1	1	1
Foreign controlled undertakings	1	1	1	1	1	1	1	1
Foreign companies (branches)	..	..	..	..	..	..	..	..
All undertakings	1	1	1	1	1	1	1	1
Total								
Domestic undertakings	58	57	61	61	61	60	59	60
Foreign controlled undertakings	41	39	44	42	40	38	37	37
Foreign companies (branches)	..	..	..	..	..	..	..	..
All undertakings	58	57	61	61	61	60	59	60
2.2 Number of employees								
Insurance undertakings	37 187	35 922	35 282	..	..	..	42 287	9 411
Intermediaries	69 621	58 004	49 126	..	..	..	..	..
Total	106 808	93 926	84 408	..	..	..	42 287	9 411

.. Not available

Note: Detailed metadata at: *http://metalinks.oecd.org/ins/20220309/73c9*.

Source: *OECD Insurance Statistics (database)*

PORTUGAL

Table 1. Selected aggregates

Million EUR

	2013	2014	2015	2016	2017	2018	2019	2020
1.1 Insurance business written in the reporting country								
1.1.1 Insurance business, by ownership								
Gross premiums								
Domestic undertakings	12 802	14 051	12 568	10 913	11 455	12 590	11 915	9 674
Foreign controlled undertakings	1 617	8 737	8 890	9 048	10 640	11 441	10 457	8 804
Foreign companies (branches)	0	0	0	0	0	0	0	0
All undertakings	12 802	14 051	12 568	10 913	11 455	12 590	11 915	9 674
Premiums ceded								
Domestic undertakings	1 144	1 118	1 194	1 214	1 307	1 338	1 638	1 771
Foreign controlled undertakings	140	836	924	992	1 180	1 209	1 505	1 667
Foreign companies (branches)	0	0	0	0	0	0	0	0
All undertakings	1 144	1 118	1 194	1 214	1 307	1 338	1 638	1 771
Net written premiums								
Domestic undertakings	11 658	12 933	11 374	9 698	10 148	11 252	10 277	7 903
Foreign controlled undertakings	1 477	7 902	7 966	8 056	9 460	10 232	8 952	7 137
Foreign companies (branches)	0	0	0	0	0	0	0	0
All undertakings	11 658	12 933	11 374	9 698	10 148	11 252	10 277	7 903
1.1.2 Insurance business on foreign risks, gross premiums								
Life	3	13	8	11	8	0	0	0
Non-life	14	13	13	4	7	8	15	18
Composite	64	92	107	127	129	195	252	119
of which:								
Life	27	53	63	70	74	132	183	42
Non-life	38	39	44	57	55	63	69	77
Total	81	118	129	142	144	203	267	137
1.1.3 Life insurance payments, by class, gross premiums								
Annuities	79	64	109	142	183	142	40	18
Unit linked	1 851	1 966	2 119	1 655	2 077	1 703	1 647	1 852
Other life insurance	7 094	8 220	6 254	4 708	4 450	5 934	5 072	2 421
Total life insurance	9 023	10 249	8 481	6 504	6 710	7 779	6 759	4 291
***of which:** Pension contracts*	..	..	..	..	..	..	..	..
1.1.4 Non-life insurance payments, by class, gross premiums								
Motor vehicle insurance	1 277	1 256	1 316	1 399	1 482	1 429	1 517	1 570
Marine, aviation and other transport insurance	33	29	28	25	27	26	29	30
Freight insurance	25	24	23	22	22	0	21	19
Fire and other property damage insurance	700	699	745	771	795	764	820	860
Pecuniary loss insurance	69	70	73	84	83	47	95	98
General liability insurance	84	87	94	99	102	101	117	128
Accident and health	1 413	1 452	1 602	1 783	1 999	2 141	2 354	2 466
***of which:** Health*	862	896	973	1 084	1 208	1 307	1 429	1 540
Other non-life insurance	178	183	205	225	235	239	201	212
Treaty reinsurance	0	0	0	0	0	..	..	..
Total non-life insurance	3 778	3 802	4 086	4 408	4 745	4 747	5 155	5 383
1.2 Gross claims payments								
Life								
Domestic undertakings	4 518	5 254	6 133	6 568	3 940	3 306	3 141	4 695
Foreign controlled undertakings	374	2 667	2 724	2 252	2 853	2 749	2 547	4 605
Foreign companies (branches)	0	0	0	0	0	0	0	0
All undertakings	4 518	5 254	6 133	6 568	3 940	3 306	3 141	4 695
Non-life								
Domestic undertakings	1 446	1 407	1 520	1 336	1 413	1 530	1 550	1 409
Foreign controlled undertakings	376	1 174	1 278	1 070	1 130	1 200	1 246	1 133
Foreign companies (branches)	0	0	0	0	0	0	0	0
All undertakings	1 446	1 407	1 520	1 336	1 413	1 530	1 550	1 409
Composite								
Domestic undertakings	5 427	5 201	5 128	4 554	4 230	5 086	4 341	4 150
Foreign controlled undertakings	562	3 991	3 922	4 501	4 180	4 606	3 877	3 847
Foreign companies (branches)	0	0	0	0	0	0	0	0
All undertakings	5 427	5 201	5 128	4 554	4 230	5 086	4 341	4 150
of which:								
Life	4 067	3 895	3 840	2 867	2 479	3 320	2 568	2 485
Domestic undertakings	4 067	3 895	3 840	2 867	2 479	3 320	2 568	2 485
Foreign controlled undertakings	167	2 904	2 839	2 815	2 431	2 843	2 106	2 183
Foreign companies (branches)	0	0	0	0	0	0	0	0
All undertakings	4 067	3 895	3 840	2 867	2 479	3 320	2 568	2 485
Non-life	1 360	1 306	1 288	1 687	1 751	1 766	1 774	1 665
Domestic undertakings	1 360	1 306	1 288	1 687	1 751	1 766	1 774	1 665
Foreign controlled undertakings	395	1 087	1 083	1 686	1 749	1 763	1 771	1 664
Foreign companies (branches)	0	0	0	0	0	0	0	0
All undertakings	1 360	1 306	1 288	1 687	1 751	1 766	1 774	1 665
Total								
Domestic undertakings	11 391	11 861	12 782	12 458	9 582	9 922	9 032	10 254
Foreign controlled undertakings	1 312	7 832	7 923	7 822	8 163	8 555	7 670	9 585
Foreign companies (branches)	0	0	0	0	0	0	0	0
All undertakings	11 391	11 861	12 782	12 458	9 582	9 922	9 032	10 254

Table 1. Selected aggregates *(cont.)*

Million EUR

	2013	2014	2015	2016	2017	2018	2019	2020
1.3 Commissions								
Life								
Domestic undertakings	144	40	77	105	103	89	132	132
Foreign controlled undertakings	7	15	41	42	85	78	116	126
Foreign companies (branches)	0	0	0	0	0	0	0	0
All undertakings	144	40	77	105	103	89	132	132
Non-life								
Domestic undertakings	156	153	178	164	183	194	220	214
Foreign controlled undertakings	38	117	133	98	115	124	141	136
Foreign companies (branches)	0	0	0	0	0	0	0	0
All undertakings	156	153	178	164	183	194	220	214
Composite								
Domestic undertakings	291	301	295	286	351	350	393	416
Foreign controlled undertakings	99	208	222	283	344	333	373	394
Foreign companies (branches)	0	0	0	0	0	0	0	0
All undertakings	291	301	295	286	351	350	393	416
of which:								
Life	98	100	82	49	58	75	86	94
Domestic undertakings	98	100	82	49	58	75	86	94
Foreign controlled undertakings	28	42	44	47	52	58	66	73
Foreign companies (branches)	0	0	0	0	0	0	0	0
All undertakings	98	100	82	49	58	75	86	94
Non-life	193	201	214	237	293	275	307	322
Domestic undertakings	193	201	214	237	293	275	307	322
Foreign controlled undertakings	71	165	178	236	291	275	306	321
Foreign companies (branches)	0	0	0	0	0	0	0	0
All undertakings	193	201	214	237	293	275	307	322
Total								
Domestic undertakings	591	493	550	554	637	633	745	762
Foreign controlled undertakings	144	339	396	423	543	534	630	657
Foreign companies (branches)	0	0	0	0	0	0	0	0
All undertakings	591	493	550	554	637	633	745	762
1.4 Gross operating expenses								
Life								
Domestic undertakings	314	212	244	300	298	280	289	291
Foreign controlled undertakings	33	136	163	168	248	246	254	280
Foreign companies (branches)	0	0	0	0	0	0	0	0
All undertakings	314	212	244	300	298	280	289	291
Non-life								
Domestic undertakings	496	495	550	467	494	513	549	539
Foreign controlled undertakings	133	398	441	357	388	402	430	414
Foreign companies (branches)	0	0	0	0	0	0	0	0
All undertakings	496	495	550	467	494	513	549	539
Composite								
Domestic undertakings	715	717	720	711	851	823	859	928
Foreign controlled undertakings	198	541	571	702	839	790	821	886
Foreign companies (branches)	0	0	0	0	0	0	0	0
All undertakings	715	717	720	711	851	823	859	928
of which:								
Life	234	230	222	148	173	206	207	222
Domestic undertakings	234	230	222	148	173	206	207	222
Foreign controlled undertakings	48	125	145	140	162	175	170	181
Foreign companies (branches)	0	0	0	0	0	0	0	0
All undertakings	234	230	222	148	173	206	207	222
Non-life	481	487	497	562	678	617	652	706
Domestic undertakings	481	487	497	562	678	617	652	706
Foreign controlled undertakings	151	416	427	562	677	615	651	705
Foreign companies (branches)	0	0	0	0	0	0	0	0
All undertakings	481	487	497	562	678	617	652	706
Total								
Domestic undertakings	1 525	1 425	1 513	1 478	1 643	1 615	1 697	1 759
Foreign controlled undertakings	364	1 076	1 176	1 227	1 474	1 438	1 505	1 581
Foreign companies (branches)	0	0	0	0	0	0	0	0
All undertakings	1 525	1 425	1 513	1 478	1 643	1 615	1 697	1 759

Table 1. Selected aggregates *(cont.)*

Million EUR

	2013	2014	2015	2016	2017	2018	2019	2020
1.5 Insurance business written abroad by branches, gross premiums								
Life								
Branches and agencies	3	13	8	11	8	0	0	0
Subsidaries	0	0	0	0	0	0	0	0
Total	3	13	8	11	8	0	0	0
Non-life								
Branches and agencies	12	12	12	1	3	0	6	14
Subsidaries	0	0	0	0	0	0	0	0
Total	12	12	12	1	3	0	6	14
Composite								
Branches and agencies	64	92	107	127	129	195	252	119
Subsidaries	0	0	0	0	0	0	0	0
Total	64	92	107	127	129	195	252	119
of which:								
Life	27	53	63	70	74	132	183	42
Branches and agencies	27	53	63	70	74	132	183	42
Subsidaries	0	0	0	0	0	0	0	0
Total	27	53	63	70	74	132	183	42
Non-life	38	39	44	57	55	63	69	77
Branches and agencies	38	39	44	57	55	63	69	77
Subsidaries	0	0	0	0	0	0	0	0
Total	38	39	44	57	55	63	69	77
Total								
Branches and agencies	79	117	128	138	140	195	258	134
Subsidaries	0	0	0	0	0	0	0	0
Total	79	117	128	138	140	195	258	134

.. Not available

Note: Detailed metadata at: *http://metalinks.oecd.org/ins/20220309/57ac.*

Source: OECD *Insurance Statistics (database)*

Table 2. Number of companies and employees

	2013	2014	2015	2016	2017	2018	2019	2020
2.1 Number of companies								
Life								
Domestic undertakings	14	16	16	14	13	12	12	11
Foreign controlled undertakings	5	10	10	9	9	10	10	10
Foreign companies (branches)	5	5	5	4	4	5	0	0
All undertakings	19	21	21	18	17	17	12	11
Non-life								
Domestic undertakings	21	21	24	23	23	23	22	21
Foreign controlled undertakings	4	15	16	15	15	16	15	14
Foreign companies (branches)	24	23	21	19	19	23	0	0
All undertakings	45	44	45	42	42	46	22	21
Composite								
Domestic undertakings	6	5	5	5	6	5	5	5
Foreign controlled undertakings	2	3	3	4	4	3	3	3
Foreign companies (branches)	6	6	7	7	7	9	0	0
All undertakings	12	11	12	12	13	14	5	5
Reinsurance								
Domestic undertakings	1	1	1	1	1	1	1	1
Foreign controlled undertakings	0	1	1	1	1	1	1	1
Foreign companies (branches)	0	0	0	0	0	0	0	0
All undertakings	1	1	1	1	1	1	1	1
Total								
Domestic undertakings	42	43	46	43	43	41	40	38
Foreign controlled undertakings	11	29	30	29	29	30	29	28
Foreign companies (branches)	35	34	33	30	30	37	0	0
All undertakings	77	77	79	73	73	78	40	38
2.2 Number of employees								
Insurance undertakings	9 224	9 252	9 441	9 387	9 381	8 781	8 781	8 566
Intermediaries	24 207	23 465	22 738	21 426	20 258	18 999	16 763	15 831
Total	33 431	32 717	32 179	30 813	29 639	27 780	25 544	24 397

Note: Detailed metadata at: *http://metalinks.oecd.org/ins/20220309/57ac.*
Source: OECD *Insurance Statistics (database)*

Table 1. Selected aggregates

Million EUR

	2013	2014	2015	2016	2017	2018	2019	2020
1.1 Insurance business written in the reporting country								
1.1.1 Insurance business, by ownership								
Gross premiums								
Domestic undertakings	2 082	2 106	2 020	..	4 186	..	2 304	2 224
Foreign controlled undertakings	1 901	1 918	1 827	..	..	..	2 044	2 037
Foreign companies (branches)	146	142	143	..	282	..	287	282
All undertakings	2 228	2 248	2 163	..	4 468	..	2 522	2 444
Premiums ceded								
Domestic undertakings	298	314	319	..	319	..	363	-258
Foreign controlled undertakings	268	283	287	..	..	..	280	-277
Foreign companies (branches)	19	17	17	..	31	..	30	30
All undertakings	316	331	336	..	350	..	365	-255
Net written premiums								
Domestic undertakings	1 785	1 792	1 701	..	3 868	..	1 941	1 877
Foreign controlled undertakings	1 633	1 635	1 540	..	..	..	1 765	1 755
Foreign companies (branches)	127	126	126	..	250	..	258	252
All undertakings	1 912	1 917	1 827	..	4 118	..	2 157	2 095
1.1.2 Insurance business on foreign risks, gross premiums								
Life	..	..	..	..	..	..	..	..
Non-life	..	..	..	..	..	..	..	..
Composite	..	..	..	..	..	..	..	..
of which:								
Life	..	..	..	..	..	..	..	..
Non-life	..	..	..	..	..	..	..	..
Total	..	..	..	..	..	..	..	..
1.1.3 Life insurance payments, by class, gross premiums								
Annuities	649	623	586	..	2	..	1	0
Unit linked	423	417	351	..	166	..	253	145
Other life insurance	164	180	171	..	950	..	947	844
Total life insurance	1 236	1 220	1 108	..	1 119	..	1 202	989
***of which:** Pension contracts*	12	12	12	..	..	..	..	..
1.1.4 Non-life insurance payments, by class, gross premiums								
Motor vehicle insurance	528	532	547	..	309	..	704	735
Marine, aviation and other transport insurance	6	6	6	..	10	..	12	0
Freight insurance	8	8	8	..	..	..	..	0
Fire and other property damage insurance	250	257	257	..	276	..	297	310
Pecuniary loss insurance	27	33	34	..	11	..	..	2
General liability insurance	73	78	78	..	80	..	79	80
Accident and health	45	49	44	..	..	..	..	106
***of which:** Health*	2	2	3	..	..	..	..	8
Other non-life insurance	34	35	39	..	397	..	100	-185
Treaty reinsurance	21	32	42	..	..	..	..	0
Total non-life insurance	992	1 028	1 055	..	1 083	..	1 366	1 046
1.2 Gross claims payments								
Life								
Domestic undertakings	91	107	98	186	76	..	74	74
Foreign controlled undertakings	91	107	98	..	73	..	71	63
Foreign companies (branches)	0	0	2	..	117	..	102	93
All undertakings	91	108	100	..	193	..	176	167
Non-life								
Domestic undertakings	0	0	0	..	..	..	..	..
Foreign controlled undertakings	0	0	0	..	..	..	..	..
Foreign companies (branches)	27	29	32	..	21	..	18	21
All undertakings	27	29	32	..	..	..	18	..
Composite								
Domestic undertakings	1 117	1 084	1 057	2 291	..	..	..	655
Foreign controlled undertakings	979	948	911	1 909	76	..	1 171	1 040
Foreign companies (branches)	14	16	16	..	21	..	46	33
All undertakings	1 131	1 099	1 073	..	..	..	1 367	688
of which:								
Life	658	646	575	..	..	..	747	206
Domestic undertakings	647	634	563	1 794	..	..	..	178
Foreign controlled undertakings	544	533	457	1 459	72	..	615	520
Foreign companies (branches)	11	12	12	..	17	..	37	28
All undertakings	658	646	575	..	..	..	747	206
Non-life	473	453	497	..	..	..	620	482
Domestic undertakings	470	450	494	497	..	..	..	477
Foreign controlled undertakings	435	415	454	450	4	..	555	520
Foreign companies (branches)	4	3	3	..	5	..	9	5
All undertakings	473	453	497	..	..	..	620	482
Total								
Domestic undertakings	1 208	1 191	1 155	2 477	76	..	74	729
Foreign controlled undertakings	1 070	1 055	1 010	1 909	149	..	1 242	1 103
Foreign companies (branches)	42	44	49	..	159	..	166	147
All undertakings	1 249	1 236	1 205	..	193	..	1 561	855

Table 1. Selected aggregates *(cont.)*

Million EUR

	2013	2014	2015	2016	2017	2018	2019	2020
1.3 Commissions								
Life								
Domestic undertakings	29	33	37	..	..	..	..	..
Foreign controlled undertakings	29	33	37	..	..	..	..	..
Foreign companies (branches)	1	1	2	..	23	..	26	29
All undertakings	30	34	39	..	..	..	..	29
Non-life								
Domestic undertakings	0	0	0	..	..	..	..	..
Foreign controlled undertakings	0	0	0	..	..	..	..	..
Foreign companies (branches)	13	15	18	..	21	..	22	23
All undertakings	13	15	18	..	..	..	..	23
Composite								
Domestic undertakings	251	259	250	..	..	..	..	..
Foreign controlled undertakings	238	244	233	..	..	..	..	..
Foreign companies (branches)	18	4	16	..	20	..	22	24
All undertakings	269	264	266	..	..	..	..	24
of which:								
Life	107	95	89	..	..	..	..	21
Domestic undertakings	93	95	77	..	..	..	..	..
Foreign controlled undertakings	90	91	73	..	..	..	..	..
Foreign companies (branches)	14	0	12	..	13	..	12	21
All undertakings	107	95	89	..	..	..	..	21
Non-life	162	168	177	..	..	..	..	3
Domestic undertakings	158	164	173	..	..	..	..	..
Foreign controlled undertakings	149	153	160	..	..	..	..	..
Foreign companies (branches)	4	4	5	..	7	..	10	3
All undertakings	162	168	177	..	..	..	..	3
Total								
Domestic undertakings	279	292	287	..	..	..	..	..
Foreign controlled undertakings	267	277	270	..	..	..	..	..
Foreign companies (branches)	32	21	36	..	64	..	71	75
All undertakings	311	313	323	..	..	..	..	75
1.4 Gross operating expenses								
Life								
Domestic undertakings	57	63	72	..	55	..	107 361 381	106
Foreign controlled undertakings	57	63	72	..	..	..	53 819 969	62
Foreign companies (branches)	2	2	3	..	51	..	58	64
All undertakings	59	65	75	..	105	..	165	169
Non-life								
Domestic undertakings	0	0	0	..	..	..	..	..
Foreign controlled undertakings	0	0	0	..	..	..	..	..
Foreign companies (branches)	30	31	32	..	41	..	39	39
All undertakings	30	31	32	..	41	..	39	..
Composite								
Domestic undertakings	522	529	505	..	502	..	641 249 475	655
Foreign controlled undertakings	492	498	472	..	..	..	..	609
Foreign companies (branches)	28	7	25	..	29	..	32	35
All undertakings	549	536	531	..	531	..	673	690
of which:								
Life	228	212	187	..	179	..	191	208
Domestic undertakings	207	212	170	..	161	..	173 023 120	178
Foreign controlled undertakings	197	202	160	..	..	..	..	165
Foreign companies (branches)	21	1	17	..	19	..	18	29
All undertakings	228	212	187	..	179	..	191	208
Non-life	321	324	344	..	351	..	482	482
Domestic undertakings	314	317	336	..	341	..	468 226 356	477
Foreign controlled undertakings	295	295	312	..	..	..	..	444
Foreign companies (branches)	7	6	8	..	10	..	14	5
All undertakings	321	324	344	..	351	..	482	482
Total								
Domestic undertakings	578	592	578	..	556	..	748 610 856	761
Foreign controlled undertakings	549	561	544	..	..	..	53 819 969	671
Foreign companies (branches)	60	40	60	..	121	..	129	138
All undertakings	639	632	638	..	677	..	877	859

Table 1. Selected aggregates *(cont.)*

Million EUR

	2013	2014	2015	2016	2017	2018	2019	2020
1.5 Insurance business written abroad by branches, gross premiums								
Life								
Branches and agencies	0	0	1	..	..	..	..	..
Subsidaries	0	1	5	..	..	..	..	..
Total	0	1	6	..	..	..	..	..
Non-life								
Branches and agencies	0	0	0	..	..	..	..	..
Subsidaries	0	0	0	..	..	..	..	..
Total	0	0	0	..	..	..	..	..
Composite								
Branches and agencies	1	2	2	..	..	..	..	..
Subsidaries	3	4	6	..	..	..	..	..
Total	5	6	8	..	..	..	..	..
of which:								
Life	0	0	0	..	..	..	..	..
Branches and agencies	0	0	0	..	..	..	..	..
Subsidaries	0	0	0	..	..	..	..	..
Total	0	0	0	..	..	..	..	..
Non-life	5	6	8	..	..	..	..	..
Branches and agencies	1	2	2	..	..	..	..	..
Subsidaries	3	4	6	..	..	..	..	..
Total	5	6	8	..	..	..	..	..
Total								
Branches and agencies	1	2	3	..	..	..	..	..
Subsidaries	3	5	10	..	..	..	..	..
Total	5	7	14	..	..	..	..	..

.. Not available

Note: Detailed metadata at: *http://metalinks.oecd.org/ins/20220309/e675*.

Source: *OECD Insurance Statistics (database)*

Table 2. Number of companies and employees

	2013	2014	2015	2016	2017	2018	2019	2020
2.1 Number of companies								
Life								
Domestic undertakings	5	5	5	3	3	..	3	2
Foreign controlled undertakings	5	5	5	3	2	..	2	1
Foreign companies (branches)	1	1	1	2	2	..	..	5
All undertakings	6	6	6	5	5	..	5	7
Non-life								
Domestic undertakings	0	0	0	0	0	..	0	0
Foreign controlled undertakings	0	0	0	0	0	..	0	0
Foreign companies (branches)	17	17	17	19	19	..	..	13
All undertakings	17	17	17	19	19	..	0	13
Composite								
Domestic undertakings	12	12	12	12	12	..	10	10
Foreign controlled undertakings	10	10	10	12	10	..	8	8
Foreign companies (branches)	2	2	2	18	2	..	..	12
All undertakings	14	14	14	30	14	..	18	22
Reinsurance								
Domestic undertakings	0	0	0	0	0	..	0	0
Foreign controlled undertakings	0	0	0	0	0	..	0	0
Foreign companies (branches)	1	1	1	0	0	..	..	0
All undertakings	1	1	1	0	0	..	0	0
Total								
Domestic undertakings	17	17	17	15	15	..	13	12
Foreign controlled undertakings	15	15	15	15	12	..	10	9
Foreign companies (branches)	21	21	21	39	23	..	..	30
All undertakings	38	38	38	54	38	..	..	42
2.2 Number of employees								
Insurance undertakings	5 778	5 937	..	..	..	..	..	..
Intermediaries	..	1 358	..	..	..	..	25 066	..
Total	..	7 295	..	..	..	..	..	..

.. Not available

Note: Detailed metadata at: *http://metalinks.oecd.org/ins/20220309/e675*.

Source: *OECD Insurance Statistics (database)*

SLOVENIA

Table 1. Selected aggregates

Million EUR

	2013	2014	2015	2016	2017	2018	2019	2020
1.1 Insurance business written in the reporting country								
1.1.1 Insurance business, by ownership								
Gross premiums								
Domestic undertakings	2 114	2 095	2 150	2 182	2 298	2 424	2 647	2 734
Foreign controlled undertakings	166	166	172	180	186	191	522	534
Foreign companies (branches)	..	..	..	..	..	..	..	..
All undertakings	2 114	2 095	2 150	2 182	2 298	2 424	2 647	2 734
Premiums ceded								
Domestic undertakings	258	274	256	269	310	320	377	335
Foreign controlled undertakings	27	28	33	39	42	42	65	73
Foreign companies (branches)	..	..	..	..	..	..	..	..
All undertakings	258	274	256	269	310	320	377	335
Net written premiums								
Domestic undertakings	1 856	1 821	1 894	1 914	1 988	2 105	2 270	2 399
Foreign controlled undertakings	140	137	139	141	144	149	457	461
Foreign companies (branches)	..	..	..	..	..	..	..	..
All undertakings	1 856	1 821	1 894	1 914	1 988	2 105	2 270	2 399
1.1.2 Insurance business on foreign risks, gross premiums								
Life	..	..	..	..	..	..	..	..
Non-life	0	0	0	..	..	..	..	..
Composite	2	1	1	..	..	..	..	..
of which:								
Life	0	0	1	..	..	..	..	..
Non-life	1	1	0	..	..	..	..	..
Total	2	2	2	..	..	..	..	..
1.1.3 Life insurance payments, by class, gross premiums								
Annuities	..	..	..	..	..	..	..	..
Unit linked	201	195	215	213	223	225	258	247
Other life insurance	273	284	283	279	293	301	293	275
Total life insurance	473	479	498	492	516	526	551	522
***of which:** Pension contracts*	45	37	37	39	41	41	50	53
1.1.4 Non-life insurance payments, by class, gross premiums								
Motor vehicle insurance	513	495	484	499	539	590	659	668
Marine, aviation and other transport insurance	15	16	18	18	19	21	24	40
Freight insurance	14	13	15	16	16	16	13	14
Fire and other property damage insurance	370	372	393	405	415	439	470	511
Pecuniary loss insurance	49	56	62	62	64	60	62	55
General liability insurance	63	65	64	72	73	79	87	96
Accident and health	585	574	591	591	623	661	738	784
***of which:** Health*	480	470	484	489	522	556	628	673
Other non-life insurance	31	24	25	28	33	34	42	44
Treaty reinsurance	..	0	0	0	0	0	0	0
Total non-life insurance	1 641	1 616	1 652	1 690	1 782	1 898	2 096	2 212
1.2 Gross claims payments								
Life								
Domestic undertakings	31	36	52	50	46	..	..	..
Foreign controlled undertakings	0	1	0	2	..	..	..	..
Foreign companies (branches)	..	..	..	..	..	..	..	..
All undertakings	31	36	52	50	46	..	..	..
Non-life								
Domestic undertakings	482	449	499	491	532	556	595	638
Foreign controlled undertakings	..	..	1	0	..	0	6	4
Foreign companies (branches)	..	..	..	..	..	..	..	..
All undertakings	482	449	499	491	532	556	595	638
Composite								
Domestic undertakings	951	941	911	903	995	1 115	1 132	1 126
Foreign controlled undertakings	93	90	91	95	104	111	326	342
Foreign companies (branches)	..	..	..	..	..	..	..	..
All undertakings	951	941	911	903	995	1 115	1 132	1 126
of which:								
Life	299	304	305	314	347	402	424	439
Domestic undertakings	299	304	305	314	347	402	424	439
Foreign controlled undertakings	51	50	51	50	50	49	94	114
Foreign companies (branches)	..	..	..	..	..	..	..	..
All undertakings	299	304	305	314	347	402	424	439
Non-life	651	637	606	590	648	713	708	687
Domestic undertakings	651	637	606	590	648	713	708	687
Foreign controlled undertakings	42	41	40	45	54	62	232	228
Foreign companies (branches)	..	..	..	..	..	..	..	..
All undertakings	651	637	606	590	648	713	708	687
Total								
Domestic undertakings	1 464	1 426	1 461	1 445	1 573	1 670	1 727	1 764
Foreign controlled undertakings	93	91	91	97	104	111	331	346
Foreign companies (branches)	..	..	..	..	..	..	..	..
All undertakings	1 464	1 426	1 461	1 445	1 573	1 670	1 727	1 764

Table 1. Selected aggregates *(cont.)*

Million EUR

	2013	2014	2015	2016	2017	2018	2019	2020
1.3 Commissions								
Life								
Domestic undertakings	3	3	3	3	4	..	..	..
Foreign controlled undertakings	0	0	0	0	..	..	..	..
Foreign companies (branches)	..	..	..	..	..	..	..	..
All undertakings	3	3	3	3	4	..	..	..
Non-life								
Domestic undertakings	4	7	8	7	8	9	1	5
Foreign controlled undertakings	..	..	0	0	..	0	0	0
Foreign companies (branches)	..	..	..	..	..	..	..	..
All undertakings	4	7	8	7	8	9	1	5
Composite								
Domestic undertakings	84	86	89	86	92	104	115	120
Foreign controlled undertakings	19	20	21	28	22	23	49	48
Foreign companies (branches)	..	..	..	..	..	..	..	..
All undertakings	84	86	89	86	92	104	115	120
of which:								
Life	32	32	34	32	32	35	34	33
Domestic undertakings	32	32	34	32	32	35	34	33
Foreign controlled undertakings	10	10	10	15	9	9	13	13
Foreign companies (branches)	..	..	..	..	..	..	..	..
All undertakings	32	32	34	32	32	35	34	33
Non-life	52	54	56	54	60	68	81	87
Domestic undertakings	52	54	56	54	60	68	81	87
Foreign controlled undertakings	9	10	11	13	13	14	36	35
Foreign companies (branches)	..	..	..	..	..	..	..	..
All undertakings	52	54	56	54	60	68	81	87
Total								
Domestic undertakings	91	96	100	96	104	112	116	125
Foreign controlled undertakings	19	20	21	28	22	23	49	48
Foreign companies (branches)	..	..	..	..	..	..	..	..
All undertakings	91	96	100	96	104	112	116	125
1.4 Gross operating expenses								
Life								
Domestic undertakings	14	15	16	12	15	..	..	0
Foreign controlled undertakings	2	1	1	1	..	..	..	..
Foreign companies (branches)	..	..	..	..	..	..	..	..
All undertakings	14	15	16	12	15	..	..	0
Non-life								
Domestic undertakings	81	86	90	97	97	105	112	109
Foreign controlled undertakings	..	..	0	1	..	1	6	6
Foreign companies (branches)	..	..	..	..	..	..	..	..
All undertakings	81	86	90	97	97	105	112	109
Composite								
Domestic undertakings	366	362	368	378	388	418	442	426
Foreign controlled undertakings	47	57	60	60	66	68	146	140
Foreign companies (branches)	..	..	..	..	..	..	..	..
All undertakings	366	362	368	378	388	418	442	426
of which:								
Life	104	99	100	99	102	116	118	100
Domestic undertakings	104	99	100	99	102	116	118	100
Foreign controlled undertakings	26	27	28	26	27	27	43	37
Foreign companies (branches)	..	..	..	..	..	..	..	..
All undertakings	104	99	100	99	102	116	118	100
Non-life	263	263	268	279	286	302	324	326
Domestic undertakings	263	263	268	279	286	302	324	326
Foreign controlled undertakings	21	30	32	33	39	41	103	103
Foreign companies (branches)	..	..	..	..	..	..	..	..
All undertakings	263	263	268	279	286	302	324	326
Total								
Domestic undertakings	461	462	474	487	500	523	553	535
Foreign controlled undertakings	49	59	62	62	66	69	152	146
Foreign companies (branches)	..	..	..	..	..	..	..	..
All undertakings	461	462	474	487	500	523	553	535

Table 1. Selected aggregates *(cont.)*

Million EUR

	2013	2014	2015	2016	2017	2018	2019	2020
1.5 Insurance business written abroad by branches, gross premiums								
Life								
Branches and agencies	..	..	..	..	..	..	..	..
Subsidaries	..	..	..	..	..	..	..	..
Total	..	..	..	..	..	..	..	..
Non-life								
Branches and agencies	..	..	..	..	1	1	1	0
Subsidaries	..	..	..	..	..	..	..	..
Total	..	..	..	..	1	1	1	0
Composite								
Branches and agencies	..	..	2	..	31	44	65	77
Subsidaries	..	..	..	..	..	..	..	..
Total	..	..	2	..	31	44	65	77
of which:								
Life	..	..	2	..	6	7	7	3
Branches and agencies	..	..	2	..	6	7	7	3
Subsidaries	..	..	..	..	..	..	..	..
Total	..	..	2	..	6	7	7	3
Non-life	..	..	0	..	25	37	58	73
Branches and agencies	..	..	0	..	25	37	58	73
Subsidaries	..	..	..	..	..	..	..	..
Total	..	..	0	..	25	37	58	73
Total								
Branches and agencies	..	..	2	..	32	45	66	77
Subsidaries	..	..	..	..	..	..	..	..
Total	..	..	2	..	32	45	66	77

.. Not available

Note: Detailed metadata at: *http://metalinks.oecd.org/ins/20220309/1e6c.*

Source: *OECD Insurance Statistics (database)*

SLOVENIA

Table 2. Number of companies and employees

	2013	2014	2015	2016	2017	2018	2019	2020
2.1 Number of companies								
Life								
Domestic undertakings	3	3	3	3	2	0	0	1
Foreign controlled undertakings	1	1	1	1	0	0	0	0
Foreign companies (branches)	0	0	0	0	0	0	0	0
All undertakings	3	3	3	3	2	0	0	1
Non-life								
Domestic undertakings	3	3	4	4	4	4	4	4
Foreign controlled undertakings	0	0	0	0	0	1	2	2
Foreign companies (branches)	4	4	4	4	4	3	3	3
All undertakings	7	7	8	8	8	7	7	7
Composite								
Domestic undertakings	8	8	8	7	7	9	9	8
Foreign controlled undertakings	3	3	3	3	3	3	4	3
Foreign companies (branches)	2	2	2	2	2	4	4	3
All undertakings	10	10	10	9	9	13	13	11
Reinsurance								
Domestic undertakings	2	2	2	2	2	2	2	2
Foreign controlled undertakings	0	0	0	0	0	0	0	0
Foreign companies (branches)	0	0	0	0	0	0	0	0
All undertakings	2	2	2	2	2	2	2	2
Total								
Domestic undertakings	16	16	17	16	15	15	15	15
Foreign controlled undertakings	4	4	4	4	3	4	6	5
Foreign companies (branches)	6	6	6	6	6	7	7	6
All undertakings	22	22	23	22	21	22	22	21
2.2 Number of employees								
Insurance undertakings	..	..	..	..	..	..	..	..
Intermediaries	..	..	..	..	..	..	..	..
Total	..	..	..	..	..	..	..	..

.. Not available

Note: Detailed metadata at: *http://metalinks.oecd.org/ins/20220309/1e6c.*

Source: *OECD Insurance Statistics (database)*

SPAIN

Table 1. Selected aggregates

Million EUR

	2013	2014	2015	2016	2017	2018	2019	2020
1.1 Insurance business written in the reporting country								
1.1.1 Insurance business, by ownership								
Gross premiums								
Domestic undertakings	58 110	57 662	59 048	66 541	65 719	66 538	66 197	62 625
Foreign controlled undertakings	12 578	12 542	11 038	..	..	..	..	..
Foreign companies (branches)	0	0	0	..	..	..	..	..
All undertakings	58 110	57 662	59 048	66 541	65 719	66 538	66 197	62 625
Premiums ceded								
Domestic undertakings	5 831	5 019	5 161	6 014	6 206	6 020	6 885	10 174
Foreign controlled undertakings	1 058	923	736	..	..	..	..	..
Foreign companies (branches)	0	0	0	..	..	..	..	..
All undertakings	5 831	5 019	5 161	6 014	6 206	6 020	6 885	10 174
Net written premiums								
Domestic undertakings	52 279	52 643	53 886	60 527	59 513	60 518	59 312	52 451
Foreign controlled undertakings	11 520	11 620	10 301	..	..	..	..	..
Foreign companies (branches)	0	0	0	..	..	..	..	..
All undertakings	52 279	52 643	53 886	60 527	59 513	60 518	59 312	52 451
1.1.2 Insurance business on foreign risks, gross premiums								
Life	22	7	11	13	9	11	0	0
Non-life	79	73	59	45	20	3	326	362
Composite	52	44	61	49	26	147	150	110
of which:								
Life	42	34	46	35	2	28	46	36
Non-life	10	9	15	14	24	119	104	73
Total	153	123	130	107	55	160	476	472
1.1.3 Life insurance payments, by class, gross premiums								
Annuities	7 946	6 406	5 881	8 746	8 318	7 583	7 053	3 707
Unit linked	3 062	2 816	2 721	2 981	4 431	4 432	4 842	4 837
Other life insurance	14 865	16 021	17 128	19 330	16 270	16 559	15 144	12 961
Total life insurance	25 873	25 244	25 730	31 056	29 019	28 574	27 039	21 505
of which: *Pension contracts*	..	..	..	..	..	..	..	..
1.1.4 Non-life insurance payments, by class, gross premiums								
Motor vehicle insurance	9 610	9 445	9 695	10 451	10 918	11 212	11 734	11 527
Marine, aviation and other transport insurance	390	361	369	369	367	389	409	466
Freight insurance	294	268	261	270	281	301	320	330
Fire and other property damage insurance	2 246	2 315	2 610	2 895	2 770	3 425	3 379	3 521
Pecuniary loss insurance	175	178	208	283	247	252	221	200
General liability insurance	1 077	1 009	1 011	1 049	1 100	1 181	1 300	1 268
Accident and health	7 888	8 227	8 449	8 879	9 329	9 744	10 057	10 539
of which: *Health*	7 031	7 356	7 536	7 902	8 224	8 652	8 997	9 488
Other non-life insurance	10 531	10 558	10 729	11 001	11 264	11 029	11 281	11 521
Treaty reinsurance	0	0	0	0	..	..	..	..
Total non-life insurance	32 211	32 362	33 332	35 197	36 275	37 532	38 702	39 372
1.2 Gross claims payments								
Life								
Domestic undertakings	14 147	16 777	18 872	3 070	3 685	3 096	2 488	2 584
Foreign controlled undertakings	1 814	1 688	1 582	..	..	..	..	..
Foreign companies (branches)	0	0	0	..	..	..	..	..
All undertakings	14 147	16 777	18 872	3 070	3 685	3 096	2 488	2 584
Non-life								
Domestic undertakings	9 463	9 250	9 593	9 453	10 280	9 702	9 940	9 650
Foreign controlled undertakings	3 947	3 890	2 592	..	..	..	..	..
Foreign companies (branches)	0	0	0	..	..	..	..	..
All undertakings	9 463	9 250	9 593	9 453	10 280	9 702	9 940	9 650
Composite								
Domestic undertakings	21 477	21 596	20 659	32 425	35 292	35 464	37 506	35 799
Foreign controlled undertakings	5 208	5 230	5 136	..	..	..	..	..
Foreign companies (branches)	0	0	0	..	..	..	..	..
All undertakings	21 477	21 596	20 659	32 425	35 292	35 464	37 506	35 799
of which:								
Life	9 702	9 986	8 948	20 670	22 722	21 474	23 064	22 136
Domestic undertakings	9 702	9 986	8 948	20 670	22 722	21 474	23 064	22 136
Foreign controlled undertakings	2 320	2 497	2 292	..	..	..	..	..
Foreign companies (branches)	0	0	0	..	..	..	..	..
All undertakings	9 702	9 986	8 948	20 670	22 722	21 474	23 064	22 136
Non-life	11 775	11 610	11 711	11 755	12 571	13 989	14 442	13 663
Domestic undertakings	11 775	11 610	11 711	11 755	12 571	13 989	14 442	13 663
Foreign controlled undertakings	2 888	2 733	2 843	..	..	..	..	..
Foreign companies (branches)	0	0	0	..	..	..	..	..
All undertakings	11 775	11 610	11 711	11 755	12 571	13 989	14 442	13 663
Total								
Domestic undertakings	45 088	47 622	49 125	44 947	49 258	48 262	49 934	48 032
Foreign controlled undertakings	10 968	10 809	9 310	..	..	..	..	..
Foreign companies (branches)	0	0	0	..	..	..	..	..
All undertakings	45 088	47 622	49 125	44 947	49 258	48 262	49 934	48 032

SPAIN

Table 1. Selected aggregates (cont.)

Million EUR

	2013	2014	2015	2016	2017	2018	2019	2020
1.3 Commissions								
Life								
Domestic undertakings	..	660	712	234	257	273	225	252
Foreign controlled undertakings	..	86	71	..	..	..	..	..
Foreign companies (branches)	..	0	0	..	..	..	..	..
All undertakings	..	660	712	234	257	273	225	252
Non-life								
Domestic undertakings	..	1 472	1 436	1 433	1 522	1 524	1 565	1 599
Foreign controlled undertakings	..	642	517	..	..	..	..	..
Foreign companies (branches)	..	0	0	..	..	..	..	..
All undertakings	..	1 472	1 436	1 433	1 522	1 524	1 565	1 599
Composite								
Domestic undertakings	..	2 270	2 635	3 328	4 629	3 786	3 897	3 947
Foreign controlled undertakings	..	669	710	..	..	..	..	..
Foreign companies (branches)	..	0	0	..	..	..	..	..
All undertakings	..	2 270	2 635	3 328	4 629	3 786	3 897	3 947
of which:								
Life	..	418	379	979	1 185	1 114	1 169	1 174
Domestic undertakings	..	418	379	979	1 185	1 114	1 169	1 174
Foreign controlled undertakings	..	94	103	..	..	..	..	..
Foreign companies (branches)	..	0	0	..	..	..	..	..
All undertakings	..	418	379	979	1 185	1 114	1 169	1 174
Non-life	..	1 852	2 255	2 349	3 444	2 672	2 728	2 773
Domestic undertakings	..	1 852	2 255	2 349	3 444	2 672	2 728	2 773
Foreign controlled undertakings	..	576	607	..	..	..	..	..
Foreign companies (branches)	..	0	0	..	..	..	..	..
All undertakings	..	1 852	2 255	2 349	3 444	2 672	2 728	2 773
Total								
Domestic undertakings	..	4 403	4 782	4 995	6 408	5 583	5 687	5 798
Foreign controlled undertakings	..	1 398	1 298	..	..	..	..	..
Foreign companies (branches)	..	0	0	..	..	..	..	..
All undertakings	..	4 403	4 782	4 995	6 408	5 583	5 687	5 798
1.4 Gross operating expenses								
Life								
Domestic undertakings	968	994	1 075	425	455	484	409	419
Foreign controlled undertakings	201	190	192	..	..	..	..	..
Foreign companies (branches)	0	..	..	..	..	..	..	..
All undertakings	968	994	1 075	425	455	484	409	419
Non-life								
Domestic undertakings	3 046	2 880	2 832	2 876	3 081	3 065	3 092	3 194
Foreign controlled undertakings	1 272	1 289	947	..	..	..	..	..
Foreign companies (branches)	0	..	..	..	..	..	..	..
All undertakings	3 046	2 880	2 832	2 876	3 081	3 065	3 092	3 194
Composite								
Domestic undertakings	5 322	5 034	5 250	6 332	6 550	6 855	7 166	7 420
Foreign controlled undertakings	1 152	1 070	1 100	..	..	..	..	..
Foreign companies (branches)	1	..	4	..	..	..	..	..
All undertakings	5 323	5 034	5 254	6 332	6 550	6 855	7 166	7 420
of which:								
Life	809	797	729	1 489	1 546	1 677	1 816	1 789
Domestic undertakings	809	797	729	1 489	1 546	1 677	1 816	1 789
Foreign controlled undertakings	162	178	186	..	..	..	..	..
Foreign companies (branches)	0	..	..	..	..	..	..	..
All undertakings	809	797	729	1 489	1 546	1 677	1 816	1 789
Non-life	4 515	4 237	4 525	4 843	5 004	5 178	5 350	5 632
Domestic undertakings	4 514	4 237	4 521	4 843	5 004	5 178	5 350	5 632
Foreign controlled undertakings	990	892	913	..	..	..	..	..
Foreign companies (branches)	1	0	4	..	..	..	..	..
All undertakings	4 515	4 237	4 525	4 843	5 004	5 178	5 350	5 632
Total								
Domestic undertakings	9 337	8 907	9 157	9 633	10 087	10 405	10 667	11 033
Foreign controlled undertakings	2 625	2 549	2 239	..	..	..	..	..
Foreign companies (branches)	1	..	4	..	..	..	..	..
All undertakings	9 338	8 907	9 161	9 633	10 087	10 405	10 667	11 033

Table 1. Selected aggregates *(cont.)*

Million EUR

	2013	2014	2015	2016	2017	2018	2019	2020
1.5 Insurance business written abroad by branches, gross premiums								
Life								
Branches and agencies	274	0	0	0	0	1	0	0
Subsidaries	..	..	..	..	..	..	..	..
Total	..	..	..	0	0	1	0	0
Non-life								
Branches and agencies	592	654	701	1 694	1 841	1 537	1 606	1 381
Subsidaries	..	..	..	..	..	..	..	..
Total	..	..	..	1 694	1 841	1 537	1 606	1 381
Composite								
Branches and agencies	885	1 286	1 361	1 262	1 385	2 155	2 184	2 113
Subsidaries	..	..	..	..	..	..	..	..
Total	..	..	..	1 262	1 385	2 155	2 184	2 113
of which:								
Life	..	..	..	518	574	812	661	527
Branches and agencies	212	559	694	518	574	812	661	527
Subsidaries	..	..	..	..	..	..	..	..
Total	..	..	..	518	574	812	661	527
Non-life	..	..	..	744	812	1 344	1 523	1 586
Branches and agencies	673	728	667	744	812	1 344	1 523	1 586
Subsidaries	..	..	..	..	..	..	..	..
Total	..	..	..	744	812	1 344	1 523	1 586
Total								
Branches and agencies	1 751	1 940	2 062	2 955	3 226	3 693	3 790	3 494
Subsidaries	..	..	..	..	..	..	..	..
Total	..	..	..	2 955	3 226	3 693	3 790	3 494

.. Not available

Note: Detailed metadata at: *http://metalinks.oecd.org/ins/20220309/36fc.*

Source: OECD *Insurance Statistics (database)*

SPAIN

Table 2. Number of companies and employees

	2013	2014	2015	2016	2017	2018	2019	2020
2.1 Number of companies								
Life								
Domestic undertakings	83	79	78	32	32	29	26	27
Foreign controlled undertakings	10	9	8	..	..	..	..	..
Foreign companies (branches)	0	0	0	..	..	..	..	..
All undertakings	83	79	78	32	32	29	26	27
Non-life								
Domestic undertakings	132	127	118	121	111	105	100	101
Foreign controlled undertakings	19	19	17	..	..	..	..	..
Foreign companies (branches)	0	0	1	..	..	..	..	..
All undertakings	132	127	119	121	111	105	100	101
Composite								
Domestic undertakings	47	45	41	75	74	74	74	71
Foreign controlled undertakings	8	8	8	..	..	..	..	..
Foreign companies (branches)	1	1	0	..	..	..	..	..
All undertakings	48	46	41	75	74	74	74	71
Reinsurance								
Domestic undertakings	2	3	3	3	3	3	4	4
Foreign controlled undertakings	0	0	0	..	..	..	..	..
Foreign companies (branches)	0	0	0	..	..	..	..	..
All undertakings	2	3	3	3	3	3	4	4
Total								
Domestic undertakings	264	254	240	231	220	211	204	203
Foreign controlled undertakings	37	36	33	..	..	..	..	..
Foreign companies (branches)	1	1	1	..	..	..	..	..
All undertakings	265	255	241	231	220	211	204	203
2.2 Number of employees								
Insurance undertakings	46 324	45 535	45 218	47 453	47 498	47 380	48 194	49 475
Intermediaries	121 427	129 549	..	..	..	..	..	..
Total	167 751	175 084	..	..	..	..	..	..

.. Not available

Note: Detailed metadata at: *http://metalinks.oecd.org/ins/20220309/36fc.*

Source: *OECD Insurance Statistics (database)*

SWEDEN

Table 1. Selected aggregates

Million SEK

	2013	2014	2015	2016	2017	2018	2019	2020
1.1 Insurance business written in the reporting country								
1.1.1 Insurance business, by ownership								
Gross premiums								
Domestic undertakings	177 197	332 028	339 533	334 834	379 418	426 318	460 661	..
Foreign controlled undertakings	66 854	66 041	62 537	67 208	78 911	97 388	101 544	..
Foreign companies (branches)	..	10 260	..	..	..	..	..	..
All undertakings	177 197	342 288	339 533	334 834	379 418	426 318	460 661	..
Premiums ceded								
Domestic undertakings	12 967	15 157	10 306	9 139	10 693	11 095	14 223	..
Foreign controlled undertakings	4 727	3 870	4 441	4 296	5 538	6 138	8 471	..
Foreign companies (branches)	..	..	..	..	..	..	..	..
All undertakings	12 967	15 157	10 306	9 139	10 693	11 095	14 223	..
Net written premiums								
Domestic undertakings	164 230	316 871	329 227	325 695	368 725	415 223	446 438	..
Foreign controlled undertakings	62 127	62 171	58 096	62 912	73 373	91 250	93 073	..
Foreign companies (branches)	..	10 260	..	..	..	..	..	..
All undertakings	164 230	327 131	329 227	325 695	368 725	415 223	446 438	..
1.1.2 Insurance business on foreign risks, gross premiums								
Life	..	581	667	60	58	58	59	..
Non-life	..	28 134	27 121	26 941	30 482	40 549	44 517	..
Composite total	..	..	..	..	..	..	..	..
Total	..	28 715	27 788	27 001	30 540	40 607	44 576	..
1.1.3 Life insurance payments, by class, gross premiums								
Annuities	73 377	205 927	169 626	94 037	107 773	126 049	139 221	..
Unit linked	1 188	2 366	75 221	85 696	97 951	107 143	106 859	..
Other life insurance	13 591	29 900	3 957	71 084	82 841	89 138	102 063	..
Total life insurance	88 156	238 192	248 804	250 817	288 565	322 330	348 143	..
***of which:** Pension contracts*	..	..	..	..	..	..	..	..
1.1.4 Non-life insurance payments, by class, gross premiums								
Motor vehicle insurance	..	30 360	21 348	..	..	..	..	..
Marine, aviation and other transport insurance	..	2 627	749	..	..	..	..	..
Freight insurance	..	..	..	..	..	..	..	..
Fire and other property damage insurance	..	29 146	36 720	..	..	..	..	..
Pecuniary loss insurance	..	459	1 070	..	..	..	..	..
General liability insurance	..	4 045	4 119	..	..	..	..	..
Accident and health	..	5 674	5 155	..	..	..	..	..
***of which:** Health*	..	..	..	..	..	..	..	..
Other non-life insurance	..	9 165	21 483	..	..	..	..	..
Treaty reinsurance	..	13 811	..	..	..	..	..	..
Total non-life insurance	84 766	95 287	90 644	83 954	90 800	103 940	112 479	..
1.2 Gross claims payments								
Life								
Domestic undertakings	64 657	60 930	64 815	76 869	76 390	77 434	73 104	..
Foreign controlled undertakings	6 337	6 055	5 719	5 852	5 784	5 704	5 652	..
Foreign companies (branches)	..	5 999	..	..	..	..	..	..
All undertakings	64 657	66 929	64 815	76 869	76 390	77 434	73 104	..
Non-life								
Domestic undertakings	69 100	75 805	64 537	65 941	66 635	77 278	82 672	..
Foreign controlled undertakings	31 398	31 024	23 701	22 495	25 544	32 791	33 257	..
Foreign companies (branches)	..	5 328	..	..	..	..	..	..
All undertakings	69 100	81 133	64 537	65 941	66 635	77 278	82 672	..
Composite, all undertakings	..	..	..	..	..	..	..	..
Total								
Domestic undertakings	133 757	136 735	129 352	142 810	143 025	154 712	155 776	..
Foreign controlled undertakings	37 735	37 079	29 420	28 347	31 328	38 495	38 909	..
Foreign companies (branches)	..	11 327	..	..	..	..	..	..
All undertakings	133 757	148 062	129 352	142 810	143 025	154 712	155 776	..
1.3 Commissions								
Life								
Domestic undertakings	..	4 167	3 782	3 063	3 545	3 494	3 648	..
Foreign controlled undertakings	..	1 302	610	274	589	587	567	..
Foreign companies (branches)	..	121	..	..	..	..	..	..
All undertakings	..	4 288	3 782	3 063	3 545	3 494	3 648	..
Non-life								
Domestic undertakings	..	4 168	4 264	3 848	3 953	3 711	4 280	..
Foreign controlled undertakings	..	2 049	2 589	2 362	2 482	2 634	2 711	..
Foreign companies (branches)	..	786	..	..	..	..	..	..
All undertakings	..	4 954	4 264	3 848	3 953	3 711	4 280	..
Composite, all undertakings	..	..	..	..	..	..	..	..
Total								
Domestic undertakings	..	8 335	8 046	6 911	7 498	7 205	7 928	..
Foreign controlled undertakings	..	3 351	3 199	2 636	3 071	3 221	3 278	..
Foreign companies (branches)	..	907	..	..	..	..	..	..
All undertakings	..	9 242	8 046	6 911	7 498	7 205	7 928	..

Table 1. Selected aggregates *(cont.)*

Million SEK

	2013	2014	2015	2016	2017	2018	2019	2020
1.4 Gross operating expenses								
Life								
Domestic undertakings	12 115	12 738	13 573	12 617	13 248	15 095	13 651	..
Foreign controlled undertakings	3 630	3 639	2 122	1 297	1 918	1 901	1 944	..
Foreign companies (branches)	..	..	..	..	..	..	..	..
All undertakings	12 115	12 738	13 573	12 617	13 248	15 095	13 651	..
Non-life								
Domestic undertakings	15 004	16 878	16 854	15 781	15 863	18 250	19 503	..
Foreign controlled undertakings	7 248	8 238	7 704	7 205	7 691	9 496	10 114	..
Foreign companies (branches)	..	..	..	..	..	..	..	..
All undertakings	15 004	16 878	16 854	15 781	15 863	18 250	19 503	..
Composite, all undertakings	..	..	..	..	..	..	..	..
Total								
Domestic undertakings	27 119	29 616	30 427	28 398	29 111	33 345	33 154	..
Foreign controlled undertakings	10 878	11 877	9 826	8 502	9 609	11 397	12 058	..
Foreign companies (branches)	..	..	..	..	..	..	..	..
All undertakings	27 119	29 616	30 427	28 398	29 111	33 345	33 154	..
1.5 Insurance business written abroad by branches, gross premiums								
Life								
Branches and agencies	..	243	279	347	347	447	421	..
Subsidaries	..	..	..	..	..	..	..	..
Total	..	243	279	347	347	447	421	..
Non-life								
Branches and agencies	..	18 630	18 207	24 226	24 226	34 479	33 631	..
Subsidaries	..	..	..	..	..	..	..	..
Total	..	18 630	18 207	24 226	24 226	34 479	33 631	..
Composite total	..	..	..	..	..	..	..	..
Total								
Branches and agencies	..	18 873	18 486	24 573	24 573	34 926	34 052	..
Subsidaries	..	..	..	..	..	..	..	..
Total	..	18 873	18 486	24 573	24 573	34 926	34 052	..

.. Not available

Note: Detailed metadata at: *http://metalinks.oecd.org/ins/20220309/b317*.

Source: OECD *Insurance Statistics (database)*

Table 2. Number of companies and employees

	2013	2014	2015	2016	2017	2018	2019	2020
2.1 Number of companies								
Life								
Domestic undertakings	39	39	38	37	36	35	37	..
Foreign controlled undertakings	8	8	8	6	6	4	4	..
Foreign companies (branches)	5	6	8	6	4	4	4	..
All undertakings	44	45	46	43	46	39	41	..
Non-life								
Domestic undertakings	130	130	127	120	117	127	127	..
Foreign controlled undertakings	44	34	24	14	15	8	8	..
Foreign companies (branches)	32	28	33	31	25	9	9	..
All undertakings	162	158	160	151	157	136	136	..
Composite, all undertakings	**0**	**0**	**0**	**0**	..	..	..	..
Reinsurance								
Domestic undertakings	1	1	1	0	..	..	..	..
Foreign controlled undertakings	0	0	1	0	..	..	..	..
Foreign companies (branches)	..	0	0	..	..	..	..	..
All undertakings	1	1	1	..	..	..	..	..
Total								
Domestic undertakings	170	170	166	157	153	162	164	..
Foreign controlled undertakings	52	42	33	20	21	12	12	..
Foreign companies (branches)	37	34	41	37	29	13	13	..
All undertakings	207	204	207	194	203	175	176	..
2.2 Number of employees								
Insurance undertakings	19 059	19 573	18 792	20 600	21 900	20 865	22 000	..
Intermediaries	2 000	3 849	3 235	3 540	3 585	3 789	1 245	..
Total	21 059	23 422	22 027	..	25 485	24 654	23 245	..

.. Not available
Note: Detailed metadata at: *http://metalinks.oecd.org/ins/20220309/b317*.
Source: OECD *Insurance Statistics (database)*

SWITZERLAND

Table 1. Selected aggregates

Million CHF

	2013	2014	2015	2016	2017	2018	2019	2020
1.1 Insurance business written in the reporting country								
1.1.1 Insurance business, by ownership								
Gross premiums								
Domestic undertakings	66 569	66 312	65 628	63 975	63 967	65 722	67 482	63 005
Foreign controlled undertakings	15 423	14 214	13 846	12 578	11 699	12 241	7 760	6 618
Foreign companies (branches)	2 267	1 923	2 091	2 522	2 768	2 198	2 064	1 821
All undertakings	68 836	68 235	67 720	66 497	66 735	67 920	69 546	64 826
Premiums ceded								
Domestic undertakings	4 536	4 346	4 141	3 363	4 085	4 283	4 600	4 262
Foreign controlled undertakings	963	831	731	506	502	613	548	200
Foreign companies (branches)	532	533	553	813	874	776	772	887
All undertakings	5 068	4 879	4 694	4 176	4 959	5 059	5 372	5 149
Net written premiums								
Domestic undertakings	62 033	61 966	61 487	60 612	59 882	61 439	62 882	58 743
Foreign controlled undertakings	14 460	13 383	13 115	12 072	11 197	11 628	7 212	6 418
Foreign companies (branches)	1 735	1 390	1 539	1 709	1 894	1 422	1 292	934
All undertakings	63 768	63 356	63 026	62 321	61 776	62 861	64 174	59 677
1.1.2 Insurance business on foreign risks, gross premiums								
Life	..	..	..	..	..	..	..	..
Non-life	..	..	..	..	..	..	..	..
Composite total	..	..	..	..	..	..	..	..
Total	..	..	..	..	..	..	..	..
1.1.3 Life insurance payments, by class, gross premiums								
Annuities	564	441	495	428	317	246	281	245
Unit linked	2 403	1 730	1 755	1 738	1 861	1 947	2 202	2 190
Other life insurance	29 707	30 478	30 359	28 518	27 445	27 607	27 514	22 253
Total life insurance	32 675	32 649	32 609	30 684	29 623	29 800	29 997	24 688
***of which:** Pension contracts*	..	..	..	..	..	..	..	..
1.1.4 Non-life insurance payments, by class, gross premiums								
Motor vehicle insurance	6 556	6 580	6 595	6 598	6 742	6 804	6 909	7 137
Marine, aviation and other transport insurance	1 060	876	732	657	681	635	724	755
Freight insurance	..	..	..	..	..	..	..	..
Fire and other property damage insurance	8 206	8 123	7 909	7 411	7 397	7 804	8 297	8 413
Pecuniary loss insurance	1 042	1 096	897	1 095	1 108	1 055	1 024	958
General liability insurance	3 558	3 658	3 562	3 293	3 447	3 416	3 768	3 834
Accident and health	13 889	13 414	13 387	14 585	15 626	16 692	17 240	17 397
***of which:** Health*	9 911	9 934	10 266	10 606	11 361	11 901	12 099	12 358
Other non-life insurance	1 351	1 378	1 525	1 649	1 715	1 361	1 214	1 292
Treaty reinsurance	..	..	..	..	..	..	..	..
Total non-life insurance	35 661	35 125	34 607	35 288	36 716	37 767	39 176	39 786
1.2 Gross claims payments								
Life								
Domestic undertakings	27 624	27 943	27 794	29 083	29 352	44 908	58 408	28 395
Foreign controlled undertakings	8 854	7 917	8 123	8 578	8 159	11 255	29 424	3 963
Foreign companies (branches)	306	3	3	3	3	7	4	15
All undertakings	27 930	27 946	27 797	29 086	29 355	44 915	58 412	28 410
Non-life								
Domestic undertakings	19 735	20 149	20 621	20 498	20 716	42 021	44 831	24 267
Foreign controlled undertakings	2 171	2 281	2 671	2 471	2 299	4 534	4 308	2 377
Foreign companies (branches)	798	874	902	1 105	1 164	1 219	1 006	1 042
All undertakings	20 533	21 023	21 523	21 603	21 880	43 240	45 837	25 309
Composite, all undertakings	..	..	..	..	..	..	..	..
Total								
Domestic undertakings	47 359	48 092	48 415	49 581	50 068	86 929	103 239	52 662
Foreign controlled undertakings	11 025	10 198	10 794	11 049	10 458	15 789	33 732	6 340
Foreign companies (branches)	1 104	877	905	1 108	1 167	1 226	1 010	1 057
All undertakings	48 463	48 969	49 320	50 689	51 235	88 155	104 249	53 719
1.3 Commissions								
Life								
Domestic undertakings	904	920	856	856	836	829	850	891
Foreign controlled undertakings	148	114	169	169	163	163	139	159
Foreign companies (branches)	11	0	0	1	1	1	1	1
All undertakings	915	920	856	857	837	830	851	892
Non-life								
Domestic undertakings	2 067	1 597	2 188	2 289	2 078	1 403	2 410	2 471
Foreign controlled undertakings	372	381	441	450	453	458	469	488
Foreign companies (branches)	95	91	78	65	24	72	66	26
All undertakings	2 162	1 688	2 266	2 354	2 102	1 475	2 476	2 497
Composite, all undertakings	..	..	..	..	..	..	..	..
Total								
Domestic undertakings	2 971	2 517	3 044	3 145	2 914	2 232	3 260	3 362
Foreign controlled undertakings	520	495	610	619	616	621	608	647
Foreign companies (branches)	106	91	78	66	25	73	67	27
All undertakings	3 077	2 608	3 122	3 211	2 939	2 305	3 327	3 389

Table 1. Selected aggregates *(cont.)*

Million CHF

	2013	2014	2015	2016	2017	2018	2019	2020
1.4 Gross operating expenses								
Life								
Domestic undertakings	1 289	1 364	1 078	1 085	1 091	1 117	1 097	1 110
Foreign controlled undertakings	176	209	156	156	160	186	186	171
Foreign companies (branches)	4	2	1	1	2	3	1	2
All undertakings	1 293	1 366	1 079	1 086	1 093	1 120	1 098	1 112
Non-life								
Domestic undertakings	3 745	5 520	2 975	2 981	3 185	3 388	3 590	3 693
Foreign controlled undertakings	416	420	341	310	316	353	337	318
Foreign companies (branches)	100	108	103	215	195	186	157	153
All undertakings	3 845	5 628	3 078	3 196	3 380	3 574	3 747	3 846
Composite, all undertakings	..	..	..	..	..	..	..	..
Total								
Domestic undertakings	5 034	6 884	4 053	4 066	4 276	4 505	4 687	4 803
Foreign controlled undertakings	592	629	497	466	476	539	523	489
Foreign companies (branches)	104	110	104	216	197	189	158	155
All undertakings	5 138	6 994	4 157	4 282	4 473	4 694	4 845	4 958
1.5 Insurance business written abroad by branches, gross premiums								
Life								
Branches and agencies	1 967	1 794	1 604	1 567	1 613	1 653	1 717	1 792
Subsidaries	..	..	..	..	..	..	..	..
Total	1 967	1 794	1 604	1 567	1 613	1 653	1 717	1 792
Non-life								
Branches and agencies	15 563	15 331	14 100	12 578	12 689	6 664	6 089	6 428
Subsidaries	..	..	..	..	..	..	..	..
Total	15 563	15 331	14 100	12 578	12 689	6 664	6 089	6 428
Composite total	..	..	..	..	..	..	..	..
Total								
Branches and agencies	17 531	17 125	15 704	14 145	14 302	8 317	7 806	8 220
Subsidaries	..	..	..	..	..	..	..	..
Total	17 531	17 125	15 704	14 145	14 302	8 317	7 806	8 220

.. Not available

Note: Detailed metadata at: *http://metalinks.oecd.org/ins/20220309/61a6*.

Source: *OECD Insurance Statistics (database)*

Table 2. Number of companies and employees

	2013	2014	2015	2016	2017	2018	2019	2020
2.1 Number of companies								
Life								
Domestic undertakings	19	18	17	16	16	16	16	16
Foreign controlled undertakings	1	1	1	1	1	1	1	1
Foreign companies (branches)	4	3	3	3	3	3	3	3
All undertakings	23	21	20	19	19	19	19	19
Non-life								
Domestic undertakings	80	79	76	74	73	70	72	69
Foreign controlled undertakings	6	6	6	5	5	5	5	5
Foreign companies (branches)	44	48	46	46	45	44	46	47
All undertakings	124	127	122	120	118	114	118	116
Composite, all undertakings	**0**	**0**	**0**	**0**	..	..	..	..
Reinsurance								
Domestic undertakings	62	62	59	55	55	54	50	50
Foreign controlled undertakings	7	7	7	7	6	6	6	6
Foreign companies (branches)	..	..	..	..	..	..	..	..
All undertakings	62	62	59	55	55	54	50	50
Total								
Domestic undertakings	161	159	152	145	144	140	138	135
Foreign controlled undertakings	14	14	14	13	12	12	12	12
Foreign companies (branches)	48	51	49	49	48	47	49	50
All undertakings	209	210	201	194	192	187	187	185
2.2 Number of employees								
Insurance undertakings	..	..	..	..	..	..	..	..
Intermediaries	..	..	..	..	..	..	..	..
Total	..	..	..	..	..	..	..	..

.. Not available

Note: Detailed metadata at: *http://metalinks.oecd.org/ins/20220309/61a6.*

Source: OECD *Insurance Statistics (database)*

Table 1. Selected aggregates

Million TRY

	2013	2014	2015	2016	2017	2018	2019	2020
1.1 Insurance business written in the reporting country								
1.1.1 Insurance business, by ownership								
Gross premiums								
Domestic undertakings	25 084	26 872	31 903	41 280	47 495	54 416	68 247	84 802
Foreign controlled undertakings	14 981	15 528	20 981	25 640	26 984	29 792	35 819	41 950
Foreign companies (branches)	68	77	126	152	201	304	553	805
All undertakings	25 152	26 949	32 029	41 431	47 696	54 720	68 800	85 607
Premiums ceded								
Domestic undertakings	6 077	6 686	7 984	9 816	13 268	15 814	19 346	22 795
Foreign controlled undertakings	3 458	3 510	4 773	5 482	6 672	7 850	8 518	9 719
Foreign companies (branches)	49	57	74	76	96	131	288	505
All undertakings	6 126	6 743	8 059	9 892	13 364	15 945	19 634	23 300
Net written premiums								
Domestic undertakings	19 006	20 186	23 919	31 464	34 227	38 601	48 901	60 416
Foreign controlled undertakings	11 522	12 018	16 208	20 158	20 312	21 942	27 300	31 549
Foreign companies (branches)	20	20	52	76	105	173	265	300
All undertakings	19 026	20 206	23 971	31 540	34 332	38 774	49 166	60 716
1.1.2 Insurance business on foreign risks, gross premiums								
Life	..	3 280	..	6 166	..	..	..	..
Non-life	..	22 711	..	34 322	..	..	..	..
Composite	..	958	..	943	..	..	..	..
of which:								
Life	..	24	..	19	..	..	..	..
Non-life	..	934	..	924	..	..	..	..
Total	..	26 948	..	41 431	..	..	..	..
1.1.3 Life insurance payments, by class, gross premiums								
Annuities	..	..	..	..	..	..	..	..
Unit linked	..	..	..	..	..	..	..	..
Other life insurance	..	..	..	..	..	..	..	..
Total life insurance	3 354	3 895	3 720	5 916	6 766	6 835	13 340	14 291
***of which:** Pension contracts*	..	..	..	..	..	..	..	..
1.1.4 Non-life insurance payments, by class, gross premiums								
Motor vehicle insurance	10 411	10 648	13 102	19 156	19 981	23 614	26 466	31 232
Marine, aviation and other transport insurance	253	321	423	455	490	706	929	1 348
Freight insurance	416	530	580	585	652	828	922	1 204
Fire and other property damage insurance	5 512	6 992	8 105	9 032	10 101	12 208	14 193	18 548
Pecuniary loss insurance	302	318	443	439	549	666	901	1 071
General liability insurance	508	679	811	863	1 028	1 389	1 698	2 190
Accident and health	3 352	4 010	4 685	4 582	6 708	8 051	9 798	12 333
***of which:** Health*	2 472	0	0	..	5 025	6 245	8 190	10 096
Other non-life insurance	74	147	99	134	226	167	197	225
Treaty reinsurance	..	..	0	..	..	..	..	..
Total non-life insurance	20 828	23 645	28 249	35 246	39 735	47 628	55 104	68 152
1.2 Gross claims payments								
Life								
Domestic undertakings	2 355	2 085	2 557	2 957	3 293	3 609	4 776	5 461
Foreign controlled undertakings	1 128	760	1 194	1 485	1 757	2 061	2 685	3 074
Foreign companies (branches)	..	..	..	0	..	0	..	0
All undertakings	2 355	2 085	2 557	2 957	3 293	3 609	4 776	5 461
Non-life								
Domestic undertakings	9 440	11 314	13 322	15 041	18 341	23 049	27 354	27 473
Foreign controlled undertakings	6 301	7 496	8 700	-9 940	11 648	13 543	15 282	15 007
Foreign companies (branches)	11	10	34	128	77	121	86	90
All undertakings	9 451	11 325	13 356	15 168	18 417	23 170	27 440	27 563
Composite								
Domestic undertakings	619	592	664	572	617	771	..	1 321
Foreign controlled undertakings	..	..	..	..	1	5	..	32
Foreign companies (branches)	..	..	..	..	..	..	..	..
All undertakings	619	592	664	572	617	771	..	1 333
of which:								
Life	7	11	6	9	15	7	..	11
Domestic undertakings	7	11	6	9	15	7	..	11
Foreign controlled undertakings	..	..	..	..	0	0	..	0
Foreign companies (branches)	..	..	..	..	..	..	..	..
All undertakings	7	11	6	9	15	7	..	11
Non-life	612	581	657	564	602	764	..	1 321
Domestic undertakings	. 612	581	657	564	602	764	..	1 321
Foreign controlled undertakings	..	..	..	..	1	5	..	32
Foreign companies (branches)	..	..	..	..	..	..	..	..
All undertakings	612	581	657	564	602	764	..	1 321
Total								
Domestic undertakings	12 413	13 991	16 543	18 570	22 251	27 430	32 130	34 255
Foreign controlled undertakings	7 429	8 256	9 894	-8 455	13 406	15 609	17 967	18 113
Foreign companies (branches)	11	10	34	128	77	121	86	90
All undertakings	12 425	14 001	16 578	18 698	22 328	27 551	32 216	34 357

Table 1. Selected aggregates *(cont.)*

Million TRY

	2013	2014	2015	2016	2017	2018	2019	2020
1.3 Commissions								
Life								
Domestic undertakings	..	..	..	..	..	..	..	..
Foreign controlled undertakings	..	..	..	..	..	..	..	..
Foreign companies (branches)	..	..	..	..	..	..	..	..
All undertakings	..	..	..	..	..	..	..	..
Non-life								
Domestic undertakings	..	..	..	..	..	..	..	..
Foreign controlled undertakings	..	..	..	..	..	..	..	..
Foreign companies (branches)	..	..	..	..	..	..	..	..
All undertakings	..	..	..	..	..	..	..	..
Composite								
Domestic undertakings	..	..	..	..	..	..	..	..
Foreign controlled undertakings	..	..	..	..	..	..	..	..
Foreign companies (branches)	..	..	..	..	..	..	..	..
All undertakings	..	..	..	..	..	..	..	..
of which:								
Life	..	..	..	..	..	..	..	..
Domestic undertakings	..	..	..	..	..	..	..	..
Foreign controlled undertakings	..	..	..	..	..	..	..	..
Foreign companies (branches)	..	..	..	..	..	..	..	..
All undertakings	..	..	..	..	..	..	..	..
Non-life	..	..	..	..	..	..	..	..
Domestic undertakings	..	..	..	..	..	..	..	..
Foreign controlled undertakings	..	..	..	..	..	..	..	..
Foreign companies (branches)	..	..	..	..	..	..	..	..
All undertakings	..	..	..	..	..	..	..	..
Total								
Domestic undertakings	..	..	..	..	..	..	..	..
Foreign controlled undertakings	..	..	..	..	..	..	..	..
Foreign companies (branches)	..	..	..	..	..	..	..	..
All undertakings	..	..	..	..	..	..	..	..
1.4 Gross operating expenses								
Life								
Domestic undertakings	2 009	1 198	1 595	1 970	2 644	2 961	4 103	5 307
Foreign controlled undertakings	1 242	765	1 033	1 241	1 724	1 926	2 376	3 025
Foreign companies (branches)	..	..	..	..	..	..	..	..
All undertakings	2 009	1 198	1 595	1 970	2 644	2 961	4 103	5 307
Non-life								
Domestic undertakings	3 726	4 309	4 648	5 579	6 263	6 689	8 211	9 770
Foreign controlled undertakings	2 564	2 944	3 110	3 847	4 170	4 183	4 821	5 700
Foreign companies (branches)	19	20	24	26	30	44	122	159
All undertakings	3 745	4 329	4 672	5 604	6 293	6 733	8 333	9 929
Composite								
Domestic undertakings	..	..	309	316	333	436	..	772
Foreign controlled undertakings	..	..	..	5	2	3	..	6
Foreign companies (branches)	..	..	..	..	..	..	..	..
All undertakings	294	289	309	316	333	436	..	772
of which:								
Life	10	8	10	10	5	8	..	13
Domestic undertakings	..	..	10	10	5	8	..	13
Foreign controlled undertakings	..	..	..	..	0	0	..	0
Foreign companies (branches)	..	..	..	..	..	..	..	..
All undertakings	10	8	10	10	5	8	..	13
Non-life	284	281	299	306	328	429	..	759
Domestic undertakings	..	..	299	306	328	429	..	759
Foreign controlled undertakings	..	..	..	5	2	3	..	6
Foreign companies (branches)	..	..	..	..	..	..	..	..
All undertakings	284	281	299	306	328	429	..	759
Total								
Domestic undertakings	5 735	5 507	6 552	7 865	9 240	10 087	12 314	15 849
Foreign controlled undertakings	3 806	3 708	4 143	5 092	5 895	6 112	7 197	8 731
Foreign companies (branches)	19	20	24	26	30	44	122	159
All undertakings	6 048	5 816	6 576	7 890	9 270	10 130	12 436	16 008

Table 1. Selected aggregates *(cont.)*

Million TRY

	2013	2014	2015	2016	2017	2018	2019	2020
1.5 Insurance business written abroad by branches, gross premiums								
Life								
Branches and agencies	..	..	..	..	..	..	..	..
Subsidaries	..	..	..	..	..	..	..	..
Total	..	..	..	..	..	..	..	..
Non-life								
Branches and agencies	..	..	..	..	..	..	..	..
Subsidaries	..	..	..	..	..	..	..	..
Total	..	..	..	..	..	..	..	..
Composite								
Branches and agencies	..	..	..	..	..	..	..	..
Subsidaries	..	..	..	..	..	..	..	..
Total	..	..	..	..	..	..	..	..
of which:								
Life	..	..	..	..	..	..	..	..
Branches and agencies	..	..	..	..	..	..	..	..
Subsidaries	..	..	..	..	..	..	..	..
Total	..	..	..	..	..	..	..	..
Non-life	..	..	..	..	..	..	..	..
Branches and agencies	..	..	..	..	..	..	..	..
Subsidaries	..	..	..	..	..	..	..	..
Total	..	..	..	..	..	..	..	..
Total								
Branches and agencies	..	..	..	..	..	..	..	..
Subsidaries	..	..	..	..	..	..	..	..
Total	..	..	..	..	..	..	..	..

.. Not available
Note: Detailed metadata at: *http://metalinks.oecd.org/ins/20220309/ffe9.*
Source: *OECD Insurance Statistics (database)*

Table 2. Number of companies and employees

	2013	2014	2015	2016	2017	2018	2019	2020
2.1 Number of companies								
Life								
Domestic undertakings	24	25	23	22	22	22	22	21
Foreign controlled undertakings	16	16	15	15	15	15	15	15
Foreign companies (branches)	..	0	..	0	0	..	..	..
All undertakings	24	25	23	22	22	22	22	21
Non-life								
Domestic undertakings	34	36	36	35	37	36	37	37
Foreign controlled undertakings	22	24	22	23	23	20	19	18
Foreign companies (branches)	2	2	2	2	2	2	2	2
All undertakings	36	38	38	37	39	38	39	39
Composite								
Domestic undertakings	..	0	..	0	0	0	..	3
Foreign controlled undertakings	..	0	..	0	0	0	..	1
Foreign companies (branches)	..	0	..	0	0	0	..	..
All undertakings	..	0	..	0	0	0	..	3
Reinsurance								
Domestic undertakings	1	1	1	2	2	2	3	..
Foreign controlled undertakings	..	0	..	1	1	1	1	..
Foreign companies (branches)	..	0	..	0	0	0	..	..
All undertakings	1	1	1	2	2	2	3	..
Total								
Domestic undertakings	59	62	60	59	61	62	62	61
Foreign controlled undertakings	38	40	37	39	39	38	35	35
Foreign companies (branches)	2	2	2	2	2	2	2	2
All undertakings	61	64	62	61	63	62	64	63
2.2 Number of employees								
Insurance undertakings	18 297	19 305	19 274	19 240	19 883	19 117	14 228	..
Intermediaries	15 603	15 587	18 931	35 992	40 231	20 605	40 000	..
Total	33 900	34 892	38 205	55 232	60 114	39 722	54 228	..

.. Not available

Note: Detailed metadata at: *http://metalinks.oecd.org/ins/20220309/ffe9*.

Source: *OECD Insurance Statistics (database)*

UNITED KINGDOM

Table 1. Selected aggregates

Million GBP

	2013	2014	2015	2016	2017	2018	2019	2020
1.1 Insurance business written in the reporting country								
1.1.1 Insurance business, by ownership								
Gross premiums								
Domestic undertakings	215 494	219 832	217 673	298 817	306 378	352 555	327 326	296 436
Foreign controlled undertakings	69 361	57 959	58 471	..	..	..	..	..
Foreign companies (branches)	2 237	2 407	2 741	247	473	498	592	712
All undertakings	217 731	222 239	220 414	299 064	306 851	353 053	327 918	297 148
Premiums ceded								
Domestic undertakings	27 456	33 780	24 299	68 763	36 957	68 169	63 873	57 510
Foreign controlled undertakings	9 270	11 048	10 801	0	..	..	..	..
Foreign companies (branches)	53	47	52	115	199	207	213	243
All undertakings	27 509	33 827	24 351	68 878	37 156	68 376	64 087	57 753
Net written premiums								
Domestic undertakings	188 038	186 052	193 374	230 054	269 421	284 386	263 453	238 926
Foreign controlled undertakings	60 091	46 911	47 670	..	..	..	..	..
Foreign companies (branches)	2 184	2 361	2 689	132	273	291	378	470
All undertakings	190 222	188 412	196 062	230 186	269 695	284 677	263 831	239 395
1.1.2 Insurance business on foreign risks, gross premiums								
Life	..	..	..	..	..	..	..	..
Non-life	..	..	..	..	..	..	..	..
Composite	..	..	..	..	..	..	..	..
of which:								
Life	..	..	..	..	..	..	..	..
Non-life	..	..	..	..	..	..	..	..
Total	..	..	..	..	..	..	..	..
1.1.3 Life insurance payments, by class, gross premiums								
Annuities	20 899	22 295	17 278	..	..	..	..	0
Unit linked	112 727	114 296	117 452	..	..	..	..	..
Other life insurance	9 393	11 834	10 622	..	..	..	..	..
Total life insurance	143 018	148 425	145 353	121 964	189 651	206 896	200 336	177 163
***of which:** Pension contracts*	104 333	132 542	128 601	..	..	..	..	..
1.1.4 Non-life insurance payments, by class, gross premiums								
Motor vehicle insurance	12 133	12 069	12 883	18 956	16 011	15 520	16 285	14 373
Marine, aviation and other transport insurance	3 805	3 098	2 604	9 395	10 521	10 636	9 687	9 908
Freight insurance	942	885	808	..	0	..	..	..
Fire and other property damage insurance	16 500	15 969	15 544	30 491	32 412	33 815	30 639	31 408
Pecuniary loss insurance	5 717	5 966	5 791	5 064	5 922	6 018	4 561	4 015
General liability insurance	10 218	10 593	10 308	16 201	18 254	18 635	17 155	17 570
Accident and health	7 895	7 662	7 821	10 872	9 591	15 548	8 971	8 035
***of which:** Health*	..	..	..	8 287	7 574	11 055	7 345	6 723
Other non-life insurance	2 859	2 962	3 177	2 407	2 341	2 497	2 436	2 289
Treaty reinsurance	..	..	..	..	..	..	..	..
Total non-life insurance	60 070	59 206	58 936	93 387	102 627	102 669	89 735	87 599
1.2 Gross claims payments								
Life								
Domestic undertakings	166 084	161 503	172 514	131 443	245 168	280 644	238 118	205 401
Foreign controlled undertakings	42 535	26 653	29 078	..	..	..	..	..
Foreign companies (branches)	-1	4	5	..	..	..	..	..
All undertakings	166 083	161 507	172 518	131 443	245 168	280 644	238 118	205 401
Non-life								
Domestic undertakings	33 152	32 079	30 897	30 260	15 238	14 938	10 613	12 006
Foreign controlled undertakings	17 593	17 062	16 387	..	..	..	..	..
Foreign companies (branches)	1 405	1 469	1 871	43	437	280	498	427
All undertakings	34 557	33 548	32 768	30 303	15 675	15 430	11 111	12 433
Composite								
Domestic undertakings	21 625	22 527	23 077	50 234	64 507	63 455	63 441	61 496
Foreign controlled undertakings	754	2 170	2 734	..	..	..	..	..
Foreign companies (branches)	0	0	0	..	..	..	..	..
All undertakings	21 625	22 527	23 077	50 234	64 507	63 455	63 441	61 496
of which:								
Life	20 366	21 254	21 794	23 337	14 055	15 285	15 686	14 271
Domestic undertakings	20 366	21 254	21 794	23 337	14 055	15 285	15 686	14 271
Foreign controlled undertakings	326	1 876	2 413	..	..	..	..	..
Foreign companies (branches)	0	0	0	..	..	..	..	..
All undertakings	20 366	21 254	21 794	23 337	14 055	15 285	15 686	14 271
Non-life	1 259	1 273	1 283	26 897	50 452	48 169	47 754	47 224
Domestic undertakings	1 259	1 273	1 283	26 897	50 452	48 169	47 754	47 224
Foreign controlled undertakings	428	294	321	..	..	..	..	..
Foreign companies (branches)	0	0	0	..	..	..	..	..
All undertakings	1 259	1 273	1 283	26 897	50 452	48 169	47 754	47 224
Total								
Domestic undertakings	220 861	216 108	226 488	211 938	324 912	359 037	312 171	278 902
Foreign controlled undertakings	60 882	45 885	48 198	..	..	..	..	..
Foreign companies (branches)	1 404	1 474	1 875	43	437	280	498	427
All undertakings	222 265	217 582	228 363	211 981	325 350	359 529	312 669	279 329

Table 1. Selected aggregates *(cont.)*

Million GBP

	2013	2014	2015	2016	2017	2018	2019	2020
1.3 Commissions								
Life								
Domestic undertakings	..	..	..	..	..	..	..	..
Foreign controlled undertakings	..	..	..	..	..	..	..	..
Foreign companies (branches)	..	..	..	..	..	..	..	..
All undertakings	..	..	..	..	..	..	..	..
Non-life								
Domestic undertakings	..	..	..	..	..	..	..	..
Foreign controlled undertakings	..	..	..	..	..	..	..	..
Foreign companies (branches)	..	..	..	..	..	..	..	..
All undertakings	..	..	..	..	..	..	..	..
Composite								
Domestic undertakings	..	..	..	..	..	..	..	..
Foreign controlled undertakings	..	..	..	..	..	..	..	..
Foreign companies (branches)	..	..	..	..	..	..	..	..
All undertakings	..	..	..	..	..	..	..	..
of which:								
Life	..	..	..	..	..	..	..	..
Domestic undertakings	..	..	..	..	..	..	..	..
Foreign controlled undertakings	..	..	..	..	..	..	..	..
Foreign companies (branches)	..	..	..	..	..	..	..	..
All undertakings	..	..	..	..	..	..	..	..
Non-life	..	..	..	..	..	..	..	..
Domestic undertakings	..	..	..	..	..	..	..	..
Foreign controlled undertakings	..	..	..	..	..	..	..	..
Foreign companies (branches)	..	..	..	..	..	..	..	..
All undertakings	..	..	..	..	..	..	..	..
Total								
Domestic undertakings	..	..	..	..	..	..	..	..
Foreign controlled undertakings	..	..	..	..	..	..	..	..
Foreign companies (branches)	..	..	..	..	..	..	..	..
All undertakings	..	..	..	..	..	..	..	..
1.4 Gross operating expenses								
Life								
Domestic undertakings	6 453	6 694	6 794	8 085	10 917	10 794	9 766	9 256
Foreign controlled undertakings	976	929	850	..	..	..	..	..
Foreign companies (branches)	0	1	1	..	..	..	..	..
All undertakings	6 453	6 695	6 795	8 085	10 917	10 794	9 766	9 256
Non-life								
Domestic undertakings	7 125	6 782	6 639	15 414	8 440	8 495	5 793	6 390
Foreign controlled undertakings	3 589	3 549	3 562	..	..	..	..	..
Foreign companies (branches)	167	174	186	59	117	119	138	155
All undertakings	7 292	6 956	6 825	15 474	8 569	8 614	6 346	6 545
Composite								
Domestic undertakings	1 978	2 127	2 325	16 675	24 078	25 164	24 209	23 611
Foreign controlled undertakings	172	277	328	..	..	..	..	..
Foreign companies (branches)	0	0	0	..	..	..	..	..
All undertakings	1 978	2 127	2 325	16 675	24 078	25 164	24 209	23 611
of which:								
Life	1 736	1 874	2 038	3 140	579	1 608	2 015	1 660
Domestic undertakings	1 736	1 874	2 038	3 140	579	1 608	2 015	1 660
Foreign controlled undertakings	91	185	211	..	..	..	..	..
Foreign companies (branches)	0	0	0	..	..	..	..	..
All undertakings	1 736	1 874	2 038	3 140	579	1 608	2 015	1 660
Non-life	242	252	287	13 535	23 499	23 556	22 195	21 951
Domestic undertakings	242	252	287	13 535	23 499	23 556	22 195	21 951
Foreign controlled undertakings	82	92	117	..	..	..	..	..
Foreign companies (branches)	0	0	0	..	..	..	..	..
All undertakings	242	252	287	13 535	23 499	23 556	22 195	21 951
Total								
Domestic undertakings	15 556	15 602	15 759	40 174	43 435	44 453	39 768	39 257
Foreign controlled undertakings	4 737	4 754	4 740	..	..	..	..	..
Foreign companies (branches)	167	175	187	59	117	119	138	155
All undertakings	15 723	15 777	15 946	40 234	43 564	44 572	40 322	39 412

Table 1. Selected aggregates *(cont.)*

Million GBP

	2013	2014	2015	2016	2017	2018	2019	2020
1.5 Insurance business written abroad by branches, gross premiums								
Life								
Branches and agencies	..	..	..	..	..	..	..	..
Subsidaries	..	..	..	..	..	..	..	..
Total	..	..	..	..	..	..	..	..
Non-life								
Branches and agencies	..	..	..	..	..	..	..	..
Subsidaries	..	..	..	..	..	..	..	..
Total	..	..	..	..	..	..	..	..
Composite								
Branches and agencies	..	..	..	..	..	..	..	..
Subsidaries	..	..	..	..	..	..	..	..
Total	..	..	..	..	..	..	..	..
of which:								
Life	..	..	..	..	..	..	..	..
Branches and agencies	..	..	..	..	..	..	..	..
Subsidaries	..	..	..	..	..	..	..	..
Total	..	..	..	..	..	..	..	..
Non-life	..	..	..	..	..	..	..	..
Branches and agencies	..	..	..	..	..	..	..	..
Subsidaries	..	..	..	..	..	..	..	..
Total	..	..	..	..	..	..	..	..
Total								
Branches and agencies	..	..	..	..	..	..	..	..
Subsidaries	..	..	..	..	..	..	..	..
Total	..	..	..	..	..	..	..	..

.. Not available

Note: Detailed metadata at: *http://metalinks.oecd.org/ins/20220309/1572.*

Source: *OECD Insurance Statistics (database)*

UNITED KINGDOM

Table 2. Number of companies and employees

	2013	2014	2015	2016	2017	2018	2019	2020
2.1 Number of companies								
Life								
Domestic undertakings	183	181	181	74	75	69	70	69
Foreign controlled undertakings	15	14	14	..	..	..	..	..
Foreign companies (branches)	1	1	1	1	1	0	1	2
All undertakings	184	182	182	75	76	69	71	71
Non-life								
Domestic undertakings	227	214	209	168	165	153	179	133
Foreign controlled undertakings	99	92	89	..	..	..	..	..
Foreign companies (branches)	10	12	7	13	11	12	14	15
All undertakings	237	226	216	181	176	165	193	148
Composite								
Domestic undertakings	21	25	25	21	22	19	15	37
Foreign controlled undertakings	7	8	8	..	..	..	..	..
Foreign companies (branches)	2	2	2	1	1	1	1	..
All undertakings	23	27	27	22	23	20	16	37
Reinsurance								
Domestic undertakings	30	29	26	16	19	17	14	19
Foreign controlled undertakings	18	16	13	..	..	..	..	..
Foreign companies (branches)	2	2	3	0	0	1	0	5
All undertakings	32	31	29	16	19	18	14	..
Total								
Domestic undertakings	461	449	441	279	281	258	278	239
Foreign controlled undertakings	139	130	124	..	..	..	..	..
Foreign companies (branches)	15	17	13	15	13	14	16	17
All undertakings	476	466	454	294	294	272	294	256
2.2 Number of employees								
Insurance undertakings	..	..	..	..	..	..	..	..
Intermediaries	..	..	..	..	..	..	..	..
Total	..	..	..	..	..	..	..	..

.. Not available
Note: Detailed metadata at: *http://metalinks.oecd.org/ins/20220309/1572.*
Source: *OECD Insurance Statistics (database)*

UNITED STATES

Table 1. Selected aggregates

Million USD

	2013	2014	2015	2016	2017	2018	2019	2020
1.1 Insurance business written in the reporting country								
1.1.1 Insurance business, by ownership								
Gross premiums								
Domestic undertakings	2 289 259	2 430 627	2 619 954	2 702 786	2 835 259	2 631 364	2 773 179	2 934 215
Foreign controlled undertakings	321 246	330 660	324 083	393 449	401 025	273 750	320 958	446 072
Foreign companies (branches)	662	696	1 129	1 007	1 034	920	737	614
All undertakings	2 289 921	2 431 323	2 621 083	2 703 793	2 836 293	2 632 284	2 773 916	2 934 829
Premiums ceded								
Domestic undertakings	657 662	609 531	713 961	743 307	810 265	429 234	430 891	495 526
Foreign controlled undertakings	175 424	134 223	139 675	195 708	226 256	108 845	175 820	216 189
Foreign companies (branches)	275	287	252	260	274	307	502	314
All undertakings	657 937	609 818	714 213	743 567	810 539	429 541	431 393	495 840
Net written premiums								
Domestic undertakings	1 631 597	1 821 096	1 905 993	1 959 479	2 024 995	2 202 129	2 342 288	2 438 689
Foreign controlled undertakings	145 822	196 437	184 408	197 742	174 769	164 906	145 138	229 883
Foreign companies (branches)	387	409	877	747	760	613	236	299
All undertakings	1 631 984	1 821 505	1 906 870	1 960 226	2 025 755	2 202 742	2 342 524	2 438 988
1.1.2 Insurance business on foreign risks, gross premiums								
Life	22 113	..	..	..	..	..	..	..
Non-life	..	..	..	..	..	..	..	..
Composite total	..	..	..	..	..	..	..	..
Total	22 113	..	..	..	..	..	..	..
1.1.3 Life insurance payments, by class, gross premiums								
Annuities	248 568	261 327	264 944	254 313	247 002	277 044	302 021	291 087
Unit linked	..	..	..	..	..	..	..	..
Other life insurance	533 515	527 280	561 674	581 948	612 083	632 578	666 265	743 257
Total life insurance	782 083	788 607	826 618	836 261	859 085	909 623	968 286	1 034 344
***of which:** Pension contracts*	..	..	..	..	..	..	..	..
1.1.4 Non-life insurance payments, by class, gross premiums								
Motor vehicle insurance	342 548	379 889	393 897	422 808	459 200	297 284	309 499	306 075
Marine, aviation and other transport insurance	3 245	3 070	2 911	4 815	2 732	2 187	2 340	2 976
Freight insurance	33 819	36 319	39 175	41 305	43 059	30 091	34 733	32 768
Fire and other property damage insurance	232 328	243 389	248 174	250 765	258 294	174 853	191 502	204 442
Pecuniary loss insurance	35 133	33 690	36 271	38 699	41 003	36 874	38 337	25 232
General liability insurance	191 562	204 069	208 722	211 362	218 298	144 286	160 208	176 819
Accident and health	566 173	646 938	714 394	761 509	799 804	803 339	852 838	922 498
***of which:** Health*	..	..	..	..	..	..	..	..
Other non-life insurance	3 505	3 780	3 728	3 921	4 493	3 716	3 720	3 361
Treaty reinsurance	..	0	0	0	..	..	..	..
Total non-life insurance	1 408 312	1 551 144	1 647 272	1 735 184	1 826 883	1 492 630	1 593 177	1 674 171
1.2 Gross claims payments								
Life								
Domestic undertakings	369 618	357 201	376 240	396 611	416 664	436 219	461 577	483 571
Foreign controlled undertakings	66 267	69 748	68 967	79 082	86 000	92 293	89 797	97 486
Foreign companies (branches)	0	0	0	0	0	0	0	0
All undertakings	369 618	357 201	376 240	396 611	416 664	436 219	461 577	483 571
Non-life								
Domestic undertakings	917 856	980 750	1 077 317	1 145 423	1 228 757	1 055 839	1 112 688	1 131 976
Foreign controlled undertakings	84 201	76 540	79 309	84 878	95 499	71 727	70 810	1 813
Foreign companies (branches)	234	240	359	504	609	649	661	337
All undertakings	918 090	980 990	1 077 676	1 145 927	1 229 366	1 056 488	1 113 349	1 134 126
Composite, all undertakings	..	..	..	..	..	..	..	..
Total								
Domestic undertakings	1 287 474	1 337 951	1 453 557	1 542 034	1 645 421	1 492 058	1 574 265	1 615 547
Foreign controlled undertakings	150 468	146 288	148 276	163 960	181 499	164 020	160 607	99 299
Foreign companies (branches)	234	240	359	504	609	649	661	337
All undertakings	1 287 708	1 338 191	1 453 916	1 542 538	1 646 030	1 492 707	1 574 926	1 617 697
1.3 Commissions								
Life								
Domestic undertakings	..	53 082	56 784	67 963	59 387	..	71 982	62 551
Foreign controlled undertakings	..	11 165	10 339	10 639	10 700	..	9 946	9 561
Foreign companies (branches)	..	0	0	0	0	..	0	0
All undertakings	..	53 082	56 784	67 963	59 387	..	71 982	62 551
Non-life								
Domestic undertakings	..	..	..	..	..	..	..	..
Foreign controlled undertakings	..	..	..	..	..	..	..	..
Foreign companies (branches)	..	..	..	..	..	..	..	..
All undertakings	..	..	..	..	..	..	..	..
Composite, all undertakings	..	..	..	..	..	..	..	..
Total								
Domestic undertakings	..	53 082	56 784	67 963	59 387	..	71 982	62 551
Foreign controlled undertakings	..	11 165	10 339	10 639	10 700	..	9 946	9 561
Foreign companies (branches)	..	0	0	0	0	..	0	0
All undertakings	..	53 082	56 784	67 963	59 387	..	71 982	62 551

Table 1. Selected aggregates *(cont.)*

Million USD

	2013	2014	2015	2016	2017	2018	2019	2020
1.4 Gross operating expenses								
Life								
Domestic undertakings	65 424	67 225	68 488	69 722	75 161	75 904	78 079	77 600
Foreign controlled undertakings	9 814	10 285	9 952	11 175	11 838	12 374	10 951	11 685
Foreign companies (branches)	0	0	0	..	..	0	0	0
All undertakings	65 424	67 225	68 488	69 722	75 161	75 904	78 079	77 600
Non-life								
Domestic undertakings	261 844	281 766	298 911	308 839	310 003	343 131	339 686	373 651
Foreign controlled undertakings	23 185	23 274	23 035	26 711	26 891	31 608	30 224	47 514
Foreign companies (branches)	165	194	410	354	360	300	146	195
All undertakings	262 009	281 960	299 321	309 193	310 363	343 431	339 832	373 846
Composite, all undertakings	..	..	..	..	..	..	..	..
Total								
Domestic undertakings	327 268	348 991	367 399	378 561	385 164	419 035	417 765	451 251
Foreign controlled undertakings	32 999	33 559	32 987	37 886	38 729	43 982	41 175	59 199
Foreign companies (branches)	165	194	410	354	360	300	146	195
All undertakings	327 433	349 185	367 809	378 915	385 524	419 335	417 911	451 446
1.5 Insurance business written abroad by branches, gross premiums								
Life								
Branches and agencies	..	..	..	..	..	..	..	..
Subsidaries	..	..	..	..	..	..	..	..
Total	..	..	..	..	..	..	..	..
Non-life								
Branches and agencies	..	..	..	..	..	..	..	..
Subsidaries	..	..	..	..	..	..	..	..
Total	..	..	..	..	..	..	..	..
Composite total	..	..	..	..	..	..	..	..
Total								
Branches and agencies	..	..	..	..	..	..	..	..
Subsidaries	..	..	..	..	..	..	..	..
Total	..	..	..	..	..	..	..	..

.. Not available

Note: Detailed metadata at: *http://metalinks.oecd.org/ins/20220309/2b6e.*

Source: *OECD Insurance Statistics (database)*

UNITED STATES

Table 2. Number of companies and employees

	2013	2014	2015	2016	2017	2018	2019	2020
2.1 Number of companies								
Life								
Domestic undertakings	995	1 031	1 030	738	735	715	728	708
Foreign controlled undertakings	156	158	158	168	157	157	149	145
Foreign companies (branches)	..	..	..	..	..	0	0	0
All undertakings	995	1 031	1 030	738	735	715	728	708
Non-life								
Domestic undertakings	3 425	3 404	3 185	3 205	3 419	3 430	3 471	3 404
Foreign controlled undertakings	403	404	390	418	405	399	388	373
Foreign companies (branches)	11	9	13	19	13	14	15	14
All undertakings	3 436	3 413	3 198	3 224	3 432	3 444	3 486	3 418
Composite, all undertakings	**0**	**0**	**0**	**0**	..	..	..	..
Reinsurance								
Domestic undertakings	247	234	354	221	228	235	228	..
Foreign controlled undertakings	65	64	76	52	44	48	48	..
Foreign companies (branches)	1	1	4	2	1	1	2	..
All undertakings	248	235	358	223	229	283	230	..
Total								
Domestic undertakings	4 667	4 669	4 569	4 164	4 382	4 380	4 427	..
Foreign controlled undertakings	624	626	624	638	606	604	585	..
Foreign companies (branches)	12	10	17	21	14	15	17	..
All undertakings	4 679	4 679	4 586	4 185	4 396	4 442	4 444	..
2.2 Number of employees								
Insurance undertakings	..	..	..	..	..	..	..	..
Intermediaries	..	..	..	..	..	..	..	..
Total	..	..	..	..	..	..	..	..

.. Not available

Note: Detailed metadata at: *http://metalinks.oecd.org/ins/20220309/2b6e.*

Source: *OECD Insurance Statistics (database)*

Printed by Libri Plureos GmbH in Hamburg,
Germany

9 789264 873131